NO EASY TASK

NO EASY TASK

FIGHTING IN AFGHANISTAN

EDITED BY COLONEL BERND HORN AND DR. EMILY SPENCER

DUNDURN
TORONTO

Copy Editor: Matt Baker
Design: Jennifer Scott
Printer: Webcom

Library and Archives Canada Cataloguing in Publication

No easy task : fighting in Afghanistan / edited by Bernd Horn and Emily Spencer ; foreword by Jonathan H. Vance.

Includes index.
Also issued in electronic formats.
ISBN 978-1-4597-0162-5

1. Afghanistan--History. 2. Afghanistan--History, Military. 3. Afghan War, 2001- --Participation, Canadian. I. Horn, Bernd, 1959- II. Spencer, Emily

DS356.N6 2012   958.1   C2011-903767-X

1 2 3 4 5   16 15 14 13 12

We acknowledge the support of the Canada Council for the Arts and the Ontario Arts Council for our publishing program. We also acknowledge the financial support of the Government of Canada through the Canada Book Fund and Livres Canada Books, and the Government of Ontario through the Ontario Book Publishing Tax Credit and the Ontario Media Development Corporation.

Cover concept courtesy of Marie Claude Delcourt.

Printed and bound in Canada.
www.dundurn.com

MIX
Paper from
responsible sources
FSC
www.fsc.org   FSC® C004071

Dundurn
3 Church Street, Suite 500
Toronto, Ontario, Canada
M5E 1M2

Gazelle Book Services Limited
White Cross Mills
High Town, Lancaster, England
LA1 4XS

Dundurn
2250 Military Road
Tonawanda, NY
U.S.A. 14150

CONTENTS

FOREWORD BY MAJOR-GENERAL JONATHAN H. VANCE   7

ACKNOWLEDGEMENTS   11

INTRODUCTION   13

1   ADJUST YOUR SIGHTS: 17
    Leading Issues Likely to Arise in Any Counter-Insurgency Campaign
    Dr. Michael A. Hennessy

2   THE QUAGMIRE OF GREAT POWERS: 29
    Dealing with the Afghan Way of War
    Major Tony Balasevicius

3   PUBLIC OPINION MATTERS: 67
    The Struggle for Hearts and Minds
    Dr. Emily Spencer

4   COALITION COUNTER-INSURGENCY WARFARE IN AFGHANISTAN   83
    Lieutenant-Colonel Ian Hope

5   CAMPAIGNING IN AFGHANISTAN: 101
    A Uniquely Canadian Approach
    Dr. Howard Coombs and
    Lieutenant-General (retired) Michel Gauthier

6   SUSTAINING THOSE WHO DARE: 123
    Logistic Observations from Contemporary Afghanistan
    Lieutenant-Colonel John Conrad

7 MORE THAN MEETS THE EYE: 139
   The Invisible Hand of SOF in Afghanistan
   Colonel Bernd Horn

8 LESSON LEARNED: 163
   Operation Medusa and the Taliban Epiphany
   Colonel Bernd Horn

9 OPPORTUNITY LOST: 199
   The Canadian Involvement in the Development of the
   Afghan National Police
   Major Alex D. Haynes

10 COUNTER-INSURGENCY VERSUS "COIN" IN
   BAZAAR-E-PANJWAYI AND PANJWAYI DISTRICT, 2008–2010:   233
   An Illustrative Study of a Canadian Problem
   Dr. Sean M. Maloney

NOTES   257
GLOSSARY OF ABBREVIATIONS   315
CONTRIBUTORS   321
INDEX   325

FOREWORD

It is an honour to be asked to write this foreword, for it offers me yet another opportunity to pay homage to our wonderful troops, their leaders, and the entire group of men and women who have served and continue to serve Canada so well in Afghanistan. From the most junior soldier to our senior non-commissioned officers (NCOs) and junior officers, unit commanders, civilians, contractors, and staff, right up to Task Force Commanders, all have given of themselves in the pursuit of excellence in the face of dire threat. To be included in these ranks is a privilege without equal.

I think it essential that we attempt to capture everything we can about our operations in Afghanistan. From the tactical to the strategic levels, there is much to learn and remember. There are truths to be maintained and myths to shatter, lessons to be learned and work to be done to prepare for continued operations in Afghanistan and the future conflict zones we will inevitably be asked to serve in. All who have served in Joint Task Force Afghanistan, in whatever capacity, have an obligation to ensure future generations of the Canadian Forces (CF) benefit from our experience, while remembering that we must never allow our service there to create an exclusive group within the CF. Let us all remember that while the CF performed well in this conflict, there were many areas in which we had to adapt, change, and improve. Similarly, we must remember that future conflicts will probably present many new challenges, some that our Afghanistan experience may well prepare us for and others that will represent new obstacles. As such, we must always learn from experience but maintain an open, analytical, and agile mind.

As we study our Afghan experience, I think it useful to place the war in some important context over time. From rotation to rotation the war evolved. Therefore, without first establishing the proper context, we risk talking past each other as we try to explain to ourselves and others what we did and why we did it. The history will be written about this conflict over a very long period, giving us all greater perspective and a fuller understanding of the many complexities that factored into decisions made and actions taken. For now, however, as we try to grapple with our understanding of the war, I will lay out my basic contextual framework. First and foremost, I maintain, and always will, that every rotation of Canadian headquarters and units did exactly the right things for the right reasons. As military factors changed, so did we. Indeed, we can celebrate the professionalism, innovation, and dedication of each rotation as they kept pace with a changing enemy, evolving strategies from Operation Enduring Freedom (OEF), and the International Security Assistance Force (ISAF), as well as the ever-important Canadian imperatives.

Our rotations fall into three important and distinct timeframes — the understanding of which is essential to place "what right looks like" in proper context. From the narrow perspective of December 2010, I believe each stage is quite distinct, and each demanded very different actions and plans from our forces. The first stage was the immediate response to the 9/11 attacks that was intended as a counter-terrorist and regime-change campaign. This stage evolved to include the establishment of the ISAF mission intended to assist the Afghan government in re-establishing itself throughout the country. Throughout this stage, in the aftermath of the regime change, an insurgency began and grew with the benefit of safe havens outside Afghanistan. Interesting to note is that it was not universally accepted, nor was it particularly evident in the official policy approach of troop contributing nations, that an insurgency was actually underway.

By 2006 the beginning of the second stage commenced, coincident with our large move from Kabul to Kandahar. It was now universally agreed, at least within informed military circles, that an insurgency was well established, particularly in the South. However — and this is an important distinction — as an international community and force, we were still resourced to conduct counter-terror and regime-change activities. The resources necessary to conduct effective counter-insurgency (COIN) operations were absent: more troops, more capacity to apply "civil effects" in a timely and focused manner, more effective indigenous forces, more emphasis on civil policing capacity, and so on. Without these enablers, we were left to use our sparse resources selectively to deal with the most urgent and immediate threats while building a base upon which future and better resourced COIN operations could be conducted.

Nonetheless, during this second stage between 2006 and 2009, we did not lose. We did not lose the airhead, the seat of the central Afghan government remained intact, albeit imperfect, and we did not allow the defeat or rout of Afghan security forces. Furthermore, we significantly hurt the insurgency, making everything the enemy tried to do hard to achieve. We bought valuable time and set conditions for the third stage.

The third stage began in 2009 with a massive reinforcement of international forces, mainly American, as well as a civilian cohort that was to grow and create increasingly larger and more focused civil effects so that the overall COIN effect could be achieved. Afghan security forces underwent better-resourced training and mentoring and they, too, grew. In this environment, where the military factor of "forces available" shifted radically, the doctrine we had wanted to apply fully for so long was finally realized. One need only think of the military transformation at a place such as Forward Operating Base (FOB) Wilson in Zharey District. In 2006 we had, at most, a platoon in that location, with hard working civil-military co-operation (CIMIC) teams working as closely as they could with the resident district staff and police. By 2010, multiple Afghan and U.S. battalions, as well as the headquarters of 2/101 Brigade Combat Team were in location. Where we once had a platoon, in 2010 we had multiple units and enablers along with a full civilian District Stabilization Team. These units, like their Canadian counterparts, lived and worked off that FOB among Afghan citizens in Zharey, providing direct and continuous security support while also assisting in the bringing to bear of important game-changing civil effects that continue to be the critical path to decent governance and the ultimate hope for a better future for Afghans.

In the end, we fought well when we had to fight, we conducted COIN operations when we could, and we consistently and continually supported our allies and coalition partners. Moreover, we provided a solid base upon which future Canadian military-civilian efforts will be applied in conflict zones around the world to increasingly powerful effect. We have much to be proud of and yet much to learn. One way to make sure we learn properly is to study and discuss the lessons of our participation in Afghanistan.

One can rarely, if ever, predict the outcome of a complex counterinsurgency. However, we do know that it requires unrelenting effort to the bitter end. Conventional wisdom puts the lifespan of effective counter-insurgency campaigns in the 10–15 year range. Given that a fully resourced campaign only began in 2009, there is still a long way to go. Part of this path is to ensure the necessary transition of the management and execution of the COIN campaign to the Afghans themselves. Nonetheless, we should be rightfully proud of the part we played. Moreover, we need to remember that to be successful in future conflict, particularly of this sort, we must nurture Canada's greatest strategic asset: the very junior but well-trained CF service members who never failed to amaze us all with that well-balanced blend of aggression, compassion, courage, and humility. Those of us who get requests to write forewords and present speeches do well to remember that we are nothing without them.

Major-General Jonathan H. Vance
Ottawa, Ontario
December 2010

ACKNOWLEDGEMENTS

A s with any written work, particularly edited volumes, many hands are at play. As such, we wish to extend our gratitude to all those who participated in the writing of this volume. Your time and effort in putting your thoughts and insights onto paper is greatly appreciated.

In addition, we would also like to acknowledge those who assisted us directly and indirectly by providing interviews, research materials, or images. In particular, we would like to thank Silvia Pecota for the use of her dramatic photographs from theatre as well as Graeme Smith for his captivating pictures from Panjwayi in Kandahar Province.

Finally, we would also like to thank Michael Carroll, Matt Baker, and the design team at Dundurn for, once again, creating such a refined volume from our manuscript. We would also be remiss if we did not thank Marie Claude Delcourt for the cover concept of this book.

INTRODUCTION

A fghanistan has long been considered the graveyard of empires. Throughout its history, its inhabitants have been forced to endure the ravishes of foreign invaders, including marauding hordes, Imperial armies, global superpowers, as well as coalitions of allied states. What has always remained constant is the fierce Afghan independence and resistance to outside occupiers. For those who have ventured into Afghanistan with notions of occupying or controlling its people, they have found that fighting in that rugged, hostile land is no easy task.

To the chagrin of those waging war in Afghanistan, Afghans have proven to be tenacious, clever, and unrelenting foes. Using the harsh, formidable terrain of their country, tribal affiliations, and relying on a warrior ethos rooted in centuries of conflict, Afghans have always employed tactics that played to their strengths and taken advantage of the weaknesses of those attempting to occupy or control their land.

Canadians have come to realize these challenges first hand. The war in Afghanistan has shocked both the Canadian Forces (CF) and Canadians in general. It has returned the CF to a combat role and shattered the long-standing Canadian peacekeeper myth.

Canadian troops deployed to Afghanistan for the first time in 2001, as part of the American response to the al Qaeda terrorist attacks in

New York on 11 September 2001. As such, in December 2001, Canadian Special Operations Forces (SOF) began operations as part of U.S. Operation Enduring Freedom (OEF). Subsequently, a light infantry battle group, based on the 3rd Battalion, Princess Patricia's Light Infantry (3 PPCLI), arrived in February 2002 and conducted combat missions with their American colleagues.

Importantly, Canadian SOF and 3 PPCLI began to rebuild the CF's reputation amongst the militaries of Allied nations. During the 1990s in the Former Yugoslavia, Canadian troops had been so limited in what they could do in theatre by the national restrictions imposed on them by their civilian and military chains of command that they had been nicknamed by some of their Allies "Can't Bat" instead of Can Bat, the abbreviated form of Canadian Battalion. However, things changed. Canadians pushed for challenging missions, and their subsequent successes made a strong impression on their allies as well as the public at home. In fact, the death of four Canadian soldiers in a friendly fire incident at Tarnak Farms, on the night of 18 April 2002, galvanized the nation. This loss struck a chord with Canadians and caused a large public outpouring of support and sympathy for CF members and, in particular, the families of the fallen. Although not realized at the time, it was a foreshadowing of what was to come.

The Canadian soldiers that had redeployed to Canada in the summer of 2002, however, returned to Afghanistan a year later at the behest of Canada's European allies. In the late summer of 2003, the 3rd Battalion, The Royal Canadian Regiment (3 RCR) joined the International Security Assistance Force (ISAF) in Kabul. The Royals had no idea what to expect. Although Taliban resistance was just in the rebuilding phase, the Royals suffered casualties, both dead and wounded, to mine strikes as well as the first suicide bomber who directly targeted the CF.

Despite this, Canada's resolve to stay the course was unaltered. Two years and several rotations later, the Canadians moved south to Kandahar Province to establish a Provincial Reconstruction Team (PRT). In addition, Canada also deployed an infantry battle group. By the summer of 2006, the Canadians were embroiled in a savage and desperate insurgency that challenged both the Government of Afghanistan and the NATO coalition forces supporting it for control of large swaths of the province. As the principal battle group in the South available for combat operations, the Canadian battle group was fed a daily diet of combat.

In September 2006, the Taliban had become so confident in their strength and control of the Pashmul area that they dug-in fortified positions and challenged the Canadians to remove them. After a tenaciously fought and bloody two-week struggle, Canadian soldiers and their coalition allies conducted Operation Medusa and inflicted severe casualties on the Taliban, finally pushing them out of the contested area.

Operation Medusa proved to be a turning point in the war in Afghanistan. The Taliban relearned the lesson that they should never confront their foe in a conventional battle of attrition, because the overwhelming technology and firepower of the coalition was just too great. As a result, the Taliban reverted to a much more deadly strategy of ambush and the use of improvised explosive devices (IEDs) and suicide bombers. The change in methodology paid off for the enemy as casualties for the Afghanistan National Security Forces (ANSF), the coalition, and the CF quickly mounted. The asymmetry in tactics that the Taliban began to employ was difficult to overcome.

Operation Medusa was a turning point in the war in Afghanistan from the Canadian perspective as well. First, it signalled to the world that Canada was once again ready to commit its sons and daughters to combat. In addition, the casualties suffered during the operation and in its aftermath, as well as the commitment in resources and effort to fight the continuing insurgency, now consumed the army and became, arguably, its singular focus.

In many ways, the war has been an enormous learning experience for the CF, and particularly the Canadian Army. The complexity of fighting in Afghanistan cannot be underestimated. The enemy is clever; he completely understands the battle space and uses it to his advantage. He adapts adeptly and quickly to changes in coalition tactics, techniques, and procedures. The Taliban is innovative, tenacious, and ruthless.

Further adding to the complexity is the weak Afghan national government that is fraught with corruption and incompetence. Moreover, competing coalition agendas and the ever-present national caveats restrict ISAF's ability to fully take the fight to the enemy.

Unfortunately, the realities that Canada, other Western governments, and their militaries face in the complex theatre of war in Afghanistan are often overshadowed by simple news bites that resonate with the public. Indeed, Canadians and other Western populations, often plagued by short attention spans, form their opinions on very complex issues through simplified 90-second news bites. This can have far-reaching consequences for Western governments, since, as democratically elected representatives, they are required to reflect the beliefs and values of their citizenry. As such, Western governments often determine national policy with public sentiment. In the end, Canadian military commanders respond to their civilian masters and must ultimately align with government wishes, regardless of any disconnect between the "reality" of the situation on the ground and the perception of the situation by the Canadian public. In difficult theatres such as Afghanistan, commanders come to grips with the Afghan paradigm and do the best that can be done in light of the challenging circumstances.

As the title of this book makes clear, prosecuting the war in Afghanistan is no easy task. Soldiers must use their limited resources to provide security, fight a difficult and savage enemy, work within a xenophobic, medieval culture, improve a backwards economy, and attempt to raise the standard of living for Afghans in a bid to provide them a reason for supporting their national government. Compounding the difficulty, soldiers must accomplish all of this in a way that resonates with their home populations, even if home and host nation populations hold quite different beliefs and values.

With a collection of essays that explore the historical and contemporary challenges to conflict and war in Afghanistan, *No Easy Task: Fighting in Afghanistan* highlights some of the complexity that Canadian commanders and soldiers now face there. Notably, each chapter is written by a Canadian practitioner or scholar, which furnishes a distinctly Canadian perspective on fighting in Afghanistan. The chapters also provide insight into the theory behind and practice of counterinsurgency, as well as specific analysis of Canadian, Afghan, coalition, and Taliban strategies and actions. In sum, they underscore the reality that fighting in Afghanistan is no easy task.

1

Adjust Your Sights

Leading Issues Likely to Arise in Any Counter-Insurgency Campaign

DR. MICHAEL A. HENNESSY

As the title indicates, this chapter will provide a short primer, or extended aide memoire, for those who find themselves embroiled in a counter-insurgency (COIN) struggle. Note the use of the word *struggle*. *War* might come to mind, but that may not be a wholly adequate, or for that matter acceptable, descriptor. That one employs the term COIN implies there is an insurgency to be countered. It is to the nature of insurgency that we must first cast our minds.

Why do men rebel? Not a small question, and not one to be avoided by the counter-insurgent. There are many theories that the student of war would be wise to consult, and we shall review several *inter alia*; however, no single theory has proven applicable to all circumstances. Rather than belabour the theory here, it suffices to note there are often multiple motives at work. Does poverty cause rebellion? Maybe. Does ideology cause rebellion? Maybe. Does ethnic/social/religious identity fuel rebellion? Again, maybe. Does state repression cause rebellion? Maybe. Does bad national government, corruption, or poor administration cause insurgency? Again, the answer is maybe. We could add to the list of attributed causes but find no definitive answer. Much theoretical work has gone toward supporting or refuting such motive causes, and no definitive answer will be given here. The truth of the matter is each or all of these elements may be present where a rebellion takes root. While there may well be other such "causes," there is neither sufficient proof nor agreement for any cause and effect model.[1] These facts should be kept in mind by those who find themselves thrust into the role of counter-insurgent, as efforts to ameliorate such causes will likely be part of the COIN strategy.

Whatever the true reasons an insurgency takes hold, almost all insurgencies have their own internal narrative that motivates and justifies the actions of the insurgents and undermines the legitimacy of the COIN forces. The narrative of grievance, injustice, and necessary change through a call to arms can vary greatly between insurgencies but is a powerful tool in harnessing recruits, undermining the established government, undercutting the vigour of partners, and sowing doubt within the minds of the many undecided members of the domestic population.[2]

While there are many insurgencies active in the world today, a study of several older campaigns from the twentieth century can help establish the contours of what one may encounter in any insurgency. As such, this chapter will provide some of those examples.

PRO INSURGENCY: PATTERNS AND OBSERVATIONS

Understanding how insurgencies work is fundamental to understanding how they may be overcome. Given the interest in COIN, one might think we have a good understanding of insurgency; however, there is little comparative work on the dynamics and successful techniques of insurgents.[3] Both solid knowledge and abstract theorizing remains contentious. Nevertheless, there are a number of individual studies that explain how a particular insurgency has fared; for brevity, only three will be examined here.

The first is the "Arab revolt" of 1917–18. Writing about how he fomented the Arab revolt, T.E. Lawrence provides a useful estimate of the situation that guided his actions. Recognizing that his adversaries, the Ottoman Empire, found it necessary to garrison population centres along the main rail lines of the Arabian Peninsula, he chose not to strike at their garrisons directly. Force against force attacks would give advantage to the Turks. His rag-tag volunteer army of tribal nomads would not stand heavy losses and required careful direction. Instead, the Turks would be left to wither on the vine. In avoiding standing fights and set piece battles, the aim was to preserve his own forces and whittle down the physical and psychological will of the enemy. Eventually, the Turkish commanders conceded the ground and abandoned their outposts. Externally supplied arms and the strategic depth for manoeuvre presented by the vast wilderness and topography of the theatre of operations made such a campaign possible — he likened it to a campaign of commerce raiding at sea.

Also factored into Lawrence's concept of operations was the inability of the enemy to swamp the theatre with reinforcements. Protracting the struggle through avoiding battle on unfavourable terms, using the theatre's physical geography, and taking advantage of the adversary's geopolitical limits figured large in Lawrence's campaign design.[4]

A similar constraint played a role in the Anglo-Irish War, or War of Irish Independence, of 1919–21. The rural insurgency that took hold in Ireland in 1919 aimed to wrest control of the countryside from the representatives and functionaries of the British-controlled government. Police stations, post offices, local courts, and tax collection were targeted, and their functions were replicated by the republican forces, who established a parallel, or shadow, government. To further their aim of rendering Ireland ungovernable, republicans ran for election to parliament. If elected, these members of parliament (MPs) refused to sit in the British parliament and instead agitated for a local parliament to be formed. Such action undercut the legitimacy of the British government and military action.

British reprisal policies, many of which originated during the Boer War at the turn of the century, included mass internment without trial for suspects and the summary eviction of families and destruction of their homes on suspicion of shielding republicans. These measures further fuelled resentment. Several well-reported breakdowns of police discipline — particularly the police riot, torching of Cork city, and later murder of the mayor — brought international criticism and concern in London.

Weary of war after the experiences of 1914–18, and recognizing that Britain had been preparing to offer Ireland its own parliament on the eve of that struggle, few in Britain favoured using all the resources of the Empire or unrestrained warfare to attack the republicans. The commander of British forces requested authority to begin a campaign of summary justice, particularly the execution (judicial or otherwise) of suspects, and suggested that, if that policy could not be followed, the government would be better off seeking a negotiated peace.

The government followed this recommendation. Although the republicans settled for the partition of Ireland, their relatively small guerrilla campaign, with probably less than 4,000 armed members at its peak during pre-peace talks, enjoyed very real, though limited, tactical success; nevertheless, it achieved its strategic purpose because of Britain's geopolitical context. The power potential of that state was not fully exercised, because of historical circumstances — such limitations should be considered in all cases of responses to an insurgency.[5]

The Irish example was not lost on others. Coming to prominence during the long struggle of the Chinese Communist Party, Mao Zedong masterminded the building of a large guerrilla army, and its eventual transformation into a large conventional army. Mao helped the party pick up the pieces after being routed from cities by Chinese nationalists, the Kuomintang Party (KMT) forces, in 1927. He studied the actions of Lawrence and the Irish republicans. Losing access to its urban support base, Mao argued, required the party to harness support from the Chinese rural peasantry.

Gaining their trust and active support became the foundation for Mao's success in resisting the conventional forces of the KMT and then the Imperial Japanese Army, which invaded mainland China in 1936. The triumph of the Chinese People's Party (CPP) against the KMT in 1949 marked the end of a 22-year protracted struggle for dominance. In that long struggle, Mao Zedong became chief political and military architect of victory.

There is a vast literature on Mao, but for our purposes only several elements of his theories need exploration here. Mao did not write a simple how-to guide. Rather, most of his writings were produced under particular historical circumstances, often after serious set-backs or on the eve of redirecting the war effort, and were aimed at mobilizing or retaining morale among his followers and encouraging the internal audience within the Party. His approach to what he termed variously as "guerrilla war," "people's war," "protracted war," "revolutionary war," and the "war of resistance" changed with the circumstances confronting him. He fought first for survival against the KMT, then made common cause with them against the Japanese, and then fought against the KMT once again.

Many writers attempting to summarize or distill Mao's military theory have reduced his writing on guerrilla warfare into an overly simple construct of a three-phased guerrilla campaign aimed at "first the mountains, then the valleys, then the cities."[6] This oversimplification ignores much. Rather than argue that he presented a single unified theory, which he did not, it is more appropriate to look for the enduring elements of his approach to organic guerrilla warfare, particularly the need to move into conventional positional warfare to obtain a final victory.

First, his forces had to remain agile and not allow themselves to be isolated and destroyed — objectives any conventional enemy would pursue. Second, building and transforming a guerrilla force into one capable of waging battle successfully against a conventional enemy would be necessary.[7] To build his forces, he would rely on mobilizing the Chinese peasantry. To that end, he espoused a series of social mobilization measures for organizing whole populations within rural villages, from elders to school-aged children, via a host of non-military structures. Sociologists might term this a form of structural functionalism aimed at channelling support for his cause.[8]

If his first aim was to survive, his second was to grow. This required harnessing the people to the cause through any means available, whether psychological, social, economical in nature, and with the use of coercion when necessary.[9] Many of these structures remain active in Chinese society today. Against both the KMT and Japanese he traded space for time, abandoning outposts and vulnerable areas rather than risking unfavourable pitched battles. Against both he also preached that the CPP was more virtuous and disciplined in its dealings with the local population than either adversary.

Mao's talk was more than hollow rhetoric. For instance, whereas both lived off the land, often stealing from the peasants, his forces paid, or promised to pay, for items taken — such acts were aimed at winning local loyalties and aimed at helping the peasants determine what side they would prefer to support. Against the Japanese, he furthered this effort by highlighting their total foreignness to Chinese culture.[10] Such measures were aimed at mobilizing deep loyalties and building support vital for first survival, then information and tacit support. Later, this support would allow further exploitation toward the cause as new circumstances, domestic and international, presented opportunities toward the ultimate ends of victory. Such measures proved invaluable for undercutting support for the purely indigenous and equally nationalist KMT regime.

INSURGENCY TODAY

The passage of time and a better understanding of past events let us speak with some confidence about the workings of previous insurgencies. The accounts above omitted tremendous detail, and they obscure how vicious or bloody the campaigns were. Internal warfare has always been particularly harsh, because so many segments of society are in conflict.[11] Acts of extreme violence by insurgent and counter-insurgent alike marked the three example cases.

Modern insurgencies are no less vicious. Some insurgencies have intentionally inflicted outrages to spark extreme reactions from security forces. Most modern insurgencies are led by a few key, highly motivated personnel seeking to make a coherent design for their campaigns, playing space for time and growing support for their struggle domestically and internationally. Many have struggled with the problem of transitioning guerrilla bands into larger forces capable of waging positional warfare. Many have sought to create parallel governments and social networks. All have striven to avoid cataclysmic defeat by taking advantage of changing circumstances.[12]

Understanding the particular and organic nature of a given insurgency is the first task of a commander dispatched to counter it. Although the challenges of COIN are not new, the response now open to Western military forces that find themselves thrust into such struggles tends to be more constrained or bounded in ways not universally recognized. Some of these bounds have to do with evolving legal protocols adopted by their nations. Some are tied to new social mores, or sensitivities, which shape the logic and acceptable forms of military action.[13] There are several ways to classify possible responses but not all are acceptable to modern Western forces — particularly those forces playing only a bit part in the campaign.

Faced with insurgency, target governments may see logic in calling for a war of extermination — an object, for instance, rejected by the British government in Ireland, but one that was demonstrated recently in the final campaign in Sri Lanka against the Tamil Tigers. There, after a very protracted stop-and-start campaign, the government proved finally able to isolate the Tigers from their external supporters. The Sri Lankan government rejected domestic and international calls for a return to the negotiating table, and heedless to other calls for restraint or calls to give quarter, prosecuted their offensives until they surrounded and killed the Tigers' leadership. The settling of accounts may have continued well thereafter within the detention centers.

The particular geo-political configuration of events that sparked and allowed such a campaign to be conducted are germane to this discussion. The Tamil Tigers had grown isolated and internally divided, with some significant defection once it resumed its armed campaign. Its repudiation of several previous ceasefires enabled the Sri Lankan government to reject its late-found calls for a ceasefire. That government also had a strong mandate for decisive action from its electorate, tired of many years of internal warfare. Further, the government was not dependent on external allies to do the fighting. With neither strategic depth nor room to manoeuvre in Sri Lanka or internationally, the Tamil Tigers were isolated and destroyed in detail.[14] So definitive an outcome is rare among Western military forces.[15]

Other COIN campaigns have sought to emulate the methods of the insurgents. The French military response in Algeria was remarkably unrestrained by due process, and it employed counter-terror, torture, kidnappings, broad-ranging psychological warfare, intrusive population control measures, and rural mobilization tactics. French military theorists argued these methods were justified merely as mirror images of what their enemy would do and moreover appeared to yield real tactical success. But these methods proved unpopular within metropolitan France and called into question the legitimacy of French actions against its own citizens, Algeria being considered not a colony but a province of France. The tactics may have dealt the guerrillas several telling blows but also brought the army into disrepute and undermined domestic support for the war effort. These actions fuelled a change in government that then reigned in the army, elements of which then launched several rebellions of their own. Such consequences brought the almost complete repudiation of French military doctrine that was written with regard to counter-insurgency theory.[16]

No Western army has attempted to follow the strict precepts of that doctrine since; rather, they have avoided all such totalitarian approaches to the problem. Instead, Western intervening forces find themselves waging protracted campaigns to help impose or restore the rule of law and assist a host government that has either sought help or been imposed by an outside power — as is the case in both Iraq and Afghanistan.[17] Acting to support a recently created government, rather than shore up an established government, poses its own unique problems, particularly regarding the perceived legitimacy by domestic political actors, neighbours, and the wider international community. If many insurgencies have enjoyed success by creating a parallel political hierarchy, a new government is challenged to make its machinery of government exist and then operate under fire — literally and figuratively. COIN forces, then, are both weeding out the insurgents and rooting in the new administration. Such activities clearly range well beyond conventional military operations; it is a different problem than supporting a well-established government.[18]

The minor players in a coalition may find themselves only supporting players in the effort to create and impose the new order while countering the rise of the insurgent order. Mere tactical military operations may be called for — indeed, may be essential in many areas — but junior coalition partners may be very far removed from influencing key higher-level activities, let alone objectives.[19] Even if one's own forces are truly able to operate with a whole of government approach, the span of influence may be limited to the tactical area of operations where one can be master of the house. Even so, knowing what to do may not be easy.[20]

What level of risk one should take, given that constraint is a thorny question, every force commander will have to answer. Consider, however, that domestic support is necessary to ensure participation in a protracted struggle, and most insurgencies are protracted campaigns of 10 years or longer — the casualty-commitment equation is of strategic significance. Our staff colleges pay little attention to the challenges of coalition warfare, but surely how coalitions maintain their cohesion through protracted struggles is not a problem unique to COIN. Such concerns are perhaps of greater importance to minor, force-contributing nations than larger questions about the course of the overall campaign, because minor nations have neither sufficient weight to dictate objectives — political or military — nor are they able to bring all their military potential to bear; they can only master their own game. Minor contributing nations face war in an increasingly and incredibly constrained environment.

Even if the Western form of COIN has now become stylized as offering tactical security operations for the enduring security of target populations, there remain many useful bromides for military leaders to absorb. Writing over forty years ago, the British COIN theorist Sir Robert Thompson distilled the lessons of post-colonial COIN campaigns into several direct principles: the government required a clear aim; it needed to follow the rule of law rather than the jungle; its entire campaign plan needed overall coherence, coordination, and control; the political counter-subversion campaign had to be active; and it should proceed slowly and only after establishing a secure base upon which to expand — it could not try to do all things, everywhere, at once. Many of these conclusions remain true today.[21]

Modern commanders must recognize the political arena they operate within. As the aim of the struggle is ultimately political, most of the actions their forces take will have political dimensions, not just kinetic targets. Maintaining or developing the political legitimacy of their forces and the host government are major objectives. Destroying the enemy, providing security assistance, rural development, or giving local security, and all other activities are means to those ends.

Ultimately, isolating the insurgent armed elements from their base of support — if possible — is both a tactical necessity and a political one. Taking steps to ensure such opportunities can be exploited fully by the host government must also be a priority. Weeding out the enemy does not ensure the "rooting in" of the government. The actions of the COIN forces must not undercut the legitimacy of the governance efforts that follow, either by promising too much too soon or by replacing one faulty system of administration, taxation, laws, and so on with one more faulty, or one so alien as to be rejected as a mere foreign imposition.

That COIN campaigns also represent a long-term commitment raises political issues. For intervening forces managing expectations of performance amongst their own forces, other entities must be part of the campaign plan, namely their allies, home front, host government, and target populations. The more that the bit players in the coalition leave such issues to others to decide, the more likely they are to be disappointed by the outcomes. Gaining a voice on such issues at the right level is difficult, and may ultimately be political, but should not be left to chance. The entrails of military history foretell that leaving such issues to others to decide will result in disharmony, discord, and disillusionment of the coalition — or defeat.

On the more strictly military side of the ledger, the number of troops available will be highly controlled. Force use will be highly constrained. Troops will be required to adapt rapidly to the complex but rather opaque operating environment. COIN warfare has long been regarded as a subaltern's campaign, epitomized most often by small unit actions. There, too, senior non-commissioned officers will play a disproportionate role in direct interaction with local population and insurgent groups.[22]

The role of good intelligence and very particular knowledge of the complex social, economic, and political environment must be generated, widely disseminated, and used to inform all local interactions, not just in generating target lists.[23] Actions to win over opinion makers, local leaders, and social groups must inform the campaign design. The rise of Provincial Reconstruction Teams (PRTs) and Human Terrain Teams

(HTTs) is testimony to these truisms, but only the names are new; the lessons have been learned before.[24]

One may never win over local hearts, but their minds will always remain fixed on the absence or presence of enduring local security. Even if these steps lead to tactical or local successes — a pacified area here, new popular leaders there — it will count for little if there is no consistent game plan and a true unity of effort between all "friendlies." This idea is very easy to assert, but, as history demonstrates, it is difficult to achieve.

Allies and partners may have mixed motives and different agendas. The host government may never perform as promised, or according to some other nation's standards, or ever be seen as popular domestically. Isolating the insurgents may prove too difficult to achieve. Other dilemmas can confound the best of intentions — and not all allies necessarily have those. Napoleon once quipped that everything in war is simple, but even the simple things prove difficult. That remains true today.

In the contemporary struggle, supporting a protracted campaign may be more important than winning. Outlasting may be more important than destroying. Providing support may be more important than getting the job done. Maintaining domestic support may be more important than bringing the enemy to death. All such considerations will cloud the campaign plan and impinge on freedom of action among the alliance. Maintaining the home fires while waging limited warfare poses one of the greatest professional conundrums any Canadian commander will face.

This *tour d'horizon* reveals some of the many contours any COIN campaign may encounter. Time, local and international circumstances, allied proclivities, the physical dictates of the terrain — human, physical, and geopolitical — will impinge all of them, as in any war. On top of those common elements will be the unique features of the particular struggle. There is no simple target. Sights must be adjusted. It is suggested fortune favours the prepared mind.

2

The Quagmire of Great Powers

Dealing with the Afghan Way of War

MAJOR TONY BALASEVICIUS

For North Atlantic Treaty Organization (NATO) coalition forces caught in the quagmire of the war in Afghanistan, the enemy's methods have proven perplexing. Although NATO has had little difficulty winning tactical victories on the battlefield, operational success in establishing security and developing governance has proven elusive. Yet, for the Afghans, this conflict is like most others they have fought over the centuries. In fact, the strategy and tactics currently being employed by the insurgents fighting against the central government's authority are little more than an adaptation of the methods that were used by their forefathers, at least since Alexander the Great's invasion of the region in 330 B.C.E. The style and longevity of this Afghan "way of war" has evolved from the country's rugged topography and its unique social structure, which is based on a tribal system.

Historically, the country's mountainous terrain and lack of well-developed transportation routes has fostered a degree of isolation between its inhabitants. This isolation has encouraged a spirit of self-reliance and circumscribed social units, fostering loyalties toward family, community, and tribe.[1] This social construct has been the cause of many historic rivalries among tribal groups and has tended to produce a great deal of localized infighting and occasionally civil war. Ali Ahmad Jalali and Lester W. Grau, authorities on the Soviet occupation of Afghanistan, describe that the country "has mostly been a loose collection of tribes and nationalities over which central governments had varying degrees of influence and control at different times."[2] They explain, "Tribal rivalries and blood feuds, ambitions of local chieftains, and tribal defiance of pervasive interference by the central government have kept the different parts of the land at war at different times."[3]

This constant infighting and lack of national unity leads outsiders to the false perception of military weakness. Combined with the country's geographic location, this misconception has helped to make Afghanistan a tempting target for takeover by powerful empires with interest in the region.[4] Although invading armies have found Afghanistan very easy to occupy, they have also learned that it is extremely difficult to conquer its people. The reason for this paradox can be largely attributed to the fragmented nature of Afghanistan's tribal-based warriors and their unique style of fighting.

Individually, each tribe is capable of quickly mobilizing a cadre of experience warriors to defend its tribal area or any specific interest it may have. However, tribes can and will also unite to fight a common enemy and when they do so, they create a potent military capability. It is this ability to transition, seemingly within hours, from independent, local irregular defence forces fighting a guerrilla war to large armies employing more conventional types of operations and back again that has confused all but the most capable military commanders.[5]

Since the beginning of the nineteenth century, a number of contemporary powers have had the unfortunate experience of dealing with this confusing quagmire of guerrilla and conventional warfare. For example, the British fought several wars in Afghanistan yet were never able to fully establish their authority over the people.[6] Since then, Afghanistan has remained fragmented by internal strife while also having to deal with two major interventions: the Soviet Union's invasion in 1979, and more recently, NATO's involvement fighting the Taliban.

Remarkably, despite a history of internal strife and frequent interventions by major powers, Afghanistan has managed to survive. Afghanistan's survival in the face of these frequent interventions has been no accident. In fact, it is based on a well-developed tribal structure and unique fighting style that takes advantage of the terrain and weather to compound its effectiveness. This chapter will explore the Afghan way of war and provide an overview of the tribal system, with specific regard to its effect on war fighting in the country. It will then look at how some invading armies have attempted to deal with the fragmented nature of Afghanistan's tribal warriors during different historical periods, proving that the Afghan way of war presents a formidable obstacle to those who wish to exert control over the Afghan people.

AFGHANISTAN'S TRIBAL CULTURE

Brigadier-General David Fraser, a former commander of the International Security Assistance Force (ISAF), Multi-National Brigade in Regional Command South once remarked, of his time as commander in Afghanistan, "I underestimated one factor — culture." He then went on to lament, "I was looking at the wrong map — I needed to look at the tribal map not the geographic map"[7] This frank admission by a senior NATO commander is interesting, in that it provides insight into understanding (or lack of understanding of) a key component of the Afghan way of war, namely the country's social makeup.

Within Afghanistan, tribes are viewed as large kin groups consisting of persons allegedly descended through the male line from a common ancestor. Tribes are also looked upon as semiautonomous political units that occupy and exert control over certain territories.[8] Within these territories, most tribal members live in small rural villages, with each village comprising a single ethnic community, and its inhabitants are usually related by a complex network of family relationships.[9] Authority within the village is usually vested with the local chief, who is referred to as *malik* and is elected into the position by the villagers. The duties of the malik can include everything from tax collection and settling local disputes to occasionally looking for and apprehending criminals. He is also the village leader and spokesperson when dealing with senior tribal or central government authorities.[10]

A local council advises the malik and is composed of the heads of the various lineages present within the village.[11] As authors Seth G. Jones and Arturo Muñoz note, "The malik is expected to make his authority felt, but at the same time he must also be guided by tribal customs and precedent in the execution of his duties. For major decisions where there is no precedent, or which may run counter to earlier practices, he is expected to consult the [council]." Thus, in many respects, the malik is viewed within the community as a first among equals rather than an absolute ruler.[12] As a result, he normally exercises his authority very loosely, unless stricter discipline is needed, such as in the case where the security of the village is at risk or when intertribal warfare is in progress.

Local security fighters are drawn from the village population and, as such, are usually only part-time soldiers mobilized for a very specific reason. To mobilize this local defence force, the village council will put out a call-to-arms, and the close relationship between the various families within the village usually aids in this process.[13] As Ahmad and Grau point out, "The kinship-based identity has been the major means of the community's political and military mobilization."[14]

Village mobilization can range from a few men being called out for local defence to much larger and better-equipped units capable of offensive operations throughout the region. In cases where regional mobilization is occurring, or when a number of tribes are being called out, the size of the forces can be significant.[15] For example, in 1919 when the Afghan regular army was getting ready to attack the British in India, they were able to field a 50,000 man conventional force and had between 20,000 or 30,000 additional tribal fighters in the Khyber area available to support their operations.[16]

GEOGRAPHY

The second component that has influenced the style of fighting within Afghanistan has been its geography. Afghanistan is a landlocked country with a total land mass of about 652,680 square kilometres, and it is shaped by physical extremes, from flat, arid deserts to towering mountain ranges.[17] The geography has made transportation and communication within this primarily rural country extremely difficult.

Although the lack of transportation infrastructure has hampered economic development and centralized political structure, it has been a significant benefit to the Afghan warrior in times of conflict. As scholar Donald P. Wright remarks, "The mountains and the lack of roads have prevented outsiders from using military force to dominate the country. Moreover, for Afghan irregular forces, which for centuries have fought ferociously to expel outsiders, the terrain served as sanctuary from which they could attack invading armies, making their hold on the country tenuous."[18]

THE AFGHAN WAY OF WAR

This focus on smaller, village-level irregular forces and the difficult geography of the country has meant that Afghans traditionally fought a version of la *petite guerre* or guerrilla warfare. Guerrilla warfare has been described as "warfare by harassment through surprise" and features the use of ambushes, hit-and-run raids, sabotage, and, on occasion, terrorism to wear down the enemy.[19] This style of fighting is often used by weak nations and has proven extremely effective in offsetting the advantages in firepower, mobility, and numbers of a larger, stronger foe. Within the context of Afghanistan, this type of warfare has evolved to include fighting from fortified strong points, sometimes even from caves within the mountains.[20] Tailored to the Afghan defenders, these tactics have proven both adaptable and extremely durable. According to Afghan scholars Jalali and Grau, the tactics used by the Afghans during the Anglo-Afghan Wars (1839–1842, 1878–1880, and 1919) were still being used during the Soviet invasion and occupation of the 1970s and 1980s. They assert, "Although technology has added range and accuracy to armies, the terrain still dictates tactics and in this respect, the Afghans are still quite comfortable applying their time-honoured tactics against a modem foe."[21]

Historically, Afghanistan's use of guerrilla warfare has also been combined with conventional operations, usually when Afghan tribes work with an occupying force or when they are developed as part of a national army. This combination of guerrilla and conventional warfare has given the country a more flexible fighting doctrine than would normally be the case. Coupled with the fighting spirit of the tribal warrior, this explains the Afghan way of war's legendary resilience.[22]

THE INDIVIDUAL FIGHTING SPIRIT

Throughout Afghanistan's history, a tribe's security and continued existence have relied on its warriors, and as such, warriors are highly regarded within the community.[23] It is therefore not surprising to see that the attributes and skills of the warrior are models that young Afghan boys attempt to emulate. In Pashtun tribal society, for example, "the admired male is the statuesque tribesman, armed with bandoleer and rifle, whose erect posture and lithe movements dispel any doubt as to his effectiveness in hand-to-hand combat against his enemies."[24] It is believed that this ideal tribal warrior overcomes his enemies by moral and physical vigour. As scholar Harvey Henry Smith has noted, "Integrity and honour are highly emphasized [and] a favourite theme of Afghan literature is that of the indomitable warrior who is always a just man, true to his word."[25]

Personal pride is an integral within Afghan tribal culture, and if a warrior feels he has been wronged or insulted, he is quick to retaliate either verbally or physically — a key aspect of redeeming personal pride is vengeance, and this concept cannot be underestimated within the context of Afghanistan's fighters. According to Smith, an authority on Afghanistan, "The awesomeness of Afghan vengeance is reflected in the Hindu saying 'Oh Gods! From the venom of the cobra, the teeth of the tiger and the vengeance of the Afghan, deliver us.'"[26] As a result, physical conflict and blood feuds have arisen over such things as "problems of water distribution, cattle rustling, pasturage trespassing and wife stealing."[27]

Afghan warriors regard death in battle as honourable, and there is little or no hesitation to give up one's life in defence of tribal honour or to resist encroachment on tribal territory.[28] As Soviet Commander Alexander Lyakhovsky, who commanded troops in Afghanistan during the Russian occupation, wrote, "[We] completely disregarded the most important national and historical factors, above all the fact that the appearance of armed foreigners in Afghanistan was always met with arms in the hands [of the population]. This is how it was in the past, and this is how it happened when our troops entered [Afghanistan]."[29] Indeed, this willingness to do battle in order to defend against any type of encroachment, a unique fighting style, and the ruggedness of the country severely challenged the Macedonian king Alexander the Great and his Greek army when they entered Afghanistan in 330 B.C.E.

ALEXANDER THE GREAT IN AFGHANISTAN

Alexander's campaign in Afghanistan was part of a much larger effort to conquer the Persian Empire. After winning a series of decisive victories against the Persians at the Battle of the Granicus, 334 B.C.E.; the Battle of Issus, 333 B.C.E.; and the Battle of Gaugamela, 331 B.C.E.; the Macedonians went on to capture Persepolis (in modern day Iran) in 330 B.C.E.[30]

During the winter of 330–329 B.C.E., Alexander began his advance into Afghanistan by marching up the Helmand River valley. He had planned to advance over the mountains past what is today modern Kabul.[31] However, he encountered difficulties with the weather and terrain and halted around Kandahar to await the end of winter before moving north in late April or early May of 329 B.C.E. As the weather began to warm, Alexander decided to set out for Kabul. Unfortunately, as the army was en route, winter storms and freezing temperatures moved into the region and created a number of problems for his ill-prepared army. The Macedonians had no experience dealing with the cold, and combined with a lack of provisions, these conditions claimed many lives.[32]

Having endured the march to Kabul, Alexander then crossed the mountains of the Hindu Kush and proceeded northward over the Khawak Pass, eventually advancing into Bactria in order to engage what was left of the Persian army.[33] When Alexander arrived in the area, Bessus, the Persian king, retreated and crossed over the Oxus River into Sogdiana, where he hoped to establish allegiances with the various satrapies and tribes in the region.[34] Concerned by the approaching Macedonians, and hoping to stop further advances by the oncoming invaders, the satrapies decided to hand Bessus over to Alexander. Unfortunately for them, the gesture was of little value, as the Greeks continued on to the Jaxartes River.[35]

Upon reaching the Jaxartes River, Alexander quickly occupied Cyropolis and a number of fortified posts that had been constructed by the Persians to guard their northeastern frontier. Having secured a quick and easy victory over what was left of the Persian Empire, Alexander felt his position within the region was now secure, and he summoned the leading nobles of Sogdiana and Bactria to a meeting with him in Bactra.

Nonetheless, he still had much to learn about the Afghan way of war. While he was on his way to the meeting, the country erupted into insurgency as Scythian[36] warriors retook Cyropolis and its forts and massacred the Macedonian garrisons.[37] The loss was a significant blow for the Macedonian king, as it meant that other Scythian tribes could now cross the river and raid Sogdiana at will. Moreover, Alexander realized that if the various Scythian tribes decided to link up with tribal forces gathering in Sogdiana, the situation might turn into a very long and exhausting campaign. He also realized that he needed to regain his authority, and to do this he felt "he would not only have to reoccupy Cyropolis and the fortified posts; he would also have to capture and execute their garrisons."[38]

Before moving on the posts, he ordered one of his commanders to lay siege to Cyropolis while he sent part of his cavalry to the more distant posts with orders to prevent their garrisons from escaping. While this was happening, he dealt with the three nearest positions.[39] Fortunately for him, the Macedonians were able to make short work of the first fort, which was surrounded by little more than a low mud wall. Once the wall was overcome, the garrison was quickly put to the sword, and Alexander moved on the next two forts, both of which were also taken quickly. The tribesmen, still holding onto the remaining positions, could see the smoke from the retaken forts and attempted to withdraw, but they were cut down by the blocking forces that had already moved into position.[40]

Unfortunately for Alexander, such operations that afforded the possibility of a quick and decisive victory were to be short-lived. The Afghans quickly realized they were outmatched in these conventional assaults and reverted to hit-and-run tactics, which played to their strengths. A return to guerrilla operations, combined with the fragmented nature of Afghan tribal fighting, put the Macedonians off balance for a period of time. As Alexander continued his attempts to stabilize the situation, uprisings in eastern Sogdia started to spread throughout much of the region. One such outbreak came when a group of Massagetae tribal warriors fighting under the capable leadership of Spitamenes, a Sogdian warlord, laid siege to Maracanda. Alexander, not fully realizing the potency of the Afghan threat or the capabilities of this particular leader, decided to send a small relief force under the command of Pharnuches, a Lycian commander, to the garrison.

While Pharnuches and his force were en route to Maracanda, Alexander got to work supervising the construction of a new city, Alexandria Eskhata (Alexandria the Furthest), on the Jaxartes River. As construction was underway, Scythian tribal nomads started harassing the Macedonians from the far side of the river. Alexander decided to take the initiative and crossed the river under covering fire from his catapults, which kept the enemy away from the river banks.[41] Once on the other side of the river, Alexander was introduced to the Scythians' guerrilla tactics, which "consisted of the mounted Scythians circling around concentrated troops firing arrows into the group then withdrawing before they could be attacked."[42]

To deal with these unconventional tactics, Alexander needed to respond quickly. He consolidated his position on the far bank. Once this was done, he massed a small force forward of his main position in an effort to make it a tempting target for attack by the more mobile Scythians. The ploy worked, as the Scythians attacked, confident that they could easily manage to outmanoeuvre the Macedonians. When the enemy had committed itself, Alexander ordered his main force forward while his Companions (heavy cavalry), which were positioned on the flanks, attempted to outflank the enemy formation. This tactic surprised the Scythians, and as they realized they were about to be surrounded, they lost their composure long enough for the Macedonians to exploit the situation.[43]

During the battle, it is estimated that some 1,000 Scythians were killed and about 150 taken prisoner, while the Macedonians lost about

60 cavalry and 100 infantry. However, the victory had far more operational significance than the number killed or captured. It resulted in the surrender of the Scythian king, who put himself at Alexander's disposal. This was an extremely important psychological victory for the Macedonian king. As historian James Ashley points out, "in Asia, the Scythians were widely believed to be invincible, and Alexander's' victory over them convinced many that it was impossible for any single nation to defeat him."[44] The victory also meant that a number of Scythian tribes either remained neutral or actively provided Alexander with support while he remained in Afghanistan. In fact, Alexander realized the benefits derived from forming alliances with tribes, and whenever possible, he tried to win them over with generous inducements.

Meanwhile, as Pharnuches approached Maracanda on his mission to relieve the city, Spitamenes was prepared for him. He broke his siege and slowly retreated to the edge of the desert, where he was joined by an additional 600 Sacae horsemen. As Pharnuches pursued the retreating guerrillas, he advanced into a well-prepared ambush. From the outset, Pharnuches was at a disadvantage, as Spitamenes commanded a light cavalry force that had greater mobility in an open area and was capable of delivering a high volume of missile fire from a distance.[45] Moreover, Pharnuches did not have Alexander's skill, and he was unable to withstand the ferocity of the assault. His troops broke formation and were annihilated.[46] When Alexander learned of Pharnuches's defeat, he quickly assembled a force of infantry, archers, and cavalry and marched 135 miles to Maracanda. After relieving the city, he instituted a scorched-earth policy and destroyed everything in the valley in order to deprive Spitamenes of food supplies.[47]

Although these battles were relatively minor affairs, they forced Alexander to confront the fact that he was fighting a completely different type of war than he was accustomed to, meaning he would have to adjust his operational approach. He returned to Balkh for the winter of 329–328 B.C.E. to come up with a strategy that could deal with this perplexing Afghan way of war. He realized that his forces were still able to succeed, but his victories were not decisive. Resistance seemed to continue even as the Afghans were consistently defeated at the tactical level, and the reason for this was simple: the Afghan tribes were far more mobile than Alexander's army and were using their long-range weapons (bow and arrows), along with hit and run tactics, to keep the Macedonians at bay, thus avoiding decisive engagement. Alexander also realized that the Afghan warriors were being supported by the local population, who provided them with food, shelter, and intelligence. This particular problem was compounded by a lack of precedent from which Alexander could draw upon. As Fuller states, "For great battles he had many masters to turn to; for mountain warfare he had Xenophon; but for a battle on the plains against an enemy who possessed neither base, nor communications, nor organization, he had no predecessor in tactics, for even Cyrus, the Great Persian ruler, had been defeated by the Scythians."[48]

In the end, Alexander's solution to the problem was both innovative and simple. He would attempt to limit the mobility of the enemy while denying them their support base. To accomplish this, Alexander established a number of fortified garrisons throughout the region at specific intervals on dominating terrain. He then divided a large part of his force into mobile columns that had the task of raiding enemy camps and rounding up the population.[49]

The plan worked, for without the local population, Spitamenes and other tribes lost their easy access to supplies, forcing them to search for food elsewhere. Wherever they moved, they came up against the strategically sited forts or ran into the mobile columns. Eventually, they were forced to conduct conventional attacks for food, and when they did, they were easily defeated. In fact, Spitamenes was forced to attack the Macedonian general Coenus and was decisively defeated, suffering heavy losses. After that battle, the Massagetae warriors decided they were nearly done with fighting,[50] and they turned on Spitamenes with lethal force.[51]

The defeat of the Persian army and the Scythians, along with the death of an innovative and charismatic leader like Spitamenes, should have ended resistance in the region, but such was not the case. Despite his impressive accomplishments, Alexander now had to focus his attention on even greater challenges: the mountain fortresses of Sogdiana. To be successful in taking the fortresses, he would not only have to conquer the will of the Afghan warrior, but also the geography of Afghanistan.

The most famous of these mountain fortresses was the Sogdian Rock, where the Bactrian noble Oxyartes had taken refuge.[52] When Oxyartes's envoys refused Alexander's demand to surrender, he decided to attack the fortress. Sogdian Rock was last major stronghold in Sogdiana, the final province of the Persian Empire still unconquered, and Alexander believed that all resistance in the region would stop if he could take it. However, taking the fortress would be a difficult task. It was protected by a rock wall on almost every approach. Moreover, it was provisioned for a long siege and had an unlimited supply of water.

To attack the fortress, Alexander asked for volunteers with rock-climbing experience. Under the cover of darkness, a 300-man team started climbing the steepest part of the rock-face, which they assumed would be the least likely to be guarded. Although some thirty soldiers lost their lives during the ascent, as dawn was breaking they were able to reach and capture the summit.[53] The sight of Greek soldiers positioned above the fortress shocked the defenders, and they decided to surrender.[54] Along with the soldiers garrisoned within, there were many women and children, including Oxyartes's wife and daughters.[55] It is said that Alexander was so taken by the beauty of Roxana, one of Oxyartes's daughters, that he made her his wife. He then appointed Oxyartes satrap of the province of Paropamisadae, India, where he remained until Alexander's death in 323 B.C.E. The marriage and appointment helped to secure alliances for the Macedonians in the region.[56]

After taking Sogdian Rock, Alexander's hope of peace was not realized, and he went on to take the Rock of Chorienes before moving into the Swat region, which was also eventually captured. Only then was he in a position to begin preparations for the conquest of India.

SUMMARY OF ALEXANDER'S EXPERIENCE

Major-General John Frederick, a military officer of great renown, best described Alexander's experience fighting the Afghans when he stated, "No great battles awaited Alexander [in Afghanistan], he was to be faced by a people's war of mounted guerrillas who, when he advanced would suddenly appear in his rear, who entrenched themselves in inaccessible caves, and when pursued, vanished into the Turkoman steppes."[57] In his analysis of Alexander's performance during the campaign, historian Charles Fuller brings out an interesting point: "In all his great battles, the organization of his enemy's army automatically created a decisive point, the brain of the organization — its command — to strike at, and in his mountain campaigns he [Alexander] could always strike at the villages of the hill men, and so attack them economically; but nomads have no villages and no organization demanding a military brain." Fuller further explains that "against such an antagonist the only sure method is to compel him by ruse to mass in an area in which his mobility will be restricted, and when such cannot be found, then by manoeuvring a hedge of moving men to fence him round and besiege him in the open."[58] Of course, compelling the tribes to fight on their enemy's terms is, at best, extremely difficult; however, that is precisely what Alexander was able to do.

Alexander's success in this regard was largely based on his ability to adjust his style of fighting to the conditions he was facing. He quickly realized that he needed to force the more mobile enemy to concentrate in areas where that mobility would be severely restricted, or he would need to surround them. To accomplish this, Alexander used a number of fighting techniques, but the most common and effective was the placement of well-situated, fortified posts. Once the forts were in place, he deployed a number of mobile columns in an attempt to round up the population. As a result, the population was unable to help the warriors with food, shelter, or intelligence. This forced the mobile fighters make conventional attacks against fixed installations, where Alexander was stronger, and more importantly, these attacks gave the Macedonians the opportunity to achieve decisive victory.[59]

Such policies showed Alexander's flexibility in dealing with unfamiliar tactical problems relating to the tribes and their particular style of warfare. Not only did Alexander quickly grasp the tactical conditions that were at the heart of the tribesmen's success, many of his innovated solutions to counter their tactics, such as fortified posts and mobile columns, are viewed as standard counter-insurgency tactics to this day.

AFGHANISTAN AFTER ALEXANDER

After Alexander left the country, the Afghans fought a succession of out-side rulers and eventually formed a number of semi-independent states. However, these local dynasties were crushed during the Mongolian inva-sions of the 1200s, which left a lasting scar on the country.

When the Mongol army invaded Afghanistan, it killed many of the people and destroyed much of the country's infrastructure, particularly the greatly valued irrigation systems.[60] According to Stephen Tanner, a military historian and author, "the fact that today Afghanistan is con-sidered a rough rather than a fragile country — inured to warfare rather than prone to passive resistance — stems largely from the wholesale destruction of its sedentary element at this time." As Tanner goes on to note, "Towns and farms based on centuries-old cultivation techniques lay naked in the path of the Mongol[s]"[61] The Mongols occupied the country until around the 1500s. Between the 16th and early 18th century, different parts of Afghanistan were governed by three major powers: the Khanate of Bukhara ruled the north, Safavid Persians controlled much of the west, and the remaining area was overseen by the Mughals.[62]

In 1747 Ahmed Shah, a Pashtu, was finally able to unify many of the different Afghan tribes. This brief period of unity would provide a glimpse into Afghanistan's military potential as a nation, for by 1751, Shah and his Afghan army had conquered an empire that extended from the Amu Darya to the Indian Ocean and from Khorasan to present-day northern India.[63] Unfortunately, after his death, his successors were unable to hold onto his legacy, and by the early 1800s, Afghanistan's central location became of increasing interest to the new world powers operating in the region, particularly the British and Russian empires.

During this period, the British were consolidating their colonial holdings on the Indian subcontinent and were looking at the Hindu Kush Mountains as a natural barrier to invasion or incursion by rival powers, such as the Russians. As the Russian Empire was expanding into Central Asia from the north, the two eventually collided in Afghanistan in what became known as "the Great Game."[64]

BRITISH EXPERIENCE IN THE AFGHAN QUAGMIRE

British concerns over Russian encroachment into Central Asia led to the "Great Game," and it was the cause of two of the three Anglo-Afghan wars. The first war (1839–1842) resulted from the arrival of a Russian diplomat in Kabul. The British demanded that Afghanistan expel the diplomatic mission and cease contact with both Russia and Iran. Moreover, it ordered the Afghan government to hand over vast tracts of Pashtun inhabited land (regions of Pakistan). Dost Mohammad, the Afghan ruler, quickly agreed to the demands, but the British decided to occupy the country anyway.[65]

The British army entered Afghanistan by way of the Hindu Kush and Kandahar. After occupying the city, they advanced onto the fortress city of Ghazni and moved on to seize Kabul with little resistance. Despite their initial success, the British, like Alexander, were soon embroiled in a popular uprising, largely because they had failed to appreciate the tribal dynamics at work within Afghanistan.

The British had assumed that if they controlled the major centres of power — the government and the ruler — by default they controlled the country. However, in Afghanistan this was not the case. Mohammed was designated as the national leader, but he had little authority over much of the country. Stephen Tanner articulates this point: "The Ghilzai tribes who oversaw the passes between Kabul and the Punjab had no use for government or taxation; [while] the Durranis, who roamed free in the south and west, were entirely content with local rule." Tanner concludes that "the cities of Kandahar, Farah, and Herat, and the entire territory north of the Hindu Kush would have to be wrested away from their princes or warlords anew if they were to succumb to the King's rule."[66]

British ignorance regarding tribal dynamics created additional confusion on the ground as uprisings were breaking out spontaneously, in different districts, apparently without any real reason and with little or no coordination. In fact, these tribal uprisings were part of the normal power structure within the country, as changes in stature of the local leaders and even the perception of reduced importance were factors that resulted in these outbreaks of fighting.[67]

As a result, the British army was thrown into the middle of a confusing situation with little understanding of what they should do next. Consequently, the occupation developed into a very distinct pattern of operations. As the British attempted to extend their control over the tribe areas, especially near the cities, they met stiff resistance. When attacked with any force, the Afghan fighters would simply fall back into the mountains; if the British did not maintain constant pressure on them, the fighters would quickly return. If the British army moved too far into the mountains, however, they were met by a series of well-sighted ambushes, where the Afghan's understanding of the terrain and control of the high ground proved decisive.

Many engagements proved even more devastating for the British, as the Afghans held a significant tactical advantage in small arms.[68] The British standard issue firearm at the time was the smoothbore Brown Bess. It was accurate to about 50 yards, and effective out to about 150, while the Afghans used the *jezail*, a hand-made muzzle loaded musket, which was effective out to 500 yards. This gave the Afghans a considerable range advantage over the British, and, in some cases, this difference had a significant effect on the outcome of battles.[69] For example, during fighting around the village of Baymaroo in 1841, a small British force tried to secure the village but was quickly pinned down by jezail fire from various buildings. As one account described, "As the battle continued Afghan fighters began arriving from the surrounding areas to help out and occupied the high ground overlooking the British positions. As the Afghans started to surge over the slopes towards the enemy's position the British formed squares, whereupon the Afghans stayed on the high ground and simply fired into the ranks with their long-range rifles."[70]

The Afghan's tactical range advantage also meant that the British were never able to bring the tribal worriers into close combat, where British discipline might prove decisive. As a result, the fighting tended to go on longer, and this extension worked to the advantage of the Afghans, as it gave them time to mobilize reinforcements from the local area, even as the battle continued. This ad hoc mobilization also confused the British, as they were never sure how many warriors they were fighting and when enemy reinforcements would arrive on the battlefield.

For the British, these problems on the ground at the tactical and operational level were compounded by a clear disconnect between what the front-line commanders were experiencing and what their political leaders in India and England were saying about the mission. As Richard Shultz and Andrea Dew explain, "While the British envoy was puffing up success in Kabul for the audience back home, General Nott was locked in an unending struggle with Afghan tribes in the south the Ghilzais and Durranis. [Meanwhile,] west of Kabul, Uzbeks and Baluchi tribal warriors roamed unchecked."[71]

Political belief that all was going well in Afghanistan from a military perspective would contribute to British defeat in the country. By the summer of 1841, the operational situation began to get much worse for the British as tribes started to unite as part of a holy war or *jihad* in order to drive the British out of Afghanistan. Amazingly, at the same time as the situation on the ground was becoming extremely unstable, with a united resistance movement gaining momentum, the British, in an attempt to save money, began to downsize their forces in the country. More incredibly, they started cutting back on bribes to the various tribes, including payments to the Ghilzais.[72] These payments were of great significance, because the tribe controlled the Khyber region, and the British were dependent on the revenue generated from tributes for safe passage through the Khyber Pass, the main British supply route between India and Afghanistan. Upon receiving news of the cuts, the Ghilzais began attacking British caravans travelling to and from India.[73]

Toward the end of 1841, discontent was so widespread that mobs were beginning to openly attack British soldiers on the streets of Kabul. As British authority eroded with the continued removal of troops from the country, outright fighting erupted within the city. Moreover, the resistance grew confident that, united, they could defeat the common enemy. In early January 1842, the British garrison in Kabul was forced to abandon the city and withdraw to India.

Paradoxically, the retreating British now had to travel through the Khyber Pass, which they believed they had secured with an agreement of safe passage. However, this was not the case, and as they moved through the pass, the Ghilzai tribesman opened fire on them from the top ledges.[74]

For the next two days, the British attempted to push through the pass but were unable to fight off the incessant attacks. Receiving constant reinforcement from the surrounding area, the tribesmen also held the tactical advantage, as they controlled the high ground overlooking the pass. In the end, due to the tenacity of the Ghilzais, who were helped by nearby reinforcements and the freezing-cold weather, every member of the British contingent that had not been captured was killed, except one.[75] With this defeat, Great Britain's first experience in Afghanistan all but ended.

THE SECOND ANGLO-AFGHAN WAR

Much like the first war, the Second Anglo-Afghan War, in 1878, had its genesis in an uninvited Russian diplomatic mission to Kabul. This time the British simply demanded that Afghanistan also accept a British contingent, but the request was denied.[76] With Afghanistan acting as a buffer zone between Russian and British territorial interest, the British perceived the move as an encroachment, and in response, in November 1878, they invaded the country with a 40,000-man force.[77]

The initial British invasion force was broken down into three military columns that penetrated Afghanistan at different locations in order to occupy key points throughout the country as quickly as possible. The initial occupation was achieved swiftly and with little difficulty.[78] The Afghan ruler, Mohammad Yaqub Khan, decided to put an end to the conflict and signed a treaty with the British in May 1879. Assured that they had achieved their aims, the British army withdrew.[79] However, on 3 September 1879, an uprising in Kabul led to the killing of Sir Pierre Cavagnari and members of his escort. This provoked the second phase of the war, and the British army returned again with a strong military presence.[80]

This second force was led by Major-General Sir Frederick Robert, who moved into central Afghanistan and quickly defeated the Afghan national forces at Char Asiab on 6 October 1879. After the battle, he moved on to occupy Kabul on 13 October. However, the character of this war would be different from the last, as the British had learned from their mistakes. The most important change to British operational procedure was their reluctance to get heavily involved in occupation duties, and they thus avoided fighting a guerrilla war, particularly in the mountains. They accomplished this by departing as soon as their political objectives were reached. Moreover, the British decision not to fight a guerrilla war was aided, to a large extent, by the Afghan decision to deploy larger, more conventional forces to engage the British.

Within a matter of weeks, the Afghan way of war had once again revealed itself, but in a more conventional form, as Ghazi Mohammad Jan Khan Wardak staged a major uprising with over 10,000 tribal warriors under his control. On 11 December, a small British detachment encountered Mohammed Jan's force advancing on Kabul.[81] Initially, the detachment was able to delay the Afghan advance, but it did so only at the cost of heavy casualties. Despite this initial setback, Mohammed Jan continued his advance, and on 15 December, he laid siege to British forces defending the Sherpur Cantonment, which was located just north of Kabul. Upon learning that British reinforcements were moving in to relieve the garrison, Mohammed Jan ordered his troops to storm the cantonment on 23 December in a conventional assault. However, the assault was defeated by superior British firepower, and Jan was forced to withdraw, effectively ending the rebellion.[82] Yet the Afghans would not remain content with the British occupation, and in July 1880, Ayub Khan, the governor of Herat, decided he would revolt in the southern part of the country with an attack on Kandahar. The British were warned about the uprising and sent a brigade from Kandahar to intercept the force, which they were able to do at Maiwand.

As the battle developed, on 27 July 1880, Ayub took advantage of the ground to outflank the British force. One British officer, after the battle, explained how this was possible: "The enemy, cleverly using dry watercourses and folds in the ground as covered approaches, now succeeded in establishing positions only about 500 yards away in a ravine running parallel to our front."[83] As the Afghans started to outmanoeuvre their forward positions, the British were forced to withdraw under the protection of a small but effective rear guard action. The rear guard was able to keep the Afghans away from the withdrawing and somewhat disorganized columns. Unfortunately for the British, Ayub Khan was able to follow them back to Kandahar and promptly laid siege to the city.

In order to break the siege, the British sent a large relief column of 10,000 soldiers from Kabul on 8 August. The resulting Battle of Kandahar, on 1 September 1880, proved to be a decisive victory for the British.[84] More importantly, the Battle of Kandahar signalled the end to the Second Anglo-Afghan War. As Ayub Khan had been decisively beaten, the British were able to position their appointee, Abdur Rahman Khan, as emir of Afghanistan. Having achieved the political aims of their invasion, the British wisely withdrew before they became embroiled in another protracted guerrilla-style war.[85]

SUMMARY OF THE BRITISH EXPERIENCE DURING THE 1800S

Alexander's success in Afghanistan was based on his ability to understand the conditions he was fighting under and adapt accordingly. He realized that the only way of dealing with the tribes was to force them into an area where their mobility was restricted. To accomplish this, he used mobile columns that were adapted for the terrain and operated from fixed bases, allowing them to raid the independent nomads while concentrating and controlling the population so that they could not help the warriors. Moreover, he understood the need to make peace and, where possible, bring the tribes onto his side.

During the First Anglo-Afghan War, the British generally lacked the leadership, political savvy, and tactical advantages to replicate Alexander's feats. From the beginning of the campaign, it was clear that the British did not understand the Afghan way of war. Even when they did employ innovative tactics, it appeared to be haphazard, and they failed to learn the valuable lessons that could have aided them in future encounters with the enemy. For example, when they entered Afghanistan, they advanced on the fortress city of Ghazni. Rather than attempt to take the city by direct assault, however, the British commander decided to employ a man with knowledge of the local language to find a way into the fortress. He accomplished this task and the city fell quickly. Richard H. Shultz and

Andrea J. Dew contend that the victory at Ghazni held many important lessons for the British on how they should fight the Afghans. They argue that these lessons included "the importance of co-opting local individuals to exploit tribal rivalries, the importance of subterfuge [a trick or ruse], and a comprehension of just how deep the sentiment ran against the infidel invaders."[86] Unfortunately, the British failed to see any lasting military relevance to the battle. They never really understood the dynamics of the tribal system or the importance of maintaining good relations with tribes, particularly ones such as the Ghilzais, who controlled important tactical features. Nor did they see the importance of playing the tribes against one another, if for no other reason than to keep them from uniting.

Thus, while victorious in 1880, the British had simply stacked the deck against themselves for future engagements. Indeed, these oversights contributed to the development of a patriotic war for the Afghans, and the tribes united to drive the British out of Afghanistan. Since they were also at a significant tactical disadvantage in small arms, the British were unable to compensate for operational deficiencies with tactical success.

During the Second Afghan War, the British were better prepared for their Afghan experience. Specifically, they were tactically more proficient and were able to capitalize on the fact that the Afghans revolted with large forces that remained intact for longer periods of time. The British seized the opportunity to bring the tribes to battle and used their superior firepower to defeat the Afghans. In fact, with the exception of the Battle of Maiwand, British firepower and discipline easily overcame the ferocity of the tribal attacks, even when heavily outnumbered.

However, despite installing a friendly government and maintaining control of the country's foreign policy, they failed to achieve a resolution of the Afghan issue. Although the British were better prepared to fight in the terrain of Afghanistan, they did not attempt to win over the tribes or come to terms with how to fight a guerrilla war, which was the likely outcome once the British army defeated Afghan forces on the field of battle. Prudently, the British departed shortly after the battle of Kandahar, avoiding what could have become a very long and costly guerrilla war. Nonetheless, this evacuation meant that they never really dealt with — or defeated — the Afghan way of war.

NO EASY TASK

THE ROAD TO INDEPENDENCE: THE THIRD ANGLO-AFGHAN WAR OF 1919

Although Afghanistan officially remained neutral during the First World War, there was a great deal of anti-British sentiment within the country, and it resulted in sporadic fighting along the Afghanistan-Indian border during the conflict. After the hostilities ceased, King Amanullah was looking for a diversion from the internal strife within the Afghan court and decided to take advantage of civil unrest in India to attack the British. His attack on British positions in India launched the Third Anglo-Afghan War.[87]

Operations began on 6 May 1919 with an Afghan army of about 50,000 attacking British positions along the border. After a brief period of skirmishing, the British gained the upper hand and started to advance into Afghanistan. However, as they started making headway, the conflict ended with an armistice on 8 August 1919. Although the Afghans were defeated militarily, they gained much from the war. The British conceded complete independence to Afghanistan with the signing of the Treaty of Rawalpindi.[88] They did not end their involvement in the country, however.

Over the next ten years, fears about Soviet encroachment into Afghanistan continued to haunt the British, and this fear led them to work with various dissident groups, who forced Amanullah to abdicate in 1929. As a result, different warlords contended for power until a new king, Muhammad Nadir Shah, was crowned. He was assassinated four years later and succeeded by Muhammad Zahir Shah, Afghanistan's final king, who ruled for the next 40 years.[89]

Zahir Shah's rule was autocratic, and while he maintained a variety of councils and assemblies to advise him, in reality they had no real power. Under Zahir's rule, political parties were outlawed and protesters were imprisoned or killed.[90] By the early 1970s, discontent was such that the Peoples Democratic Party of Afghanistan (PDPA) decided to aid Mohammed Daoud Khan, who was the cousin and brother-in-law of King Zahir, in seizing power. In return the party was to receive a number of government posts. However, once Daoud had consolidated his power, he instead ordered a crackdown on the party.[91]

In 1978 the PDPA was able to seize control of the government from Daoud in a military coup. Shortly after they had taken over the reins of power, they announced a number of broad but ill-conceived reforms that alienated large segments of the population. Moreover, they did little to actually implement the reforms, thereby also alienating those groups that might have supported them.[92] The discontent became violence when rebellion broke out in the Nuristan region of Eastern Afghanistan and, in the following months, spread to other parts of the country. In order to contain the growing unrest, the PDPA requested increases in Soviet military assistance. Unfortunately, this assistance did little to alleviate the problem, and by October 1979, rebellion had become widespread. The situation had become so dire that the Afghan government formally requested Soviet intervention.

SOVIET EXPERIENCE IN THE QUAGMIRE

Although initially hesitant, the Soviets eventually acquiesced to the requests and deployed the 40th army into Afghanistan in December 1979. The force consisted of three motorized rifle divisions, an airborne division, an assault brigade, and two independent motorized rifle brigades along with five separate motorized rifle regiments.[93] Like the British in the 1800s, they rapidly took control of the large population centres and quickly secured all government buildings along with the key lines of communication.[94] While the occupation of the country was both swift and impressive in its military efficiency, pacification of Afghanistan's rural warrior society would prove impossible.

Almost from the beginning of their occupation, the Soviets were confronted by the same difficulties that had plagued the British's first experience in dealing with the Afghan way of war. Specifically, the Soviets had agreed to deal with a national rebellion that was complicated by the geography of the country, a fragmented society that held no allegiance to a central authority, and a security force structure that proved totally inadequate for the type of conflict they were engaged in.[95] Moreover, the Soviets, like the British, had also underestimated the reaction of the

Afghan people to their presence and ended up fighting an Afghan tribal society that was engaged in holy war. These warriors were referred to in the Western media as the *mujahideen*.[96]

Like their predecessors, the mujahideen fought the Soviets under the guidance of tribal leaders, using the assortment of proven guerrilla tactics such as ambushes of convoys along key supply routes, sabotage and raids on key government infrastructure, and various acts of terror. However, operations were updated to include defensive operations to counter raids, helicopter insertions, cordon and search, counter ambush, and fighting against and in encirclement.[97]

Tactics were also adjusted for new technology, as most of the weapons that were used by Afghan fighters were taken from the Soviets. These included the AK-47 and RPG-7 antitank grenade launcher, which became the mujahideen's weapon of choice. This favouritism was due to the fact that the grenade launchers were capable of taking out tanks, armored personnel carriers, and in some cases helicopters.[98]

Armed with these weapons, the Afghans were cunning at executing ambushes. For example, a mujahideen warrior recounted:

> We were 11 Mujahideen with an RPG-7, seven Kalashnikovs and two Enfields. We moved into the area the night before, spent the night in a village and set up our ambush site the next morning north of Kolangar District Headquarters. We were told that a column was coming from Kabul to Gardez, and so we had time to set up during the daylight before the column arrived, since the convoys always left Kabul in the morning well after dawn. Kabul is about 50 kilometers north of the ambush site. We set our ambush just south of the Tangi Waghjan Gorge. There, the river continues to run parallel to the road and restricts maneuver while providing better firing positions for the ambush force. We had a collapsed electric pylon that we stretched across the road as a road block. We put in an RPG firing position for Mulla Latif, our RPG gunner, and

put two other Mujahideen on the edge of the river in positions.

At about 1000 hours ... the lead tank in the column came to our roadblock. The tank driver stopped his tank, got out of the tank and moved the barrier. He had gotten back into his tank and driven past as we reached our positions. Mulla Latif ... hit the tank this time and it burst into flames ... This burning tank stopped the convoy since there was no room to maneuver or pass. Other Mujahideen from other areas and groups ran to the area and moved up the gorge by the trapped column and started firing at the vehicles. There was not much resistance from this supply convoy.[99]

Like both Alexander and the British, the Soviets initially attempted to overcome this type of warfare with a large conventional army designed for battle against other heavy conventional forces. Ahmad and Grau point out that during the initial stages of the Afghan conflict, "the Soviet army was trained for large-scale, rapid-tempo operations. They were not trained for the platoon leaders' war of finding and closing with small, indigenous forces which would only stand and fight when the terrain and circumstances were to their advantage."[100] Initially employing techniques that the Western media referred to as "Hammer and Anvil" operations, the Soviets attempted to establish blocking positions and then conduct massive mechanized sweeps over wide areas, intending to crush any tribal fighters that were caught between the two forces.[101]

These large-scale operations proved futile because they were totally inappropriate for fighting the Afghan way of war. Eventually, the Soviets realized the limitations of these tactics and adapted their organizations and operations accordingly. Moving away from their reliance on motor rifle units, they started employing lighter, better trained, and more professional soldiers, including airborne, air assault, and special purpose (*spetsnaz*) forces. They also introduced new types of lighter, more mobile formations, such as mountain motor rifle battalions, and developed training and tactics that were more suited to the operational requirements in-theatre.[102] Despite these reforms, which increased their tactical efficiency, the Soviets were unable to achieve decisive operational results. Much of this failure can be attributed to their inability to destroy the mujahideen's ability to fight a guerrilla war and, similarly, the Soviets' inability to effectively exploit the fragmented nature of the country's tribal structure.

The Soviets did initially attempt to bring the Afghans, particularly in the south, on side by trying to convince them of the legitimacy and benefits of their occupation, but these efforts proved to be unsuccessful, and they eventually ended all programs aimed at winning over the people in these areas.[103] Instead, they tried gaining control of the population by using reprisals and harsh punitive measures to frighten the populace into supporting the security forces.[104] Over the course of the war, such harsh measures became a key part of Soviet strategy in areas where the mujahideen had firmly established their authority. Unable to put sufficient forces into these areas, the Soviets ruthlessly attempted to separate the mujahideen from the villages. Using Mao Zedong's metaphor that guerrillas are supported by the population the way fish swimming in the sea are supported by the water, the Soviet approach in Afghanistan was to progressively empty the water out of the bowl, thereby killing the fish.[105]

The Soviets also used reprisal attacks, causing what has often been referred to as migratory genocide.[106] This strategy was based on rapidly responding against any rebel attack on Soviet troops with an overwhelming military retaliation against villages in the immediate area of the assault.[107] In certain rural areas where the rebel forces were strong, the Soviets deployed heavy mechanized forces with the simple goal of exterminating the local population.[108] During these operations, the Soviets destroyed the agricultural system upon which the rural population depended. Irrigation facilities, livestock, orchards, vineyards, water wells, and crops were actively targeted with the express purpose of forcing civilians to choose between flight and starvation.[109] After one such attack, a Swedish official reported that "Russian soldiers shot at anything alive in six villages — people, hens, donkeys — and then they plundered what remained of value."[110]

The scope of this effort and the results were staggering. At the end of 1986, the United Nations High Commission for Refugees (UNHCR) stated there were approximately 3.2 million Afghan refugees in Pakistan with a further fifty thousand scattered in Europe, India, and the United States.[111] Toward the end of the war, it was believed that there were upwards of five million refugees in Pakistan and India, with a further two million rural Afghans seeking refuge in Kabul and other Afghan population centres. In their efforts to eliminate potential bases of support, it is believed that the Soviets killed as much as 9 percent of Afghanistan's pre-invasion population.[112] However, despite this destruction and massed killings, the will of the Afghans to keep fighting remained intact.

Critical to the mujahideen's ability to continue fighting was preventing the Soviets from destroying their bases. In addition to the bases located in various villages and in the mountains, the mujahideen had also established a number of sanctuaries along both sides of the Afghan-Pakistani border where they were able to regroup and continue operations.[113]

Understanding the significance of these safe havens, the Soviets made a concerted effort to close the border area in an attempt to cut the rebels off from their sanctuaries.[114] Initially, they attempted to do this by creating government posts along the Afghan-Pakistani border from which they could launch attacks against mujahideen columns. This proved unsuccessful due to the sheer length of the border and the inability to establish sufficient posts or manpower to interdict the infiltrations. As a result, the Soviets tried to financially co-opt tribes living in the area to harass the mujahideen bands as they attempted to move back and forth, which also proved ineffective.[115]

In the end, various measures to separate the mujahideen from the people and their sanctuaries did not work. The Soviets' failure to destroy the sanctuaries allowed the mujahideen to continue long-term operations, meaning they could wear down the Russians' strength with the cumulative effect of fighting.[116]

One interesting aspect of Soviet tactics was their attempt to disrupt rebel actions and gain information through subversion operations, which were carried out by the Soviet intelligence services, using Afghan spies and collaborators. Exploiting the fragmented nature of the country, the Soviets were able to persuade some villages to form a truce and reject rebel demands for logistic support. Such villages were often found near major population centres and would form their own militia groups that protected the village and enforced law and order within the community. In certain cases, rebel groups were bribed into switching allegiances, while tribal chiefs were bribed with land and money to renounce support for the mujahideen. These techniques of co-opting the population have the effect of creating "a stratum of people in the countryside that have a vested political and economic stake in the system and are likely to defend it."[117] Subversion was particularly successful when used to spread conflict and division among the various resistance groups. Afghan society, and the rebel groups it produced, was inherently fragmented and fraught with disunity.[118] The Soviets repeatedly attempted to exploit these divisions and turn the groups against one another. Agents infiltrated these rebel organizations and attempted to assassinate mujahideen leaders, or they tried to turn the insurgent organizations against one another by providing information on insurgent movements and tactics. Agents also spread rumours between resistance groups and employed disinformation to create conflict between bands or to discredit the mujahideen leaders in the eyes of others. The fact that the rebels acted independently and did not possess modern means of communication to resolve these artificial conflicts made this technique all the more effective. One mujahideen leader discussed the effectiveness of these techniques in some areas, stating, "The KHAD (Democratic Republic of Afghanistan's secret police) agents have rendered mujahideen groups completely useless by getting them to fight among themselves." He added, "Why should the Soviets worry about killing Afghans if the mujahideen do it for them?"[119]

Despite some success, the Soviet policy of pitting the various mujahideen bands against each other proved to be of limited value. The Soviets found their subversive tactics were often disrupted by the same weaknesses they were trying to exploit: the fragmented nature of the Afghan tribal system. "At the root of the Soviet difficulties, military as well as political," one military analyst noted, "lies the fact that Afghanistan is less a nation than an agglomeration of some 25,000 village-states, each of which is largely self-governing and self-sufficient."[120] As one scholar put it, "Much has been written about the lack of unity within insurgent ranks, but little note has been taken of the extraordinary difficulties that such disunity poses to the counter-insurgent."[121]

Although overcoming the disunity of the country would have been key to the Soviets winning the counter-insurgency campaign and pacifying Afghanistan, the reality on the ground was that they were never really able to start the process. This is because they lacked the necessary resources to do the job they were asked to carry out. As General (Ret.) M.Y. Nawroz and Lieutenant-Colonel (Ret.) L.W. Grau state, "The Afghanistan War forced the 40th Army to change tactics, equipment, training, and force structure. However, despite these changes, the Soviet army never had enough forces in Afghanistan to win. Initially, the Soviets had underestimated the strength of their enemy. Logistically, they were hard-pressed to maintain a larger force and, even if they could have tripled the size of their force, they probably would still have been unable to win."[122]

By 1988 the Soviets had mostly given up, and their first contingent departed in May of that year. Before departing completely, though, the Soviets attempted to transfer the burden of fighting to the Afghan armed forces by increasing their numbers and training. As a result, the Soviets restricted their support of the Democratic Republic of Afghanistan (DRA) to providing artillery, air support, and technical assistance. It was hoped that over time the DRA armed forces would number 302,000; however, these numbers were never achieved. The second and final Soviet pullout occurred in February 1989. In order to ensure a safe passage, the Soviets negotiated ceasefires with local mujahideen commanders, so the withdrawal was generally executed without incident.[123]

SUMMARY OF THE SOVIET EXPERIENCE

Like the British during First Anglo-Afghan War, the Soviets entered Afghanistan not fully understanding the conditions under which they would have to fight or how effective and resilient the Afghan way of war could be. They started off with tactical operations focused on large-scale conventional heavy mechanized forces, which were totally inappropriate for the counter-insurgency operations required in the mountainous terrain of Afghanistan. Tactical deficiencies were compounded by the inability of the Soviets to achieve surprise anywhere they went. Moreover, the Soviets were unable to control the population or eliminate rebel bases and their sanctuaries in Pakistan.

Despite some success in pitting the various mujahideen tribes against each other, the overall effort proved to be of limited value; the Soviets never really understood the tribal system or the resilience of the Afghan people. Evidence suggests that the Soviets initially entered Afghanistan with the limited mandate of providing support to the established authority. In fact, declassified U.S. reports suggest that the Soviets imposed limitations on the size of their forces in Afghanistan because they believed "that the primary purpose of [the] Soviet intervention of December 1979 was to take over security responsibilities in the cities so that [Afghan] government forces could concentrate on putting down the ever-growing insurgency."[124] Although the Soviets may have initially expected the Afghan army to carry the main burden of the fighting against the insurgents, the idea quickly proved unrealistic — at least in the short term.[125]

The most significant problem the Soviets faced, and one they never rectified, was a lack of resources, specifically the necessary "boots on the ground" to establish the necessary security of the country.[126] In fact, the Soviets never had sufficient resources to move beyond these major centres, as almost 85 percent of the approximately 100,000 troops they had available in theatre were used for basic security tasks, such as protecting key locations within their strategic bases and the outposts along vital supply routes to and from the Soviet Union.[127] This shortfall proved costly for the Soviets, as more than 80 percent of the country's population lived in rural areas and these people were left to the mujahideen's influence.[128] This single factor prevented them from creating the basic security conditions necessary for winning over or controlling the people, and without their support, defeat was inevitable.

RISE OF THE TALIBAN

In 1989 the Soviets withdrew, leaving the People's Democratic Party of Afghanistan (PDPA) government to deal with the situation by itself. However, with the common threat from the outside gone, the tribal factions again turned inward to deal with old rivalries and began fighting as much between themselves as with the government forces. As a result, it was not until 1992 that mujahideen fighters were able to topple the PDPA.[129] Nonetheless, the collapse of the government did not mark the end of Afghanistan's civil war. Different tribal leaders and warlords claimed and occupied different cities and regions of the country. These warlords continued fighting as they collected the spoils of victory and sought to enlarge their regions at the expense of their rivals.[130] Pakistan also maintained a keen interest in the country.

Seeking to end the civil war that threatened the stability of their own country, the Pakistani intelligence service aided in the creation of a new Islamic fundamentalist movement, known to the West as the Taliban. The word *Taliban* is Pashto and means "students." The movement was born in the Islamic schools that had sprung up in Afghan refugee camps inside Pakistan. Scholars who studied the Taliban noted, "Its leadership and the bulk of its initial ranks were made up of young religious students, primarily Pashtuns, motivated by the zeal of religion and the belief that they were ordained to bring stability and the ways of Allah back to their war torn land."[131] As the Taliban mounted a military push to take over the country in 1994, they were well received by a war-weary population. Taliban expert Ahmed Rashid observed, "As they gained momentum and success their ranks were filled by rank and file Mujahideen fighters and young idealists from inside the country, and city-by-city they were able to occupy much of the country."[132]

According to Rashid, the Taliban's first major military operation was carried out in 1994, "when they marched northward from Maiwand and captured Kandahar City and the surrounding provinces, losing only a few dozen men."[133] In 1996 they captured the capital city of Kabul and had forced the remaining warlords into the far north of the country. These warlords subsequently formed a defensive alliance termed "the United

Front," but it was often referred to in the Western media as the Northern Alliance. Fighting between the two groups continued off and on until the Northern Alliance, with the help of the Americans, drove the Taliban out of the country in the fall of 2001.[134]

NATO INVOLVEMENT IN THE QUAGMIRE

Following the 11 September 2001 World Trade Center bombings in New York, the United States had evidence to suggest that Osama Bin Laden, the leader of al Qaeda, was responsible for the attacks. At the time, Bin Laden was living in Afghanistan and the American government demanded that the Taliban hand him over. However, the request was refused based on insufficient evidence of Bin Laden's involvement.

Within weeks of the 9/11 attacks, the United States began providing active support to the Northern Alliance in their efforts to overthrow the Taliban. With the addition of a significant military commitment in the form of Special Operations Forces (SOF) and close air support, the Northern Alliance quickly succeeded in routing the Taliban and seizing the city of Mazaar-e-Sharif before moving on and taking Kabul. With the fall of Kabul, the Taliban began abandoning other major cities as they retreated into the mountains along the Pakistani border.[135]

As the Americans started to consolidate their military position in Afghanistan, things were moving on the diplomatic front as well. The United Nations Security Council passed Resolution 1386, creating the International Security Assistance Force (ISAF), and NATO took over command of the force from the U.S. in August 2003. The security council then passed Resolution 1883, which called upon NATO to provide "security, law and order, promote governance and development, help reform the justice system, train a national police force and army, provide security for elections, and provide assistance to the local effort addressing the narcotics industry."[136]

Since their initial deployment into Afghanistan, NATO forces have had little success at adapting to the Afghan way of war. Although they have proven they have a clear firepower and mobility advantage over the

Taliban, they are still perplexed by the dynamics of the conflict. According to Brian Hutchinson of the *Edmonton Journal*, "after four years of effort and heavy sacrifices, Canada's military is still confounded by this place, the seat of Taliban power and home to a tiny, unhappy populace. Panjwaii is not secure. Insurgents continue to assemble here, kill troops and plan attacks on Kandahar City and places beyond."[137]

Canadian frustration is not unique within NATO, and evidence suggests that the Taliban clearly understand NATO's limitations and have evolved their tactics to attack perceived weaknesses. Since 2004 there has been a clear shift in the Taliban tactics in order off set NATO's firepower and take advantage of the coalition's limited resources.[138] At the tactical level, the Taliban's strategy is now in line with the Afghan way of war and is based on guerrilla warfare, improvised explosive device (IED) attacks, and suicide bombing.

These tactics have been used successfully in attacks along coalition supply routes in different parts of the country. Using small arms, mortars, and rocket-propelled grenades, insurgents have also attempted to attack NATO strong points and have stopped only in the face of superior firepower. Moreover, over the past three years the Taliban appears to be getting stronger, as attacks have increased both in scope and numbers. For example, in January 2008, a report issued by the Afghanistan Study Group claimed that "the year 2007 was the deadliest for American and international troops in Afghanistan since the 2001 invasion of Afghanistan."[139]

On 18 August 2008, eighteen French soldiers were killed and twenty-one were wounded when a joint French and Afghan force was ambushed by the Taliban in Kabul province, just thirty-five miles from the capital.[140]

Swapna Kona of the Institute of Peace and Conflict Studies offers the following assessment of the situation:

> The Taliban attacks, the coalition forces counter attack and the Taliban retreats. After a period of time they return to some other part in the country and the process starts again.... Taliban tactics seem to focus on wearing out the coalition forces and to diminish their credibility among the Afghan population.... These attacks have helped to

create a security void that insurgents are stepping in to
fill by setting up shadow administrations, offering people
a chance to cultivate their drugs unmolested and promising a return to law and order they [the Taliban] enforced
before 2001.... In carrying out this strategy the Taliban
have some important advantages over the coalition forces.
First they have a wide recruiting base as long as they can
maintain the support of the population and this will give
them the necessary staying power.[141]

As the coalition forces' credibility diminishes, the number of individuals who volunteer to serve with the Taliban increases. More importantly,
the Taliban continues to have access to sanctuaries in Pakistani borders
that provide them with both shelter and training camps.[142]

In an attempt to overcome this problem, President Barack Obama
developed a new strategy in 2010 that was designed to increase resources
for the stabilization effort in Afghanistan. The strategy called for an additional seventeen thousand American combat troops to be deployed into
the volatile southern and eastern regions of Afghanistan. Moreover, it
directed that an additional four thousand U.S. military personnel be
deployed as training cadre for the Afghan National Security Forces
(ANSF). The Obama administration believed that this level of training
support would allow the Afghan National Army (ANA) to achieve its
target of 134,000 troops (from its existing strength of eighty-five thousand) by 2011. The strategy also emphasized the need to strengthen and
reform the Afghan government, increasing civilian expertise in order to
help the central government, but at the provincial and local levels.[143]

How these reforms and troop increases will impact NATO's current
stalemate in Afghanistan is difficult to assess. As we have seen, the major
problem with the Soviet deployment in Afghanistan was the lack of manpower — much more was needed to establish security throughout the
country. The Soviets deployed and maintained a force of about 100,000
troops in Afghanistan, which was generally believed to have been totally
inadequate for the task they were expected to undertake. CIA estimates at
the time reveal how underequipped the Soviets really were: "An increase

of perhaps 100,000 to 150,000 men might [have allowed] the Soviets to clear and hold major cities and large parts of the countryside or block infiltration from Pakistan and Iran, although it probably could not do both.... An even larger reinforcement of 200,000 to 400,000 men probably would [have allowed] Moscow to make serious inroads against the insurgency if the efforts could be sustained." This assessment compares to the current ISAF troop strength of about 119,819, with 47 troop-contributing nations providing support.[144]

To date, NATO has not been able to destroy the foundation of the Afghan way of war, separate the population from the Taliban, or eliminate the sanctuaries in Pakistan that provide the Taliban with shelter and training camps for its fighters. According to a March 2008 report issued by the Atlantic Council of the United States, the situation on the ground has settled into a strategic stalemate. It states that "Afghanistan's political transition was completed with the convening of a parliament in December 2005, however, after seven years of a new national government neither the government in Kabul nor the international community has made much progress toward its goals of peace, security, and development." The report suggests NATO and Afghan forces cannot eliminate the Taliban threat by military means as long as they have sanctuary in Pakistan, and the civil development efforts are not bringing sufficient results.[145] The Atlantic Council concludes that currently "the Taliban's strategy appears to be working as they are holding out until NATO goes home."[146] Additionally, it appears that NATO does not have the will or resources to counter this strategy. Moreover, time is always on the side of the Afghan Warrior.

CONCLUSION

The longevity of the Afghan way of war derives from the country's unique tribal structure, which has served to evolve a version of *la petite guerre* or guerrilla warfare, sometimes in the form of regular forces from the country's central authority and other times by combining warriors of different tribes. This model of combining regular and irregular forces is what has made fighting Afghans so difficult.

As a result, Alexander, the British, and the Soviets all started off employing unsuitable tactical operations focused on large-scale conventional heavy forces, which were inappropriate for the counter-insurgency operations that were needed in the mountainous terrain of Afghanistan. Moreover, the evidence shows that each initially failed to see any military relevance to the tribal system. As a result, each was forced to readjust their tactics to deal with the Afghan war of war.

The British and the Soviets in particular had little understanding of the tribal dynamics at play and found little use for developing or maintaining good relations with tribal leaders. During the First Anglo-Afghan War, this oversight contributed to the development of a patriotic war, as the Afghan tribes united to drive the British out of Afghanistan. Although the British were better prepared to fight in the terrain of Afghanistan in their second attempt, they never tried to win over the tribes or deal with following guerrilla war that, based on history, was likely to come after the major military defeats of large Afghan forces in the field. Prudently, the British departed shortly after the battle of Kandahar, avoiding what could have become a very long and costly guerrilla war, yet, in the process, they never really dealt with the key issues of the Afghan way of war. For their part, the Soviets were embroiled in a holy war from the beginning of their occupation; however, their attempts to play the tribes against one another other did not work. This failure was due in large part to the fact that the Soviets also never really understood the dynamics at work within the tribal system or appreciated the resilience of the Afghan people.

The Soviets also had to contend with the problem of not having sufficient resources to deal with the problems they were facing. The Soviets never had the required "boots on the ground" to establish the levels of security they needed to effectively control the country. In fact, the Soviets never had sufficient resources to move beyond Afghanistan's major centres. This shortfall proved costly for the Soviets, as more than 80 percent of the country's population lived in rural areas, and these people were left to the mujahideen's influence.

Alexander had the greatest success in fighting the Afghan way of war. His ability to subdue the Afghan tribes had to evolve, and his skill in adjusting his style of fighting to the conditions he was facing played no small part. Specifically, he was able to compel the Afghans to mass in areas where their mobility was restricted. Operationally, he developed this concept by using a number of different fighting techniques, but the most common and effective of these was the placement of well-situated fortified posts.

Once the forts were in place, he deployed mobile columns to round up the population and attack the mobile warriors. As a result, the population was unable to help the warriors with food, shelter, or intelligence. This forced the tribes to make conventional attacks against fixed installations, where Alexander was strongest, but more importantly these attacks gave the Macedonians the opportunity to achieve decisive victory. The British were able to achieve similar successes during the Second Anglo-Afghan War, because they were able to capitalize on the Afghans' tendency to revolt with large forces that remained intact for longer periods of time. This situation gave the British an opportunity to use their superior firepower to defeat the tribes in battle. However, it should be pointed out that historically such opportunities have been few and far between, as the Afghans prefer fighting a guerrilla war. More importantly, the Afghans have learned that when an enemy occupies their land, the clock starts ticking and time is on their side. The terrain, the extremely durable type of warfare, and the unpredictability of tribal motivations and participation have proven to be too much for even the best armies in the world.

Vestiges of a former conflict. The wreck of a Soviet armoured personnel carrier on the outskirts of Kandahar City lies as silent testimony to the failed Soviet occupation of the 1980s.

A Soviet MI-17 Hip helicopter shot down during the Soviet occupation.

Canadians on patrol in an Iltis jeep (with interpreter in the back) in Kabul, 2003.

Members of Para Company, 3 RCR conduct a patrol with an Afghan transitional authority policeman.

Para Coy, 3 RCR personnel on patrol in Kabul. The Queen's Palace is in the background.

Members of 3 RCR conduct a security check while on patrol in Kabul.

Courtesy Steve Sikora

The Canadian base in Kabul, Camp Julien.

Photo by MCpl Brian Walsh, Courtesy 3 RCR

A detainee taken by 3 RCR during OP Tsunami in Kabul.

The challenging terrain of Pashmul: vineyards and concrete hard-mud grape drying huts.

An aerial view of a portion of Kandahar City.

Right: *Mullah Omar's abandoned bunker on the outskirts of Kandahar City.*

Below: *One of the Arghandab irrigation canals on the northwestern side of Kandahar City, March 2006. The Arghandab, part of one of the four major river systems in Afghanistan, serves the south as an instrument of irrigation. Canadian international investment has spent over 50 million dollars in repairs on the Dahla Dam of the Arghandab irrigation system.*

A Heavy Logistics Vehicle Wheeled (HLVW), the old Canadian workhorse of the Cold War, serves in Afghanistan as an immediate replenishment platform for the battery of new Canadian guns in northern Kandahar Province, 2006. Note the "after-purchase" air conditioner perched on the roof of the vehicle. Air conditioners are an essential piece of equipment for operations in Kandahar.

The infamous white school house that was the scene of vicious fighting between Canadians and Taliban forces in the summer of 2006.

Members of 1 RCR systematically clear their objectives during heavy fighting in Operation Medusa, September 2006.

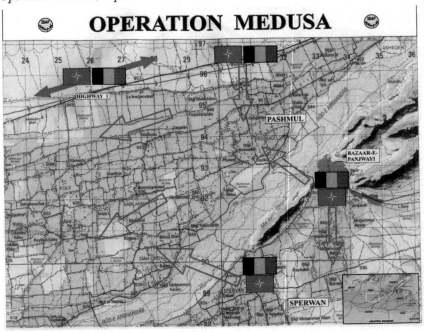

ISAF information operations hand-out to explain OP Medusa.

3

Public Opinion Matters

The Struggle for Hearts and Minds

DR. EMILY SPENCER

Machines don't fight wars. Terrain doesn't fight wars. Humans fight wars. You must get in the minds of the humans. That's where the battles are won.[1]
— Colonel John R. Boyd

The nature of war has not changed with the passage of time. Essentially, the goal of warfare — to impose your will on your opponent — has been constant. What has changed, however, is how wars are fought. Tactics, techniques, and procedures (TTPs) have evolved in light of new technologies and, most importantly, changing social constructions as to what is acceptable in war. Indeed, different levels of warfare, from limited to total war, elicit differing views on what is acceptable conduct during periods of belligerence, as do the varying types of warfare, from conventional to unconventional, including counter-insurgency (COIN).[2] Perhaps most significantly, the different beliefs, values, and attitudes of the groups engaged in conflict delineate how wars are waged and, especially in the context of limited, unconventional wars such as the ongoing COIN in Afghanistan, what will determine success or failure.

In these days of instant mass media, the battle for public opinion, both at home and abroad, is especially important for success in the contemporary operating environment (COE). This is particularly true of the ongoing war in Afghanistan. The democratic nations of the West require the will of their populations to have a continued presence overseas. Additionally, they must simultaneously win over the "hearts and minds" of local Afghans, a group that represents a totally different culture from our own. For their part, the insurgents must erode or simply prevent the Western public's support of their governments' decisions to commit troops to the struggle in Afghanistan while also deterring the local Afghan population from supporting the Western-backed Afghan government.

In essence, the war for public opinion determines who will be the victor in the field, so winning the battle of public opinion in both arenas is vital to success in the conflict in Afghanistan. As Westerners fighting in Afghanistan are beginning to realize, "people are the prize."[3]

In its simplest form, public opinion reflects the beliefs held by a nation's adult population. While it remains difficult to measure,[4] the study of public opinion is rooted in the development of democracy.[5] Within democratic nations, it is essential for elected representatives to maintain public support in order to retain power. This connection, as Abraham Lincoln so eloquently captured in his famous Gettysburg Address in November 1863, reflects a "government of the people, by the people, for the people." While it would be wrong to deny that this principle of democracy has not on occasion been perverted, its basic tenets ring true. Thus, democratically elected governments must somehow enlist the will of their populations in order to survive. At no point is this connection more true than during periods of conflict.

During periods of belligerence, it is arguably always necessary to mobilize public opinion. During some wars this process has been relatively easy; for example, Western nations held the belief that the Second World War was a "good war." During other conflicts, such as Vietnam, and more recently Iraq and Afghanistan, however, Western public opinion remains divided as to whether or not the wars are "proper and morally sound."[6]

The degree to which public opinion needs to be mobilized in order to win a conflict depends largely on how invested governments are in the outcome. Unlike a total war, in which governments mobilize all national resources toward the destruction of the enemy's ability to wage war, a limited war, as the term suggests, is much narrower in scope. A limited war refers to a conflict in which a nation does not harness all of its resources or demand total defeat of the enemy. Rather, political aims and resources are limited to a level seemingly proportional to the desired objective.[7] The challenge often lies in determining the correct balance between costs and desired objectives, a task that is further aggravated as each item is in a constant state of flux. The difficulties of limited wars are even increasingly complicated when opponents have different cultural constructs of war as well as unequal access to resources. In such a circumstance, the belligerents lack symmetry, thereby having an inequality of resources or will to engage in conflict.[8]

As is evident in Afghanistan today, fighting a limited, asymmetric COIN campaign is no easy task. A large part of the difficulty is because of the challenging nature of gaining and retaining public support with limited resources, for a limited goal.

An important way to garner public opinion is to win hearts and minds. Generally, referring to winning the loyalty and trust of a subjugated population, the principles are equally applicable to home populations, where democratic governments vie for votes by appealing to an electorates' intellectual and moral reasoning. While public opinion may be swayed by more than just an appeal to a nation's hearts and minds, acts of intimidation and terror — although arguably effective at influencing the public — are usually ignored by Western governments in favour of a softer approach. As such, the Western war of public opinion is often fought through battles for hearts and minds.

Overwhelmingly, military and strategic analysts agree that public opinion, and subsequently winning hearts and minds, is a crucial component for victory in modern war. Within the domestic domain, having public opinion on your side allows democratically elected governments to carry out their agendas without the fear of alienating electorates. With regard to defence issues, a military that serves a democratic nation cannot be successful if it is not supported by the will of the home population. As former deputy commander of Task Force Afghanistan Colonel Fred Lewis commented, "The will of the Canadian people is our centre of gravity. So define centre of gravity as strength. If our strength fails, we lose."[9]

Equally important is the need to have public opinion from the host nation population on your side. This is absolutely critical, since it means that host nation nationals will be less likely to be antagonistic toward you and more likely to co-operate with government and coalition forces, which could translate into physical support for reconstruction and development, as well as the provision of information of enemy activity. The reverse is also true: it means that the population is less likely to sympathize with the enemy, who then may not receive physical support or information on government or coalition activities.

The omnipresent media of the twenty-first century further requires Western governments to have the support of their populations in order to continue expeditionary operations. As such, not only do militaries have to win the kinetic battles on the ground, they must also win the battle for hearts and minds. In fact, no amount of victory in combat will make up for the loss of public support. As professor Cori E. Dauber argues, "The military force fighting today against a terrorist organization in defense of a democratic state is really fighting a two-front war." She further explains:

> There is on the one hand the *ground war*, meaning the war that has to actually be won on the ground, the state of play on the ground as it exists in reality.... But there is also the *air war*, meaning the war as it exists on the nation's front pages and television screens.... For a democracy, winning one and not the other will always mean losing, and losing in a very real sense, because the loss of public support means that the war will come to an end, period.[10]

Thankfully, there is now starting to be a recognition amongst Western governments and militaries that public opinion — both "ours" and "theirs" — is crucial to success in COIN. As retired Colonel Bruce Jackson aptly notes, "A counterinsurgency is a battle for a decision that we want from the population."[11] Additionally, as Russell Hampsey and

Sean P. McKenna, retired U.S. military officers now working on the International Security Assistance Force (ISAF) Counterinsurgency Advisory and Assistance Team in Afghanistan, comment, "Relationships are a salient piece to the success of a COIN strategy. They could actually be the single point of failure." They assert that "a COIN fight is not won in briefings and working groups, but through the actions of the units on the ground interacting with the population."[12] In fact, in a recent Canadian COIN campaign assessment, it was noted that the situation in Afghanistan has "become a matter of which side can demonstrate to Afghanistan's population that it has the will and the means to win." Notably, the document highlights, "the coalition must convince their own national populations that they can win at an acceptable cost and that progress is being made toward that goal."[13]

While the logic of winning hearts and minds, and thus influencing public opinion, may indeed be simple, its application is often anything but easy or straightforward. It is one thing to say that you are committed to winning the trust of others and swaying them to your way of thinking, but it is quite another thing to actually do so.[14] As U.S. chairman of the Joint Chiefs of Staff Michael G. Mullen acknowledged, "… Our biggest problem isn't caves; it's credibility. Our messages lack credibility because we haven't invested enough in building trust and relationships, and we haven't always delivered on promises."[15]

Moreover, this task can often be time consuming and involve behaviours that do not initially resonate with ideas of task accomplishment held by some military members. For example, influencing public opinion in Afghanistan may involve partaking in many daily activities with local Afghans, such as drinking tea or attending a lengthy *shura*, which may superficially appear to some military members as a waste of valuable time.[16] Nonetheless, because of the value that Afghans place on developing personal bonds through ceremonial social acts such as these, the time spent in such a process may provide more actual dividends than hours spent in the field. Locals are much more willing to share knowledge about insurgent activities once they have developed trust in their potential confidents. Respecting Afghan customs is an important way to develop trust and respect, each a valuable asset in the quest for public opinion.

Clearly, it is no easy task to simultaneously win the trust and support of different groups of people with varying beliefs, values, attitudes, and behaviours (essentially, different cultures). Therefore, exhibiting high levels of cultural intelligence (CQ), meaning understanding these aspects of a group of people and using that knowledge to further national objectives, is fundamental to victory in COIN, because it can contribute gaining public support for your objectives.[17] Understanding how others view the world and appreciating how they see your place in it is a crucial first step in being able to effectively work together toward a common goal. Since "the centre of gravity in all counterinsurgency operations is the population," as Australian major Jason Hayes aptly remarks, "you must have an ability to influence and shape a population to dislocate the insurgents through lethal and non-lethal means." Hayes concludes that "in order to be able to do this you need to 'truly get to know the population, you must really understand it.'"[18]

In fact, the need to better comprehend local populations and win the war of public opinion provided the impetus for the U.S. military to employ human terrain analysts. These individuals are trained to focus on cultural aspects of a specific region and then create maps that military members can use to garner socio-cultural information in addition to the regular geographic and terrain features. These maps also include beliefs and values prevalent in distinct areas and whether or not certain behaviours tend to occur in these zones. As such, they help military members determine what is important to the group of people they are working amongst, which in turn helps them in the battle for hearts and minds and ultimately the war for public opinion.[19] Notably, the Americans are not the only ones who recognize the benefits of and need for this type of analysis.[20]

Adding to the complexity of understanding the host nation population and demonstrating respect for their culture is, again, the omnipresent twenty-first century media. The media assures that actions in any cultural milieu will likely be judged in other domains, where people may have different sets of beliefs and values. While this might simply be construed as a harsh fact for some, many are keenly aware of the advantages that this type of media environment can provide. As Dauber explains,

"Sophisticated propagandists ... are not only constructing sophisticated texts meant to simultaneously reach multiple audiences, they are also constructing multiple texts targeted to reach a variety of different categories of audience."[21] For example, it was recently reported that Taliban detainees were locked in "dog pens." Subsequently, there was a large public outcry about the treatment of these detainees, particularly since in the Muslim faith dogs are considered impure. In the end, it did not really matter that the story was fabricated and that the detainees had never been treated in any such manner. Propagandists had already taken advantage of the situation, and once that image had been formed, it was impossible to separate perception from reality.[22]

Since the media is a common tool used to influence public opinion and create perceptions about reality, making effective use of the media is "mission critical" in the COE.[23] According to Dauber, "Waging war against terrorists (or insurgents using a terrorist playbook) is a qualitatively different enterprise from earlier, or different, wars." She further explains, "By definition, terrorists are too weak to fight conventional battles." Rather, she asserts, "They fight a battle to shape the perceptions and attitudes of the public — a battle over the public's very will to continue fighting, whether that is the indigenous public insurgents seek to intimidate or the domestic American public they seek to influence so as to force counterinsurgents to withdraw from the battlefield prematurely." As Dauber concludes, "In the modern world, this will, of necessity, be a battle to shape media coverage."[24]

Unfortunately, however, the West has not always been good at waging the war for public opinion, often neglecting the need to gain and retain home support for the war in Afghanistan as a crucial component for victory. As scholars Lee Winsor, David Charters, and Brent Wilson note of the 4 July 2007 Improvised Explosive Device (IED) attack in Afghanistan that claimed six Canadian lives, "The [attack] caused exactly the kind of media effect that the Taliban commanders sought." They go on to explain that "back in Canada there were more questions about vehicle safety and whether or not the Afghan mission was succeeding." While they acknowledge that the line of inquiry was understandable, they remark that

... those raising [those questions] seemed to have only one measure of mission success or failure: the Canadian body count. They paid little attention to the fact that Panjwayi's irrigation system had improved and was yielding bumper crops. Or the fact that a better crop yield undermined drug trafficker control and improved quality of life of the people. Nor did they take note of the fact that Afghan soldiers and police were assuming much more of the security burden.[25]

Additionally, as retired Canadian general Paul Manson observed as late as 2010, "The media's preoccupation with ramp ceremonies at the expense of analytical reporting of events in the field has distorted the picture as has editorial pressure to focus on bad news while ignoring less newsworthy successes."[26]

Nonetheless, there is an element within the Canadian Forces and government that recognized early on the need for the Canadian public to stand behind the mission and the big role that the media plays in this process. As early as 2003, when Canada began its tour in Kabul as part of ISAF, then Major-General Andrew Leslie, a former Canadian deputy commander of ISAF, realized that "we weren't going to succeed in the mission and with the Canadian public without the media. The media was to be welcomed and not excluded, but included."[27] Additionally, as Canadian journalist Graeme Smith, who has spent enormous amounts of time reporting from Afghanistan, remarked, "The military learned in 2006 that if they gave us lots and lots of access, we would tell their story, rather than someone else's."[28] Smith elaborates: "That was a PR [Public Relations] coup for the military. Canadians knew what was going on. They saw the operations."[29]

Recognizing some of same concerns that were highlighted by Windsor, Charters, and Wilson, as well as Manson, by mid-2006, senior public officials in the Government of Canada were noticing and being bothered by the mostly negative news coming from Afghanistan, particularly following several Canadian casualties. As a result of the new levels of concern, public affairs officers in Afghanistan were tasked with "aggressively selling or 'pushing' development and reconstruction stories to journalists embedded with the Forces in Afghanistan."[30] It was hoped that these more positive stories would resonate strongly with the Canadian public and encourage increased support for a Canadian presence in Afghanistan.

While the attention given to gaining and retaining domestic support for the war in Afghanistan continues to ebb and flow in Canada, winning the hearts and minds of Afghans, in an attempt to win the war of public opinion, has notably received more attention from Western nations. There is no doubt that Western nations are currently putting forth great effort to win the hearts and minds of Afghans in order to curry favour in the war of public opinion. Indeed, a former ISAF commander, retired American general Stanley McChrystal, was quite vocal about winning over Afghans in order to defeat the Taliban in that nation. He remarked, "I have made it clear to our forces that we are here to protect the Afghan people, and inadvertently killing or injuring civilians undermines their trust and confidence in our mission. We will re-double our efforts to regain that trust."[31]

In fact, McChrystal is often touted as having "recommended implementing a counterinsurgency strategy in which troops give top priority to protecting Afghans rather than seizing terrain or killing insurgents."[32] Echoing these sentiments, a former Canadian commander, Brigadier-General Daniel Menard, commented, "I'm not after killing every single insurgent ... I don't really care about the insurgents. What I do care about is to make sure the population understands they don't need to be threatened by them, and this is not the way that they should be living."[33] Similarly, U.S. Army major-general Michael Scaparrotti was also succinct and clear when he remarked, "the fight, essentially, is about the support of the people."[34]

The Western attempt to influence Afghan public opinion, often via winning Afghan hearts and minds, has focused on gaining their trust and ensuring that they do not need to fear supporting the Western-backed Afghan national government. The U.S. Army Training and Doctrine Command has acknowledged that "in order to defeat future enemies they must put emphasis on influence, specifically 'the shaping of opinions and attitudes of a civilian population through information engagement, presence, and conduct."[35] "Success in the long term," however, as McChrystal points out, "will be when the people of Afghanistan develop trust and faith in their own government and military."[36]

In the short term, though, the Western focus is on winning the trust of local Afghans and one way to do so is to try to minimize Afghan civilian casualties. Quite simply, civilian casualties provide the Taliban with propaganda victories. Under such circumstances, the West looks callous and uncaring toward the Afghan people. Consequently, the Taliban can easily prey on the growing disenchantment within the local population.[37] In fact, even when collateral damage has occurred, coalition members are now realizing it is better to accept responsibility and attempt to make amends rather than simply ignore the issue. For example, following the death of a pregnant woman and two young men after U.S. Special Forces erroneously opened fire on a house where a family had gathered to celebrate a recent birth, the commander of the American Joint Special Operations Command, Vice-Admiral William H. McRaven, visited the family. He stated, "I am the commander of the soldiers who accidently killed your loved ones. I came here to send my condolences. I also came to ask your forgiveness for these terrible tragedies."[38]

Importantly, coalition members are realizing that winning Afghan trust requires more than simple verbal persuasions in a world where actions speak volumes. Reconstruction and development projects help out in a multitude of ways, particularly by providing a visual landmark to note the aid that is being distributed. The effect is underscored when the aid projects reflect an acceptance of Muslim religious faith, such as the rebuilding of a mosque, rather than a more secular project such as the construction of a well. This approach in the Kandahar District has been extremely effective. As one official report explained, "These projects have been winners in three ways: 1) in terms of the message, they demonstrate that international forces in fact honor the local religion; 2) the improvements cannot be easily vandalized by the Taliban, who do not want to burn down mosques; and 3) appreciation for the mosque projects transcend some of the petty local rivalries commonly associated with development projects." The document further elaborated on the benefits of this type of aid. "Whereas wells and other 'secular' projects in one locale tend to stoke the jealousies of the neighbors," revealed the report, "the mosque improvements have been more broadly accepted by the community as a whole."[39]

It is important that the West is finally realizing that the battle for Afghanistan is truly a war for public opinion, often waged through battles for hearts and minds. Certainly, momentous strides have been taken by the West in recent years, but we are fighting a formidable foe who seems to have realized from the outset that victory is all about winning public opinion to your side. As Dauber assessed, "Today's terrorists and insurgents have been brilliant at capitalizing on this environment in their operational art."[40]

Indeed, the Taliban seem to have been continuously more aware of the importance of the war of public opinion to victory in the contemporary operating environment than Western nations. Notably, they are also less restrained in their actions; they openly use threats and coercions to get their way, as opposed to Western nations who adhere to international laws of war. The Taliban use all available networks — political, social, economic, and military — to further their cause and convince their opponents that the costs outweigh perceived benefits.

One way that the Taliban has been effective in conveying this message is through the use of suicide bombers and improvised explosive devices (IEDs). These attacks require little manpower and have a large impact on popular support, as do the use of other "spectacular" events, which the media broadcasts around the world.[41] As an American military officer lamented, "Unfortunately, we [Americans specifically and Westerners in general] tend to view information operations as supplementing kinetic [fighting] operations. For the Taliban, however, information objectives tend to drive kinetic operations ... Virtually every kinetic operation they undertake is specifically designed to influence attitudes or perceptions."[42] Sadly, as Hampsey and McKenna comment, "The insurgents recognize the importance of media attention, and they plan operations to gain that attention. The COIN information-operations practitioner must seize the initiative from the insurgent."[43]

In fact, from the onset, the Taliban has been aware that in order to be victorious, they need to erode Western public support for the war, as well as deter Afghans from aligning with the Western-backed Afghan national government. As Windsor, Charters, and Wilson explain, "The Taliban were keenly aware that mass-casualty media events created by spectacular vehicle hits were victories that ate away at the Canadian public's stomach for staying the course in Kandahar."[44] More recently, retired Canadian general Paul Manson echoed this sentiment: "One thing the insurgents are good at is propaganda … Ironically, while they are not really winning the war in Afghanistan, they appear to be winning over the Canadian people." He elaborated, "Greatly disturbed by the deaths of so many of our military … the average Canadian has grown weary of a conflict that has now gone on longer than the Second World War."[45]

Eroding Western support of the war is but one aspect of the complex propaganda initiative that the Taliban has undertaken. The other major piece of the battle of public opinion lies in swaying local Afghans to their side. With varying degrees of success, the Taliban has accomplished this task by vilifying the West in the eyes of local Afghans through an effective information operations (IO) campaign, intimidation and acts of terror and punishment directed toward Afghan nationals, as well as apparent appeasements, more often than not applying a combination of these three tactics. As the International Crisis Group observed, "Within Afghanistan the Taliban is adept at exploiting local disenfranchisement and disillusionment."[46]

One way that the Taliban has been able to take advantage of the tumultuous mood in the country is by downplaying or outright denying access to foreign aid. In this way, the Taliban is able to enforce a distance between ISAF forces and the local populations and, in doing so, also appears to bear legitimate control of an area. As Carl Forsberg, a research analyst at the Institute for the Study of War, explains, "By banning the use of government development aid, the Taliban further separates the population from ISAF and reinforces the psychological perception that the Taliban is the legitimate local government."[47]

This situation is further exploited by the Taliban's adept use of media channels to propagate their message. As the International Crisis group describes, "Using the full range of media, [the Taliban] is successfully tapping into strains of Afghan nationalism and exploiting policy failures by the Kabul government and its international backers." They identify the result as a "weakening [of] public support for nation-building, even though few actively support the Taliban."[48]

Forsberg provides data that supports this claim. He demonstrates that although "from May to September 2009, civilian casualties caused by the Taliban rose by twenty percent, while civilian casualties caused by NATO [North Atlantic Treaty Organization] in that same period decreased by eighty percent[,] … the Taliban have worked to mitigate backlash against the violence they have inflicted through an effective information operations campaign blaming NATO for violence and casualties inflicted by the Taliban."[49]

Simultaneously, the Taliban has also been employing a strong campaign of intimidation and terror directed at supporters and would-be supporters of the Western-backed Afghan national government. They have directly targeted key individuals in government, pro-government mullahs, as well as Afghan National Security Force (ANSF) and ISAF forces by assassinating key figures to send the message to the wider population that backing Western forces is not beneficial.[50] As reporters Ruhullah Khapalwak and David Rohde proclaim, "Since being toppled in 2001, the Taliban have mercilessly targeted tribal elders who support the Karzai government, apparently viewing them as one of their greatest potential rivals." They add that "at the same time, President Karzai's weak government has struggled to protect and strengthen tribal elders, hundreds of whom have been killed in assassinations and bomb attacks."[51]

The results of these acts of intimidation and terror have debatably achieved their objective of minimizing Afghan public support of the West. Taliban assassinations, suicide bombings, and other acts of intimidation have demonstrated to locals that the Government of Afghanistan is unable to defend against such acts and create a secure environment for Afghans. "Fear, combined with functioning Taliban tribunals and governance structures in the populated areas surrounding Kandahar City," argues Forsberg, "has given the Taliban de facto influence over much of the population of Kandahar City."[52]

Additionally, a third key tactic that the Taliban has been employing in order to sway the local population to their side — or, at a minimum, to prevent locals from backing the opposition — has been to demonstrate some moderation in beliefs and thereby appease popular wishes, as well as to provide functioning "governmental" structures in order to accommodate the needs of Afghan nationals. As British journalist Jonathan Steele states, "An understanding of what fuels popular opinion may also be the motive behind evolving Taliban messaging." Steele cites a Tajik woman who had "noticed Taliban members presenting themselves as nationalists more than Islamists these days." As the Tajik woman elaborated, "There are two kinds of Taliban: those who want a strict implementation of sharia law, and those who want to get rid of U.S. forces."[53]

Some American officials also suggest that the Taliban is overtly trying to "soften" its image in order to appeal more widely to the Afghan people.[54] "The Taliban's desire to win public support in occupied areas through their judicial code," asserts Forsberg, "is also demonstrated by their willingness to moderate the harsh legal prohibitions on entertainment they had taken during their tenure in power during the 1990s." He further explains that "radio, television, and the shaving of beards are no longer outlawed by the Taliban in Kandahar ..."[55]

Moreover, not only has the Taliban effectively diminished the utility of the Government of Afghanistan in the eyes of many, they have also stepped in to fill the void of governance. For example, in areas under Taliban control, as Pulitzer Prize winning journalist John F. Burns opines, "The insurgents have succeeded in establishing at least a facsimile of government." He elaborates, "They have named shadow governors, raised taxes and set up courts. Relying on their own lessons learned, they have relented on some of their harsher measures; now they allow children to fly kites and villagers to play soccer, and they have banned ... public beheadings for alleged miscreants."[56] Similarly, Forsberg describes how the Taliban has fostered a kinder image in society: "The Taliban professed limited aims at their inception, promising to wipe out corruption, provide security, and establish a fair judiciary based on sharia (Islamic law)." He argues that the result is that "the Taliban's dramatic demonstrations and noble promises convinced many that [Mullah] Omar and his followers were committed to good governance and could provide relief from the oppression and extortion of local strongmen."[57]

In combination, these three tactics have been quite effective in the battle for public opinion. As the international Crisis Group explains, "The Taliban seeks to create the illusion of inevitability and invincibility, while trying to defend the legitimacy of its actions. It has succeeded in conveying an impression of coherence and momentum far greater than reality, both within Afghanistan, among a population that is weary of war, and outside, with those in Western capitals also weary of commitments to a far-distant conflict." The report concludes that the insurgents "cannot win on the battlefield, but they do not have to. All they need to do is wear out their opponents — and influencing perceptions at home and abroad are a vital component of this strategy."[58]

One should never forget that wars are not necessarily won or lost on battlefields, but rather in the political arena that supervises and legitimizes the fighting. For democratic nations, public opinion forms the backdrop for elected government. As such, it is essential to have the support of the domestic population in order to be successful in conflict and war, but this is just one key element in winning a COIN campaign. Equally important is to gain the trust and support of the host nation's population or, at a minimum, to prevent the opposition from achieving this end. Notably, these outcomes are not easy tasks.

The difficulty is especially noticeable when fighting across cultural milieus comprised of individuals with sometimes drastically different beliefs, values, attitudes and, consequentially, behaviours. Moreover, when the opponent is also culturally different and applies asymmetric means that would not resonate with your home population — for example, the Taliban's use of terror and intimidation to elicit a desired response from Afghan nationals as well as Westerners — the task at hand is again further complicated, doubly so when one considers the influence of the twenty-first century media.

This is the situation that the West is facing in Afghanistan. On the positive side, we are finally recognizing that public opinion matters — ours and theirs. But the Taliban seem to have been playing this card since the beginning. Additionally, we are stuck in the mindset of fighting a limited war — a war to which we engage limited resources and have limited goals — against an opponent who is not holding back.

In the end, what it comes down to is that the battle for public opinion is going to be the crucial element in determining the outcome in Afghanistan. We should be asking ourselves two questions: Can we convince our domestic populations to stay the course? If so, can we convince Afghans that we will stay the course and provide them with a better life?

4

Coalition Counter-Insurgency Warfare in Afghanistan

LIEUTENANT-COLONEL IAN HOPE

Coalition operations and counter-insurgency (COIN) operations are two of the most complex types of military undertakings that armies may embark upon. As such, the intricacy of each will be treated individually in this chapter before we consider the more ominous nature of combined coalition counter-insurgencies. Due to the complex nature of each, it is best to proceed incrementally, first discussing the general characteristics of coalition operations, their various permutations, and the factors which contribute to their success or failure. Next, the general characteristics of insurgencies and the military challenges they create will be examined.

To properly understand the nature of contemporary COIN, it is important to ground the analysis in the revolutionary warfare theory of Mao Zedong and the counter-insurgency theory of General David Galula, as each work provides a foundation that is still is use today. Additionally, this theoretical approach will allow for a solid understanding of the challenges confronting troops of Operation Enduring Freedom (OEF) and the International Security Assistance Force (ISAF) in their efforts to reverse the Taliban insurgency in Afghanistan, the backdrop to the chapter. The conclusions drawn from this analysis are not positive. As will be demonstrated, applying a theoretical lens to the current situation in Afghanistan suggests that ISAF faces the distinct possibility of defeat.

NO EASY TASK

THE AD HOC POLITICAL NATURE OF COALITIONS

Coalition operations are as old as warfare itself. Coalitions are now precisely defined as ad hoc arrangements between two or more nations for a common action.[1] While this definition pertains to state entities, the fact is all social groupings have, in the past, combined efforts with other groups in pursuing common military objectives. Homer described the coalition of Achaean clans that combined to capture Troy, and the ad hoc nature of that coalition was demonstrated in the squabble between Achilles and Agamemnon. Thucydides described the coalitions of Greek city states that fought each other throughout the Peloponnesian War and the political compromises made to keep coalitions intact. Closer to our time, British imperial history reads as a narrative of continually shifting military coalitions, evidenced clearly in the campaigns of Marlborough and Wellington.

Coalition warfare is today the norm, and multiple coalitions are operating concurrently in Afghanistan. ISAF itself is a coalition based upon the North Atlantic Treaty Organization (NATO) alliance, and it operates in tandem with the American-led coalition under the mandate of OEF. Both work alongside coalitions of security contractors and development workers.

A coalition is distinct from an alliance, the latter being defined as a relationship that results from a formal agreement between two or more nations for broad, long-term objectives that further the common interests of each.[2] The formal nature of alliances brings more strict obligations for each partner, more diplomatic finessing over what are and what are not common interests, and what constitutes acceptable commitments to the achievement of these interests. Such diplomatic and political formality makes the establishment of alliances far more difficult than coalitions. But, once established, they can also be more capable in formulating combined strategy and more beneficial to each participant in the achievement of long-term policy goals. They are, because of their formal nature, also more closely controlled by political authorities of each of the participating countries. The political control exercised by the Supreme War Council in 1918 over the operations of the Allied Powers, as well as the influence of the Combined Chiefs of Staff system established in the alliance of England and the United States in 1942, are notable examples. In both cases, diplomacy determined the compromises to sovereignty that each alliance member would make for the sake of common alliance action.

In contrast, coalitions have more narrow military purposes, and there is comparatively less diplomatic wrangling over aims and commitments and less collective political oversight over operations. Under OEF, for instance, no formal multi-nation forum exists for political oversight of coalition operations or for diplomatic debate over national interests, objectives, or strategy. This ad hoc political nature allows many participant nations to retain a degree of sovereignty over their military forces by limiting action through the use of national caveats and restrictive national rules of engagements (ROE). Such caveats and individual ROE are substitutes for the harder activity of sitting in collective council to determine the limits of common military action based upon a common strategy and common interests that are acceptable politically to all nations.

Another characteristic that distinguishes coalitions and alliances from each other is in the differences regarding mutual understanding and respect. Alliance partners tend to understand one another, tend to know what to expect from one another in terms of commitments and capabilities, and, aided by standing combined committees and councils, they can formulate strategy acceptable to all partners.[3] While this may take some time and effort, once a strategy is agreed upon, the partners can more easily hold one another responsible for delivering upon commitments. Each member tends to understand the limitations imposed by domestic politics and domestic elections. At the same time, an alliance partner can point to long-term alliance agreements to substantiate military commitments to their national electorate. Alliances enhance legitimacy.

Comparatively, in coalitions there is less understanding of one another, less knowledge of military capability, and more suspicion regarding national interests. The process of strategy formulation frequently lies exclusively with a powerful "lead nation," who decides the military campaign plan that the rest of the coalition will accept. Input into strategizing in modern coalitions is achieved through confidential bilateral talks between the lead nation and a partner, and the influence of the latter upon the former varies greatly.

In these types of relationships, inequalities of influence and trust often cause jealousy and resentment. This is most obvious when coalitions organize how military intelligence will be disseminated. America, Britain, Canada, and Australia (ABCA) have established protocols for intelligence sharing that never fail to invoke resentment amongst other nations participating in a coalition with this "Four Eyes" community.[4] I have witnessed this frequently, first during my employment in the United States European Command Joint Planning Group, wherein the Coalition Planning Cell for the Global War on Terrorism (GWOT) was established in November 2001. The sharing of intelligence between ABCA members, excluding the French, Spanish, Italian, German, and Turkish coalition partners, caused considerable tension. This was also the case in ISAF headquarters in 2004, where I worked as a strategic planner and had to attempt to use American intelligence without disclosing classified information to my non–Four Eyes ISAF partners.

The tension over intelligence sharing arose again during my time in command of a Canadian battle group in Kandahar in 2006, when I was unable to share information with Romanian and French soldiers under my command. In 2007 I would encounter these difficulties again, when I served in the Headquarters United States Central Command, working between the Four Eyes community and the remainder of the sixty-nation OEF coalition. I have seen intelligence-sharing discrepancies invoke reactions that range from mild jealousy to irate condemnation.[5]

MEASURING COALITION PERFORMANCE

Bearing in mind their ad hoc political nature, coalitions' operational performance and endurance are determined by four factors: the nature of the threat to each of the coalition partners, the length of the military operation, the intensity of combat involved, and how command and control is exercised.

Nature of Coalitions

- Ad hoc political construct
- Strategy of a lead nation, remainder contribute tactical forces
- Success dependant upon
  - Enemy threat to coalition partner
  - Duration of the mission
  - Intensity of combat and amount of casualties
  - Command and control arrangements

Coalitions can perform well in short, intense combat operations such as Desert Shield/Desert Storm in 1990–91. In that conflict, Arab partners felt the immediate (in some cases, such as Qatar, the mortal) threat posed by Iraqi aggression. Western and Asian partners felt the threat posed by Iraqi control of Kuwaiti oil. This perception of threat had a direct correlation to the ability of each coalition partner to accept casualties, and Arab states made their forces available for combat operations. Canada, on the other hand, having perceived no direct threat from Iraq, was unwilling to send large combat formations for fear of casualties.

The relatively short duration of the offensive military operations in Desert Storm prevented the stress on resolve that occurs with any long-term military commitments. That the coalition involved in Desert Storm suffered relatively light casualties during this short operation helped to avoid diminishment of resolve in coalition partners.

Partner resolve was also sustained in Desert Storm because the command arrangements allowed each nation a degree of agency to discuss interests and strategy behind military operations and to exercise command over their forces. The United States operated an integrated headquarters (with Western military representation embedded), while the Saudis operated a parallel but distinct Arab headquarters, with the two linked by a combined coalition coordination centre. Therefore, during Desert Storm, even small partners such as Bahrain could voice opinion and diplomatic position on overall coalition strategy. The desire of the United States and England to conduct ground offensive operations into Iraq was countered by the concern voiced by smaller Arab partners. Acceptance of the Arab position ensured the continuance of coalition collective action until the sanctioned objective was achieved — the liberation of Kuwait.

Coalitions can also perform well in operations of long duration when the threats to each partner are limited and combat casualties are low. The efforts of the Australian-led International Force in East Timor, between 1999 and 2005, provides good example of this.[6]

PERFORMANCE FACTORS AND ISAF/OEF

The idea of a coalition fighting a long-term combat operation in an environment of limited direct threat to the partners is highly problematic. This is revealed when considering the factors of threat, length, intensity of combat operations, and command and control in assessing ISAF and OEF in Afghanistan.

While some Western countries still perceive al Qaeda as a direct threat, none consider them to constitute an omnipresent global threat, and the minds of Western citizens are not plagued by fears of this terrorist group. The threat posed by the Taliban is real for Afghanistan and Pakistan but does not project itself as a direct challenge to nation states involved in the ISAF and OEF coalitions. Western perception of the threat is limited. At the same time, by necessity the operations in Afghanistan require long-term commitments. Combat casualties have increased steadily since the re-emergence of the Taliban in 2006, and there are no signs that casualties will be reduced. To this day, command and control over military operations is highly bureaucratic, and few partners in either the ISAF coalition or the OEF coalition have agency in defining objectives and formulating strategies.

The ad hoc political nature of the OEF and ISAF coalitions has, from their beginnings, led to incremental evolution of both missions. The OEF coalition commenced in 2001 and aligned itself with anti-Taliban Afghan warlords (most notably of the Afghan Northern Alliance) and has prosecuted rigorous counter-terrorist operations since then, as well as substantial counter-insurgency operations between 2005 until 2007, when ground operations across Afghanistan were handed over to ISAF.

The ISAF coalition commenced in 2002 as a separate and distinct entity from OEF and was restricted to conducting stability operations in Kabul, coming under NATO sponsorship in 2003. ISAF gradually expanded stability operations to other parts of Afghanistan until subsuming most OEF forces in 2007. The attempts to integrate OEF and ISAF in 2006 and 2007 occurred at the same time that the Taliban escalated their activity into a full-blown insurgency. Evolutions in command and control of ISAF/OEF continued nonetheless, without reconciliation of different partner perspectives of military strategy. European partners, comfortable with limited stability operations, have become stressed over the growing insurgency in their individual areas of operation in Afghanistan. The United States has accepted counter-insurgency requirements but continues to oscillate between emphasis on a counter-insurgency strategy and one with greater focus upon counter-terrorism.

In the ad hoc political nature of these coalitions, there is no standing international body charged with political oversight or diplomatic discussion regarding strategic ends and means. After eight years, we are still unsure whether or not to nation-build in Afghanistan using a mix of counter-insurgency and stability operations or contain threats there using strictly counter-terrorism methods.

Confusion over military strategy and a lack of partner action has been exacerbated by a highly convoluted evolution in command arrangements. The bifurcation of theatre headquarters in Kabul, namely ISAF Headquarters and Headquarters Combined Forces Command — Afghanistan (OEF), officially ended in 2007, but divisions in command still exist and unified command still eludes coalition efforts. The commander of ISAF reports nominally to one boss in Europe (supreme allied commander Europe), and actually to another in Tampa, Florida (commander United States Central Command — CENTCOM). NATO nominally runs the ground war in Afghanistan, but CENTCOM coordinates all air effort, theatre intelligence, surveillance, reconnaissance, theatre special operations, Afghan training strategies, relations with Pakistan, and theatre strategic planning. NATO plays no part in these critical activities and has no political oversight. There is no formal relationship between CENTCOM and the alliance. Responsibility for civil development and reconstruction, law reform, and counter-narcotics rests with agencies other than the ISAF and OEF coalitions, and coordinating these activities with military action has proven to be extremely difficult.

Ad hoc arrangements also dominate operational command and control. Since 2001 there have been no less than eight senior American OEF commanders and nine European or Canadian ISAF commanders in charge of coalition operations in Afghanistan.[7] There have been at least seven different attempts to produce a unifying campaign plan.[8] No campaign plan has survived a change of command parade, as each new commanding general has felt compelled to begin theatre strategic planning afresh. Coalition partners appear content to avoid the difficult effort and accountability associated with campaign planning, preferring instead to place their general officers in ISAF/OEF headquarters positions or in charge of subordinate tactical commands.

Because each headquarters structure must appease the sensitivities of a large number of coalition nations, there are a disproportionately large number of general officers in ISAF. To accommodate these appointments, each headquarters now contains several deputy commanders and multiple chiefs of staff and assistant chiefs of staff. While theatre strategy rests exclusively with American planners and senior staff, tactical level command and planning is being conducted by myriad generals representing dozens of countries, each with unique perspectives on how to conduct operations within their areas of operation.[9]

The threat posed by the Taliban in Afghanistan remains an abstraction to most coalition partners, and the ad hoc political nature of ISAF and OEF prevents collective strategic analysis and debate regarding what the real threat may be and what might be the best strategy to deal with it. Meanwhile, casualties mount amongst coalition partners and there appears to be no success in winning the strategic initiative from the Taliban. This has led to cracks in coalition resolve, apparent in the recent Dutch decision to withdraw from the coalition effort and pending Canadian and British withdrawals. The critical factor that is causing tension is the very late realization amongst coalition members that the war they are involved in is one of insurgency and counter-insurgency, which is far more complex and deadly than the peacekeeping and stability operations upon which most of the coalition leadership was weaned.

THE NATURE OF INSURGENCY

Insurgencies are not well understood, and there is no consensus on how best to describe — or win, for that matter — counter-insurgencies. Nonetheless, many believe that Mao Zedong's work on revolutionary warfare is foundational. As such, this examination will use Mao's theory of revolutionary warfare as a basis for understanding complex insurgency. There are two further good reasons to do so: first, Mao formulated the most comprehensive and effective theory of insurgency; and second, it is Mao's strategic guideline that the Taliban are following.[10]

Nature of Insurgency

- Protracted warfare
- Focus at strategic level
- Three strategic phases
  - Strategic Defensive (Taliban 2002–2005)
  - Strategic Stalemate (Taliban 2006–present)
  - Strategic Offensive (Taliban once coalition has withdrawn)

Insurgency is an organized effort to overthrow a political authority of a nation. A wide spectrum of activities are used to achieve this end. Indoctrination and the organization of civil unrest can be an important first stage to insurgency. Terrorism, targeted intimidation, and small-scale but widespread guerrilla operations are conducted in the second stage. Conventional military action or large-scale mobile guerrilla warfare characterizes the third and final stage. Insurgents use these means to attempt to coerce or persuade the population to accept the insurgent cause instead of government political authority. While insurgencies can be highly political movements, they can achieve their aims without widespread popular support. In most cases, insurgents need only to encourage large-scale popular apathy toward government processes.

The Maoist model of insurgency prepares the insurgent forces for protracted warfare.[11] Insurgents perceive their commitment as generational, and they are willing to train their children and grandchildren to carry on the struggle. Maoist insurgencies are also characterized by a strategic focus. Most effort is expended achieving strategic impact, not chasing tactical successes that have no real enduring effect. Insurgents are also prepared to allow tactical setbacks if there is strategic gain. The most oft-cited example of this was the 1968 Tet Offensive in the Vietnam War. There was a similar occurrence in Kandahar in summer of 2006, when Taliban massed outside of Kandahar City, initiating vicious ground combat that cost the insurgency hundreds of lives.[12] However, across the provinces of south Afghanistan, and in Kabul, their efforts in 2006 demonstrated to all that the Taliban sphinx was emerging once again. In the mind of the local Afghans, the optimism of 2003–2005 ended during the fighting of July 2006.

Another characteristic of Maoist insurgency is that it follows specific strategic stages. The first is Strategic Defensive, which occurred for the Taliban between 2001 and 2005. In this stage, they withdrew into sanctuary in remote areas of Afghanistan and into Pakistan, where they reorganized and spent considerable time acquiring information on the forces of both OEF and ISAF. In the southern and eastern parts of Afghanistan, they also devoted time and effort in preparing people and villages for their return. They inserted fighters into these areas and became involved in local and regional economies by providing transportation security for the expanding opium trade. They inserted religious instructors into these regions who became involved in village mosques, preaching an anti-Western and anti-government form of radical Islam. During this phase, the Taliban made efforts to recruit and mobilize support across the south and east, using a sophisticated array of incentives, all of which demonstrated their willingness to once again exert the real authority over the people. Failure by the coalitions and the government of Afghanistan to provide an alternate credible and legitimate authority at the district level facilitated the Taliban return into most districts in the south and east.

In 2006, the Taliban initiated the second strategic phase of their insurgency — Mao's Strategic Stalemate stage. Not coincidentally, this was the year that saw NATO begin to assume control for most ground operations in Afghanistan. The aim of this phase is to wear down government resolve and gain widespread support of the population, or at least public promises to not support government efforts and to grant movement rights, as well as food and recruits, to the insurgency. In 2006, to connect with the people, the Taliban pushed thousands of fighters from Pakistan into Afghanistan to establish bases of operations. They formed shadow governments at district and provincial levels and began to circulate Taliban judges between villages to dispense justice over local disputes in the absence of any government judicial system. Acts of intimidation and terrorism, including assassination, were meted out against those villagers who wished to allow children education at the government schools or to those under employment of the government or with coalition forces. Assassination has now become widespread, a daily occurrence in Kandahar City, and a clear indication of Taliban confidence in this Strategic Stalemate phase.

In this second stage, the Taliban's military aim is to deny the coalition legitimacy and disrepute all government action. They also seek to seize and maintain the strategic initiative by conducting small but widespread guerrilla operations, pinning and wearing down government and coalition forces through attrition. Taliban forces attempt to cut off and defeat isolated military posts, prevent freedom of movement and action of coalition tactical forces — mainly through use of improvised explosive devices (IEDs) — and attack the political resolve of coalition partners. They pay close attention to the election cycles of coalition nations in the hope that rising ISAF casualty figures will become election issues. They have been careful to never threaten direct action against Western coalition nations outside Afghanistan, knowing that perceived direct threat to countries like Canada might well stiffen our resolve. Here, the Taliban concentrates on strategic success, delivering propaganda through both local and international media, including widespread use of video on

Muslim websites. They measure success by the degree of support they receive for their insurgency.

Afghanistan today is in the midst of the Strategic Stalemate phase, with a strong Taliban presence in most districts of Afghanistan. This phase will last for some time. While difficult to forecast accurately, it is probable that the Taliban will be satisfied in keeping second phase activities going until the Western military coalitions have withdrawn the bulk of their military forces from Afghanistan. Once those forces have left, the Taliban may attempt the final strategic phase — the Strategic Offensive — by initiating large-scale guerrilla operations across the whole of the country, leading to the overthrow of the government. Should the Taliban suffer a reversal at any time, they can revert back to the Strategic Defensive and await another opportunity to escalate into the second phase again.

COUNTER-INSURGENCY

Counter-insurgencies are military operations that work alongside government and developmental partners to arrest insurgent group activities and reverse any gains they have made. This is accomplished by correcting socio-economic and political grievances that might be contributing to insurgent success. In this respect, counter-insurgencies are multi-dimensional.

Counter-insurgencies may be conducted unilaterally by a government within a nation's own national boundaries. This was the case of the South African counter-insurgency against Cuban-backed guerrillas, who attempted to overthrow South African rule in Namibia between 1975 and 1985. Counter-insurgencies are also fought by governments aided by the military forces of another nation or a group of nations, as was the case in Vietnam and South Vietnam between 1950 and 1972.

A great deal has been written about counter-insurgency (COIN) operations in the past half decade in attempts to explain the conflicts in Iraq and in Afghanistan. Operations in both of these areas involve a coalition of military forces attempting to assist indigenous governments in fighting militant Islamic insurgents. New military manuals and think-tank publications abound. Most Western armies, however, are led by officers unschooled in the complexity of such counter-insurgency theory and without direct experience in such operations. Unfortunately, they have preferred to distill the written breadth of knowledge into a few abstract principles, such as "COIN is all about protecting the population," or "COIN is entirely about the Whole-of-Government approach." There are many useful prescriptions now published regarding COIN tactics and techniques, but there is very little in the way of COIN strategy. As such, the past provides as useful a guide as the present, and this chapter adheres to the observations of Colonel David Galula in his classic 1964 text, *Counter-Insurgency Warfare Theory and Practice*, to assess what specifically must be included in strategies that win in a counter-insurgency war.[13]

Galula lists four goals that, if not accomplished, will aid and abet the insurgent: negating or countering the appeal of insurgent cause, denying the insurgent free cross-border movement and sanctuary within the country, preventing outside support to the insurgent, and strengthening government institutions to prevent weakness that is exploitable by the insurgent.[14] If the insurgent can be denied two or three of these factors, the counter-insurgency has a chance. If the insurgent can exploit three or four of these factors, it may be impossible to defeat him.

Counter-Insurgency Imperatives

- Counter the insurgent cause
- Deny the insurgent of sanctuary and freedom of movement
- Sever outside support to the insurgency
- Eliminate weakness in government institutions

Again, the first of Galula's factors is the countering of the insurgent goal that has popular appeal and that cannot be accommodated by the government. The Taliban's cause is the withdrawal of foreign troops from Afghanistan and the replacement of the Karzai regime with a fundamentalist government that will enforce a uniform system of law and order. While few in Afghanistan want the harshness of Taliban rule, they deplore the systemic corruption of the Karzai administration and the lack of a justice system, and more and more Afghans are growing weary of coalition presence or, at a minimum, they lack confidence that the coalition will remain committed to Afghanistan.

The Taliban has been very successful in portraying their struggle in terms of a traditional Afghan effort to oust foreign invaders and re-establish Afghan independence, and they are quick to frame all small-scale Taliban tactical actions and efforts as strategic aspects of that cause. If the ISAF and OEF coalitions were following a Galula-guided strategy, these themes would be actively countered and diminished by a strategic information campaign that would project an alternate message in an attempt to rob the Taliban message of its appeal. However, coalitions are ill-suited for such strategic initiatives. The liberal sensitivities of coalition members, the very tight controls put upon use of information by coalition units, and inconsistency in command have made it impossible for the coalition to engage in their own propaganda and counter-propaganda campaigns. Therefore, at the strategic level, the Taliban message is heard much louder than the voice of the coalition. Coalition focus on tactical-level issues, combined with the lack of single unified strategic command in Afghanistan, have ensured that Taliban retained the moral high ground in the minds of the Afghan people and those outside of Afghanistan who support the Taliban in this Strategic Stalemate phase.

Porous borders and rugged, isolated terrain allow the insurgent freedom of movement and the opportunity to establish bases of operations that are unassailable by government forces. This presents a particular challenge to coalition forces working in Afghanistan, where open borders and vast areas of highly compartmentalized and rugged terrain have enabled Taliban movement and sanctuary within the country. It is impossible for the coalition and the government security agencies to muster sufficient forces to close all borders, interdict all movement corridors, and occupy and pacify all of the districts of Afghanistan simultaneously. Therefore, of all of Galula's four factors, this must remain the one that is least likely to change, even should a proper counter-insurgency strategy emerge.

The third factor in Galula's list is outside support for the insurgency. This is manifested as general monetary, materiel, and human resource aid to the insurgents, and the allowance of cross-border movements and sanctuary in neighboring countries. If counter-insurgent forces cannot deny or arrest a significant degree of outside support, the potential for the conflict to drag on or escalate into a regional affair will be significant. The Taliban today enjoy considerable outside support. In fact, they are not truly indigenous to Afghanistan, and western Pakistan remains the geographic centre of gravity for the entire movement. They have relatively easy border access along the southern and eastern borders of the country, which — despite large-scale efforts of Pakistan's army — remain open. Materiel and recruits flow into Afghanistan from support bases in Pakistan, and this reflects the fact that the Taliban is a Pashtun social movement that is independent of the national governments that are supposed to have lawful authority over these areas. Monetary aid to insurgent Taliban groups also comes from Iran and more distant Muslim states.

The Taliban has received wide social approval for their violent actions because of their intelligent use of the media, especially the Internet, to propagate their message. Apart from American and British bilateral efforts to compel Pakistan to pressure the Taliban within that country, the coalitions in Afghanistan have no mandate or capability to sever the umbilical cord that has sustained and augmented the small number of Afghan-grown Taliban. Most coalition nations want no part in broadening their responsibilities to include cross-border operations. The tactical focus of most coalition contingents and their governments prevents partners from comprehending the magnitude of the problem of outside support.

The last of Galula's factors is weakness in the government administration caused by corruption, lack of capacity and leadership, and lack of legitimacy. Government institutions that cannot adequately address the socio-economic problems of a country automatically grant an insurgency space to vie for legitimacy and power. In Afghanistan this problem is acute. Western efforts to create democratic mechanisms within Afghanistan have clouded our ability to understand Afghan culture, how power has traditionally been divided and exercised in that country, and how best to establish institutions that are both efficient and credible throughout the nation. Ignorance of culture has allowed largely corrupt practices to become deeply entrenched and widespread. A complex network of family, clan, tribal, and business relationships — constantly shifting and adapting — has diluted Western efforts to institute reform in government. Corruption is rampant, and in many districts the Afghan people feel victimized by their own politicians and police. Western military initiatives to "protect the population" in accordance with the maxim of COIN doctrine have had limited success, largely because coalition military efforts fail to understand that the population feels threatened by the government as well as the Taliban alike. The ISAF and OEF coalitions have also failed to appreciate or modify the highly localized and compartmentalized power structures — with acute family, tribal, and business biases — that rule in Afghanistan. The assumption by coalition forces that all district and provincial leaders are legitimate serves to cast our military contingents as supporting agents to corrupt power brokers, a stigma which reinforces the Taliban cause. No strategy exists within the coalitions to ameliorate this situation.

Galula maintains that an insurgency in a country with all four conditions stands a good chance of success. ISAF and OEF failure to undermine or provide an alternative to the Taliban cause, our inability to deny the Taliban sanctuary within most Afghan districts or mobility across borders, our similar incapacity to end foreign aid to the Taliban, and, most importantly, our inability to correct the inherent weaknesses in the government administration have, using Galula's estimate, provided the Taliban with the essential ingredients for success.

PUTTING IT ALL TOGETHER

Coalition warfare is inherently complex but can be characterized by its politically ad hoc nature. The chances of success in coalition warfare are dependent upon the perception of the threat by coalition partners, the duration of military operations and extent of casualties, as well as the effectiveness of command and control arrangements to formulate and execute strategy and campaign plans. In Afghanistan today, the NATO-led coalition (ISAF) and the American-led coalition (OEF) face incredible challenges in all four factors. Perhaps the largest is the challenge posed by command and control. Unified command structures and unity of command have been forsaken during the ad hoc evolution of the ISAF and OEF missions. If we are to learn anything from the much vaunted efforts or generals Briggs and Thompson in the Malayan campaign, it is that unity of command — optimally with *all* aspects of the counter-insurgency (political, military, economic, and social) coming under a single omnipotent leader — is essential. Modern tendencies to replace this time-tested principle with highly nuanced ideas of "unity of effort" and "whole-of-government" are contributing to the failure of the coalitions in Afghanistan.

Equally challenging is the nature of the Afghan insurgency. Maoist in character, it is protracted and strategic in its focus. The Taliban is following a model of strategic progress over time. They have taken advantage of the lack of centralized control, the ruggedness of the terrain, and the guarantee of outside support inherent in Afghanistan to promote their cause and discredit an infamously corrupt government. They are now engaged in a strategic phase aimed at neutralizing and decimating foreign forces that are almost entirely focused at the local tactical level.

The ISAF and OEF inability to fight at the strategic level, to establish unity of command, and to appreciate and mitigate the challenges posed by Afghan terrain and culture, harp of military failure. While forecasting is always difficult, it appears more and more probable that Western military efforts in Afghanistan will be supplanted by Western-supported anti-Taliban warlords, and international initiatives to establish civil society in that country will steadily diminish. When Western militaries seek to understand what happened during our decade-long counter-insurgency struggle, they will be best served to assess our efforts against substantiated doctrine and theory. From 2002 onward, political and military leaders in the coalitions failed to engage in proper strategy formulation for counter-insurgency, failed to understand the strategy of their opponents, failed to define appropriate coalition strategic objectives and determine adequate resources and, most importantly, failed to establish coherent command and control structure over civil-military action in Afghanistan. If Western militaries seek to become more proficient in the complexity of coalition and counter-insurgency operations, we would do well to now start more rigorous study and assessment.

5

Campaigning in Afghanistan

A Uniquely Canadian Approach¹

DR. HOWARD G. COOMBS AND
LIEUTENANT-GENERAL (RETIRED) MICHEL GAUTHIER

Ideas of campaigning have permeated Western military thought for centuries.² In the early nineteenth century, the military theorist Carl von Clausewitz formalized Western views of the relationship between campaigning and military theory by expressing it in its true context. He asserted that war "is not merely an act of policy but a true political instrument, a continuation of political intercourse, carried on by other means."³ Clausewitz strove for broad explanatory concepts of war and viewed the connection between policy and the violence of war as modified by various gradients of strategy and tactics.⁴ These ideas, as understood today, were codified within the crucible of United States doctrinal debate in the early 1980s through the adoption of the operational level of war as a formal part of this hierarchical construct to organize and plan military activities.⁵ These American perspectives were later adopted verbatim by the Canadian Forces.⁶ However, as a result of the peace support activities of the 1990s, and more so the recent war-fighting experiences of Afghanistan, the Canadian Forces has had the opportunity to not only implement the concepts of "campaigning," but do so in a fashion that is uniquely Canadian.

Campaigns are mostly planned at the operational level of war, which is the conceptual realm that exists between the politics of strategy and the violence of tactics. A campaign has two main components: campaign planning and operational art. The former is the process of translating strategic objectives in a manner that can be understood and used at the tactical level, while the latter is a far more complicated skill and refers to the creative aspects of arranging engagements, battles, and campaigns to achieve national ends.[7] The operational level of war is an extremely important professional idea, as it formalizes the connection between strategy and tactics, in theory, if not in practice, ensuring the link between military activities and political direction. Also, implicit in contemporary visions of this construct are ideas of establishing a common enduring vision amongst the participants in order to fulfill the objectives of alliance, coalition, or national strategy.

Between 1987 and 1995, when the operational level of war was being adopted by Canada, along with accompanying doctrinal ideas like that of structured campaign planning, there was not a great deal of professional debate by Canadian military practitioners concerning its utility. This lack of debate can be attributed to the legacy of Canadian military operations during both the Second World War and the Cold War. By the cessation of hostilities in 1945, it was evident that Canada's acceptance as a middle power lay in its ability to establish relevancy on the international stage by participating in constructive international action through multilateral organizations. The subsequent entanglement of alliances, particularly the North Atlantic Treaty Organization (NATO, 1949) and North American Air Defence Command (NORAD, 1958),[8] and to a lesser extent the United Nations (U.N., 1945), as well as the necessity of constructing saliency within these alliances, *de facto* determined how Canada would use its military.

While the broad strokes of immediate post-war foreign policy did chart an initial course, early in the Cold War emphasis moved from multilateral to bilateral arrangements for defence. In the absence of coherent and durable political guidance during succeeding decades, the use of the Canadian military as an instrument of national power became fragmented and disjointed.[9] By default, the unifying factor in Canadian defence activities became support of a *Pax Americana*.[10] Consequently, doctrine development became a matter of simply adopting the doctrine of our closest partner.

While this latter statement may seem contentious, it is borne out by the instruction that was conducted at the Canadian Forces College in Toronto, Ontario, during the Cold War.[11] From the first course, a significant part of the curriculum was the adoption of the United States Joint Planning System (US JPS) as the predominant method of creating inter-service, or joint, plans. Its importance was underscored in 1980–1981, when it was included as a portion of achieving the learning outcome, "understanding of the staff functions of all environments in the joint planning process."[12] Significantly, a few years later, by 1985–1986, due to the lack of a Canadian joint doctrine, the JPS had become the preferred model for Canadian joint planning. The college *Calendar* from that year notes:

> The US JPS has been chosen as a model for joint planning because it is the most highly codified, broadly diversified, and well documented system. Senior Canadian officers must be familiar with the US JPS because of North American bilateral security arrangements as well as the close historical association between the armed forces of the two nations.[13]

Interestingly, in 1991, when Canada was originally in the midst of adopting the operational level of war, Canadian military historian Dr. Bill McAndrew questioned this practice of adopting American doctrinal concepts word for word. McAndrew put forward the idea that embracing this construct was problematic and risky. He explained that the search for answers by the United States Army during the post-Vietnam period resulted in the adoption of the operational level of war. A similar pattern of crisis and response had not taken place in Canada and, consequently, McAndrew asserts:

> The Canadian Forces have not experienced that vital intellectual search for first principles. Instead of stimulating an exchange of ideas on which to construct a sound intellectual base, a bureaucracy arbitrarily directed that

Operational Art was to be adopted. Unfortunately, this came at a time when, elsewhere, categories were hardening and insights were being engraved in doctrinal manuals. Accepting those manuals without having experienced or really understood, the essential first phase builds on a precarious foundation...It is doubtful that a way of thinking can be changed by fiat, nor is it likely that the way an army thinks about itself can be imported. Trying to absorb foreign doctrines second hand will be as fruitless as transplanting tropical plants in the tundra.[14]

Despite this seeming non-interest, in the early 2000s there was debate within the Canadian profession of arms, most originating from the Canadian Forces College, as to whether these ideas were applicable to Canada.[15] One can attribute this discussion to a number of causes, from the experiences gained in the turbulent military interventions of the post-Cold War period to the revitalization of the Canadian profession of arms, which initiated as a result of incidents arising from Canadian Forces participation in the U.N. peacekeeping mission in Somalia during 1992–1993.[16] In the course of this early discourse, some, such as recent Joint Task Force (Afghanistan) (JTF (A)) commander Brigadier-General Jon Vance argued that the Canadian Forces did not campaign, but simply organized itself tactically to meet strategic needs without operational thought.[17] Others advocated that although the doctrine for these constructs was not rigorously followed, commanders at various levels exercised the thought processes required to translate the nebulous objectives of policy into concrete realities of tactics.[18]

This last point of view contended that the mental constructs required for operational thought had been used in the past and continued to be implemented, albeit not always in a doctrinally coherent or orderly manner. It was because of the exercise of these elements of operational art that the Canadian Forces functioned at the operational level of war. Moreover, instances of Canadian officers commanding at the operational level of war within coalitions in Bosnia and the Persian Gulf and

Afghanistan during the period in question demonstrated the continued requirement of converting policy to military actions.[19]

Consequently, in order to achieve this translation of strategic direction to definable activities, operational-level Canadian military leaders do create campaign plans. These plans arrange military and other activities to enable the sequential or simultaneous attainment of strategic objectives and fulfill a set of conditions visualized as the ultimate goal of that campaign.[20] Canadian practitioners of operational art use theory and doctrine to dissect complex military problems and to develop and sequence campaigns. Commanders exercise operational art as a method to translate strategic aims (ends) into campaigns (ways) using elements of operational design that will ultimately permit the allocation of resources (means) to be utilized at the tactical level to achieve the original strategic objectives. Elements of operational design are used to create a practical expression of operational art: the campaign plan. They include concepts like military end state, or the desired conditions that are required to fulfill the strategic objective. Ideas such as centre of gravity, decisive points, and lines of operation assist in determining the manner in which the military end state will be achieved.

The centre of gravity refers to the physical or moral quality considered to be the centre or hub of power for an opponent. It is essential to attack the centre of gravity to cause defeat. Normally it is unwise to attack the centre of gravity directly, as it is strongly protected, so it becomes crucial to discern decisive points. Decisive points are intermediate objectives whose attainment would enable one to affect the centre of gravity. The line created by joining a series of decisive points in the order that they will be influenced is a line of operations. This permits the construction of a model that sequences military activities in time and space. It is very important to arrange military events so that they occur simultaneously, in order to overwhelm an opponent. When that is not possible, it is necessary to complete these activities in a continuous, sequential manner, without creating a pause that would enable the other side to gain a respite. This idea of sequencing is also an element of operational design.[21]

As a result of the professional revitalization of recent years, this construct, as used by Canadians in the early years of the twenty-first century, was neither as hierarchical or process-oriented as that of some allies, and it depended on the intellectual visualization of concepts as opposed to geographical constructs of theatres of war with subordinate theatres of operations or significant military forces. Canadian officers exercised the thought necessary to organize resources, personnel, and the associated systems in response to sometimes vaguely articulated political direction in a "bottom-up" fashion significantly different from the formal constraints of the doctrines of those years. In any case, this proved to be a superb starting point for the evolution of Canadian campaigning in Afghanistan.

Of particular importance is that Canada's international leadership role in Southern Afghanistan, beginning in 2006, gave Canada's military a unique opportunity to practise operational art to a degree not previously seen in its military history. As the mission unfolded, the Government of Canada progressively built a strong strategic framework focused on achieving "whole-of-government" results in Kandahar Province.[22] National policy and programming objectives became both explicit and relatively specific, and at the political level, responsible ministers communicated mission results to Canadians through series of Quarterly Reports. And with this growing whole-of-government framework came an expectation, at the political and bureaucratic levels, that the Canadian military campaign in Afghanistan would conform to national policy and strategy.

In this context, it can be argued that, to a greater extent than perhaps ever before, the Canadian military has been challenged to direct and shape the tactical actions of its deployed troops over time in full consonance with this very dynamic national political and strategic framework — the essence of operational thought. The complex Afghan mission context required Canadian operational-level leaders and planners to weave together a number of disparate strands into their campaign planning and ongoing guidance; the sometimes conflicting imperatives of national whole-of-government policy and practices and international military, primarily NATO and United States, operational direction; an exceptionally fragile Afghan government and security apparatus; an insurgency, the strength of which has consistently been underestimated by the international community; evolving international and national views of best practices in both counter-insurgency and nation-building operations; and the need to take account of a cyclical force generation process that introduced fresh troops from across the Canadian Forces into operations at six and nine month intervals.

Given the lack of Canadian experience in directing and guiding military campaigns, the process has certainly been a learning experience at all levels of government and within the military, and, of course, it has been imperfect in many ways. But what has emerged from the experience — despite modest military force levels — is a relatively unique approach to both military campaign planning and operational art aimed at providing clarity of purpose, consistency, and continuity to the Canadian effort over a period of several years in a very complex operating environment at the strategic, operational, and tactical levels.

In 2001 the American-led Operation Enduring Freedom (OEF) had focused primarily on defeating al Qaeda and Taliban opponents. Over time, this mission evolved to one that was primarily under the auspices of NATO leadership and oriented toward setting security conditions for an international nation-building effort, albeit without the necessary military resources actually committed to accomplishing this task. The International Security Assistance Forces (ISAF) mandate was at first limited to the provision of security in and around Kabul. During October 2003, the U.N. approved Security Council Resolution 1510 and extended this mandate to cover the whole of Afghanistan, paving the way for an expansion of the mission across the country.[23] Simultaneously, the United States had become more preoccupied with achieving military success in Iraq, which diverted its focus from Afghanistan. However, with the success of the 2007 American military "surge" in Iraq and the 2008 election of U.S. President Barrack Obama, the United States became invested in the dilemmas of the ongoing conflict in Afghanistan, namely providing a strategic vision and the resources necessary to create a multinational counter-insurgency campaign in Afghanistan. This improved strategic coherence, and the allocation of American personnel and material renewed international interest in Afghanistan and gave impetus to NATO efforts to resolve the expanding violence.

Unfortunately, the absence of a consistent and clearly articulated international strategy for Afghanistan between 2006 and 2009 gave rise to what has been described by critics as a series of "locally designed" national campaigns across the Afghan area of operations, such as that conducted by Canadians in Kandahar, the British in Helmand, and the United States in the eastern provinces. With the influx of tens of thousands of American troops, and more clearly defined international campaign leadership in late 2009, these national campaigns have only recently been fully integrated into broader international counter-insurgency and nation-building campaigns that have now begun to coalesce. But it is in this context that, of necessity, a relatively robust Canadian whole-of-government campaign was able to evolve in Kandahar Province.

Canada's current involvement in southern Afghanistan resulted from ISAF enlargement to that region in 2006. At that time, the NATO mission took over from United States-led coalition forces in the region. During this period of transition, Canadian Forces elements that had been supporting ISAF in the area of Kabul were withdrawn and the infrastructure and material that had been part of the primary Canadian base, Camp Julien, were moved to Kandahar.

While Canada had initially deployed a battle group to the Kandahar region as part of OEF for a limited period during 2001–2002, before committing to ISAF in the Kabul region in 2003, the large-scale substantive engagement of Canadian Forces personnel in combat in southern Afghanistan actually commenced in 2006. Brigadier-General Dave Fraser and his staff formed Multi-National Brigade (South) (MNB (S)), with units from 1 Canadian Mechanized Brigade Group, based in western Canada, and for the initial period MNB (S) was part of the American coordinated OEF before transitioning to ISAF control. MNB (S) became part of Regional Command (South) (RC (S)) on 31 July 2006. Since then, the command of RC (S) has rotated amongst a number of NATO nations, including Canada, and as of the time of writing is changing over to American control.

Also significant was the fact that 2006 marked the initial implementation of the Canadian intergovernmental approach to addressing the complex challenges of the contemporary security environment. This approach, while at first nascent and ill-defined, has become much more coherent and well-understood, with integration of high-level Canadian governmental officials into Canadian military operations. It also includes Privy Council Office and Cabinet interest in, and coordination of, a comprehensive governmental approach along with corresponding detailed quarterly assessment of activities at the national level. Today, this whole-of-government process includes the Department of National Defence/ Canadian Forces, Department of Foreign Affairs and International Trade (DFAIT), and the Canadian International Development Agency (CIDA), as well as more recent additions of other government departments, such as the Royal Canadian Mounted Police (RCMP) and Corrections Services Canada (CSC).[24]

In the best traditions of Clausewitz, Canadian domestic politics have had a direct bearing on the military campaign in southern Afghanistan from its earliest days. At the very moment when Canadian soldiers were beginning to deploy to Afghanistan in January 2006, the national political landscape shifted fairly dramatically with a minority Conservative Government coming to power. Over the course of the Canadian campaign, there have been two relatively divisive parliamentary votes (May 2006 and March 2008) concerning the extension of the mission and its essential character, the convening of an independent panel to make recommendations on the future course of the mission in 2007 (the Manley Report), and a very politicized public discourse on the government's detainee transfer policy, which began in 2007 and continues to this day.[25]

This fragile political environment has given new meaning to the notion of the "strategic" corporal, with Canadian casualties, Afghan civilian casualties, issues around detainees, and a plethora of tactical level incidents regularly garnering front-page headlines from the outset of the mission. Just as important, it has engendered a level of precision and detail in the articulation of strategic policy and a degree of political and bureaucratic control over the military mission, including associated public messaging, that has likely not been previously seen.

In a more positive sense, in recognition of the breadth and complexity of the Afghan challenge, there has been a substantial evolution in both the strategic whole-of-government coordination framework in Ottawa and the corresponding mission structure and civilian resourcing in Afghanistan. Since early 2008, Canadian efforts in Afghanistan have been overseen by a Cabinet committee on Afghanistan, supported by the Afghanistan Task Force in the Privy Council Office and an ad hoc committee of deputy ministers that, today, meets on a weekly basis.

The deployed Canadian civilian and police contingent has also grown from a handful in 2006 to more than 100 in 2009, with a relatively robust civilian leadership cadre at the embassy in Kabul, at Kandahar Airfield under the leadership of the representative of Canada in Kandahar (RoCK), and a senior civilian director of the Kandahar Provincial Reconstruction Team (KPRT). In 2010 the latter two positions were amalgamated and the RoCK is now also the director KPRT.

Following the Manley Report and the parliamentary vote of March 2008, the government unveiled a detailed set of policy objectives for the mission and soon thereafter developed a framework of benchmarks to measure and report on the progress achieved on each of its six key policy priorities. It is noteworthy that just one of these priorities involves security, and its focus is entirely on building the capacity of Afghan National Security Forces (ANSF) to sustain a more secure environment and promote law and order. Consequently, this dynamic and complex national strategic policy and political landscape had a very direct bearing on how the Canadian military campaign in Afghanistan was planned, adjusted, and communicated to the public.

With significant increases of American military personnel in the region since 2009, Canadian military forces have been able to focus efforts and resources on increasingly smaller areas — most recently the districts of Panjwayi, Dand, and Daman, within the province of Kandahar. At this time, the MNB, the Canadian-led Task Force Kandahar (TFK), has an American unit, which adds significantly to the military capabilities of this Joint Task Force (JTF).

The foundation of the current Canadian campaign can be said to have been laid in 2004 by General (retired) Rick Hillier, then a lieutenant-general and commander ISAF. In January 2004, Hillier was presented with a number of problems by President Hamid Karzai, who at that time was the leader of the Afghanistan Transitional Authority (ATA).[26] Most important of these was the lack of unified action by the myriad foreign governments and organizations. This resulted in less than effective development and caused a weakening of potential effects. Also, as a result of the lack of a shared approach, ISAF could not move beyond lower order, or tactical military activities, in order to achieve higher-level and enduring strategic objectives.

Hillier believed that without a coherent strategic concept in which all involved parties — military, international organizations, non-governmental organizations, donor institutions, the international community, and most importantly the ATA and Afghan people — could partake, no operational-level campaign could be created. Accordingly, he used his ISAF staff, and later two Canadian officers tasked from Canada, to assist the ATA in articulating a strategic concept.[27] This model was eventually released in the form of an idea paper entitled "Creating a National Economy: The Path to Security and Stability in Afghanistan." While primarily developmental in nature, it also specified ideas that would later be used to assist with governance and security. These core ideas later emerged within in the Afghanistan National Developmental Strategy (ANDS), which continues to be an overarching Government of the Islamic Republic of Afghanistan (GIRoA) policy document governing multiple activity streams by all contributing to the rebuilding of Afghanistan.[28]

When General Hillier assumed the position of chief of the defence staff (CDS) for the Canadian Forces from 2006–2008, he implemented a relatively bold vision for the projection of Canadian Forces influence abroad by substantially realigning the operational command and control structure of the Canadian military. Part of this restructuring was the establishment of Canadian Expeditionary Forces Command (CEFCOM).[29] Hillier charged the newly-formed CEFCOM with the construction of a Canadian campaign that would integrate military efforts to meet the needs of Afghanistan and harmonize these activities along three major thrust lines, or lines of operations — governance, development, and security — delivering fully integrated strategic effects for Canada in full concert with national "3D" (Diplomacy, Defence and Development) partners and international allies:

CDS INTENT

> The CF [Canadian Forces] commitment to Afghanistan
> is all about helping Afghans: help them move towards
> self-sufficiency in security, stabilize their country,
> develop their government and build a better future
> for their children. Our commitment, as part of a wider
> Government of Canada and International Community
> commitments, will aim to achieve effects at three lev-
> els: at the national level, by providing mentoring and
> advisory capabilities; at the regional level, by taking
> the lead of the multinational brigade; and provincially
> in Kandahar, by providing a robust battle group and a
> capable Provincial Reconstruction Team.[30]

In line with this intent, CEFCOM became the enabling platform to guide, shape, and set the conditions for Canadian tactical and operational outcomes for the multi-year campaign in Afghanistan. It led the effort to produce and oversee the execution of a military campaign for the Afghan mission — something quite unprecedented in Canadian military operations of the past several decades. In this role, it became the Canadian Forces focal point for translating strategic policy into military operational guidance, for ensuring alignment with other government departments, and for coordinating internationally with sister headquarters, such as the United Kingdom Permanent Joint Headquarters, United States Central Command, Netherlands Ministry of Defence, ISAF Headquarters, and Afghan operational authorities. Also, just as important, it provided guidance and direction to the Canadian military force generation effort to over time ensure convergence with a very dynamic Afghan operating environment.

Another important structural element of Hillier's vision was his desire to empower and set the conditions for a single national theatre commander with full operational authority over all Canadian elements deployed to that theatre: air, land, maritime, and special operations forces.

To this end, the traditional approach of relying on a small deployed national command element, focused on national administrative and support matters, quickly evolved. By 2007 the command and control element in Afghanistan was a relatively robust JTF headquarters responsible for operational control and national command of all Canadian military forces. Uniquely, this headquarters has, for the past three years, had one foot at the tactical level, directing and controlling day-to-day tactical activity, and the other at the operational level, planning and guiding operations over the course of a deployment in accordance with their theatre concepts, developed in the context of the both the ISAF and CEFCOM campaigns.

The two structural aspects of Hillier's operational vision that are the basis for this relatively unique approach to Canadian campaigning in Afghanistan are an empowered theatre commander with the mandate to plan, direct, and co-lead, with whole-of-government counterparts, the execution of a comprehensive theatre campaign for a fixed period, and at CEFCOM, an Ottawa-based operational commander who functions at the strategic and operational interface. This commander has the responsibility of interpreting national policy and strategy to guide, shape, and maintain a multi-year military effort fully integrated with intergovernmental and international partners, as well as the force generation authorities of the Canadian Forces.

In the earliest days of Canada's mission in Kandahar, in 2006, a Canadian and subsequently a CEFCOM campaign plan were published and expanded upon over the ensuing years. Above all, this latest planning document was intended to serve two fundamental purposes: to assure shared commander's intent at the strategic, operational, and tactical levels of command and to provide a framework from which to assess and communicate progress. In traditional fashion, the campaign plan specified the commander's overarching intent, and it emphasized key lines of operation, consistent with international plans and strategies. Within each line of operations were decisive points, which defined intermediate objectives or touchstones that would, over time, lead to the attainment of a series of operational objectives flowing from Canada's overarching strategic objectives for the mission.

It is important to note that, at first, there was neither a whole-of-government equivalent of a campaign plan, nor for that matter whole-of-government doctrine or procedures to support this approach to overseas missions. At the strategic policy level, memoranda to Cabinet were the principal planning vehicle, and these documents tended to focus on broad policy, macro-level resourcing, and strategic communication strategies, not operational plans and programs. Hence, in many respects, CEFCOM's early campaign planning effort was aimed as much at coalescing other government departments' planning and management frameworks as it was on providing a shared vision for the mission within the military. In fact, a close look at the lines of operations, decisive points, and associated measures of campaign effectiveness would reveal that the majority of these design features were the purview of other government departments.

Linked to this was the necessity of developing a coherent and useful campaign assessment framework — one fully linked to Afghan, ISAF, and whole-of-government imperatives. This unavoidable necessity also consumed much command and staff attention. While it is not always well understood at all levels, a politician's most important weapon is communication with the public, and key messages are their ammunition. In this strategic context, arguably the most critical role played by CEFCOM was to assess and communicate campaign progress in a way that was helpful to the bureaucracy and to policy makers. It was a function that was emphasized as essential by Hillier early on in the campaign effort. To this end, considerable effort was devoted to developing a rigorous campaign effects measurement framework as an adjunct to the campaign plan. Subsequently, weekly, monthly, and quarterly campaign assessment process — a very dynamic and demanding process involving commanders at all levels — emerged as a central component of the operational conceptualization practised by CEFCOM.

Over time, and long after the first iteration of the campaign plan, basic elements of operational design and understanding emerged in this unique Canadian construct. The theoretical aspects of campaign planning are well institutionalized within the Canadian Forces. But the same cannot be said for the procedures and processes used by commanders and staffs to implement a campaign concepts in an incredibly complex operating environment — that can only be gained through practice. That preparation was obtained in a setting where government policy constantly changed in very important ways in response to a fragile political situation, international strategies, and evolving allied theatre level plans. Also, the nature of the opposing forces, the supported government, as well as the regular Canadian military rotations, all had a significant influence on the pace of progress on the ground. It was within this very complex dynamic that some of the more useful elements of planning and management became more evident. These included:

1. A cyclical planning process emerged, designed to influence the force generation of units and JTF headquarters six months or more before deployment.

2. Within the basic campaign plan framework that defined decisive points within lines of operation leading to specified objectives, this cyclical evaluation and planning focused on adapting force structure, desired operational effects linked to geography and people, and priority tasks and balance of effort — in other words, ends, ways, and means — for a particular troop rotation.

3. A system of CEFCOM orders to force generation authorities and directives to deploying JTF commanders. These were effectively the dynamic component of what would otherwise have been a less than helpful static campaign plan.

4. In the interests of campaign continuity and common intent shared at all levels, perhaps the most important element of operational level battle procedure was the series of meetings, or "leadership engagements," held between CEFCOM and deploying forces commanders and staffs for each rotation on at least three occasions prior to a deployment.

5. Weekly and monthly assessment reports were produced by the JTF commanders, and CEFCOM quarterly campaign assessment reports were briefed to the senior leadership of the Canadian Forces and the Department of National Defence. All of these, of course, were complementary to

the frequent CEFCOM command and staff level visits into Afghanistan and end-tour briefings by the deployed JTF and unit commanders.

6. Later in the campaign, a system of whole-of-government progress benchmarks was managed by the Privy Council Office — Afghanistan Task Force with quarterly reports signed by the involved ministers.

7. A government level mission management framework of ministerial and cabinet-level committees which have been meeting regularly since 2008.

There were numerous other factors that needed to be catered to in development of the integrated Canadian campaign in Afghanistan, some of which have been alluded to previously. The GIRoA has had a number of elections resulting in President Karzai's continuation in office, which have been accorded various degrees of legitimacy by external authorities and the Afghan people. Along with this have been accusations of corruption undermining national governance. Despite this, great gains have been made in increasing the capacity of the Afghan National Army (ANA), but less so with the Afghan National Police (ANP). Our major ally in Afghanistan, the United States, has become Afghanistan-focused, to the point where ISAF has been, for a number of years, based on a framework of American leadership. Furthermore, ISAF's strategy has become increasingly determined by the United States and dependent on ever-larger American troop contributions.

Throughout this process, Canadian goals and approaches have become more and more defined until today, when we have a clearly articulated set of objectives for our national involvement in Afghanistan to assist Afghans with creating "a more secure Kandahar that is better governed and can deliver basic services to its citizens, supported by a more capable national government that can better provide for its security, manage its borders and sustain stability and reconstruction gains over the longer term."[31]

Canada has implemented six priorities and three signature projects which support this vision. These priorities range in scope from endeavours designed to address regional challenges to those oriented toward national issues:

1. Increasing ANSF capacity and assisting with implementation of the rule of law in Kandahar province.
2. Augmenting basic services available to the people of Kandahar and enhancing regional growth.
3. Providing humanitarian aid to those in need.
4. Facilitating an augmentation in border security by encouraging bilateral discussion between Afghan and Pakistani officials.
5. Promoting democratization through public accountability of national institutions and transparent electoral processes.
6. Encouraging Afghan-led political reconciliation.

Canada's three concomitant signature projects are reconstruction of the Dahla Dam and its associated irrigation system, significant investment in regional education capacity, and support to polio eradication across Afghanistan.

When examining Canadian operations in Afghanistan since 2006, one can discern that combat operations, like counterinsurgency, assist with setting the conditions for a secure and stable environment. However, military operations are just one part of a complicated puzzle and make no sense without being put in context with the other parts. In order to create the shared understanding required by the multitude of entities involved in Afghanistan within the context of the many influences in that environment, a campaign concept with a holistic perspective was developed.

It was recognized by those involved in formulating a campaign approach that the three lines of operation — governance, development, and security — could not be viewed in a linear, synchronized fashion with objectives, or decisive points, being achieved in a methodical fashion by military agencies. Instead, they were non-linear and asynchronous with a host of contributing Canadian participants. In addition, these activities were aligned with the actions of Afghan and international authorities.

It was necessary to explicitly acknowledge the complex dynamic system created by the interaction of the areas of governance, development, and security, which reinforced the cross-cutting nature of Canada's whole-of-government efforts in Afghanistan. The campaign concept also highlighted the critical need to maintain close collaboration and co-operation amongst Canadian contributors. The Canadian JTF commander was and is responsible to ensure continuity of purpose and intent in the pursuit of the achieving Canadian objectives, as well as having appreciation of progress in the broader context. This broader context includes Afghan directives like the ANDS, NATO/ISAF plans and directives, as well as Canadian governmental strategy. It is a non-hierarchical and interactive, iterative process.

In the final analysis, the Canadian campaign idea that evolved over time provided a common vision that allowed for a continuity of approach across successive deployments and amongst the interagency team unprecedented in recent decades. While it may seem intuitive, building on the successes of previous Canadian task forces requires constancy of vision, directives, and plans that arises only a coherently articulated and relevant campaign concept. Our military operations in southern Afghanistan have all been oriented toward achieving a secure environment for the population and the most recent iteration of ISAF Commander's guidance reiterates this theme. General David Petraeus emphasizes the need to protect and serve the Afghan people, as "only by providing them security and earning their trust and confidence can the Afghan government and ISAF prevail."[32] However, at the same time these military activities are part of an overall Canadian effort that Dr. Doug Bland, of Queen's University, described in 2007 as "Canadian 'whole-of-government' operations in Afghanistan are part of what can best be understood as a 'stability campaign,' in which military operations conducted under warfare doctrines and experiences aim to create 'harmonious law-based conditions' in which legitimate governments (aided or directed by the U.N.) can develop in turn a more peaceful, liberal-democratic, consensual and self-sustaining national, regional, or international order."[33]

The amalgamation of these perspectives and corresponding

objectives has directly underpinned the creation of a Canadian campaign approach in Afghanistan over the last several years. This concept involves Canadian field partners, members of the international community, and Afghan authorities at all levels. It is creative and responsive to the exigencies of Canada's most current intervention, but at the same time in a fashion unlike earlier operational level doctrine, it provides for the development of a common vision and unity of effort through consensus building and coordination of all parties across major efforts in governance, development, and security. Canada's campaign framework ultimately provides a flexible method to prioritize the challenges facing Canada's military with the purpose of assisting whole-of-government capacity building in Afghanistan, and as a result provides for the security and prosperity of Afghan citizens and contributes to regional and global stability.

Furthermore, with the purpose of facilitating Canadian efforts toward development and governance in Afghanistan through security assistance, the Manley Report recommended prolongation of the Canadian military commitment beyond 2009. Parliamentary approval was given to extending Canadian Forces involvement until the end of 2011. Consequently, the Canadian military strategy until 2011 includes training the ANSF, providing security for reconstruction and development efforts in Kandahar, the continuation of Canada's responsibility for the KPRT, and preparing for changeover of the current security mission in southern Afghanistan to American or other allies in 2011.

From the earliest days, the Canadian Forces campaign was guided in its most fundamental sense by General Hillier's stated intent for the mission: helping Afghans build national capacity and create a secure environment for themselves and future generations. Of course, just as "no plan survives first contact with the enemy," the approach to campaigning in Afghanistan evolved as lessons were learned and things changed. It was heavily influenced by three key dynamics among many others: first, in Afghanistan, the growing understanding of an increasingly powerful insurgency, the relative weakness of Afghan authorities at all levels to respond to capacity-building efforts, and the pragmatic indifference of the Afghan people to both of these; second, the imbalance in the equation between these and the international resources being applied to the challenge; and third, the evolving Canadian policy and communication strategy, with its strong emphasis on everything but combat operations.

Both the strength and the weakness in the guiding intent for the mission was the overarching focus on building Afghan capacity. As much as the international community collectively underestimated the strength of the insurgency, it overestimated the capacity of Afghan leadership, in governance and security efforts, to assume full responsibility for responding to the challenges in Kandahar Province. Under these circumstances, the Canadian challenge revolved around balancing its efforts to enable Afghan authorities and security forces and at the same time keep the insurgents at bay with a single battle group, or augmented infantry battalion, in an area of operations that required a much larger military commitment. Almost five years later, the basic intent remains the same, but both Afghan and international security force levels are only now reaching the point where it can begin to be met.

Canada's approach to campaigning in Afghanistan has been replete with flaws but also rich in lessons learned. Above all, Canadians should take great pride in the role the Canadian Forces played in holding Kandahar for more than three years, pending the arrival of more than twenty thousand additional troops. Canada's unique and highly successful approach to mentoring ANA troops has earned our soldiers and combat leaders the enduring respect of our Afghan brethren and allies alike. The Canadian decision to form military teams to mentor the ANP has since been widely adopted by NATO and our American allies in particular. Likewise, the Canadian approach to substantially strengthening the civilian presence on the ground has been emulated more recently in the United States' civilian surge. Finally, the essential elements of the counter-insurgency strategy adopted by the Canadian Forces in early 2009 — predicated on protecting the population at the village level and empowering Afghans — has, in many respects, served as a foundation for the more recent NATO approach.

Historians will ultimately be the judge of the strengths and weaknesses and the success of Canada's approach in Afghanistan. Ironically, one of the underlying challenges of this mission has been for the international community and each of its key players to clearly define success, and in many ways this facet of the mission remains a work in progress. What can certainly be said about Canada's approach to campaigning in Afghanistan is that it has provided a relatively unique opportunity for its non-commissioned members and officers, its military, and its government to play a significant leadership role as part of these topical international efforts in southwest Asia.

6

Sustaining Those Who Dare

Logistic Observations from Contemporary Afghanistan

LIEUTENANT-COLONEL JOHN CONRAD

When you're wounded and left on Afghanistan's plain
And the women come out to cut up what remains,
Jest roll to your rifle and blow out your brains
An' go to your Gawd like a soldier...
— Rudyard Kipling

I was trying to stay calm, but the suffocating heat in the diesel truck kept convincing me that I could not draw a full breath. The sweat beneath my blast vest was oozing. My driver and I guzzled water and snatched rabbit breathes as we kept our eyes glued to the road and our lumbering necklace of logistics vehicles.

The air conditioner had quit in our big diesel fuel truck on the way out to Helmand that morning, a thousand hours ago. In this country, a broken air conditioner will ground a vehicle, keeping it in the field workshop for repair; such is the dire human need for air-conditioned cabs, underneath the layers of mandated personal equipment and protective gear. Corporal Shawn Crowder and I had traded our Mercedes G-Wagon with the diesel crew so they could have a break from the heat on the long road back to Kandahar Airfield.

Crowder was throwing darts at me with his eyes just as I became aware of the Toyota Hiacre truck: a squat, cab-over style contraption that was gently picking its way west along the edge of our convoy. With a dreamlike slow-motion quality, the Tonka toy rip-off suddenly detonated in front of us. I felt the blast in the same split second my eyes processed what was happening. In startling clarity, twisted chunks of metal and gore went flying over our cab and onto the reinforced window and grill of our truck. The Bison Light Armoured Vehicle (LAV) II to our front broke column and careened into the north shoulder of the road. One minute Crowder and I were worried about heat and dehydration, the next we were on the floor of the heavy fuel vehicle hoping to live.

I climbed down from my co-driver position to begin the process of overseeing the protection of our stricken convoy. I was keen to ensure that our escorts had begun evacuating our seriously wounded, but I had yet to learn that we had lost two fine Canadian boys in the blast. Like a caught-out U-Boat skipper gritting his teeth and setting his trim and depth to await the onslaught, we battened down our cordon around the halted string of vehicles. Our first, albeit uninspired, move in the two hour ambush had been made. As it turned out, there was more dark business yet to come from our opponent, more blood yet to be spilled.

Those soldiers who have served on Afghanistan's plain recognize the hard little country for what it is: a land whose infrastructure and geography offers precious little logistic advantage to armies of occupation. Military commanders from Alexander the Great to Lieutenant-General Stanley McChrystal have all had to wrestle with this reality before even rolling up their sleeves to deal with the enemy. Here is a land that is as lean on indigenous capacity as it is harsh on poor preparation.

The Canadian Forces (CF) have come to know southern Afghanistan and all her supply chain perils well these past few years. Afghanistan is one of the toughest places to soldier on the planet, and, by extension, a difficult country in which to project military logistics. Contemporary experience fighting a determined insurgency in southern Afghanistan has brought certain logistic truths home to roost for military planners. Highest among the lessons is the reaffirmation of a warrior ethos for logisticians that must focus on the moral plane as much as the physical. Ninety percent of the fighting a logistics soldier will do in Afghanistan is with himself, in the kingdom of the mind. A review of some hard-won lessons from the tactical perspective on my own tour as a Canadian logistics battalion commander in Kandahar as part of Operation Enduring Freedom in 2006 will punctuate this fact.

To appreciate fully the singular tactical pressures of plying military logistics in Afghanistan, one must first acknowledge certain harsh truths. Even a cursory review of Afghanistan's operational logistics foibles leads one to some quick realizations.

Commanders and their logisticians seek to move the staples and sinew of combat power in bulk, and the first consideration for doing so is shipping by water. In terms of strategic projection, sea transport must always be a consideration for a protracted Canadian deployment.[1]

TRANSPORTATION

Afghanistan is a landlocked country, however, completely bordered by Iran, Turkmenistan, Uzbekistan, Tajikistan, China, and Pakistan. The absence of any seaports for disembarkation in Afghanistan forces operational planners to become imaginative in their approach to this area of operation. In the Canadian case, during the winter of 2005–2006, sea transport was used to move the equipment of the First Battalion, Princess Patricia's Canadian Light Infantry (1 PPCLI) to interim staging bases (ISBs) in Turkey. Two ships were contracted and loaded out of Montreal to move the battle group fighting vehicles and equipment in scale. The first was in late November and the second in early December 2005. After arriving at the ISBs from the sea, fighting vehicles and major equipment were moved via an air shuttle to the Kandahar Airfield (KAF).

We recognized early in the planning stages that any materiel coming into Kandahar for use with the Canadian Task Force would have to come over land through Pakistan or by air right onto the Kandahar Airfield (KAF). The empirical consumption characteristics of a modern infantry battle group in combat, festooned with enablers, were of keen interest to us, as the Canadian Army had been away from sustained combat missions since the Korean War. We quite simply did not know how much of any given materiel, from axles to bullets, we would need to match consumption. Getting more materiel was always going to involve some form of an air bridge leading into KAF from either an interim staging base, Camp Mirage, or Canada itself. Without a seaport on the doorstep of your area of operations, there is less ability to stockpile and little margin of error for irrelevant stock and ammunition natures. Landlocked Afghanistan puts pressure on a logistics staff to get in-country holdings right and be dead accurate from then on, with the prioritization of additional materiel coming from over the horizon.

Nonetheless, interior waterways are always worthy of military attention as well, a feature that Afghanistan does possess. Rivers can figure prominently in an operational level distribution system or as an aid to the administrative movement of forces.[2] There are four major river systems in Afghanistan: the Amu Darya, the Hari Rud, the Helmand-Arghandab, and the Kabul.[3] All four major systems have the same headwater source in the high watershed of the central mountains.

Relevant to the Canadians in southern Afghanistan is, of course, the Helmand-Arghandab system. However, the alluring turquoise pulse of the Arghandab River offered no military distribution benefit. The Arghandab, along whose shoulders Alexander once bivouacked with an invading force of thirty thousand soldiers, runs some four hundred kilometres from its origins in the highlands of eastern Hazarajat. The river winds its way through Kandahar and Helmand Provinces and eventually joins with the Helmand River at Qala Bist just beyond Lash Kar Gah. In other words, the Arghandab River cuts a swath through a good portion of Regional Command South (RC South)[4]. The river, however, is seasonally fed and can become quite shallow late in the year, particularly in its southern extremity. Any logistics investment on the river would not have been profitable in the short or medium term in 2006. Furthermore, the Arghandab River was used predominantly over the years as an instrument of irrigation for southern Afghanistan before falling into serious neglect. The Canadian government has undertaken the project of restoring this large but damaged irrigation tool.[5]

The next mode of transport preferred for moving materiel in an area of operation is rail. The logistic advantages of rail seem subtle at first but are quite telling over the long haul, and their positive effects are cumulative.

I would submit that a glaring gap in the maturation of Afghanistan as a healthy functioning state is the absence of rail. There are only twenty-four kilometres of railway in all of Afghanistan, laid in two sidings to assist with the evacuation of the Soviet 40th Army in 1988–89. This paltry amount of track exists in the north, far from the Canadian task force in RC South, far from any practical use to a tactical Canadian supply chain.

When one rules out intra-theatre waterways and rail distribution networks as means of transportation, all that remains to accomplish these tasks are trucks and airplanes. The Soviets demonstrated that aviation could be used to good logistic effect in an asymmetric battle space like RC South. This is a country and a battlefield that demands helicopters for logistics support, however, and our Canadian task force did not have any of its own in 2006, or at least not the right sort.[6] Fortunately, we were able to bid on the pooled coalition aviation assets for logistics tasks through the daily parcelling out of aviation sorties at Coalition Joint Task Force 76 (CJTF 76) — the division headquarters in Bagram, Iraq. Despite this, the reality was that very few logistic helicopter sorties were awarded to us. Our American colleagues leaned heavily on movement of materiel through the air, and although aerial medical evacuation was always there for our Canadian wounded, getting precious helicopter capacity to move Canadian combat supplies was rare on our tour.

The lack of access to helicopters meant that, during my tour, the tactical supply chain was almost entirely ground based. While the U.S. Army mounted a logistics convoy almost as an exceptional operation in southern Afghanistan, Canadians needed to run convoys nearly daily.

Ground-based supply chains mean convoys, and convoys require the use of roads, which are arguably one of Afghanistan's most challenging distribution frailties. In Sarajevo's Ilidza district, in the shadow of the old NATO Stability Force (SFOR) headquarters, you can walk from the venerable Hotel Herzegovina down to the Pizzeria Ilidza over the paved remains of an old Roman road. The path has been glazed over with asphalt, but the underlying crown of the road is as true as it was millennia ago. The Romans understood well the value of a good road, and evidence of the well-constructed Via Roma network is still plentiful all over the former Roman Empire.

Roads, however, often bring mixed blessings. For example, they initially brought the Roman Legions, but the tax collectors, sheriffs and merchants — all vestiges of governance and sovereignty — followed close behind. The challenge of governance and prosperity throughout the current NATO campaign plan supporting the growth and development of President Hamid Karzai's Islamic Republic of Afghanistan is at least partially due to the poor road infrastructure throughout the country. The creation of more and better roadways must figure prominently into any campaign that sees Afghanistan returning to full health. But its topography poses a challenge that establishment of a comprehensive road network that links the entire country.

Afghanistan's most defining feature, its mountainous topography, further complicates logistics issues. The region is known as the rooftop of the world, with many elevations over twenty thousand feet. The Hindu Kush Mountains extend from the southwest portion of the country and reach well beyond its eastern borders to join up with the fabled Himalayas. The rugged elevations of central Afghanistan give way to great flood plains in the south, and it is here, around the periphery of the country's mountainous centre, that Afghanistan's anemic road network has been eked out — roughly two thirds of the country's mountainous landmass is impassable to vehicles.

In all of Afghanistan, there are only forty-one thousand kilometres of road, only twelve thousand of which are paved. Many of the roads are of ancient origin, from silk routes that predate Alexander. Over the years, however, they have not profited from a uniform investment in maintenance and upgrade. Nonetheless, there are many examples of high quality stretches where it was obvious that Soviet or American aid money had recently been spent on upgrades. The first thirty-seven kilometres of Highway 4 leading southwest from Kandahar to the Pakistan border serves as a fitting example. At kilometre thirty-eight, the investment capital quite dramatically appeared to have had run out. At this juncture, Highway 4 becomes a rustic, axle-snapping country road.

The poor quality of many of the roads posed a challenge for vehicle maintenance and keeping the battle group combat effective. Differentials and axles for the LAV III fighting vehicle were worn and consumed at a greater rate than normally experienced. Vehicle suspension systems and transmissions also expired much faster than in Canada, and tires were routinely destroyed on every patrol or convoy. A further challenge generated by the poor road network involved the tires on the brand new M777 Howitzers. The M777 was a United States Marine Corps (USMC) weapon system that Canada fielded in Kandahar in February 2006.[7] The gun has a number of classified innovations bred in the bone, but it is no secret that the weapon is light enough to be airlifted by helicopter. This advent was perfect for the USMC manner of fighting but of little import to a Canadian task force without dedicated national aviation assets. In other words, the M777 was towed by a truck everywhere it had to go in southern Afghanistan. The need for the life-saving capability of the new guns forced the Canadian gunners to be on the move almost constantly, and their guns' tires began to pop like popcorn. We learned in quick order that the tires on the gun were of a civilian grade, a sensible compromise for a gun intended to travel through the skies.[8] With every increased tactical demand, be it tires or other repair parts and major assemblies, there accrued an additional demand on the operational-level problem of getting the right *type* of materiel into KAF, and then stocking relevant parts in an acceptable quantity to meet the wear and tear of the rugged Afghan terrain.

The other challenge with the roads in southern Afghanistan is their limited number. Put simply, there is not enough of a selection of roads to offer a tactician a variety in route planning and certainly not many that lead into the difficult highland terrain (north–south orientation). Predictability and habit are the stock and trade of a successful enemy improvised explosive device (IED) cell. Sound tactics on a counter-insurgency battlefield like the one presented by Kandahar call for the variation of routes and the avoidance of pattern in order to defeat IEDs. The limited numbers of roads for convoy leaders to pick from made this task difficult. For example, for the greater portion of our tour, "A" Company, 1 PPCLI maintained a platoon patrol house, known as the Gunbad Safe House, in the northern part of the province. There were really only two roads to get into the safe house to sustain the platoon, and a modicum of choice in that complex terrain was simply not there. As an alternative, in many cases, *wadis* (dried-out river beds) and sheer cross-country driving were used by Lieutenant-Colonel Ian Hope's troops instead of explosive-infested roads, like those leading to Gunbad, or Highway 611 in Helmand, which ran north to the Sangin District.[9]

ENEMY THREAT

The first thing a logistics soldier needs to grasp in this battle space is that the enemy attacks when and where he chooses. As a young officer training on those sun-baked sandy fields of Canadian Forces Base Borden, I remember that our instructors demanded that we begin the presentation of a tactical solution in the field by pointing out the direction from which the enemy was coming. The orientation of observation measures, limited weaponry, and early warning for a diesel commodity point were always defined by the physical location of the enemy. Imagine the luxury. The layouts of our training battlefields were largely linear: a distinctive construct that had brother units or formations to one's left and right and a communication zone in the rear giving way to the forward combat zone. The further forward one moved along the line toward the front of the combat zone, the closer one got to the fighting.

The postcard battlefield of contemporary Afghanistan does not permit such niceties. This battle space is more analogous to a sixties-style lava lamp. The blobs in the lava lamp represent our defended forward operating bases (FOBs) and the oil medium between these blobs is the new-age no-man's land.

Furthermore, the insurgents active in southern Afghanistan do not wear distinctive uniforms as our foes tended to in the Cold War era. It is difficult to determine who is Taliban and who is not unless you are being engaged directly or you catch them in the act of digging in an improvised explosive device (IED) on a roadside. The civilian clothing of the Taliban warrior makes him indistinguishable from the man you have hired to supervise your civilian labour force on KAF.

Much could be written about the essence of the insurgents in this raw little country. The warrior ethos ingrained in the Afghan culture is almost tangible. The country is populated by a collection of different tribes who, as a collective whole, have endured a lot. Regardless of the potpourri assortment of tribes, a common thread that runs though all of their bloodlines is bravery and an admirable mental toughness. The Afghans I came to know in my time were tough — physically and morally. Angry young Afghan men, unfortunately, provide superb grist for the insurgent mill.

I remember visiting my logistics detachment in Kabul, on the British Camp Souter, literally a few hundred metres from the Kabul International Airport. This little detachment ensconced on Camp Souter sustained the dispersed Canadian elements in various headquarters and staff across Afghanistan's capital and the large Division headquarters at Bagram.[10] The afternoon of our arrival, my regimental sergeant major (RSM) and I decided we had just enough time to work in a run inside the tight confines of the British camp. Some Afghan workers were engaged in minor construction on one corner of the garrison, and they watched dispassionately as the two pasty, white North Americans jogged by them time after time on our tight camp-based circuit. One of the workers suddenly burst alongside us, pushing a wheelbarrow filled to the gunwales with handmade bricks. The grin on his angular face was wide, and even though the RSM and I were struggling with Kabul's elevation and our aching lungs, the worker jogged effortlessly along, pushing his heavy load. His sense of glee and satisfaction was very evident. Eventually, the Afghan worker sprinted away from us with his load of bricks, filling the air with his cackles. Chutzpah. Our soldiers must face this common gumption in all of their convoy fights.

Further complicating matters in this theatre, the first move in a convoy fight belongs to the enemy. This means that the combat logistician rides Afghanistan's roads with the intense but passive hope that he or she will have a chance to fight — you can be extremely proficient at your anti-ambush drills and superb with your rifle, but you still need to survive the opening move. Whether you live or die depends on proximity to the blast, the quality of your vehicle armour, and sheer luck. These facts, however, are very difficult for the logistics soldier, and for any soldier really, to accept. The biggest fear among the troops on my deployment was to die on convoy without the chance to fire off a shot, to at least deliver a blow to the enemy before succumbing. These things matter and they matter a great deal.

My friend and colleague Lieutenant-Colonel Omer Lavoie commanded the First Battalion, The Royal Canadian Regiment Battle Group (1 RCR BG) and came in after our tour to replace 1 PPCLI. In his post-tour reflections, Omer spoke of the catharsis that his infantry soldiers felt when they were able to go on the offensive.

The moral release of the offense makes eminent sense, but it is a release that is denied the sustainment soldier. The logistician fights in reaction to an attack. Surrendering the first move to your opponent puts an immense amount of psychological pressure on a soldier. Soon every erratically driven civilian car looks like a bomb; every suspicious looking Afghan is an IED quarterback.

AN ENVIRONMENT THAT CAN KILL

Dealing with the environment is just one more matter that a logistics soldier must add to his load. For example, the powdery, insanely fine dust that crept into the throat, between bearings, behind dust boots, and inside seals worked in all cases to corrupt the various purposes of the parts. A dust storm in Afghanistan could elicit the same claustrophobic feeling inspired by a driving in a dense blizzard brushing in over Lake Ontario. The dust storms in Afghanistan sweep in with little warning and reduce your immediate world to the shelter that you can find. Visibility dissolves to zero. All the while, tiny particles of southwest Asian dust work their way aggressively into the cracks and crevices of one's body, machinery, weapons, and clothing, as if the tiny particles acted out of informed belligerence. The powdery dust demanded a condensed maintenance schedule for all of our vehicles. For example, the fuel filter on the LAV III is to be changed for every 1,000 kilometres of use in Canada, and yet we found that it needed to be swapped out every 200 to 300 kilometres in Afghanistan. Left unchecked, the dust clogged up air and fuel filters at an accelerated rate and caused premature component failures.

The dry, desert-like conditions that prevail in southern Afghanistan ushered in frigid nights, but more challenging for vehicle maintenance were the relentlessly hot days. During the day, temperatures soared into the high forties (Celsius) during the summer months of the tour, with high points frequently exceeding fifty degrees. Heat heightens wear and tear and decreases the shelf life of almost all components, especially the highly technical inner workings of our fighting vehicles — the more complicated the machinery, the more detrimental heat can be. The guts of the LAV III or the LAV II-based "Coyote" reconnaissance vehicle make the avionics of their infantry/armoured reconnaissance predecessors look like Henry Ford's Model T by comparison. High technology in many ways is a clear calling card for asymmetric possibilities, and it is all a field workshop can do to close off the potential advantage that the weather may cause for a low-tech opponent. While not specifically designed for this type of environment, the Canadian suite of vehicles and equipment generally performed well with diligent operator maintenance and a robust corrective maintenance program. The soldier in Afghanistan is also in constant combat with the oppressive climate, and it became clear that the infantryman must worship at the same altar of vehicle custodianship as the logistician and the mechanic.

The oppressive heat and dust of Kandahar constantly chipped away at the combat effectiveness of soldiers unaccustomed to such circumstances. Afghanistan's heat imposed a psychological and physical tax on the Canadian soldier that had to be proactively resisted. Air conditioning units in all vehicles were considered *essential* equipment that had to function for a vehicle to be deemed serviceable. Water, one of the big four in terms of combat supplies, was on steady push replenishment in Kandahar. The average soldier needs eight to ten litres of drinking water per day and more when fighting. Stockpiles of bottled water were maintained in the FOBs along with refrigerated vans to keep the caches cool. The challenges to the human system remind us that, in southern Afghanistan, a significant investment in soldiering has to be made just to get to the fight.

RETRO EQUIPMENT: THE GOOD, THE BAD, AND THE UGLY

You have what you have. I have always admired General Lee's gritty handling of the Army of Northern Virginia in the decisions and actions that led up to Chancellorsville, May 1863. The Confederate Forces, although not having the initiative and being the smaller force, divided twice and lashed out at the superior Union force commanded by General Joe Hooker.

Chancellorsville still speaks to me. The main lesson is that as a military leader you have only what you have on hand to deal with the tactical problems in front of you. In projecting combat power in Kandahar Province in 2006, we had two particularly prominent cases of aged, sub-standard logistics equipment: the sixteen-thousand-ton Heavy Logistic Vehicle Wheeled (HLVW) bulk-fuel tanker trucks and an awkward HLVW wrecker/flat bed trailer solution for recovery of the LAV III.[11] One has to take the rough with the smooth that comes from retro equipment.

In terms of the bulk-fuel trucks, we had the capacity to move diesel fuel all over Kandahar and Helmand Provinces. The preferred method among our allies for shipping bulk fuel was to contract out the job to civilian truck companies, known as jingle truck companies. There were five major warlord owners of these jingle truck companies in Afghanistan during my tenure. In October 2005, while conducting the last of a series of reconnaissance for our deployment to Kandahar from Kabul, the big problem surrounding the jingle trucks was theft. A ten-thousand-litre jingle truck would arrive at the customer's doorstep with only seven thousand litres or perhaps five thousand. The cause: clean, simple theft. In May 2006, the problem had evolved slightly. Nearly two million litres of fuel had been lost among Coalition members in RC South in that month.[12] The tactics in this case, however, were more damaging than in 2005. A jingle truck would arrive seemingly full, but a theft had occurred all the same. The thieves had taken what they wanted and inserted water to make up the empty difference, thereby contaminating and wasting the entire load. I remember at the June 2006 Multinational Brigade Logistics Brief that our allies around the table were apoplectic. There was acrid panic in the air, as contingents could not function without robust jingle truck delivery.

We continued to use the jingle trucks in 2006, but only sparingly as we now had our own dated HLVW military lift as well. Having our retro military bulk-fuel trucks made me feel very good. Throughout the highs and lows of the jingle truck game, we always had the old-fashioned ability to move fuel with military trucks and the gutsiest of soldier-drivers.

One lesson that should be taken away is that we must never again buy an equipment fleet without a proper recovery variant (a vehicle that is specifically designed to tow or recover from the battlefield broken or damaged vehicles of a similar type) as was done for the LAV III purchase in the late 1990s. Afghanistan's physical makeup in particular demands the omnipresence of a suspension towing capability in a credible combat force. Suspension towing is the nirvana of vehicle casualty extraction. It provides the fundamental ability of the recovery machine to pick up the front end of the casualty and muscle it away when it is battle damaged. The sickly cousin to suspension towing is direct towing, and although it can be conducted by a less powerful machine, it pales in comparison to suspension towing when real bullets are involved.

Given our lack of suspend-tow capability, the HLVW tractor and Arnes trailer combination was the bread and butter of recovery operations during our tour.[13] The HLVW wrecker was the only vehicle, short of another LAV, that could directly tow a LAV casualty. Crews, however, were challenged by the inherent off-road limitations of the HLVW wrecker and low-bed combination, as the latter piece of equipment was a civilian pattern trailer. We only had five of these civilian Arnes trailers in Afghanistan to do the job, and these five pieces of major equipment were fussed over like a prized set of great-grandmother's fine bone china. Nonetheless, owing to the poor roads, which were lethal to the long civilian pattern Arnes equipment, almost every recovery operation resulted in the big trailers requiring repairs. Rarely were more than three of the five trailers available for use at any given time.

When the LAVs were used to direct tow other LAVs, the infantry was to use the old artillery towing bar from the M109 155 self-propelled howitzer. This steel leviathan tow bar was to be a key component in pulling damaged LAVs to safety.[14] A further complicating factor was the amount of preparatory maintenance that had to be done prior to direct towing a LAV III. This list included power pack preparation and disengagement of the driveshaft and transfer case to cite but a few. If this bookish checklist of things was not performed prior to towing, then more harm would occur to the vehicle casualty. In the thick of battle, LAVs were used to tow other LAVs and in extreme situations, my own Bison Mobile Repair Teams in their smaller LAV II chassis were used for direct tow of casualties.

The use of these LAV frames for direct tow recovery was a dangerous practice, magnified by the fact that the greater percentages of recovery operations undertaken were under effective enemy fire. Recovery operations in southern Afghanistan, particularly the recovery of battle-damaged equipment, elicited some of best examples of soldier ingenuity and resourcefulness I have yet observed. Routinely, a vehicle recovery operation would take twelve to fifteen hours to complete. The length of time was determined by the terrain, vehicle serviceability en route, and the necessary battle procedure that an active enemy puts on a convoy.

Although the majority of tasks for the Arnes trailers and HLVW wreckers were in support of recovery operations, we also used them to move engineer equipment — both for our own purposes and those of the Afghan National Army (ANA) — and large bulky stores in support the construction of FOBs. Despite having recovery challenges while we awaited better Canadian solutions, we were selected to move a large amount of ANA equipment out of the Sangin District and up into northern Kandahar Province.

NATO does not own the logistics equipment that underpins its combined joint task forces, but it certainly catalogues what equipment lurks in the fabric of National Support Elements (NSEs) that constitute the multi-national logistics quilt in a given area of operation. We knew that the U.K. had proper and better equipment for heavy recovery than Canada did. We also knew that the Netherlands had better equipment suited to these sorts of tasks than us. Even though the ANA equipment was in close proximity to the U.K. forces in Sangin District and was to be moved to a portion of RC South that was to assist the Dutch effort, the Canadians, with our sub-optimum recovery equipment, were tasked to do the transport. We did the job and did it well. This is the sort of detail that never ends up in a history book, and yet it is one of the logistic accomplishments of our task force, replete with some old-fashioned equipment, of which I am the most proud.

CONCLUDING REMARKS

Strategic logistic pathways into Afghanistan pose a challenge to all who dare soldier there. Once materiel makes it into the country, a military force is confronted with an environment and an infrastructure that is lean and harsh. This is precisely the way that generations of tough Afghan warriors have wanted it: a fine accentuation of logistical challenges that sets the table for the most profound home-field advantage this side of the Ho Chi Minh Trail. Once on KAF, onward movement of the gear to our infantry combat teams dispersed around Kandahar Province posed a formidable task, given climate, topography, and the presence of a determined insurgency.

In dealing with these challenges, we have learned a great deal about our logistics soldiers and what it takes to make a battle group successful on Afghanistan's plain. We have reaffirmed that military logisticians in this sort of battle space must be combat capable — morally and physically tough. I doubt that many of us will ever again think of a battlefield in terms of those stilted black-and-white photographs of mud and slop from Passchendaele or the Regiment de Chaudière heading inward from the beach at Bernière-sur-Mer. For Kandahar veterans, Afghanistan represents among the worst of what the new security environment has to offer both the logistician and the soldier. Kandahar has moved the feel of battle from sepia-tinged photographs of linear combat zones to the full-colour spectrum of a biblical city street replete with vendors, adobe walls, dust, and the omnipresent potential of explosive devices. Kipling described her oh so very well. Now it would appear it is our turn.

Corporal Corey Betik takes a break from combat operations during OP Medusa.

Warrant Ray McFarlane coordinates actions between his platoon and a co-located ANA detachment in response to a reported Taliban incursion, October 2006.

A LAV III acts as a mobile observation post on Route Summit in the Panjwayi district.

ANA soldiers stop an ANP patrol to discuss suspected Taliban activity, October 2006.

A view of the surrounding countryside as seen from an observation post at Patrol Base Wilson in Panjwayi.

A "C" Coy, 1 RCR LAV positioned in the heart of Strong Point Centre, on Route Summit in the Panjwayi, provides observation and security for the road development project.

A Canadian soldier on OP Dragon captures the essence of the infanteer's struggle in Afghanistan — close terrain, heat, and heavy loads.

Canadian troops and their interpreter speak with locals during a patrol in Kandahar Province during Operation Array.

Above: *Canadian troops grab a ride on a Canadian Leopard tank during clearance operations in Kandahar Province.*

Left: *A member of the ANA conducting operations with 3 RCR takes a break to cool off and drink from a local stream.*

Command conference. Brigadier-General Denis Thompson, commander Task Force Afghanistan, confers with 3 RCR CO Lieutenant-Colonel Roger Barrett and one of his sub-unit commanders, Major Rob McBride.

India Coy soldiers on patrol during Operation Take-Out in Siah Choy, Zhari, May 2007.

ANA troops conducting operations with Canadian battle group in Kandahar Province.

Canadian and Afghan soldiers discover a major Taliban weapon cache in southern Kandahar Province, August 2008.

Right: *Soldiers from "N" Coy, 3 RCR prepare to blow a Taliban ammunition cache.*

Below: *"Hearts and Minds" — A Canadian soldier befriends children in Kandahar Province.*

1

More than Meets the Eye

The Invisible Hand of SOF in Afghanistan

COLONEL BERND HORN

The past three decades have not been kind to the concepts of trust and blind faith. A continuous stream of scandals and malfeasance by senior corporate executives and politicians, coupled with a seeming abrogation of responsibility and accountability by such trusted institutions as the church, police, and military, to name a few, have left most citizens with a healthy dose of cynicism and skepticism. For most, the adage "I'll believe it when I see it" rings true. But is it?

For special operations forces (SOF) in the Afghan theatre of operations, this concept is problematic, as most of their operations are veiled in a cloak of secrecy.[1] Generally, the only information that trickles out about such forces is negative and deals with allegations of wanton violence and huge collateral damage. It is also often tinged with the scent of "black op" forces running wild with little oversight or control.

The truth about SOF, however, is far from the widespread speculation by those who have little understanding of SOF roles or actions. Although their effects are not always visible or publicly touted, SOF are an important enabler in the Afghanistan theatre of operation. SOF were one of the first forces on the ground after 9/11 and were instrumental in driving the Taliban and al Qaeda (AQ) from Afghanistan in 2001–2002. They have continually adapted and evolved their roles since then, with great success in meeting requirements of the theatre. Although not widely known, SOF acts as the invisible hand that provides campaign-winning results to the Afghan theatre of operations.

SOF's pivotal influence in Afghanistan was apparent from the very beginning. On the morning of 11 September 2001, millions watched their television screens, mesmerized as events unfolded in New York City. In the early dawn hours, a passenger jet had ploughed into the top storeys of the World Trade Centre (WTC) in the financial core of the city. As most were trying to absorb what happened, a second large commercial airliner came into view and slammed into the twin towers of the WTC. It would only be a short time later that both towers collapsed and crumbled to the ground, killing almost 3,000 people. A third aircraft crashed into the Pentagon, killing and injuring hundreds more, while a fourth hijacked jetliner heading for Washington D.C. smashed into the ground in Pennsylvania, short of its objective due to the bravery of its passengers.

Within days of 9/11 it was clear that the Americans would take military action to strike at the terrorists behind the well-planned and coordinated attacks and those that supported and abetted them. Osama Bin Laden and his AQ terrorist organization, sheltered in Afghanistan by Mullah Omar and his Taliban government, quickly became the centre of attention.[2]

On 7 October, after ensuring the necessary political groundwork was laid, the United States and the United Kingdom informed the United Nations (U.N.) Security Council that they were taking military action in self-defence, specifically that they were undertaking operations to strike at AQ and Taliban terrorist camps, as well as training and military installations, in Afghanistan. That day, Operation Enduring Freedom (OEF) commenced with the heavy bombing of Taliban bases and infrastructure throughout the country, as well as strikes against the fifty-thousand Taliban troops outside of Kabul, who were manning the frontlines against the Northern Alliance (NA), a loose coalition of Afghan forces that were opposed to the Taliban. In addition, the Americans deployed CIA paramilitary forces and U.S. SOF, who, working in conjunction with the NA anti-Taliban resistance movement, quickly launched an offensive to oust the Taliban from Afghanistan and capture Bin Laden and his associates.

In an extremely short period of time, approximately three hundred American Special Forces (SF) soldiers were on the ground in Afghanistan.[3] These operators rallied and forged cohesive teams out of the unorganized anti-Taliban opposition groups, and equally as important, using a small amount of high-tech targeting equipment, brought the weight of American airpower down on Taliban and AQ fighters. Approximately four weeks of bombing finally created the necessary effect. On 9 November 2001, the NA, who were supported by U.S. SF and CIA operatives, as well as American air support, broke through the Taliban lines at Mazaar-e-Sharif. The Taliban collapsed and were totally routed.[4]

Within the next three days, all of northern, western, and eastern Afghanistan fell to the NA and their U.S. SF partners. The remaining Taliban forces fled south to Kandahar, the birthplace and headquarters of their movement. Throughout their retreat, they were harassed and pounded by U.S. air power.[5] On 5 December, Mullah Omar, the Taliban leader, surrendered Kandahar and fled to Pakistan.

In total, it took only forty-nine days from the insertion of the first SF teams assigned to NA forces for Kandahar to fall. After the collapse of the Taliban regime, small SOF teams, composed of about a dozen personnel each, established outposts deep in contested territory and continued to work with Afghan units against some Taliban and AQ hold-outs. For example, Bin Laden, his senior AQ leadership, and a large number of his forces dug in at the Tora Bora mountains in eastern Afghanistan. However, a concerted U.S. offensive with a heavy SOF involvement forced them to abandon their positions and flee to eastern Pakistan. By early 2002, the Taliban and AQ in Afghanistan were largely defeated. Military estimates put the Taliban losses at eight to twelve thousand men, representing approximately 20 percent of their total force. Additionally, twice that number were wounded and a further 7,000 taken prisoner.[6] In total, the estimates placed the Taliban casualties at over 70 percent of their strength.

It should be no surprise that SOF played a critical role in this outcome. Their ability to respond quickly and effectively was no revelation to those who actually understood SOF. After all, small teams of highly trained SOF operators working with indigenous forces have proven effective before. The addition of precision effects just made a good capability that much better. Nonetheless, despite tremendous losses, the Taliban continued to fight, and the war in Afghanistan seemingly carried on unabated. This persistent threat underscored the enduring importance of SOF.

This should be no surprise. After all, SOF provide a self-contained, versatile, and unique capability, whether employed alone or complementing other forces or agencies to attain military, strategic, or operational objectives. In contrast to conventional forces, SOF are generally small, precise, adaptable, and innovative. As a result, they can conduct operations in a clandestine, covert, or discreet manner.[7] They are capable of organizing and deploying rapidly and can gain entry to and operate in hostile or denied areas without the necessity of secured ports, airfields, or road networks. In addition, they can operate in austere and harsh environments and communicate worldwide with integral equipment. They deploy rapidly, at relatively low cost, with a low profile, and have a less-intrusive presence than larger conventional forces.

To fully understand SOF's capability and role, it is important to understand some basic SOF theory and precepts, beginning with the actual definition. Special Operation Forces are organizations containing specially selected personnel that are organized, equipped, and trained to conduct high-risk, high-value special operations to achieve military, political, economic, or informational objectives. They do this by using unique operational methodologies in hostile, denied, or politically sensitive areas to achieve desired tactical, operational, or strategic effects in times of peace, conflict, or war.[8] The key factor to SOF effectiveness, however, is in fact its people. SOF equip the operator rather than man the equipment. Selection and screening are fundamental principles of all SOF organizations. And the individuals who are attracted to SOF, who volunteer, and who are ultimately chosen to serve in SOF as a result of highly refined selection procedures and standards, are what provide the SOF edge — that is the key element for mission success. Quite simply, SOF organizations seek individuals with these qualities:

1. *Risk accepting*: Individuals who are not reckless, but rather carefully consider all options and consequences and balance the risk of acting versus the failure to act. They possess the moral courage to make decisions and take action within the commander's intent and their legal parameters of action to achieve mission success.

2. *Creative*: Individuals who are capable of assessing a situation and deriving innovative solutions, kinetic or non-kinetic, to best resolve a particular circumstance. In essence, they have the intellectual and experiential ability to immediately change the combat process.

3. *Agile Thinkers*: Individuals who are able to transition between tasks quickly and effortlessly. They can perform multiple tasks at the same time, in the same place, with the same forces. They can seamlessly transition from kinetic to non-kinetic or vice versa, employing the entire spectrum of military, political, social, and economic solutions to complex problems to achieve the desired outcomes. They can react quickly to rapidly changing situations and transition between widely different activities, ensuring they position themselves to exploit fleeting opportunities. Moreover, they can work effectively within rules of engagement (ROE) in volatile, ambiguous, and complex threat environments and use the appropriate levels of force.

4. *Adaptive*: Individuals who respond effectively to changing situations and tasks as they arise. They do not fear the unknown, but rather embrace change as an inherent and important, dynamic element in the evolution of organizations, warfare, and society.

5. *Self-reliant*: Individuals who exercise professional military judgment and disciplined initiative to achieve the commander's intent without the necessity of constant supervision, support, or encouragement. They accept that neither rank nor appointment solely define responsibility for mission success. They function cohesively as part of a team but

also perform superbly as individuals. They continue to carry on with a task until it is impossible to do so. They take control of their own professional development, personal affairs, and destiny, and they strive to become the best possible military professional achievable. They demonstrate constant dedication, initiative, and discipline and maintain the highest standards of personal conduct. They understand that they are responsible and accountable for their actions at all times and always make the correct moral decisions, regardless of situation or circumstance.

6. *Eager for challenge*: Individuals who have an unconquerable desire to fight and win. They have an unflinching acceptance of risk and a mindset that accepts that no challenge is too great. They are tenacious, unyielding, and unremitting in the pursuit of mission success.

7. *Naturally oriented to the pursuit of excellence*: Individuals who consistently demonstrate an uncompromising, persistent effort to excel at absolutely everything they do. Their driving focus is to attain the highest standards of personal, professional, and technical expertise, as well as competence and integrity. They have an unremitting emphasis on continually adapting, innovating, and learning to achieve the highest possible standards of personal, tactical, and operational proficiency and effectiveness.

8. *Relentless in their pursuit of mission success*: Individuals who embody a belief that, first and foremost, service to country comes before self. They have an unwavering dedication to mission success and an acceptance of hardship and sacrifice. They strive to achieve mission success at all costs, yet within full compliance of legal mandates, civil law, and the law of armed conflict.

9. *Culturally attuned*: Individuals who are warrior-diplomats, who are comfortable fighting but equally skilled at finding non-kinetic solutions to problems. They are capable of operating individually, in small teams, or in larger organizations

integrally, or with allies and coalition partners. They are also comfortable and adept at dealing with civilians, other governmental departments (OGD), and international organizations, as well as non-governmental organizations (NGOs). They are culturally attuned and understand that it is important to "see reality" through the eyes of another culture. They understand that it is not the message that was intended that is important but rather the message that was received. They strive to be empathetic, understanding, and respectful at all times when dealing with others. They comprehend that respect and understanding build trust, credibility, and mission success.[9]

Armed with exceptional individuals as well as cutting edge technology and equipment, SOF bring a wide range of kinetic and non-kinetic options to pre-empt, disrupt, react to, or shape operational or strategic effects within theatre.[10] Simply put, they provide a force or theatre commander with a wide range of capabilities not resident in conventional forces. They are capable of

1. conducting surgical precision operations with lethal or non-lethal effects;
2. deploying specially configured SOF task forces that tailor organizational design and force structure to meet the specific need of a mission or task;
3. operating seamlessly in combined, joint, or integrated environments or force structures;
4. infiltrating and extracting from hostile or denied areas, and operating within those designated areas in an overt or clandestine manner;
5. surviving and operating in a variety of harsh and hostile environments for extended periods of time;
6. operating in a self-sufficient manner for extended periods of time;

7. bringing expertise and influence to an area due to their level of cultural awareness, training, and operational methodologies; and

8. bringing a dominance in command, control, communications, computers, intelligence, surveillance, and reconnaissance (C4ISR) to the battle, providing informational superiority, which in turn allows for rapid decisive action that can shape an area of operation (AO).

Given this theoretical backdrop, one can fully appreciate the dramatic effect that SOF have had in the Afghanistan theatre of operations (ATO) since 2001, although not much has been heard of SOF's contribution or role, with the exception of some negative publicity.[11] Since the early days following 9/11, SOF have remained a critical enabler, akin to an invisible hand that continues to evolve and transform itself to best conduct those key tasks that assist conventional operations and shape the ATO. Quite simply, SOF are a vital enabler for conventional force operations in that they provide indigenous capacity, force protection through host nation (HN) engagement and direct operations, as well as the destruction of enemy capability.

SOF achieves these effects by conducting a number of their doctrinal roles. Although each discrete task on its own provides impressive impact on the ATO, most of the tasks are actually mutually reinforcing and create a synergistic effect of immense proportion. For the sake of clarity, however, each contribution will be examined individually.

The first way that SOF contributes to the fight in Afghanistan is through its unconventional warfare (UW) role, which is defined as "military and paramilitary operations, normally of long duration, predominately conducted by indigenous or surrogate forces who are organized, trained, equipped, supported, and directed in varying degrees by an external source." UW includes "guerrilla warfare and often direct offensive, low visibility, cover, or clandestine operations, as well as the indirect activities of subversion, sabotage, intelligence gathering and escape and evasion."[12]

The original work with the Northern Alliance by U.S. SF post-9/11 was a classic example of UW. However, SOF continued to work with indigenous forces to create specialized strike platoons, companies, and even battalions. These forces were normally superior in training, equipment, and capability to their Afghan National Army (ANA) counterparts and provided great impact.

Once the Taliban was overthrown and an interim government installed, later replaced by the Government of the Islamic Republic of Afghanistan (GIRoA), SOF evolved to a more Security Assistance Force (SFA) role as opposed to classic UW. This second major function has made a tremendous contribution to operations in the ATO. SFA, in accordance with U.S. doctrine, refers to "the unified action to generate, employ, and sustain local, host-nation, or regional security forces in support of a legitimate authority."[13] It basically involves the conduct of action programs, such as developing capacity within the security agencies, military, or police of another country to assist them in protecting their society from subversion, lawlessness, and insurgency. The SFA role is an evolution of the former task of Foreign Internal Defence (FID).[14] Not only does SFA lead to improved employment of HN forces, it also enables SOF to develop strong networks of influence that assist them in effectively creating the desired operational effects.

This critical role has allowed SOF to build a more effective internal Afghan security capability. For instance, SOF have created a number of highly effective counter-terrorist forces and have worked closely with the National Directorate of Security (NDS) in sharing intelligence to conduct operations, as well as in developing the NDS ability to assist with the concept of governance by improving its evidentiary capability to bring suspected terrorists and insurgents to trial and successful prosecution.

SFA has also been instrumental in developing additional host nation capacity that in turn can more effectively prosecute the counter-insurgency (COIN) effort, provide basic security, enhance force protection, and free up coalition forces for other more complex operations. For example, since 2008, SOF have trained Pakistani Frontier Corps troops, which are locally recruited paramilitary militia in the volatile Taliban-infested Federally Administered Tribal Areas (FATA).[15] Despite continuing limitations, this has created some capability where arguably none existed before.

During this time period, SOF have also taken a key role in training the ten-thousand-strong police force that was established in villages across Afghanistan. This was part of Afghan president Hamid Karzai's decision to enhance the delivery of security through locally recruited "community watch" forces under the local defence initiative (LDI). This village stability program was one of SOF's highest priorities in theatre. It not only creates additional forces and presence for the COIN fight, but it also serves to connect remote villages to the Afghan government, thereby achieving not only tactical results but also strategic effects.

The impact of these initiatives has become readily visible. In the Zerkho Valley, in Herat Province, for example, there is reportedly a greater presence of people out and about in the villages and fields. Tribes who had previously not spoken to one another now attend shuras together to solve village problems. Moreover, the accompanying economic development has meant that fewer people need to travel to nearby Iran to work. The SOF efforts have been so successful that other villages have asked to be included in the program.[16]

SOF was also targeted to provide additional training to 40 percent of Afghan's elite police force, the Afghan National Civil Order Police (ANCOP). SOF trained eight ANCOP *kandaks* (battalions) and is partnered with four of them. The training and partnership directly results in lower attrition rates and greater effectiveness of the Afghan forces.[17]

Arguably, however, there is no bigger success than the SOF commando program. The U.S. SF has created and partnered with a force actually called Afghan Commandos. Over the past three years, this force has become known as "Afghanistan's premier direct action force, specializing in air assault missions that kill or capture insurgents."[18] The effort has had great effect. The first commandos trained were the training cadre. From that point, Afghan commandos have trained other aspiring commandos, thereby increasing internal capacity. In addition, the commandos provide the Afghan face to SOF missions. Colonel Don Bolduc, a former commander of Combined Joint Special Operations Task Force — Afghanistan (CJSOT-A), stated, "We're using them effectively to insert into an area and be that first presence." He added that "people wake up and they have commandos talking to them about security governance and development."[19]

In fact, Afghans have come to revere the Afghan Commandos. "People know that if the commandos come in, they're not going to tear up the place," observed one SOF officer.[20] It is their reputation of professionalism and tactical aggression on the battlefield that has allowed the commandos to create a strategic effect. The enemy fear them, not only as fierce fighters but also as proud representatives of the Afghan nation. Their reputation is such that they are known and respected by Afghans across the ATO. "The Commandos just bring confidence to the people," asserted Lieutenant-Colonel Matt McFarlane, a senior U.S. commander in Wardak province. He explained, "They have trained orators who talk about the future and how we're all going to do this together ... and the people walk away more confident in their army and their government."[21] As one government official noted, "Having Afghan soldiers of that level of competence, that level of performance, is the kind of thing that affects national will."[22] This has only been enhanced as commandos are trained to become "full-spectrum units," meaning they can communicate effectively with village and tribal elders and conduct humanitarian assistance missions, which complements their reputation as fierce warriors.

To date, 5,300 commandos in nine *kandaks* have graduated. The Afghan government intends to deploy seventy-two Afghan SF teams around the country to secure the rural tribal population. They will partner with U.S. SF in "village stability operations," which have been nicknamed "precision counterinsurgency" operations. This follows the directive by General David Petraeus, commander of the International Security Assistance Force (ISAF), to "live with the people."[23]

The benefits of the SFA program go deep. On one level, SOF have created a larger and more effective national security force, which is desperately needed. However, on a much deeper level, they have strengthened the relationship between Afghan National Security Forces (ANSF) and the coalition. "We are working like brothers," confirmed one Afghan commando.[24] In the larger COIN context, SOF have enhanced governance by providing a direct link between the population and government or coalition troops.

This linkage is crucial, since as noted by Colonel Chris Kolenda, special assistant to the ISAF commander, "All problems in Afghanistan, or at least all social local problems, are solved at the community level. And so enfranchising communities with ownership in local governance, local security, localized development, will help bring communities together and help create the pressure and attraction to bring young men back into peaceful existence."[25] Notably, SOF have been on the forefront of the battle of building internal governance and credibility. "Our biggest problem isn't caves; it's credibility," conceded General Mike Mullen, who further stated that "our messages lack credibility because we haven't invested enough in building trust and relationships, and we haven't always delivered on promises."[26] SOF, however, have done far more than their share in building relationships.

Nonetheless, SOF energy has not been focused exclusively on winning hearts and minds. It has also proven significant in its direct support to conventional operations. First, it enables the COIN mantra of "clear-hold-build." SOF are able to penetrate denied areas and shape follow-on action by a larger conventional force. For example, prior to a conventional "clearance," SOF infiltrate the designated areas and conduct surgically precise direct-action missions to target enemy leadership capacity and improvised explosive device (IED) networks. Although not eliminating all resistance, this precision strike function disrupts command and control, thereby lessening the enemy network's ability to respond effectively.[27]

A number of examples provide insight into the impact SOF operations provide. In September 2006, ISAF was involved in a major operation to expel a large Taliban force that had dug in and was contesting the Pashmul area near Kandahar City. The enemy intent was to actually seize the city itself. In turn, ISAF launched Operation Medusa to destroy the concentration of Taliban forces. The task fell to the Multi-National Brigade (MNB), which was deployed in Kandahar Province.[28] The operation was ultimately successful but owed a great deal of its success to SOF participation.

In direct support of the conventional operation were SOF forward air control (FAC) parties to assist with delivering air support to the battlefield. In addition, British SOF operated in the Regestan Desert to cut off the Taliban supply lines as well as to interdict any reinforcements coming from or retreating enemies attempting to escape to Pakistan.

Furthermore, U.S. Task Force (TF) 31 had the responsibility of screening the MNB's western flank.[29] As the operation unfolded, the brigade commander, Brigadier-General David Fraser, ordered TF-31 to move north into Sperwan Ghar at the same time as the conventional forces started clearance operations. The mission of TF-31 now changed from one of flank security to the task of disrupting the Taliban command and control node in Sperwan Ghar. TF-31 entered into a fight that lasted over three days. Against superior numbers, TF-31 seized a key mountain from the Taliban, then held the position against concentrated attack. The coalition now owned the vital ground for the whole area. From this position they could observe the entire area of operations. The SOF effort prompted the MNB operations officer to state, "That was one of the most profound acts of bravery I've seen since I've been over here." He elaborated that "about 24 American Special Forces soldiers, reinforced by an American rifle company, and some ANA actually took that feature from about 200 Taliban."[30]

That night, the Taliban attempted to retake the hill, and it resulted in a sustained battle lasting approximately four to five hours. However, close air support and mortar and artillery fire pummelled the enemy, and by the end of the battle, the Taliban were forced to stay on the north side of the river. They had given up their attempts to recapture the strategic mountaintop. The MNB headquarters estimated enemy casualties at two hundred dead and approximately three hundred wounded. Lieutenant-Colonel Shane Schreiber noted, "TF-31 had done the disrupt. They had completely dislocated the Taliban from that area."[31]

Captain Chris Purdy, a Canadian intelligence officer, summarized the situation:

> We had a concern that the enemy would try to flank us. And indeed, I think they would have, had TF-31 not been there [in Sperwan Ghar — the western flank].... They inflicted a significant number of kills in that area and that was one of the main enemy command and control nodes as well.... They cut off the head while we were dealing with the main body of fighters. And when

that command and control started to get a little skewed
the enemy decided to suck back.[32]

Additionally, other SOF elements targeted the AO and provided so
much pressure, according to an American intelligence officer, that ultimately enemy leadership was forced "to step onto the battlefield to lead
their fighters, exposing themselves in ways they typically avoid."[33] In the
end, during this brief two week time span, five Taliban commanders
were killed in action.

In the summer of 2010, the same approach was taken as the Taliban
once again contested control of the Kandahar area with the GIRoA and
coalition forces. Predictably, SOF deployed first to shape the battle space
for conventional operations. The latest battle for Kandahar was described
almost universally by journalist and defence analysts as "the make-or-
break offensive of the eight-and-half-year war."[34] It is for that reason that
the offensive was deliberately initiated by SOF. Using intelligence-driven
operations, SOF carried out an extremely effective campaign to identify, isolate, and remove local insurgent commanders. In a period of four
months, SOF eliminated up to 70 mid-level commanders in order to
shape the battlefield for conventional forces.[35]

SOF also assists during actual operations. On a number of occasions, SOF forces have been used in blocking positions once Taliban
forces have been engaged and fixed in order to prevent their escape.[36]
Moreover, SOF assistance extends to better coordinating the efforts of
conventional forces as well. In Shinkay District in Zabul Province, a
SF A-Team deployed to help bring security to a population of fifteen
thousand to twenty-five thousand people spread out between twenty-
five towns and villages where three hundred ANA, an Afghan National
Police (ANP) element, and a company from the 82nd Airborne Division
were deployed. The SF team worked at knitting the disparate coalition
forces together. They took over some of the training of the ANA and
ANP, allowing 82nd Airborne Division more freedom of movement
to carry out operations. They were successful in bringing the military
elements and civilian components together, and they built up cohesion, trust, and confidence within the different players with remarkable

results. One intelligence sergeant noted that the Taliban held little sway in the district since the SOF effort and further said, "Now we're seeing the Taliban commanders fighting each other."[37]

SOF also perform the necessary task of sanctuary disruption. Not surprisingly, insurgents who survive clearance operations escape to safe areas where they are able to refit, plan, and train for future operations. Although it is not always possible to occupy these safe areas, SOF can effectively disrupt sanctuaries and deny the enemy the ability to prepare for future action unmolested. This sanctuary disruption function provides time and space for conventional forces to conduct their clear-build-hold operations.[38] For example, the 3 September 2008 Joint Special Operations Command (JSOC) Angor Adda cross-border raid into Pakistan's FATA was the third such attack into a safe area.[39]

Finally, Remote Area Operations (RAO) are yet another means of supporting conventional forces. In accordance with U.S. FM 3-05.202 *Foreign Internal Defense 2007*, RAO are operations undertaken in insurgent-controlled or contested areas to establish islands of popular support for the HN government and deny support to the insurgents. They are not designed to establish permanent HN government control over the area, since remote areas may be populated by ethnic, religious, or other isolated minority groups, which may be located in the interior of the HN or near border areas where major infiltration routes exist. However, the intent is to deny the enemy freedom of movement and action. RAO normally involve the use of specially trained paramilitary or irregular forces supported by SOF teams, with the aim of interdicting insurgent activity, destroying insurgent base areas in the remote area, and demonstrating to local populations that the HN government has not conceded control to the insurgents. RAO are also important for collecting and reporting information concerning insurgent intentions in more populated areas. These operations indirectly support conventional forces by providing intelligence, force protection, and destruction of enemy capacity.

Another critical SOF contribution has been in the realm of intelligence, surveillance, and reconnaissance (ISR). Although technology has increased exponentially in its capability and reach, even the newest, most-dynamic systems have their limitations. For example, during

Operation Anaconda in March 2002, American and Afghan forces went into the Shah-i-Kot valley in Afghanistan ill-prepared, without the proper force structure, because they had focused their available surveillance and target acquisition capabilities, including satellite imagery, Unmanned Aerial Vehicles (UAVs), and signals intelligence, to develop the enemy situation. The failure of the technology to actually find and define the enemy positions meant that the inserted light infantry forces were surprised. The Americans discovered that "a motivated and capable enemy had eluded detection, requiring the force to develop the situation in close contact."[40] In fact, they had failed to detect the majority of the most important enemy fighting positions until the first arriving forces got out of their helicopters.[41]

Four years later, not much had changed. The MNB commander, Brigadier-General Fraser, still lamented, "You don't ever have 100 per cent intelligence. Metaphorically speaking on a good day I would get 20 per cent."[42] Moreover, the xenophobic, tribal nature of Afghan culture, compounded by language barriers and fear of ruthless Taliban retaliation, makes generating human intelligence (HUMINT) difficult.

As such, SOF has become a critical enabler in filling in the intelligence gap and thereby shaping operations across the ATO. This is critically important in a contemporary operating environment (COE) that is almost entirely dependent on intelligence-driven operations. General David Petraeus has repeatedly underscored how SOF in the COE has assisted operations. "JSOC played a hugely significant role by killing or capturing many high-value targets as well as collecting valuable intelligence," he insisted.[43]

As a result of their contributions to developing the intelligence picture, SOF seriously degrades the effectiveness of the enemy, thereby assisting conventional forces to achieve their missions with less risk and casualties. They achieve this through the efforts of small SOF teams conducting special reconnaissance and reporting on enemy movement, activities, or dispositions. In addition, Special Operations Intelligence Cells (SOIC) fuse information from multiple sources to provide actionable intelligence. They also direct action teams that strike targets and immediately exploit information or leads that fall out of those missions, which all leads to building and enhancing the overall intelligence profile of the enemy.

The final SOF contribution to be discussed is arguably the most important in outright impact on the ATO. It is direct action (DA), which is defined as "short duration strikes and other precise small-scale offensive actions conducted by special operation forces to seize, destroy, capture, exploit, recover or damage designated targets. Direct action differs from conventional offensive actions in the level of physical and political risk, operational techniques, and the degree of discriminate and precise use of force to achieve specific objectives."[44]

Not surprisingly, a U.S. Department of Defense official stated that SOF has become the "instrument of choice for kinetic activity."[45] After all, SOF can effectively execute small surgical strikes over a vast geographical area, even in hostile or denied areas. The number of missions SOF has conducted has seen a spike of 40 to 50 percent. Between May and August 2010, SOF was operating at its highest tempo since entering the ATO, conducting approximately three thousand missions.[46] From June to August 2010, JSOC alone has conducted over five hundred missions. One senior official said that during this timeframe, SOF "killed or captured 235 insurgent leaders, killed 1,066 insurgents and captured another 1,673."[47] Their success only increased with time. Between November 2010 and May 2011, NATO revealed that SOF "conducted 3,240 operations, killing or capturing about 870 insurgent leaders." Furthermore, NATO released that "more than 4,340 insurgents were captured and more than 1,170 were killed."[48] Undeniably, this type of devastation to an enemy's command and control network has a tremendous impact on the ATO.

The actual DA missions, however, have several distinct purposes. One requirement for precision DA strikes is to conduct hostage rescue or combat search and rescue. To date, a large number of reporters, aid workers, businessmen, and some soldiers have been kidnapped or captured. The resultant recovery action often falls heavily on SOF. For example, on 20 August 2008, as they were on their back from a funeral, an American businessman and his Afghan partner were kidnapped in Wardak Province. They were held in a mud hut in a remote mountain range in Afghanistan and moved around frequently. The American was held for two months by members of Gulbuddin Hekmatyar of the Hezb-i-Islami militant group.

The SOF task force was able to locate the hostage by using a variety of information collection measures, but rescue had to be conducted in very "treacherous terrain." Nonetheless, on the night of 14–15 October 2008, three Chinooks flew approximately thirty soldiers into the remote mountains and dropped them approximately three miles from the objective. They successfully rescued the hostage. According to one ISAF official, "It was an overwhelming success."[49]

Another case was Linda Norgrove, the British non-governmental organization (NGO) aid worker who was kidnapped on 26 September 2010, when her car was forced off the road in Kunar Province near the Pakistan border. She too was taken to a stronghold in a steep-sided valley eight thousand feet up in the mountains. SOF attempted her rescue and fast-roped right onto the objective. Unfortunately, she was killed in the rescue attempt.[50] These are just two examples, but SOF has had its hand in many more missions that were planned or conducted. In short, only SOF has the expertise, skills, and capabilities to exercise such high-risk operations in hostile, denied, and treacherous terrain.

Hostage rescue and combat search and rescue are important for demonstrating governmental and national control, as well as support to one's citizens and soldiers, all of which is important for morale and national pride. With that said, no DA task is more important to operations in the ATO than capture or kill missions targeting enemy commanders. There is a SOF philosophy that advocates maintaining pressure on enemy commanders to the point that they have no rest or respite, thereby forcing them to constantly be on the move, to sleep in a different location every night, and to bed down in fields or other inhospitable areas to avoid detection and capture. Former Canadian chief of the defence staff General Rick Hillier declared:

> What we want to do is take out the commanders who are engaged in orchestrating, facilitating, paying, leading, planning and driving folks to attack us or attack the Afghans or attack the innocent. And our special forces

are focused very much on that.... I said, during a recent speech, that we had removed from the battlefield six commanders who were responsible for the deaths of 21 Canadian soldiers. Well that's changed. We've removed seven commanders who have been responsible for the deaths of 27 soldiers.[51]

Similarly, one senior NATO official explained, "If you hit a network hard enough, you'll wind up taking out the mid-level leaders. The senior leaders who are sitting across the border [in Pakistan] are now faced with a choice: how do they reconstruct what's been taken apart and motivate those who are left?"[52] A senior SOF officer echoed those sentiments. "The mid-level leaders' arrival in Afghanistan presents us with targets. What you really want to do," he observed, "is you want the network to start eating itself from within, you want the dissension, you want folks deciding, 'Hey, this just isn't worth it.'"[53]

There is reason to believe SOF has had this effect. Canadian scholars studying counter-insurgency operations in Kandahar have noted that SOF operations targeting Taliban leadership in 2007 created a lack of cohesion, coordination, and planning in enemy activities, which resulted in poor command and control, making enemy operations less effective.

The SOF pressure has been maintained ever since. For instance, SOF has hit the Haqqani network very hard. Some mid-level Haqqani leaders are abandoning what had been their Pakistani safe haven and are returning to Afghanistan, in part out of a desire to throw the CIA and its lethal drones off their trail, but also, as one journalist noted, "because their networks are taking a battering over in Afghanistan, and other folks need to come in and start fixing that or dealing with gaps that have been created by folks that have been detained or folks that have been killed."[54]

The effect has been wide-ranging. In Kabul, one NATO official proclaimed, "The ISAF SOF has just ripped them [Kabul Attack Network] apart. There have been very, very few attacks inside of Kabul because of ISAF SOF."[55] To the south, in Kandahar Province, a Canadian battle group commander noted the impressive effect SOF had on his area of operations:

The SOF strikes had a chilling effect on the Taliban. In one strike they killed an important leader and 16 of his fighters. The Taliban leadership in Kandahar City felt a lot of pressure from SOF. They were moving every day so we saw a reduction in activity. They were being disrupted — they were on the move, on the run.[56]

A group of scholars who studied the Canadian sector noticed similar results:

Insurgent operations in 2007 were increasingly characterized by lack of co-ordination and poor planning, which could be attributed to the growing effectiveness of ISAF's Special Operations Forces (SOF). SOF units from all ISAF contributor nations in the south were pooled for the task of arresting known bomb-making cell leaders, drug lords, and a legal case prepared for their arrest, Canadian (and other ISAF) SOF troops would be deployed to apprehend the suspect. As often as not, if the target was a Tier 1 Taliban leader, he would try to shoot his way out, with predictable results. Consequently, Taliban command-and-control capacity in the south in 2007 was less effective than the previous fall.[57]

Finally, increased operational tempo by SOF over the past year has begun to bite into the insurgent network in the central part of Helmand Province as well. U.S. intelligence has tracked a breakdown in regular communications between local commanders in Helmand and their leadership in Quetta.[58]

There is also anecdotal evidence according to officials that "resentment is building in the midlevel ranks of the Taliban, aimed at the top commanders who are safely ensconced in Quetta or in the North Waziristan area of Pakistan."[59] Additionally, Nick Vickers, the assistant secretary of defense for special operations and low intensity conflict, revealed that over the last year, although "al-Qaeda's senior leadership is reconstituted, to some degree, in Pakistan, they have suffered significant setbacks." He further explained the impact on AQ leadership: "If you look at the number of al-Qaida leadership and, more importantly, operatives, part of its network, that have been lost to the organization in the past year, I think it could be characterized as a pretty significant disruption to their ability to plan and operate."[60] This was direct result of SOF action.

Another Pentagon official, while not providing numbers of AQ killed, conceded "it is significant." With regard to insurgent losses, he added, "It is having an effect on direct [AQ] operatives, it is altering behaviour and we're certain that it impacts direct AQ operatives or those that are immediately involved in facilitating their operations or their safe havens." He reinforced that "there is an altered pattern of behaviours that is being tracked through multiple other organizations in the government."[61]

The Australian perspective is comparable. Major-General Jim Molan expressed that Australian SOF contribution to the ATO is concentrated mainly on anti-leadership operations in the area where most of the population lives and where most of the Taliban activity occurs. He reported that the disruptive effect is "huge."[62]

To provide a final level of granularity to the issue, on 9 October 2009, SOF killed Ghulam Yahya Akbari, the so-called "Tajik Taliban" commander, who, together with his two sons, had carried out a reign of terror across parts of western Afghanistan. After his two sons were killed, Yahya became even more relentless in his prosecution of suicide and rocket attacks into Herat Airfield. One journalist noted that SOF conducted

a very effective man-hunting campaign against him, and it eventually paid off. When he was killed it was like the weight of the world was taken off a couple of fairly large swaths of people. The prices of foodstuffs went down in certain bazaars and markets out there because Yahya was jacking them up ... More bazaars opened up. And then, of course, once this sort of weight of intimidation came off of the shoulders of these people, many of the fighters said, "I'm done." As a result of the coalition killing "a guy who acted as though he was invincible ... somewhere between a hundred and 200 fighters [have given up]."[63] By anyone's account, that is very significant.[64]

Finally, the last DA function, which is equally as important as capturing or killing enemy commanders, and is often intertwined with that task, is the disruption of IED networks.[65] SOF DA raids targeting IED networks, whether their leadership, facilitators, financiers, logistical coordinators, or bomb makers also make a significant contribution to the COIN fight in the ATO. For that reason, General Petraeus has made SOF the "pointy end" of the anti-IED stick. "Certainly you want to protect the force," he noted, "by killing or capturing those at the point of planting the IED, but what you really want to do is go after the network."[66] Their effect, as described above, has been significant. In the end, for every DA precision strike that nets commanders, facilitators, financiers, logistic coordinators, or bomb makers, SOF have taken a bite out of the insurgency and saved lives.

And so, although seldom trumpeted or even acknowledged, SOF have been, and continue to be, the invisible hand in Afghanistan. Though conducting a war in the shadows, SOF have a significant impact on force protection, increases in host nation governance and security, as well as destruction of enemy capability. Moreover, SOF are a vital contributor to the successful fight for the hearts and minds of the population. It is for this reason that General Petraeus has begun to speak openly, "turning aside years of keeping the SOF capability in the shadows, to try and convince sceptics that the war could be won." In fact, he has repeatedly emphasized SOF missions to kill or capture key insurgents.[67]

It is also the reason why ISAF SOF have tripled in number and why despite fiscal restraint everywhere, SOF budgets have remained untouched and in some instances have even grown. For instance, the U.S. will add 2,800 SOF troops to their inventory over next six years. This represents a 5 percent increase.[68] In sum, as has often been said, SOF have become the force of choice. As one defence analyst noted, "In many ways, SOF are now serving as both a nucleus of action and as the center for a community of practice, frequently driving interagency discussions on operations and activities against al-Qaeda and its affiliates as well as other national security threats and challenges."[69]

Nowhere has this leadership role been greater displayed than in Afghanistan. The invisible hand of SOF has influenced and shaped the Afghan theatre of operations in a significant way, saving lives, strengthening the counter-insurgency, and destroying enemy capability and capacity. They are a classic example of the adage "there may be more than meets the eye."

8

Lesson Learned

Operation Medusa and the Taliban Epiphany

COLONEL BERND HORN

In mid-September 2006, NATO and International Security Assistance Force (ISAF) commanders proclaimed a decisive victory over Taliban insurgents in Kandahar as a result of Operation (OP) Medusa. The two-week combat operation was credited with killing approximately 1,500 insurgents, including a number of key tactical commanders. Taliban forces had massed considerable combat power and entrenched themselves in fortifications on the outskirts of Kandahar city in a brazen attempt to take control of it, and NATO hailed its victory over the insurgents as singular proof of its capability and effectiveness.[1] Politicians and military commanders credited NATO's first battle with nothing short of saving Afghanistan and the interim Karzai government.

Unfortunately, however, OP Medusa was no panacea, and Taliban influence continued to spread throughout much of Afghanistan. Less than four years after OP Medusa, American and ISAF forces announced the implementation of a troop build-up in Kandahar Province for another large push to eject the Taliban and stop the insurgents' imminent offensive to seize Kandahar City. "This is the edge of the moon," asserted Lieutenant-General Andrew Leslie, the Canadian Army commander, to a reporter. "If you go 100 metres that way you will die."[2] Significantly, the admission of Taliban de facto control of much of the districts around Kandahar City mirrored the state of the insurgency throughout Afghanistan. In fact, intelligence operators painted a grim picture of the effectiveness of the counter-insurgency. For example, by 2009, the U.S. intelligence community estimated "that 19,000 to 27,000 insurgents [were] operating in Afghanistan, a roughly tenfold increase from 2004's estimate of 1,700 to 3,200."[3] Moreover, a Pentagon report to Congress in April 2010 assessed that 48 of 92 districts were supportive of the Taliban. This was up from 33 districts only three months prior.[4]

So what happened? Why did the pervasive victory over the Taliban in September 2006 not translate into a greater success? A component of the answer to this complex question lies in the Taliban epiphany that emerged from their crushing defeat. In effect, they learned, or one could argue re-learned, a valuable lesson of insurgency in the overwhelming pounding they experienced at the hands of NATO's modern, well-equipped forces. Put simply, their experience in OP Medusa underscored the point that one should never wage a battle of attrition based on firepower and static defence against a technologically and materially superior opponent. The Taliban emerged convinced that they should leverage asymmetric advantages and wage "the war of the flea." Consequently, the Taliban's subsequent recalibration of their tactics made them a more lethal and formidable enemy and allowed them to achieve a degree of ascendency in the insurgency.

BACKGROUND

Few realized in the early morning hours of 11 September 2001 that the world was about to change. The brazen attack by the terrorists, who, armed with only cheap ninety-nine-cent box cutters, hijacked fully fuelled commercial airliners and used them as precision munitions to strike not only the two separate towers of the World Trade Centre in New York but also the Pentagon in Washington D.C. A fourth hijacked jetliner heading for Washington D.C. slammed into the ground in Pennsylvania, short of its objective due to the bravery of its passengers. In total, almost three thousand people were killed in the attacks.

Not surprisingly, Washington responded quickly to the 9 /11 attacks in order to protect the American homeland and U.S. facilities and installations abroad. The Americans suspected that Osama bin Laden and his al Qaeda (AQ) terrorist network, who were protected by the Taliban regime in Afghanistan, were responsible for the attacks. They also realized that they would need to strike their antagonists overseas, and on 14 September, the American Congress authorized President George W. Bush to "use all necessary and appropriate force against those nations, organizations, or persons [who] planned, authorized, committed, or aided the terrorist attack on September or harbored such organizations or persons."[5]

The Americans also called on their NATO allies for help. As a result, NATO's North Atlantic Council met on 12 September to discuss the U.S. request to invoke Article 5 of the North Atlantic Treaty, which defines "an armed attack against one or more of the Allies in Europe or North America" as "an attack against them all" and thereby requires each ally to "assist the Party that has been attacked by taking such action as it deems necessary."[6] This would be the first time that the Article 5 clause was invoked.

By 2 October, the Americans provided their allies with "clear and compelling evidence" that AQ had in fact been behind the 9/11 attacks. Two days later, NATO Secretary General Lord Robertson announced that the Alliance would indeed take collective actions to assist the United States.[7]

In addition, NATO, in accordance with treaty requirements, also notified the U.N. that it intended to invoke Article 5 under the framework of the United Nations Charter provision, affirming the inherent right of member states to individual and collective defence. The U.N. Security Council had come to a similar conclusion, having also met to address the 9/11 attacks on 12 September. They subsequently urged all states to work together "to bring to justice the perpetrators, organizers, and sponsors of the attacks."[8] Then, on 7 October 2001, the United States and the United Kingdom informed the security council that they were taking military action in self-defence, specifically that they were undertaking operations to strike at al Qaeda and Taliban terrorist camps and training and military installations in Afghanistan. That day, Operation Enduring Freedom (OEF) commenced with the heavy bombing of Taliban bases, infrastructure throughout the country, as well as the 50,000 Taliban troops outside of Kabul manning the frontlines against the Northern Alliance (NA), which was a loose coalition of Afghan forces that were opposed to the Taliban.

Approximately four weeks of bombing finally created the necessary effect. On 9 November 2001, the NA, who were now supported by U.S. Special Forces (SF) and CIA operatives, as well as American air support, broke through the Taliban lines at Mazaar-e-Sharif. The Taliban collapsed and were totally routed. Within the next three days, all of northern, western, and eastern Afghanistan fell to the NA. The remaining Taliban forces fled south to Kandahar, the birthplace and headquarters of the movement. Throughout, they were harassed and pounded by U.S. air power.[9] On 5 December, Mullah Omar, the Taliban leader, surrendered Kandahar and fled to Pakistan.

Nonetheless, some hold-outs remained. Bin Laden, his senior AQ leadership, and a large number of his forces dug in at the Tora Bora mountains in eastern Afghanistan. However, a concerted U.S. offensive forced them to abandon their positions and escape into eastern Pakistan. By early 2002, the Taliban and AQ in Afghanistan were largely defeated. Military estimates put the Taliban losses at eight thousand to twelve thousand men, or 20 percent of their total force. In addition, the number of wounded were estimated to be twice as much, with a further seven thousand taken prisoner.[10] In the end, the Taliban lost over 70 percent of their strength. Importantly, however, their entire leadership structure remained intact and was safely ensconced in Pakistan.

RESURGENCE

With Afghanistan arguably rid of the Taliban, a huge opportunity was largely squandered in 2002. Subsequently, the Americans began to focus their attention on the impending invasion of Iraq and quickly pulled the majority of their forces from Afghanistan, leaving a largely token conventional presence and a number of special operations forces (SOF), which focused almost entirely on hunting down AQ leadership. The Americans turned the task of rebuilding the country to the newly installed NA warlords, who were mostly the same corrupt, ruthless thugs who had created the conditions for the emergence of the Taliban in 1994 in the first place.[11] In addition, the Americans counted on their European allies and the newly created ISAF to provide some stability, but ISAF focused almost exclusively on Kabul and other cities and had virtually no presence in the rural areas.

Given these circumstances, it is not difficult to see that the prognosis for success was not strong: the Americans were becoming more and more distracted with Iraq, the Europeans were seemingly not wholly committed to the mission, and the newly installed Afghan government appeared to be back in the control of corrupt warlords who had neither the support of the population nor their best interests at heart. The Afghan expectation that billions of dollars of U.S. and European investment would flow into the country to rebuild infrastructure, agriculture, and industry, improving their economy and standard of living, failed to materialize. Instead, Afghans were once again terrorized by the same warlords and militias that the Taliban had routed years before, and the Kabul regime seemed distant and unresponsive to their needs. To make matters worse, the American presence that remained seemed only interested in bombing suspected Taliban and AQ targets and conducting night raids, all of which resulted in collateral damage and more Afghan resentment and anger.

It wasn't long before the Taliban leadership in Afghanistan took advantage of the situation. By the end of 2002, the majority of Taliban senior leadership had re-established itself in Pakistan, specifically in Quetta, spawning the title "Quetta Shura" for the senior Taliban decision-making body. It was this group that developed, and still heads to this day, Taliban strategy and direction, which they pass down to subordinate tactical commanders.[12]

The first overt signs of a Taliban resurgence came that same year, 2002, when *shabnamah* (night letters) began to appear, warning citizens against cooperating with the government. Taliban fighters began to stockpile weapons in Afghanistan and develop supply lines from neighbouring Pakistan. By 2003, Taliban fighters were stopping traffic on main road networks and murdering Afghans and foreign aid workers. The first battles with U.S.

troops also occurred that year, and by the end of 2003, the Taliban had established almost complete control over Zabul and Helmand provinces.

The Taliban, cleverly taking advantage of the American preoccupation with Iraq, re-established itself.[13] They were astute in their efforts to exploit the rising popular dissatisfaction in the south with regard to high popular expectations of Western economic assistance and the dismal reality of virtually no such support materializing. Small groups of Taliban fighters also conducted minor attacks in urban centres, such as Kandahar City, as well assassinations of pro-government mullahs, sporadic rocket and mortar attacks, and general intimidation of the population. These tactics, by the end of 2003, succeeded in driving most international non-governmental organizations (NGOs) out of the country, further exacerbating the dearth of Western aid.[14]

During this period, the Taliban also received visits from Arab and Iraqi mujahideen, who, according to Taliban fighters, "began transferring the latest IED [improvised explosive device] technology and suicide-bomber tactics they had learned in the Iraqi resistance during combat with U.S. forces."[15] The Taliban experimented with the new tactics, and in June 2003, in the first attack of this kind in Afghanistan, a suicide bomber killed four German ISAF soldiers, an Afghan national, and wounded many others in Kabul as their bus was headed to the airport to take them home after completion of their tour of duty.[16]

Despite its success, the Taliban did not yet fully embrace the tactics of suicide bombing and IEDs. They saw no need to. Their traditional methodology of combating government and coalition forces seemed to be working just fine. In fact, by 2004, the Taliban had developed solid lines of communication (LoCs) into Afghanistan from Pakistan and consolidated control over the mountainous region spanning the borders of Kandahar, Zabul, and Uruzgan.[17] So confident were they with their advances that they attempted to advance against Kandahar City from their bases in Uruzgan, Zabul, and Shah Wali Kot. However, they were successfully blocked by a battalion of U.S. infantry that was deployed in Kandahar as part of Task Force (TF) Bronco.[18]

Not to be deterred, the Taliban turned their focus westward. From such areas as Baghran and Sangin in Helmand, the Taliban hoped to penetrate into Panjwayi and Zhari. From here they desired to launch their campaign to control Kandahar City in 2006. The Taliban hoped to isolate this target by intimidating local leaders and the population with violence, gaining control of the areas surrounding Kandahar City. By the beginning of 2005, they started to murder police officers, government officials, "spies," and elders who were working with the Americans.[19] They also established a judicial system to increase the Taliban's legitimacy and began to infiltrate the area with fighters to challenge the government and ISAF for control of the physical terrain.

DIRECT CHALLENGE TO KANDAHAR CITY

Canadian involvement in Afghanistan began immediately following 9/11, under the code name Operation Apollo. Canada deployed a number of ships, aircraft, and SOF, as well as a light infantry battle group based on the 3rd Battalion, Princess Patricia's Canadian Light Infantry (PPCLI), in February 2002 to support American OEF operations in the Kandahar area.[20] Throughout the next six months, members from 3 PPCLI and Canadian SOF, in support of the American initiatives to destroy Taliban and al Qaeda forces, conducted combat operations with their American counterparts in the Tergul Mountain range in the Sha-i-Kot valley in eastern Afghanistan, as well as in the Gardez area. By late July 2002, Canada redeployed these ground forces back home, as the government felt the Taliban threat was largely eliminated.

However, Canadian ground participation in Afghanistan quickly resumed when, on 12 February 2003, Canada's European allies requested Canadian participation in ISAF for the U.N.-mandated mission in Kabul.[21] As a result, Canada, under the code name Operation Athena, once again deployed a battle group and a brigade headquarters for a period of one year, commencing July 2003.[22]

Operation Athena officially ended on 18 October 2005 with the withdrawal of the last of the Canadians from the Kabul area.[23] But Canada did not leave Afghanistan. Rather, she redefined her contribution as part of Stage 3 of ISAF's expansion across all of Afghanistan. Canada agreed to take responsibility for a Provincial Reconstruction Team (PRT) in the increasingly volatile and violent insurgent-rich Kandahar Province. It assumed command of the PRT in August 2005.[24]

The 350-strong Canadian PRT represented the same multi-disciplinary focus of the American PRTs that stressed development as well as security. It became a multi-departmental effort, employing personnel from the Department of National Defence (DND), Foreign Affairs and International Trade Canada (DFAIT), the Canadian International Development Agency (CIDA), the Royal Canadian Mounted Police (RCMP), and other Canadian police forces. Still ongoing, its mission is to help extend the authority of the Afghanistan government in Kandahar Province by promoting local stability and security, improving local governance structures, and engaging in reconstruction activities.[25]

Equally important to the Canadian commitment was the deployment in February 2006 of an infantry battle group of approximately a thousand soldiers to work with the American forces to conduct stabilization and combat operations throughout Kandahar Province. The American forces were still operating under the framework of OEF, and the introduction of the Canadian battle group became an integral component of the transition from the American OEF framework to the ISAF Stage 3 transition of NATO control of coalition forces in Afghanistan.[26] Subsequently, it fell to the 1st Battalion, the PPCLI, or TF Orion as its commanding officer (CO) Lieutenant-Colonel Ian Hope titled it, to conduct the combat tasks in Kandahar Province.[27]

For the Taliban, the transition from OEF to NATO control of southern Afghanistan proved to be a golden opportunity to deepen and consolidate their control of Kandahar Province. They had already infiltrated the districts and created shadow governments that were effectively displacing the weak Government of the Islamic Republic of Afghanistan (GIRoA) structures in place. In addition, through a campaign of intimidation and fear through night letters and selective assassination, they terrorized the population into submission. They now began to concentrate their fighters to openly challenge the coalition and GIRoA. And, as the Taliban grew in strength and numbers, they became more and more aggressive.

By the spring of 2006, much of the resurgent Taliban fighting fell to the Canadians. Lieutenant-Colonel Hope was responsible for covering an area of approximately fifty-four thousand square kilometres. Adding to the huge task was the fact that another Canadian, Brigadier-General David Fraser, as part of the transition, took command of the southern region, including the province of Kandahar for which the PPCLI Battle Group was responsible. Fraser had jurisdiction for the other southern provinces, including the hot spots of Helmand and Uruzgan provinces, an area measuring 220,744 square kilometres. Not surprisingly, Fraser leaned heavily on Hope. In essence, the Canadians were the bridge between the U.S.-led OEF mission and NATO's ISAF mission.

By June 2006, as the annual fighting season was in full swing, the surge in Taliban activity became evident — it was indicative of a full blown offensive. Between May and June there was an alarming increase in the number of enemy contacts. The Taliban began to confiscate cell phones from local nationals as a counter-intelligence measure and also established plans for setting up checkpoints and moving into Kandahar City itself. On 30 June 2006, the task force received reports indicating that the Taliban were issuing night letters directing Afghan locals to leave the Panjwayi and Zhari areas immediately, as Taliban elements were planning to engage GIRoA forces and Canadian Forces (CF) elements.

The state of chaos and violence reached such levels that, by June 2006, the Senlis Council reported, "Kandahar now is a war zone, with suicide bombings, rocket attacks, ambushes and repeated outbreaks of open warfare, resulting in numerous Canadian fatalities and many more injuries."[28] They concluded, "Kandahar is a province at war: there is no peace to keep."[29] Statistics backed their assertions. By June 2006, there was a "600% increase in violent attacks."[30] In that year, the Taliban burned down 187 schools and murdered 85 teachers and more than 600 policemen.[31]

Consequently, the 1 PPCLI Battle Group focused its energies on security operations, specifically to find, fix, and destroy the enemy. In July, due to the increasing Taliban presence and activity, Lieutenant-Colonel Hope developed a concept of operations that entailed concentrating his combat power in Pashmul to disrupt the Taliban. The Taliban, however, refused to go quietly, and were in a constant state of combat with the

Canadians. Embedded reporter Christie Blatchford summarized that month: "July was a daily diet of long battles that went on for hours and stretched the battle group thin over six hundred kilometres in seven separate districts over some of the most treacherous terrain in Afghanistan."[32]

By August, intelligence reports continued to paint a grim picture of ongoing Taliban activity, namely key leader engagements and increasing numbers of troops in contact (TICs), all of which indicated that the enemy was massing forces in the Panjwayi valley. The Taliban focus on the area was not hard to understand: Panjwayi has always been critically important to the Taliban because it is fertile, densely populated, and economically lucrative. It has also been the traditional staging area for attacks against Kandahar City, as well as an area for resupply for troops staging in Zhari district.

In addition, Kandahar province and its capital, Kandahar City, have always been of interest to the Taliban because the region has consistently maintained a kind of autonomy from any of the various central governments in Kabul. It is also the second largest province in Afghanistan, located in the harsh desert environment of the volatile southeastern corner of the country. It is bounded on the north and northeast by the mountainous Uruzgan and Zabul provinces, in the west by Helmand, and it shares a very porous 402 kilometre-long border with the Pakistan province of Balochistan. Kandahar City is situated at the junction of Afghanistan's main highways and is the major southern link to Pakistan. The highway system passes from Spin Boldak on the Pakistan border through Kandahar City to Kabul.

Kandahar also holds a seminal importance to the Taliban and its senior leadership. Many of them, including Mullah Omar, Mullah Osmani, and Mullah Obaidullah, were born and raised in the area. Furthermore, they preached Islam and fought in Kandahar and hoped to repeat the success they achieved during the anti-Soviet jihad in the 1980s, when Panjwayi became the epicentre of resistance in the south. During the fall of 1982, mujahideen fighters had inflicted severe casualties on the Soviets and thwarted Soviet ability to exert control over the area. They did this with the support of the local population and the expert use of the close terrain — canals, dense orchards, vineyards, walled compounds, and fields of crops, for example. The Taliban believed they could once again prevail over an "occupying force" with the same ground and tactics as they had in 1982.

Kandahar is the birthplace of the Taliban and continues to be its heartland. So, somewhat ironically, Kandahar had also become a centre of gravity for both the GIRoA and the coalition in the fight for the confidence and support of Afghans. Furthermore, NATO had begun to establish Afghan development zones (ADZ) as secure bubbles around a nucleus where the GIRoA and NATO could push resources and redevelopment — this is known as the ink spot method.[33] These efforts were all part of the governance, security, and reconstruction strategy for rebuilding a modern Afghanistan. Conversely, for the Taliban, victory in Kandahar Province would discredit the GIRoA and coalition forces in the eyes of Afghans.

For all these reasons, it became clear to coalition commanders and GIRoA leaders that the Taliban were massing in Panjwayi to establish a permanent base of operations there, with a view to attacking Kandahar City. It was apparent that the Talibes were committed to winning. "The Taliban emptied Quetta and other centres to conduct offensive operations in Regional Command (South) (RC (S)) in 2006," confided one senior NATO staff officer. "It was a window of opportunity for them as we focused on elections and the hand-over from U.S. control in Kandahar to NATO control as part of Stage 3 expansion."[34] Lieutenant-Colonel Shane Schreiber revealed the extent of Taliban forces in the area: "Our intelligence estimated that they [Taliban] brought in, as a minimum, 12,000 foot soldiers."[35]

In early August, continuing reports of major enemy activity and massing of troops triggered yet another coalition foray into the area. On 3 August 2006, Lieutenant-Colonel Hope and his battle group found themselves in the Pashmul/Panjwayi area once again. After a vicious day of long combat that saw several armoured vehicles destroyed and a large number of casualties, Hope was forced to pull back.[36] The size and defensive posture of the Taliban made it clear that they intended to stay. Moreover, any attempt to remove them would need to be a brigade-size operation.

Brigadier-General Fraser, the multi-national brigade (MNB) commander for Regional RC (S) assessed that Panjwayi was going to be the Taliban's "major fight for the summer." He explained, "The third of August was the defining day that we knew exactly what we were facing, and what the enemy wanted to do, the enemy's intent."[37] In Fraser's estimation, the enemy's intent "was to isolate Kandahar City, not directly but indirectly, to demonstrate the weakness and the inability of the national Government to come after them with a conventional force."[38] He stated, "This also indicated to us that the Taliban were actually progressing with the evolution of their own operations to the next stage[39] where they thought they were capable enough to go and challenge the national government and coalition forces in a conventional manner."[40]

Fraser added, "We also assessed that their intent was to engage the international community in a battle of attrition on ground of their tactical choosing to cause as many casualties as they could to attack our centre of gravity (i.e. domestic public support)."[41] He concluded that the Taliban plan "was designed to defeat us from a 'political will' point of view; to illustrate weakness in the Government of Afghanistan and thereby set the stage where the Taliban could attack the city and defeat not only the provincial government there but also attack the national government in Afghanistan in a fairly sophisticated and substantive way."[42] As a result, Fraser briefed his plan to General David Richards, the British commander then in charge of NATO's ISAF forces in Afghanistan at NATO headquarters. "I said this is a fight we can't lose," remembered Fraser. "This is the main, main fight."[43]

NATO RESPONSE — OPERATION MEDUSA

It became obvious to Canadian and NATO commanders, particularly after the grim combat engagements throughout the summer, that the enemy was skilled, tenacious, and well-established in the Pashmul district. To Fraser and his multi-national brigade, ISAF headquarters assigned the mission of defeating the Taliban in Pashmul in order to set the conditions for the establishment of the Kandahar ADZ.[44] Subsequently, Fraser issued his intent: disrupt the Taliban in the district, achieve security for the local population and freedom of manoeuvre for aid agencies, complete Quick

Impact Projects (QIPs) to achieve rapid reconstruction, and subsequently develop the region's governance and economic capacity.

He intended to shape the battlefield to disrupt Taliban forces through the conduct of leadership engagements, namely brigade manoeuvre and the intensive application of air and indirect fires (e.g. fighter aircraft, Spectre C-130 gunships, artillery). In addition, shaping would also be affected through the conduct operations (i.e. decisive strike, link-up of forces to secure the area of operations (AO)). In sum, he believed these actions would clear the enemy out of Pashmul/Panjwayi.

The plan lacked one major component — combat forces. The MNB operations officer, Lieutenant-Colonel Schreiber, acknowledged that issue: "We were spread pretty thin on the ground between Martello, Spin Boldak, Kandahar City and Panjwayi. Therefore, what we wanted to do was concentrate that battle group and essentially fix the Taliban in Pashmul to make sure that they couldn't push any further into Kandahar or Highway 1." He then described that they had hoped to use the coalition's superior ISR (intelligence, surveillance, reconnaissance) assets and firepower to "begin to pull apart the nodes and take apart the Taliban defense." Schreiber conceded:

> We didn't have enough [combat power] to clear it. At that point we assessed it would have taken a brigade attack and there was no way we were ever going to generate a four, or even a three battle group brigade to be able to do that, nor did we want to because of the collateral damage that would have caused. So instead, what we decided to do was to defeat the Taliban build-up by isolating and disrupting and pulling the Taliban apart in chunks, hoping that at some point they would say 'okay it's not worth it.'[45]

In essence, Fraser's intent was to separate the Taliban forces by putting deliberate kinetic and non-kinetic pressure on them. He explained that they had the Taliban contained: "They were fixing themselves, or rather they had fixed themselves." Fraser elaborated, "They were bringing forces in from everywhere — infiltrating through the Reg[estan] Desert, up from Pakistan and they assembled a lot of commanders in the pocket."[46]

Remarkably, despite the abundance of historical data on insurgencies, the Taliban had chosen to concentrate and posture themselves in such a way as to directly challenge the GIRoA and NATO forces in a truly conventional manner, namely by digging in, building fortifications, and holding ground. Despite this brazen decision, the Taliban were not about to make themselves easy targets. The enemy operated in teams of roughly platoon-equivalent size (twenty to thirty fighters), over which effective command and control was maintained. As they had already shown, and would further confirm, they were sophisticated enough to conduct tactical reliefs-in-place and coordinated attacks against their opponents. More importantly, their defences were prepared as strong points, which made extensive use of natural and man-made obstacles. These points all had interlocking arcs of direct fire with small arms, RPGs, and recoilless rifles. In addition, their indirect fire from mortars was responsive and well-coordinated, and obstacles on roads were particularly prevalent, with extensive use of pressure plate IEDs. For example, in one area five such devices were found in a fifty-metre span of road leading into a Taliban defensive position. They had also widened the existing canal with light equipment so that it could act as a tank trap.

Although NATO and the Canadians did not initially have a full picture of the Taliban defensive dispositions, no one was fooled into thinking it would be easy to clear the enemy from the region. The challenge was imposing. Schreiber notes, "Especially after the 3 August attack we realized that we were facing a battalion size defensive position based upon complex obstacles covered by surveillance, indirect and direct fire and incorporating kill zones." He affirmed, "So this is what we faced, two company positions with strong points from which they [Taliban] would sally forth to conduct ambushes along Highway 1. We were having anywhere between three to five ambushes a day on Highway 1, every day late July and early August." Schreiber further declared, "And then they had another company defensive position to control the Arghandab River with a C2 [command and control] node in the middle."[47]

As a result of the apparent sophistication of the enemy, the brigade and battle group staffs devoted a great deal of effort to Phase 1 planning and gathering intelligence. Subsequently, the emphasis shifted in the early stages of Phase 2 to "building up," specifically to assembling the combat forces and enablers (ISR platforms, aviation, close air support (CAS), direct and indirect fire assets), as well as the necessary logistical support to take out the Taliban completely.

It was the Taliban's excellent use of fieldcraft that mitigated some of the vulnerability they had imposed on themselves by engaging in a conventional battle of attrition. Trench lines were well-prepared by hand and superbly concealed to evade detection by ground and airborne ISR assets. Trenches were tied into thick mud walls that proved extremely resilient against both direct fire weapons (for example, 25mm cannon and small arms) and C4 explosives. In fact, they had developed a sophisticated strongpoint replete with entrenchments that resembled a Soviet defensive position. Communications trenches were dug to connect the larger trench system and bunkers. Lieutenant-Colonel Schreiber concluded that "[the Taliban] had a battalion defensive position fully dug in with complex robust command and control capability with mutually supporting positions and advanced surveillance and early warning."[48]

The Taliban were highly motivated and fought in place. Their fire discipline was strictly imposed in order to draw coalition forces into their kill zones, and they aggressively launched counterattacks from the flanks with small mobile teams to attack the depth of assaulting forces.[49]

Undeniably, the Taliban had chosen their ground well. Beyond the fortifications they had built, the natural lay of the land worked in their favour. Pashmul was a green belt with thick vegetation, and seven-foot-high marijuana fields hid movement and masked the thermal imagery of the LAV.[50] One official report noted this difficulty in detail:

> The terrain was extremely difficult due to the combination of natural and built up features. Enemy defences were anchored on the Arghandab River that provided a natural impediment to high-speed manoeuvre to the defensive position. Although dried up for the most part,

the steepness of the banks canalized movement to ford-
ing sites where we were vulnerable to enemy direct and
indirect fires. Canals criss-crossed the manoeuvre space
and proved an impediment to off-road movement for
LAVs. Corn and marijuana fields (with stalks extending
to a height of 6-8 feet) limited visibility and provided
excellent concealment for both TB [Taliban] fighters
and natural obstacles. The most significant terrain features were arguably the mud walls and the vineyards.
Mud walls approximately eight feet high and two feet
thick dominated the terrain. In one case 10 blocks of C4
were required for a single breach. The vineyards covered
earth mounds approximately 3–5 feet high with rows
arranged every three feet.[51]

And so Fraser deployed his forces around the objective area to
provide as much containment as he could. The containment force maintained a dynamic disposition in order to provoke the enemy to move
inside the "circle so [Fraser's forces] could shape the battle and advanta-
geously engage the enemy."[52] Coalition forces also dropped psychological
pamphlets to warn non-combatants, civilians, and less-fanatical enemy
personnel to vacate the area. "For the three weeks before we launched
Operation Medusa, we talked to and gave money to every village leader
in the area," revealed Fraser. "In exchange, we asked them to get rid of
the Taliban." Ultimately though, he conceded, "We had limited success."[53]

In the aftermath of the bloody August battle, Brigadier-General
Fraser briefed General Richards on the plan for OP Medusa. In turn, the
ISAF Commander confirmed to Fraser that Operation Medusa was the
ISAF main effort. He went even further and pronounced that Operation
Medusa was actually the "NATO main effort."[54] This sentiment was supported by NATO secretary general Jaap de Hoop Scheffer, who publically
announced, "If we fail and this nation becomes a failed state again, the
consequences will be felt in Ottawa, in Brussels, in the Hague, in Madrid,
in New York and elsewhere. That is what is at stake."[55]

THE FIGHT

The stakes were clearly high. The fight for Pashmul, or more accurately for Afghanistan, as Brigadier-General Fraser and other senior NATO military leaders described, no longer rested with Hope and TF Orion. By early August, they were already conducting a relief in place (RIP) with the 1st Battalion, The Royal Canadian Regiment Battle Group (1 RCR BG) or Task Force 3-06 as it was officially termed. At 1600 hours, 19 August 2006, a small ceremony to mark the Transfer of Command Authority (TOCA) between the outgoing and the incoming units was taking place at Kandahar Airfield (KAF) between Lieutenant-Colonel Hope and Lieutenant-Colonel Omer Lavoie, the CO of TF 3-06. Within hours of the TOCA, before Operation Medusa could even be launched, and with portions of his force having only been in theatre for a few weeks, Lavoie was fighting his first major battle.[56]

Reports from locals indicated a continuation of the infiltration of insurgent fighters, as well as new leaders, into the Panjwayi district. More troublesome were the reports that a large portion of the reinforcements moving into Pashmul were assessed as the more-experienced Taliban fighters from out of area who were likely augmented by foreign fighters. They continued to reinforce their defensive positions in Pashmul but also began conducting noticeably more and better-coordinated attacks. They also demonstrated a large improvement in their use of fire and movement, as well as their ability to coordinate and concentrate their fires. The insurgents began to conduct almost daily ambushes along major routes, targeting ISAF and ANSF elements.

The new Task Force reacted quickly and pushed out its companies to monitor enemy activity. On 19 August, Afghan Independence Day, with the TOCA ceremony barely finished, "A" Coy, 1 RCR BG was deployed to the dominating high ground at Ma'Sūm Ghar to observe the enemy. They arrived at approximately 1730–1800 hours and linked up with the ANP, who maintained a presence on the high feature. This activity initiated a prompt response from the enemy. At approximately 1845 hours, the Taliban launched a major assault against the Bazaar-e-Panjwayi District Centre. "I had not anticipated," conceded Lavoie, "having my first command combat experience within hours of transfer of command authority."[57] But Lavoie had no say in the matter, as an estimated three hundred to five hundred insurgents, armed with small arms and RPGs, and using disciplined section fire and movement, began to manoeuvre to overrun the ANP and "A" Coy positions on Ma'Sūm Ghar. Their assault entailed dismounted coordinated attacks from three different directions. Lavoie recalled, "Within a span of a few hours, 'A' Coy came under attack at night by an enemy that seriously outnumbered them."[58]

The assaulting insurgents proved to be nothing less than tenacious. The fight had lasted over three hours when "A" Coy pulled off the feature in darkness and under contact. "You just couldn't tell who was who," said Warrant Officer Mike Jackson. "And we were very lucky we didn't have any blue on blue [casualties]."[59] Moreover, "A" Coy could no longer secure their position and were running low on ammunition. Therefore, the OC, Major Mike Wright, decided to pull back to more defensible ground about three kilometres outside of Bazaar-e-Panjwayi to resupply and regroup. At that point, the Quick Reaction Force (QRF) platoon from Patrol Base Wilson met up with the sub-unit and delivered the much-needed ammunition. Wright then pulled back to the outskirts of Bazaar-e-Panjwayi and formed a leaguer for the last few hours of darkness that remained.

In the end, the defence of Ma'Sūm Ghar, which represented the outer defensive perimeter of the district centre, had blunted the attack against the ANP headquarters (HQ) inside Bazaar-e-Panjwayi. Coalition battle damage assessment indicated that approximately eighty to one hundred insurgents were killed. Local security forces recovered the bodies of at least thirty-seven insurgents — a remarkable feat in itself, as the Taliban were meticulous in policing the battlefield so as not to leave any indication of their losses.

Having beaten off the Taliban attack, Lavoie now focused his task force on the approaching mission. However, he still had to ensure the Taliban were kept in check until he was ready to launch Operation Medusa. As such, between 22–29 August, his task force undertook deterrence patrolling to prevent the Taliban from attacking the district centre. Meanwhile, the planning for Operation Medusa was in its final stages.

Lavoie gave formal orders for Operation Medusa on 27 August 2006. The CO outlined that he intended to achieve his mission by denying the enemy freedom of movement or action within the Panjwayi-Zhari-Kandahar-Arghandab greenbelt, which had historically served as a significant sanctuary and transit route in past efforts to seize Kandahar City. The operation was to be a joint Afghan National Security Forces (ANSF) and ISAF initiative, with the ANSF leading wherever possible. Lavoie explained, "The key to success of this operation lies in our ability to match our strengths against enemy weaknesses in order to constantly disrupt his decision cycle and prevent his C2 [command and control] assets from being able to react to our manoeuvre." As such, he directed that the battle group would "make maximum use of joint fires, ISR, EW, [electronic warfare] superior direct firepower capability, mobility and C2 to dominate the three dimensional battle space and overwhelm an enemy capable of operating on only one plane of the battlefield."[60]

Lieutenant-Colonel Lavoie planned on deceiving the enemy into believing that a major assault was imminent on their lines of communication as well as on their command and control nodes. He hoped to achieve this by advancing aggressively from east to west on two separate axes with two respective balanced company group (Coy Gp) teams — one advancing from the north and the other from the south. The plan was premised on the notion that once the Taliban understood that their critical vulnerabilities were being threatened by a major ground force, they would mass to defend themselves. This would allow ISAF assets to destroy them using precision fire from close air support (CAS), aviation, and artillery.

Lavoie and his battle group were originally given eight days to clear the objective. The precursor to the operation began on 1 September, when the Coy Gps moved to their waiting areas close to their objectives and conducted battle procedure in preparation for their opening roles. "B" and "C" Coy Gps were responsible for conducting feints north and south of Pashmul respectively, with a view to drawing the enemy out of their defensive positions. Concurrently, "A" Coy Gp was to isolate Bazaar-e-Panjwayi in order to provide flank protection to "C" Coy Gp due to the nature of the threat and terrain. If successful in their actions, the enemy would be pummelled and annihilated by precision-guided munitions and indirect fire.[61]

The following day, 2 September 2006, at 0530 hours, TF Kandahar manoeuvre elements deployed into their battle positions centred on enemy objectives in Panjwayi/Pashmul. "C" Coy, under command of Major Matthew Sprague, was responsible for seizing Ma'Sūm Ghar. Lavoie wanted to ensure he took possession of the high ground first, namely the Ma'Sūm Ghar feature, from which he could dominate the area by both observation and fire. "C" Coy did so without incident, arriving on the objective at 0600 hours, which was the intended "H-Hour."[62]

So far, all was going well. But a wild card remained: where exactly was the enemy? There was still no clear picture as to the Taliban's actual positions. On the afternoon of 2 September, Brigadier-General Fraser visited the forward lines. That night, based on the success to date and pressure from NATO command not to allow any Taliban to escape the pocket, he ordered an attack on the Taliban position across the river, deciding to speed up the planned sequence of events.[63]

Although unhappy with the loss of several days of preparatory bombardment, the CO ordered Charles Coy Gp to attack the following morning. Due to the lack of preparation time, the only clear flat crossing point was alongside the main road directly in line with the famous white school complex in the village of Bayenzi, which had caused so much grief for TF Orion a month prior during the desperate combat of 3 August.[64] And so, at 0600 hours, on 3 September 2006, Charles Coy Gp commenced their assault.

Initially, all went well. The attacking sub-unit had overwhelming indirect fire support. "We crossed and got into a decent defensive posture and established a good foothold," explained Sprague. "We were in a half circle with 8 Platoon facing West, 7 Platoon facing North, the ANA and their American Embedded Military Training (EMT) team facing North-East and the engineer Zettlemeyer and bulldozer and other support elements in the flat area behind us."[65]

Sprague then pushed his force farther inland to attack the Taliban positions, which they believed were around the white schoolhouse. As the lead elements pulled up approximately fifty to a hundred metres away from the building, all hell broke loose. The Taliban unleashed a fusillade of fire against the Canadians, who were caught in a horseshoe ambush. After several hours of bitter fighting against a foe they could not see, and having taken heavy casualties, Major Sprague realized that there was not much more he could do, so he directed more fire forward and calmly organized the withdrawal of his forces, ensuring that neither casualties nor disabled vehicles were left behind. The attempted assault on the enemy positions had been costly: four killed and eight wounded in the task force.

That evening, an intelligence report summarized the situation: "The enemy believe that they are winning, and their morale is assessed as high." The Taliban quickly claimed victory following the withdrawal of Charles Coy Gp back to their battle positions on Ma'Sūm Ghar. Moreover, despite the loss of a significant amount of Taliban fighters, the intelligence report concluded that their heavy losses did not have a demoralizing effect on the remaining Talibes. The defence of Pashmul had become a rallying point for the local Taliban insurgents and they began pushing reinforcements into the area and re-manning many of the abandoned ambush positions.

For the Canadians, there was no respite, and Fraser ordered another attack the next morning. However, misfortune once again played its hand. As Charles Coy Gp awoke and began to prepare for another attack against the white schoolhouse, an American A-10 "Warthog" close air support aircraft that was called in to attack an enemy position across the river became momentarily disoriented, and before he realized his error, the pilot unleashed a partial burst of deadly fire from his seven barrelled 30mm Gatling gun, killing one Canadian and wounding thirty-five others, including the Charles Coy Gp OC.

The latest calamity was disastrous. Having lost most of its command structure and almost a third of its strength in the friendly fire incident, Charles Coy Gp was now combat ineffective. "Twenty minutes away from an assault river crossing and Omer [Lieutenant-Colonel Lavoie] lost half a company," lamented Brigadier-General Fraser. "We delayed 24 hours but at the end of the day we had to get it done."[66]

The brief pause allowed Lieutenant-Colonel Lavoie the opportunity to recalibrate and amend the plan. He would no longer attack into the Taliban's kill zone. Rather, he now put the emphasis on the north and east, where he would conduct a push using overwhelming force through terrain of his choosing. The 1 RCR BG was now going to use three dismounted companies clearing from the east, moving down the canals to get into the area and then clear out the enemy.[67]

After reallocating and reorganizing forces, the renewed push by "B" Coy started on 6 September 2006 in the north, when they breached the treeline that marked the divide between friendly and enemy territory. The 1 RCR BG now hit its stride. One sub-unit would move forward and dominate intervening ground, provide a firm foothold, and act as a firebase. Artillery would then be called in to hammer the respective objective, and then the next sub-unit would surge forward, break through the objective, and then fight through the target area.

According to almost all who participated, the clearing of objectives resembled Cold War techniques designed to fight the Soviets. Since the entire civilian population had been evicted by the Taliban and the area turned into a fortified defensive zone, matters were somewhat simplified; it became an exercise of unrestricted compound clearance. The soldiers would toss grenades into a building or room and then, immediately upon the explosion, pour into it and hose it down with fire. Major Andrew Lussier acknowledged, "The Taliban did us a big favour; essentially they had kicked out all the civilians … It made life so much easier for us." He declared, "Essentially we just shot and bombed the crap out of these guys for the better part of four or five days while the battle group made their way from the north."[68]

Lieutenant-Colonel Lavoie echoed these sentiments. "When the operation commenced, it seemed as if it were a Cold War training exercise," he observed. "There was nothing new in war fighting." He explained the specifics further:

> We used air [support] to hit deep and danger close artillery at 300 yards or less. Dismounted infantry rushed in before the smoke cleared and seized the objective. Engineers cleared a route with bulldozers and dealt with IEDs. We pushed LAVs up to support infantry to the next objective and to the next bound. At night we conducted

fighting patrols and Reconnaissance Platoon seized the line of departure for the next bound the next day. And much like predecessors in Vietnam who said they had to destroy the village to save it — we had to do the same.[69]

In essence, as the operation began to play out, it became increasingly "conventional" in nature. Fraser described it as "a conventional duke it out fight." He said, "The enemy wanted the ground and had prepared the area well for a defensive battle. In the end, it was all about putting the proper resources into the fight. We knew we would win because losing just was not an option."[70]

Major Ivey concurred with the brigade commander's assessment:

> We went right back to using conventional ammunition, high explosives. The air burst we found was outstanding for neutralizing soldiers that we suspected were hiding under trees, using the shade as concealment or using the thick brush to move back and forth. So we used air burst a lot, as well as 155mm delay ground burst to pierce through those complexes to get whatever effect we were trying to achieve, which was basically just to kill people and to destroy whatever bunkers they had.

Ivey related that they also reverted to using smoke to blind the enemy, screen their movement, and mark targets for close air support.[71]

In essence, the choreography of the advance was in keeping with the conventional warfare playbook that most of the senior leaders in the battle group had practised since joining the army. "What we ended up doing was hours before the launch of an advance, each of the respective Forward Observation Officer (FOO) parties with the two lead companies commenced their preparatory fires," explained Major Ivey. He added, "There was no flashes of brilliance — what we wanted to achieve was to destroy as much of the compound structures as we could that we thought were housing enemy OPs or firing positions and neutralize anybody and anything in the objective areas." As a result, higher headquarters pushed the necessary enablers (CAS, attack aviation, and guns) to the FOO parties so they could pound the Taliban into submission.

The enemy was now pinned down due to the heavy fire and deliberate tactics. Moreover, the Taliban fighters were becoming extremely frustrated with their inability to fight back. Captured enemy communications revealed statements such as, "We cannot achieve our objective while we're getting bombarded."[72]

By 14 September 2006, the fight was largely over, and 1 RCR BG elements pushing from the north linked up with their sister elements pushing from the south. They had seized every last bit of ground from the Taliban, including the village of Bayenzi, which was the home of the infamous white schoolhouse complex that was at the centre of the death of so many Canadians.[73]

AFTERMATH

With the taking of the white schoolhouse, which represented the centre of Objective Rugby, the combat phase of Operation Medusa was over. In the end, Fraser assessed, "after all that pressure, after all that time, the enemy just collapsed and they went to ground."[74] The brigade commander declared that the conditions for TF 3-06 to move from Phase 3 (exploitation) to Phase 4 (reconstruction), namely the creation of a secured area of operations in the Pashmul district, were now at hand.

Once again, a phased approach was taken. A three stage plan was developed. The first stage entailed restoring security through the visible employment of ANSF throughout the area with RC(S) forces in support, and it was also to be the commencement of an enduring ANA/ANP presence in the Pashmul/Panjwayi area.

The next stage called for resettlement. In coordination with the Disaster Management Committee and key district leaders, as well as U.N. and appropriate civil agencies, ISAF forces were earmarked to assist with the return of the civilian population to the area. Finally, the third and last stage of the reconstruction phase of OP Medusa was the development piece, where the larger and more enduring projects targeted for long term development could take place. After all, Brigadier-General Fraser had pronounced that the end state to OP Medusa would be achieved when "the people of Afghanistan have freedom of movement along Highway 1, the villagers of Pashmul and greater Zhari have returned to their villages, and the Taliban have been denied freedom of action in the vicinity of the Kandahar ADZ."[75]

By 15 September 2006, the various task forces began pushing farther out from their original objective areas. Although there were no enemy engagements, there were locals observed fleeing the area, which normally portends no good fortune. However, in this case no combat ensued, and the Government of Afghanistan and ISAF began radio and television broadcasts to encourage locals to return to their homes, explaining that the fighting had stopped. By 16 September, some of the elements of the OP Medusa task forces were redeployed to the Kandahar Airfield (KAF). The next day, 1 RCR BG began to rotate its companies through KAF for rest and refit, maintaining two company groups on security and clearance operations in their area of responsibility. It seemed that by 17 September 2006, OP Medusa, aside from the non-kinetic Phase 4 reconstruction phase, was over.

It appeared that the ISAF multi-national brigade, but particularly the 1 RCR BG — which bore the brunt of the fighting in the Pashmul area — had indeed defeated the Taliban. The cost, however, was not inconsequential. In total, the Canadians had lost five and approximately forty were wounded. The victory was hailed as a monumental success. A NATO statement was swiftly broadcast, announcing the victory:

NATO launched its largest ever combat operation, against a well-prepared and determined enemy. It was fought to the south west of Kandahar City, in the Panshwaye and Zhari districts. It was here that the Taliban filtered in large numbers of insurgents in to first take and then, far more significantly, hold the area. It was a trial of strength that will have a lasting effect both militarily and on the hearts and minds of the Afghan people.[76]

Another NATO missive announced, "The operation has met its initial aims by dealing a severe blow to the leadership and forces of the extremists so that they are no longer a cohesive force and have had to dispense after suffering important losses."[77] A political official was less restrained. He remarked that OP Medusa "wiped the floor with the Taliban."[78]

Not surprisingly, NATO leadership used the success to push select messages. ISAF Commander Lieutenant-General David Richards boasted:

> Operation Medusa has been a significant success and clearly shows the capability that Afghan, NATO and coalition forces have when they operate together. I always said that I would be robust when necessary, and that is what I have done. The Taliban had no choice but to leave ... Having created a secure environment in the area, it is now time for the real work to start. Without security, there can be no reconstruction and development. Without reconstruction and development there can be no long-lasting security.[79]

According to Lieutenant-General Richards, OP Medusa was a key battle against the Taliban insurgency. "If Kandahar fell," he explained, "and it was reasonably close run last year, it did not matter how well the Dutch did in Uruzgan or how well the British did in Helmand. Their two provinces would also, as night followed day, have failed because we would have lost the consent of the Pashtun people because of the totemic importance of Kandahar."[80]

The Afghan government also hailed the success of OP Medusa. Provincial Governor Assadullah Khalid stated on 17 September 2006, "Six nations fought side by side to inflict significant casualties on the entrenched insurgent forces, who could have avoided this sad loss of life by reconciling with the legitimate Afghan government."[81] He added, "The ability of the Taliban to stay and fight in groups is finished. The enemy has been crushed."[82] Khalid assessed, "This operation in Panjwai and Zhari is one of very few successes in recent years."[83]

The rather effusive praise from senior NATO and Afghan leadership was echoed by some scholars and analysts. Author Barnett Rubin, a respected global authority on Afghanistan, credited "Canada's military for turning back 'a frontal offensive by the Taliban' in Panjwai last summer and for rescuing Afghanistan from what [Rubin] considers 'a tipping point.'"[84]

The largely Canadian ground action did not go unheralded by its national command, either. The chief of the defence staff (CDS), General Rick Hillier, asserted, "Afghan ministers will tell you that operation [Medusa] saved Afghanistan. If Kandahar had been encircled, if Highway 1 had been shut down and if the Panjwai had been held by the Taliban, the government in Kabul would have fallen."[85] The MNB commander concluded, "We defeated the Taliban with only five of our casualties [killed]. Then the Taliban tried to bug out one night. Not many made it out. We saved the city, and in so doing, [we] saved the country."[86] Lieutenant-General Mike Gauthier, commander of Canadian Expeditionary Force Command (CEFCOM), believed that OP Medusa and follow-on operations signalled a major success in Kandahar. He bluntly elaborated: Kandahar City did not fall; the Taliban heartland was lost by the enemy; the Taliban were unable to maintain momentum in the winter; and the capacity of the ANA was increased.[87]

NATO's initial assessment claimed 512 Taliban were killed and 136 captured.[88]

Lieutenant-Colonel Schreiber stated, "It is a conservative estimate that the Taliban suffered 1,500 casualties (1,000 wounded, 500 dead)."[89] Brigadier-General Fraser's assessment was similar: "We think we probably killed about 300 to 400 and captured 136, which includes the death of approximately five senior commanders on the ground." He added, "That's a significant defeat, the worst defeat the Taliban ever experienced in probably 40 years according to the Afghan Minister of Defence."[90]

The effects of OP Medusa seemed impressive. Brigadier-General Hayfield, the ISAF chief of operations proclaimed, "Operation Medusa was a huge success."[91] Similarly, media reported, "Medusa was, in military terms, a roaring success. The enemy was routed and more than 1,000 insurgents were killed, giving what British and NATO commanders call 'psychological ascendancy' over the Taliban."[92]

The local Afghans had a different perspective, however. "The bombing and the fighting destroyed our mosque, our homes and our vineyards," said one farmer. "The Taliban are gone, but so is most everything else."[93] Haji Abdullah Shah, another local Afghan, stated, "The cause of the fighting was the Taliban, but with the bombing NATO made big mistakes ... They killed our children, they killed our families. Every canal is collapsed. Every field needs water. We don't have enough food."[94] Abdul Hai lamented, "We have only dirt, nothing else."[95]

TALIBAN RECALIBRATION

The longer term impact of OP Medusa is more difficult to assess. The Taliban attempt at concentrating and holding ground was convincingly defeated. However, being an adaptive and clever foe, they analyzed their defeat and quickly concluded that their future survival and success depended on an asymmetric approach to fighting the ANSF and coalition forces. They became a far more significant threat and effective insurgent force, as Brigadier-General Fraser explained:

> So, when the enemy left we knew we had won this fight. However, we also realized that they would evolve. We knew the enemy would go back, they would go to ground for a bit [disperse and regroup in safe areas] and that they would do an after action review, after which they would come back at us in a far more sophisticated and dangerous way. They always do, they always adapt. The only question we had was how long was it going to take them to replace their leaders and how long was it going to take for them to come back at us again and what form would it take. When they did come back at us, they did so very quickly. They hit us with suicide attacks, IEDs and ambushes. So was it a surprise? No. Are they more dangerous now? Yes.[96]

An official Canadian report agreed: "It is expected that the kinetic effects of OP Medusa will be transitory." It elaborated, "The TB [Taliban] has demonstrated that they are adept at infiltrating fighters into the region and it is expected that enemy force numbers will be replenished in the coming months. Consequently, there is no belief that the TB movement has been defeated in Kandahar province, nor in RC(S).... Ironically, there is some unofficial suggestion that the TB will enter into a more dangerous posture reverting back to terrorist tactics involving the use of suicide bombers and IEDs to inflict casualties on ISAF forces."[97]

The "unofficial suggestion" would come home to roost in a substantial way. After all, the Taliban had not been convinced that they were defeated — in an attempt to regain the initiative, as early as 18 September 2006, the Taliban carried out three separate attacks, which to that point in time became one of Afghanistan's bloodiest days. In Kafir Band, a suicide bomber hit a foot patrol, killing four soldiers and 24 children. In Kabul the same day, a car bomber killed four ANP, and that same night in Herat, another suicide bomber killed 11 people outside city's main mosque.[98] And they were certainly not prepared to surrender the Pashmul area to the GIRoA or the coalition forces. One Taliban fighter stated, "No Muslim wants the human garbage of foreign soldiers in Afghanistan." He explained, "We were ready to fight, but there was lots of bombs, lots of dust. It was hard to see. So we decided to fight somewhere else."[99]

In essence, realizing their error in attempting to fight in a symmetrical manner, the Taliban recalibrated their efforts and returned to their former methodology of intimidation, assassinations, and terror. But significantly, they also seemed to abandon any reservations they may have had about suicide bombers and the widespread, unrestricted use of IEDs. They now embraced whatever methods required to beat their foe.

So, despite NATO's declaration of victory, there appeared to be some confusion as to the long term impact or actual victory that was won as a result of the Canadian and coalition forces actions in Pashmul between 3 and 14 September 2006. Although they had soundly defeated the Taliban's attempt at concentrating forces and holding ground, they had also pushed the Taliban to evolve into a much more dangerous and difficult foe to fight. In essence, OP Medusa forced the Taliban to adopt asymmetric attacks as their operational methodology. The fight would evolve into a much more complex, frustrating, difficult, and dangerous war.[100]

It was the period of reconstruction that proved to be deadlier than OP Medusa itself, as a combination of roadside bombs, suicide bombers, as well as combat and mine strikes killed another 10 Canadian soldiers in the month that followed the capture of Bayenzi (Objective Rugby). "Kinetically we had great effect," said Lieutenant-Colonel Peter Williams. "In stark terms, the number of casualties we inflicted on the enemy was significant. We disrupted their leadership to the point where they realized from a conventional point of view they would not be able to take us on and achieve any sort of success." However, he conceded, "We found that they tended to reverse their tactics ... so after Medusa there has been an increase in the number of IEDs and suicide bombers."[101]

"The Taliban reverted to their asymmetric tactics, which has made them far more dangerous," acknowledged Lieutenant-Colonel Schreiber, the MNB operations officer. "They've now re-infiltrated into this area, small groups of highly motivated fighters, tier one Taliban, many of them foreign fighters, Chechens, Tagiks, Arabs and they're now conducting a very effective asymmetric campaign that relies mostly on IEDs and IED ambushes."[102]

An official report explains this change in tactics: "After the Taliban lost hundreds of fighters in a battle launched under ISAF's Operation Medusa in late 2006, the insurgents evolved to use more guerrilla-type tactics, including operating in small groups and adopting IEDs as a primary, and effective, tactic. Suicide bombings, virtually unheard of in Afghanistan before 2001, have also become common."[103] The coalition assessments were reinforced by the Taliban themselves. One enemy fighter explained, "Our resistance became more lethal, with new weapons and techniques: bigger and better IEDs for roadside bombings, and suicide attacks."[104]

IEDS — THE TALIBAN'S NEW WEAPON OF CHOICE

IEDs became, as CNN aptly described, "the Taliban weapon of choice."[105] Since 2006, the use of IEDs jumped 350 percent in Afghanistan.[106] Soldiers quickly learned that it was often "safer to go by foot than by vehicle, due to the IEDs."[107] In 2007 there were approximately 2,600 attacks using homemade bombs.[108] The frequency of attack just continued to increase. ISAF officials acknowledged that, from 2007–2008, there was a 33 percent increase in the overall number of kinetic events against Afghan or coalition forces. Those same officials confirmed that IED events were the single largest cause of casualties, and these increased by 27 percent.[109]

Strategist Carl Forsberg revealed that the Taliban IED campaign of 2007 was designed to counter the Canadian presence in Zhari and Panjwayi. He noted that the IED attacks became increasingly powerful and frequent. By April, the Taliban began rigging several bombs together, effectively destroying the almost impregnable LAV IIIs and inflicting fatal casualties on their crews. In Forsberg's assessment, IED attacks became an almost daily occurrence on the section of Highway 1 running through the Zhari district.[110]

With continuing success, not surprisingly, the Taliban steadily increased the frequency of their IED attacks in 2008 and even more in 2009. IED attacks from April to June 2009 were 108 percent higher than in the same period in 2008. Frequently, IEDs were deployed on motorcycles or bicycles, although the Taliban also used rickshaws — and even donkeys.[111] Correspondent Adam Day tallied that "based on a literally seat-of-the-pants survey done in the spring of 2008, roughly one in seven trips outside the wire of Kandahar airfield resulted in some kind of IED incident."[112] More accurately, as of 13 November 2009, IEDs accounted for over two thirds of all coalition deaths.[113] A 2010 U.N. report revealed that "the number of attacks involving improvised explosive devices increased by 94 per cent over the same period in 2009, while assassinations of Afghan officials rose by 45 per cent."[114]

The Pentagon confirmed the increase of IEDs and the Taliban's continued reliance on their tactic of choice. A Pentagon report indicated that 1,059 IED incidents transpired in April 2010. This was one of the highest monthly numbers on record and more than double the amount that occurred in April 2009. The Pentagon further confirmed that IEDs continue to be the single greatest cause of military casualties in Afghanistan and were central to the Taliban's strategy. "The overall Afghan insurgent strategy going into 2010," the Pentagon report acknowledged, "is to counter (NATO) expansion and cause casualties to international partner forces with the expanded use of IEDs and suicide bombings."[115]

The effect was deadly, and the impact and trend is not hard to comprehend. In a comparative study of casualties for the September 2007–2009 timeframe, the numbers showed a clear pattern:

Killed in Action (KIA) / Wounded in Action (WIA)

September 2007 — 9 KIA / 37 WIA
September 2008 — 21 KIA / 66 WIA
September 2009 — 37 KIA / 285 WIA[116]

The overall coalition fatalities due to IEDs since 2002 tell a similar tale:

2002 — 4
2003 — 4
2004 — 12
2005 — 21
2006 — 42
2007 — 78
2008 — 152
2009 — 400[117]

Following this, 2010 was adding up to be similarly deadly for coalition troops. IEDs killed 18 troops in April 2010, up three-fold from the same month the previous year. Moreover, in the first five months of 2010, IEDs killed 99 coalition forces in Afghanistan and wounded 785 others.[118] The Taliban clearly had chosen their tactics well.

THE EFFECT

The evolved Taliban methodology proved incredibly troublesome, as intelligence officer Captain Tim Button assessed:

Medusa achieved a 12 month effect. We watched how the Taliban changed the way they did business in a major way. We will never again see them mass together to attack. We drove their commanders underground and they were unable to openly exercise their command. But not concentrating force also makes it harder to find them. We reinforced their need to act asymmetrically.... We don't see large opportunities to target them.[119]

The Taliban also focused on disrupting reconstruction, and in sum the Taliban tactics were now more difficult to counter, making the struggle for the support of the local people increasingly challenging.

As Button concluded, the effect of the Taliban recalibration of tactics and techniques had a demonstrable negative impact on the counter-insurgency. In the year following OP Medusa, the Afghanistan Study Group claimed it was the deadliest year for coalition troops in Afghanistan since 2001. It noted that violence continued to escalate in 2008, with a 30 percent increase in violence nationwide.[120]

It was not only formal reports that conveyed the sentiment of a growing insurgency. After embedding himself within the Taliban, journalist Nir Rosen concluded that they were winning.[121] He was not alone. An informal survey of tribal leaders and former mujahideen commanders in Kandahar City conducted in November 2008 showed the effect of the Taliban strategy in the south. The vast majority of those surveyed believed Kandahar City would fall to the Taliban within the next twelve months.[122]

As a result of that fear, in conjunction with the existence of a very effective system of functioning Taliban tribunals and governance structures in the populated areas surrounding Kandahar City, the Taliban were able to exert a very real and pervasive influence over much of the population of Kandahar City. In the end, fearing likely Taliban control, the population continues to be unwilling to contest Taliban authority, and a wide range of local and mid-level leaders since 2007–2008 refused to take sides against the Taliban, out of sheer terror. As strategist Carl Forsberg concludes, "In this way, the Taliban has made significant progress in taking over Kandahar City without having to wage a conventional battle."[123]

Somewhat predictably, then, during that same timeframe, two years after OP Medusa, two high ranking coalition officers stated the war was not winnable. British brigadier Mark Carleton-Smith, Britain's top military officer in Afghanistan, said publicly that people should "lower their expectations" with regards to how the conflict in Afghanistan would end. "We're not going to win this war," he bluntly stated. "It's about reducing it to a manageable level of insurgency that's not a strategic threat and can be managed by the Afghan army."[124] Several days later, he was supported by the head of France's military, when General Jean-Louis Georgelin commented, "[The British officer] was saying that one cannot win this war militarily, that there is no military solution to the Afghan crisis and I totally share this feeling."[125] Their underlying message was reinforced several months later. In December Norine MacDonald, president and lead field researcher of the International Council on Security and Development, formerly known as the Senlis Council, insisted that "the West is in genuine danger of losing Afghanistan."[126] At the same time, a former head of the U.N. Assistance Mission to Afghanistan (UNAMA), Lakhdar Brahimi, wrote, "The Afghan government is losing ground every day to insurgents and other outlaws who now control at least a third of the country."[127]

All of these assessments pale in light of announcements made by the vice president of the United States and the prime minister of Canada in March 2009. Joe Biden unambiguously stated, "We are not winning the war in Afghanistan," while Stephen Harper declared, "We are not ever going to defeat the insurgents."[128] These assessments were not much different from the observations of the ISAF commander. In September 2009, American general Stanley McChrystal noted, "Eight years of individually successful kinetic actions have resulted in more violence."[129] A month later, he acknowledged that the insurgency was growing, concluding that success could not be taken for granted.[130] Later estimates reflected his perception, and in November 2009, NATO conceded that 30 percent of Afghanistan was under strong Taliban leadership.[131] Other analysts declared that half of Afghanistan was either contested or controlled by the Taliban.[132] The director of intelligence for General Stanley McChrystal's headquarters, Major-General Mike Flynn, conceded that the expansion of Islamic extremist groups across the Afghanistan-Pakistan region was "the worst [he had] seen it."[133]

The Canadian government's official position also acknowledged the Taliban ascendency in the insurgency: "Eight years since the allied ouster of the Taliban regime, the Afghanistan balance sheet presents both pluses and minuses," assessed an official report. It explained, "The latest coalition analysis acknowledges that the insurgents have seized the initiative, both in the armed conflict and by creating a crisis of confidence among the populace through the equally important 'silent war' of fear, intimidation and persuasion."[134]

A U.N. report in March 2010 painted an even bleaker picture: "The deterioration of Afghanistan's security situation has continued, with 2009 being the most volatile year since the fall of the Taliban in 2001, averaging 960 security incidents per month, as compared with 741 in 2008. The situation worsened in January 2010, with the number of security incidents 40 percent higher than in January 2009."[135] According to one OP Medusa veteran who returned to serve another tour in 2010, despite how dangerous it had been during 1 RCR's first tour in Kandahar, "Panjwayi is a harder fight now." Master-Corporal Manser explained, "The enemy is definitely present. They are right outside the camp and are a lot craftier with the IEDs than they used to be."[136]

Not surprisingly then, by the spring of 2010, declarations that the war was unwinnable and that negotiations with the Taliban should be considered no longer created a backlash of indignation. Negotiation with the Taliban was now generally accepted as a reality and could be used as a possible exit strategy for Western nations embroiled in Afghanistan.[137]

The Taliban clearly demonstrated that they could quickly adapt in the face of adversity. They were able to take their defeat in Panjwayi in September 2006 and quickly recalibrate their strategy to one consistently asymmetrical, which allowed them to wield their strengths against the GIRoA and take advantages of coalition weaknesses. Abandoning any attempt to hold ground or confront superior NATO forces in a conventional battle in favour of IEDs and other terror tactics such as assassinations, kidnapping, and bombings, combined with shadow governance techniques, allowed them to gain ascendency in the insurgency.

Arguably, the Taliban defeat during OP Medusa sparked an epiphany that led the Taliban to relearn their lessons of counter-insurgency and find a more effective manner to achieve their aim. Meanwhile, although militarily superior, NATO members continue to be unable to fully leverage their tactical victories into strategic gains, proving once again that fighting in Afghanistan is no easy task.

9

Opportunity Lost

The Canadian Involvement in the Development
of the Afghan National Police

MAJOR ALEX D. HAYNES

The Canadian Forces (CF) mission to help stabilize Afghanistan has faced numerous challenges throughout the past eight years. Not least among these has been the effort to develop the nascent Afghan National Police (ANP). This daunting task of creating, from scratch, an effective national police force in the midst of a counter-insurgency campaign can be likened to building an aircraft in flight. Yet, the CF's role in this endeavour has been limited throughout much of Canada's mission in Afghanistan to the provision of a handful of police trainers and mentors within Kandahar Province, as well as some funding and equipment for the ANP. Even this modest effort has been hindered by a lack of personnel, resources, and interest from some within the CF. The net result has been a lost opportunity for the CF in its counter-insurgency campaign in Afghanistan.[1]

The CF's effort to aid in the development of the ANP raises a number of issues that warrant examination. First among these is the critical role of police forces within a counter-insurgency campaign. Police represent a vital link between the legitimate government and the populace of a country. As such, they are often the most visible manifestation of the government's authority. A counter-insurgency campaign is essentially a battle for the allegiance of the population — the insurgents and the government are each trying to convince the people that they are the rightful stewards and leaders of the state. The police, through the provision of security and the support of the legal system, can be a significant tool in a government's arsenal. By protecting a population terrorized by insurgents, and by upholding the nation's laws, police demonstrate that the government works for the benefit of the people. As one observer stated, "Reducing criminality and providing security to the public provides the most widely shared and distributed public good."[2] Conversely, ineffective or corrupt police have the exact opposite effect — namely, pushing the populace toward supporting the insurgents.

Unfortunately, the efforts of the international community to create and develop the ANP have not been commensurate with the importance of this task. Inadequate resources, uncoordinated programs, inappropriate approaches, and generally a lack of interest have all served to delay the critical task of building up Afghanistan's police force. Canada shares in the blame for this lost opportunity, as the CF and other government departments have been slow to recognize the need for developing the ANP as a critical component of success in Afghanistan. Furthermore, the initial efforts undertaken were often hampered by a lack of personnel and resources. Much of this low prioritization was due to a deficiency in the CF's understanding of the importance of developing police forces in a counter-insurgency campaign.[3]

Examining a number of historical examples provides a contextual foundation for the importance of police development in counter-insurgency campaigns. The second half of the twentieth century provides a number of case studies. Police forces are not extensively covered in much of the academic research that exists about these campaigns, but, nonetheless, that which is written does provide an insight into the critical role they play. Studying these examples, while by no means providing a template for Afghanistan, can illuminate some of the best practices used in counter-insurgency campaigns. They can also offer a warning as to what happens when police forces are poorly trained, organized, or employed.

The British experience in Malaya from 1948 to 1960 furnishes a good example of the successful use of indigenous police in a counter-insurgency campaign. This conflict witnessed the British and their Malay allies faced with a communist insurgency that drew its strength from the ethnic Chinese minority and who used Malaya's vast unpopulated jungles as a base area. The threat consisted of communist guerrilla units operating from these jungle bases, attacking populated areas, and threatening key infrastructure. Communist forces also included a political wing that conducted subversion, terrorism, and propaganda activities in the populated rural countryside and in towns.

Lacking manpower, training, and equipment, Malaya's British-led police initially were not up to the challenge of confronting and defeating the insurgents. Preliminary British efforts at stemming the insurgency included a large expansion of the police and the poorly-armed, untrained civilian home guards and auxiliary security units. The training of the expanded police force occurred largely "on the job." Predictably, these neophyte policemen had difficulty with even the most basic of tasks, such as vehicle maintenance or communications, to say nothing of tackling a determined insurgency.[4] While this expansion helped stabilize the situation, it could not defeat the insurgency or confront the insurgents in their jungle bases. Furthermore, poorly trained police were ill-equipped to handle covert political and subversive cells that hid amongst the population. Such a task requires skilled police officers supported by an efficient police intelligence system. Additionally, the auxiliary police were too poorly trained and equipped to do much more than static security tasks of vital infrastructure.

As a remedy to these shortcomings, special police jungle companies were formed that could penetrate deep into insurgent base areas in an effort to deny them sanctuary. Jungle training school taught policemen jungle survival, navigation, patrolling skills, and marksmanship.[5] Additionally, the arrival in 1952 of the commissioner of the London Metropolitan Police, Sir Arthur Young, helped encourage improvements in police training. Young began a program to retrain the entire Malayan Police force in only eighteen months. To achieve this objective, he deployed highly qualified British instructors from England to conduct the training. Emphasis was placed on developing the leadership skills of Malayan police officers and non-commissioned officers (NCOs) while also expanding the force's intelligence-gathering and investigative skill-sets. In a seemingly counterintuitive move, Young cut ten thousand personnel from the force. However, this decision to focus on quality instead of quantity was a wise one: he removed some of the most poorly trained, incompetent, and corrupt police from the force and ultimately improved the overall quality.[6]

Commissioner Young also recognized the value an effective police intelligence system and placed considerable emphasis on the improvement of the Malayan Police Special Branch. This branch became responsible for gathering and analyzing intelligence on guerrilla units and subversive cells, not just for the police but also for the army. A Special Branch training centre was established in 1952, and skilled Malay and British police officers were hand-picked by Young to lead the branch. In a further effort to improve intelligence gathering, ethnic Chinese Malayans were recruited into the force. Additionally, British and Malay police were sent on Chinese-language courses.

Emphasis on police intelligence soon paid dividends, as the police and the army were able to locate and destroy guerrilla forces with greater frequency. Improvements also enabled the police to more ably locate and eliminate political and subversive elements in populated areas. The importance of good intelligence of this type was clear to British counter-insurgency expert and Malaya veteran General Frank Kitson, who wrote, "The problem of destroying enemy armed groups and their supporters... consists very largely of finding them."[7]

Once the army and police field forces found and cleared insurgents from a district or province, the regular police had another key role to play: holding what had been won. In Malaya there were never enough army units to hold all districts and prevent infiltration by the communist guerrillas. Furthermore, army units are seldom trained or equipped to conduct the kind of community policing roles that are required in a "hold" operation of this sort. Infantry battalions are better suited to the initial clearing operations and interdictory penetrations into the guerrilla jungle strongholds. Police, on the other hand, are ideally suited to living amongst the population and offering protection from subversion and terrorism. Indeed, when subversion and terrorism are viewed as criminal-vice military problems, it becomes clear that countering it is rightly the role of police forces. Operating in small units in villages and patrolling rural areas, police can maintain regular contact with locals and provide the constant security that the populace requires. Such close contact also improves police intelligence-gathering efforts as police get to know the population and determine who supports the insurgency and who does not.

Police units also present the locals with tangible evidence of government authority and in some cases the only evidence of a central government. If the government decides to impose curfews, food controls, and restrictions on movement in contested zones to restrict support to the insurgents (as was done in Malaya), it is likewise the police who implement these measures. This approach of using police to hold what had been won in Malaya allowed the army to focus on fighting the insurgents where they were strongest rather than diluting forces to cover vast cleared areas.

Due to the multitude of key roles that police played in the counter-insurgency campaign in Malaya, decision makers quickly realized the importance of the need to expand and professionalize the police. General Sir Robert Thompson, another Malayan veteran — and former British advisor to the Americans in Vietnam — underscored this point when he stated, "The government's immediate need is to expand its police force, including the intelligence organization."[8] He insisted that this action must take precedence over expanding the military, as the latter was generally strong enough to confront the insurgents.

Nonetheless, a key lesson drawn from the Malayan experience was that police numbers alone matter less than training and competence in a counter-insurgency. By 1954 the improved Malayan police were developing actionable intelligence about insurgent groups that enabled targeted and effective sweeps of insurgent-held territory. In addition to high-quality intelligence, the Special Branch was producing professional Malay police officers who would later assume command of Malayan police when the British left. Well-trained police field-units and jungle companies were working alongside army units to clear guerrillas from populated areas and to strike into jungle bases. Finally, regular police units were holding what government forces had cleared, thereby freeing up forces for further clearances. In this manner, a more professional police force enabled the British to leave Malaya as the insurgency weakened in 1960. U.S. counter-insurgency expert James Corum concluded, "The British could withdraw forces, confident that the Malaya Police and the army could take over responsibilities, thanks to their thorough training and the presence of a cadre of competent indigenous officers."[9]

In stark contrast to the successful development of police forces in Malaya is the British experience battling a Greek insurgency in Cyprus from 1953 to 1959. A British possession since its capture from the Ottoman Empire in 1878, the eastern Mediterranean island's population was largely Greek with a small Turkish minority. A small element of that Greek population sought union with Greece and resorted to subversion and terrorism to oust the British when diplomatic pressure from Greece was unsuccessful. Unwilling to cede control of the strategically important island, the British government felt it must fight the insurgents.

At the beginning of that campaign, the Cypriot police were poorly organized, trained, equipped, and led. Consequently, they were unprepared to deal with the insurgency. The inadequate pay of both local policemen and British colonial police meant morale was low and the force had difficulty attracting quality personnel. Quite simply, the colonial administration was reluctant to spend scarce resources on police forces. Officers lacked basic items such as flashlights and police posts were often dilapidated shacks.[10] Not surprisingly, the Cypriot police were corrupt and largely ineffective. On meagre pay and with little equipment, few were willing to risk actively hunting determined insurgents.

To add to these problems, the Greek insurgents infiltrated the police force. This provided the insurgents with key intelligence regarding counter-insurgency operations and security-force intentions. There were also sympathizers within the Cypriot police force who would protect wanted insurgents, greatly impeding counter-insurgency efforts. Finally, those in the police force who refused to support the insurgents were targeted and often killed.

The British colonial administration responded by hiring more Turkish Cypriot police and establishing a poorly trained auxiliary force.[11] This response did nothing to address the underlying causes of inefficiency within the Cypriot police. Moreover, no effort was made to improve police training, leadership, pay, or equipment problems. Far more damaging, however, was the decision to employ large numbers of *Turkish* Cypriots in the expanded force. Predictably, this action alienated the Greek population while also diminishing the police's ability to gather intelligence from locals. Rather than being seen as a force that provided security and represented the rule of law, the corrupt and ethnically unbalanced Cypriot police provoked animosity from the Greek population.[12]

A commission of senior British police officers visited Cyprus in 1956 to evaluate the police and made several recommendations: improving pay and training, disbanding the auxiliary forces, and improving the indigenous police leadership. However, the governor general of Cyprus ignored these recommendations and instead continued to expand the police and auxiliaries (mostly with Turkish Cypriots). No efforts were made to improve training, as had been done in Malaya. The British strategy focused on destroying insurgent cells and interdicting their supply routes rather than on developing police intelligence capabilities.

This strategy proved to be a failure. The poorly trained police, drawn mostly from one ethnic group, used heavy-handed tactics and sparked communal violence between the Greeks and Turks on the island. Furthermore, the lack of intelligence meant that the British-Cypriot security forces of almost 40,000 were unable to defeat or even effectively disrupt an insurgent force of only 200.[13]

The Cypriot example demonstrates what can occur when poorly trained, organized, recruited, and led police are unleashed on an insurgency. At best they are ineffective, and at worst they only serve to fuel the conflict. The British colonial administration emphasized numbers over efficiency and effectiveness. Moreover, they were blind to the critical role police can play in winning the allegiance of a population. Likewise, no effort was made to use the police to gather critical intelligence from the population. Rather, the police were a valuable source of intelligence for the insurgents and a threat to the counter-insurgency forces' operational security. Much of what was done in Cyprus can be regarded as a negative example of developing and employing police forces in a counter-insurgency campaign.

The U.S. experience in South Vietnam during the 1960s against a communist insurgency mirrors some aspects of the British experience in both Malaya and Cyprus. Faced with a fierce and active insurgency supported from communist North Vietnam, the U.S. and the South Vietnamese governments recognized the need to bolster police numbers. "Police were considered a crucial element in the process of holding areas once cleared of Viet Cong guerrillas," author and counter-insurgency expert Robert Taber explained. He insisted they were vital to "check on all movements within the country, to ferret out suspected Viet Cong agents, and to maintain law and order in the villages, where the official links with the central government have broken down."[14] This was in recognition of the previously mentioned fact that police are often best suited to holding an area cleared of insurgents, due to their contact with and intimate knowledge of the people. It was also an admission of the reality that, for many rural Vietnamese, their only contact with the government was the National Police.

In keeping with this concept, in 1961 the government reinforced the South Vietnamese police force, bringing it up to seventy-two thousand personnel deployed in eleven police institutes throughout the country.[15] Despite this effort, training was of poor quality and there was no attempt made to mentor the new policemen once they had deployed to the districts. With poor supervision and little follow-up, the South Vietnamese National Police remained largely ineffective.[16] Consequently, the police never completely fulfilled the mandate to hold cleared areas or represent government authority in villages and hamlets. Nor were the South Vietnamese police able to provide much in the way of actionable intelligence as did the police forces in Malaya. In part, this was due to the lack of integration between the National Police and the armed forces of South Vietnam and the U.S.

Rather than address these shortcomings, the American and South Vietnamese authorities instead developed a number of different paramilitary local defence forces to provide the needed security. This diluted the resources that otherwise could have been allocated to training and equipping a more effective police force. For example, the Civil Guard and Popular Forces both took on roles that fall within the realm of policing or a rural constabulary force, but did so with even less training than the National Police. Similar to Cyprus, South Vietnam provides an example of the inadequacy of a policy that emphasizes quantity over quality. Unlike Cyprus, however, the counter-insurgency campaign in Vietnam provides an instructive lesson regarding the consequences of diluting focus and responsibility with a number of police-like forces.

In recent years, commentators, experts, and academics have begun to argue more clearly and forcefully for the necessity of developing police forces, especially in Afghanistan. These writings echo much of what counter-insurgency experts like Sir Robert Thompson and Frank Kitson wrote in the 1960s and 1970s. Political scientist Seth Jones clearly articulated this point in a study on the campaign in Afghanistan for the RAND Corporation. "Building the police in counterinsurgencies," he argued, "should be a higher priority than the creation of the army because the police are the primary arm of the government in towns and villages across the country."[17] The International Crisis Group places even greater emphasis on the issue in a report concerning the ANP: "In countering an insurgency, the police are the first line of defence as the interface with the community."[18]

This growing chorus of expert opinion about the development of indigenous police forces is indicative of the realization that progress in Afghanistan is linked in many ways to progress in developing the ANP. This belated recognition of the need to develop police forces started a drive among many Western militaries to create doctrine describing this activity.

Prior to the U.S.-led liberation of Afghanistan and the subsequent invasion of Iraq, no manuals existed in either the U.S. or British militaries to articulate the principles and techniques for the development of indigenous police forces. After 2001, however, the need to create, train, equip and mentor the ANP and the Iraqi Police provided a strong impetus to develop such doctrine. Granted, much of this new doctrine is subsumed within manuals relating generally to counter-insurgency or the development of security forces as a whole. Nonetheless, the effort devoted to the creation and adoption of police-force-development doctrine underscores the importance of that task in current operations in Afghanistan and Iraq. Doctrine provides the basis for armed forces training and education and therefore is a good indicator of what the armed forces consider important.

Although the CF has often been criticized for not always strictly adhering to its own doctrine, a review of Canadian doctrine is still important, as it provides insight into how the CF approaches police mentoring. The new CF doctrine on counter-insurgency recognizes the importance of indigenous police forces and states that they "may play a valuable role in the conduct of a COIN [counter-insurgency] mission and will be a key element in a comprehensive approach."[19] However, what is not covered in any detail is the development of those indigenous police forces by Canadian military forces, beyond the statement that "military forces may be used, at least initially in a campaign, to train indigenous civilian police."[20]

Indeed, most of the discussion in the manual assumes that indigenous police are generally competent and able to contribute to the counter-insurgency fight. Recent experience in Afghanistan has demonstrated that this is not always the case. What is lacking from the CF publication *Counter-Insurgency Operations*, and likewise from CF doctrine as a whole, is a description of how indigenous police forces are to be developed, trained, and mentored by Canadian military forces. This dearth of doctrine is indicative of the degree of importance the CF accords to indigenous police force development.

In contrast, the new joint United States Army–United States Marine Corps manual *Counterinsurgency* devotes an entire twenty-two-page chapter to the topic of developing indigenous security forces, and it goes into considerable detail regarding how that is to be done. Concerning indigenous police development, the manual underlines its importance by stating, "The primary frontline COIN force is often the police — not the military."[21] Although not exhaustive, the manual does provide a threshold level of detail regarding the organization and training of indigenous police forces, as well as principles and techniques for combined military-police operations.

The U.S. military recently expanded upon this doctrinal foundation with the publishing of a new manual on Security Force Assistance (SFA), which is defined as "the unified action to generate, employ, and sustain local, host-nation, or regional security forces in support of a legitimate authority."[22] While SFA refers to assistance provided throughout the spectrum of war, the tenets and methods within the manual are well-suited to the development of indigenous forces in a counter-insurgency campaign. Much of the effort to develop and promulgate SFA doctrine, lessons learned, and best practices is spearheaded by the Joint Centre for International Security Force Assistance at Fort Leavenworth, the director of which is a lieutenant-general who is double-hatted as the commander of the U.S. Army Combined Arms Centre.[23] The considerable effort devoted by the U.S. military to the creation and implementation of doctrine relating to the development of indigenous security forces reinforces the importance attached to such activities.

Similar to U.S. doctrine, the manuals of British forces place a greater emphasis and provide more detail on indigenous police force development than does Canadian doctrine. The joint manual *Security and Stabilization: The Military Contribution* includes an entire chapter on security-force capacity building, which includes the development of police forces. Indeed, this manual goes so far as to assert that "police primacy should be the ultimate goal,"[24] thereby underscoring the importance attached to police development above even the development of military forces. The manual includes advice on how military forces can contribute to the development of indigenous security forces, from the tactical to strategic level.

This progress in creating police-force development doctrine has only occurred within the last two years (2008–2010), however. The multinational coalition fighting the Taliban insurgency has been operating for almost eight years though, and much of what was done to develop the ANP since 2002 has transpired in a doctrinal vacuum. Accomplishments by the coalition in that time were based on ad hoc approaches with little theoretical grounding. Those developing the ANP could not open a manual to find possible solutions to the myriad problems encountered when creating a force from scratch. No military officers or civilians were trained in the methods and precepts that should govern the development of indigenous police forces, nor did any of the member nations of the coalition possess recent experience in creating a national police force under such circumstances. As would be expected, the need to learn on the job meant that the coalition's efforts to develop the ANP did not always go smoothly.

In the vacuum that followed the 2001 defeat of the Taliban, Afghanistan's police forces largely consisted of untrained and poorly equipped members of various warlord militias. There was no system of law and order that most in the west would understand; rather, the police, such as they were in Afghanistan, existed to protect the interests of warlords and extort tolls on Afghanistan's highways. In fact, the country did not have a national police force since the fall of the communist regime almost a decade before the defeat of the Taliban. There was little memory of a formed police force among the population, and there were few trained police officers in the country when the coalition arrived. The ANP had to be created from scratch.

Following the demise of the Taliban, the development of the ANP began in the spring of 2002. Under an agreement reached between members of the multi-national coalition, Germany assumed responsibility for the development of the fledgling ANP. The German effort focused on the creation of a professional, highly trained police force structured toward the maintenance of public law and order. To this end, a police academy was built in Kabul and staffed with German police instructors.

Prospective police officers and non-commissioned officers received formal and extensive training on the model of a professional, Western police force. For the former, this training entailed a three-year course, and for the latter, a year-long course (later reduced to nine months). The intent was to build a strong leadership cadre that would guide the ANP toward professionalization and greater competency.[25] The decision by the German government to focus on a police force of this type, instead of a force optimized for counter-insurgency, would have repercussions as the development of the ANP progressed. While the ANP needed professional police leadership, they also needed policemen and officers trained in the intricacies of counter-insurgency tactics.

This system addressed the need for professional police officers and non-commissioned officers but did little to prepare the rank-and-file ANP policemen for their role. Furthermore, the German focus on law-and-order training instead of paramilitary counter-insurgency training meant that even the professionals their system produced were ill-suited for the fight against the Taliban.[26] Aggravating this problem was the fact that the ANP who completed the German training program deployed to the provinces and districts of Afghanistan with no follow-up training or mentoring. This deficiency went all the way up to the Afghan Ministry of the Interior, the ministry responsible for the ANP. That ministry was poorly staffed and was widely known for corruption and inefficiency.[27]

The system devised and implemented by the Germans, although admirable in its goals, did not meet the needs of counter-insurgency campaign then taking shape in Afghanistan. Nor did it provide the numbers of police required to provide security throughout the country's lawless provinces. The first class of professional police officers was not due to graduate from the Kabul Police Academy until well into 2005, but there was an urgent need to grow the ANP well before that date. Despite that reality, no effort was made to train junior policemen, and other than a handful of vehicles and some infrastructure projects in Kabul, the Germans did little to address the other deficiencies of the ANP. [28]

Consequently, in 2003 the Americans decided to take over responsibility for training the bulk of the ANP. Germany retained its status as the "lead nation" for police development, and the U.S. diplomatically claimed only to be helping with the German effort. In reality the U.S. contribution of both money and trainers quickly dwarfed anything the Germans had accomplished. The U.S. Department of State's Bureau of International Narcotics and Law Enforcement Affairs (INL) assumed responsibility for the U.S. police-development effort and began pouring hundreds of millions of dollars into developing the ANP. A Central Training Centre was established in Kabul, as were seven Regional Training Centres (RTCs) throughout the country. The private security company DynCorp received the INL contract to staff and run these training centres, which relied largely on retired U.S. police officers as instructors. Soon, thousands of ANP policemen were graduating from two-week basic training courses and were deployed throughout the country.

While the American approach appeared to meet the need for large numbers of policemen quickly, there were conspicuous problems. As with the German program, there was no follow-up or mentoring of ANP in the provinces and districts once they had deployed. This meant that many of the hastily-trained ANP reverted to virtual tribal or warlord militias and returned to their old habits of extortion and theft — only this time in police uniforms.[29] Unlike the German program, the DynCorp training program produced only low-quality, undisciplined, and poorly equipped policemen. Courses ranged in length from two to eight weeks, depending on a candidate's literacy and previous experience. Most trainees only received the two-week course, since 70 percent of ANP recruits were illiterate and therefore ineligible for the longer courses.[30] The U.S. program placed far too much emphasis on quantity over quality, with consequences that have been seen before.

By mid-2005, the U.S. recognized that the Department of State's approach was no more successful than the German plan in providing the police force Afghanistan so desperately needed. The American government decided to shift responsibility for developing the ANP to the U.S. Department of Defense, although DynCorp retained its training contract. The multi-national Combined Security Transition Command — Afghanistan (CSTC-A), which was already charged with the development of the Afghan National Army (ANA), assumed responsibility for the implementation of police development. Early efforts by CSTC-A included a program to reform the inept Afghan Ministry of the Interior through the provision of military advisors and strategic planners. Also, CSTC-A placed considerably more emphasis on equipping the ANP and providing suitable infrastructure in the form of police stations throughout the country. The ANP rank and pay system was revised to increase pay for the rank-and-file while decreasing the large number of senior police officers.

However, as with earlier German and INL programs, the CSTC-A approach was still far from perfect. A 2006 combined U.S. Department of State–Department of Defense report noted that the program, while improving the training and equipping of the ANP, still lacked a mentoring system that would follow up on the DynCorp training. This deficiency meant that CSTC-A could not accurately report on the number of ANP in the field, nor could it account for the equipment issued to the police. More importantly, as with earlier efforts, there was no system in place to ensure the ANP were effectively performing their role as police officers.[31] CSTC-A had little visibility on what the ANP were doing once they left the training centres. Accordingly, while CSTC-A was reporting that over seventy thousand ANP had been trained since 2003, only thirty thousand could be considered trained and equipped to function as police.[32]

The over-reporting of police numbers was indicative of a larger problem within the ANP. One conclusion is that many of the trained police were either deserting or were casualties. However, this did not account for the entire discrepancy, and it was learned early on in the CSTC-A program that many provincial and district chiefs-of-police were over-reporting the number of policemen in their commands in order to claim the excess salaries. This was possible because chiefs-of-police were responsible for paying their subordinates with money delivered from the Ministry of the Interior in Kabul. With no system in place to verify actual police numbers on the ground, corrupt chiefs-of-police could inflate the reported numbers of their subordinates and pocket the surplus money. Particularly unscrupulous chiefs-of-police took this a step further by withholding salaries from the majority of their policemen, both real and fictional. Graft was not limited to pay, and senior ANP officers stole equipment and supplies before they could reach the field forces. Morale in the ANP plummeted because of this corruption, and retention of trained policemen became increasingly difficult.

Once again, coalition forces realized that a new approach was needed to address the shortcomings of previous police-development programs. Under American leadership, CSTC-A developed a program called Focussed District Development (FDD). Under FDD, entire districts of ANP would be removed to a RTC for eight weeks of training or re-training under DynCorp instructors. While the ANP were at the RTC, the newly formed and better-trained Afghan National Civil Order Police (ANCOP) would assume responsibility for policing in the vacated district.[33] Better equipment was issued at the RTC, including body armour, boots, and sufficient weapons to equip all policemen. To address the issue of graft and corruption, all policemen processed through the RTC were issued with an identification card as well as access to a bank account where their pay would be deposited. Chiefs-of-police would no longer be responsible for distributing pay to their subordinates and could therefore no longer skim salaries for their own profit.

In a significant departure from previous programs, American Police Mentor Teams (PMTs) would accompany the newly trained ANP upon the completion of their training at the RTC. These teams, one assigned per district, were made up of about ten U.S. military officers and soldiers, as well as one or two civilian police mentors provided by DynCorp. The team would mentor the ANP over a period of at least six months and would provide the mentorship, oversight, and accountability that had been lacking in previous approaches. Once the ANP of a district had reached a certain level of capability, whereby they could operate without close mentoring and supervision, the PMT would move to another district and begin the process again.

Under FDD, CSTC-A anticipated that it would take approximately nine months of training and mentoring before a district would no longer require PMT support. With 365 police districts in Afghanistan, a limited number of American PMTs, and only seven RTCs to conduct the training, FDD was by necessity a long-term project. By January 2009, fifty-two police districts had undergone FDD — less than one-seventh of all districts. Furthermore, a shortage of PMTs and civilian police mentors limited the number of districts mentored following the RTC training program. In 2009 the U.S. was only able to provide one-third of the PMTs required to implement the program.[34]

Exacerbating this was the realization by American PMTs that it took much longer than nine months to improve a police district to the point where mentors could leave. In April 2008, the U.S. Government Accounting Office noted that none of the ANP's 433 units (districts, headquarters, and special units) were capable of performing without coalition support, and 75 percent were at the lowest capability rating.[35] Even so, FDD represented the first attempt at developing the ANP in a more holistic manner. Training, mentoring, equipment, and pay were all addressed.

Also in 2007, as FDD was being developed and implemented by CSTC-A, Germany formally relinquished its role as the lead state for police development in Afghanistan. The European Union assumed Germany's responsibilities with the formation of a police mission known as EUPOL. The mission had an authorized strength of four hundred European police officers and was charged with mentoring and advising the ANP on the establishment of a professional civilian police force. In other words, EUPOL focused on the law-and-order aspect of policing as opposed to the counter-insurgency aspect of the ANP's development.

Despite its limited mandate and size, the EUPOL mission was hindered by a number of challenges almost from inception. EU member states were reluctant to contribute the necessary numbers of police officers to staff the mission. Also, a lack of force protection for the few EUPOL officers prevented them from operating outside of secure locations like coalition bases. Coordination between CSTC-A and EUPOL left much to be desired, meaning ANP often received divergent advice and support from the two organizations.[36]

As CSTC-A and EUPOL increased efforts to improve Afghanistan's police throughout 2007, the CF took on a greater role in developing the ANP. Prior to this development, the CF had played a limited role in training the ANP. In Kabul, where Canada first deployed in 2003, this support was limited to some low-level training and partnering with police in the city. Elements of the Canadian battle group would conduct joint patrols and cordon-and-search operations with police forces. However, there was no formal mentoring program in effect, and much of what was done was the result of the initiative of commanders on the ground rather than top-down direction.

Once the CF moved to Kandahar in 2005, the newly established Provincial Reconstruction Team (PRT) in Kandahar City took on the role of training the ANP in that province. CF military police taught ANP policemen basic soldiering and policing skills and accompanied them on some missions. Similarly, elements of the Joint Task Force — Afghanistan (JTF-A) Battle Group often partnered with ANP for operations where it was necessary or beneficial to have Afghan police present to interact with the local population. As in Kabul, much of the effort to develop and partner with the ANP was based on bottom-up initiatives.[37]

The establishment of the Kandahar PRT also saw the introduction of Canadian civilian police officers, known as CIVPOL. Drawn from police forces across Canada, the CIVPOL element in the PRT was charged with training ANP in policing skills as well as advising the ANP on administrative, logistical, policy, and operational issues. CIVPOL officers, much like EUPOL officers, were reliant on coalition forces for mobility and force protection. In the PRT, this reliance not only meant a close working relationship developed with the CF forces but also that CIVPOL were often confined to the PRT camp.

The early Canadian low-level efforts to train the ANP in Kandahar province did not fully fulfill the requirements of the CF or the ANP, however. Too few ANP were mentored and what little was done was confined mostly to Kandahar City. In September 2007, the CF hastily formed a new sub-unit in Afghanistan that was intended to mentor and train the ANP in the Zhari and Panjwayi districts of Kandahar Province.[38] This new sub-unit was designated the Police Operational Mentoring and Liaison Team (P-OMLT). It was formed by reassigning a team from the Operational Mentoring and Liaison Team (OMLT) designed to mentor an ANA *Kandak* (battalion) and combining it with a platoon of military policemen (MPs) from the JTF-A Military Police Company.[39]

The formation of the P-OMLT was not linked in any formal way to the CSTC-A FDD program and was not part of a larger Canadian government plan to contribute to the development of the ANP. Rather, it was a local initiative started by JTF-A to address two urgent needs: to improve the survivability of the ANP operating in JTF-A's area of responsibility and to generate much-needed forces to retain terrain in the critical districts of Zhari and Panjwayi. In 2007 the ANP in Kandahar Province were taking considerable casualties in the fight against Taliban insurgents, due in large part to their poor equipment and training. JTF-A also had to contend with the issue of holding ground in Kandahar Province with only one battle group (BG) of Canadian soldiers and less than a brigade of ANA troops.[40] The ANP provided the additional manpower that JTF-A needed for operations, and the P-OMLT provided a solution to the tactical problem of holding ground.

The fix involved sending teams of eight to ten combat-arms soldiers and MPs from the P-OMLT to live and operate with the ANP in small "forts" called Police Sub Stations (PSS) that were spread throughout Zhari and Panjwayi districts. The CF leadership in Afghanistan hoped that directly embedding Canadian soldiers with the ANP would help train, professionalize, mentor, and coordinate the activities of that fledgling police force. The OMLT had already demonstrated the template for embedding with and mentoring ANA units, which the P-OMLT replicated with the ANP. OMLT teams trained their ANA counterparts, coordinated and de-conflicted their activities with other coalition forces, and brought enablers like artillery, close air support, and medical evacuation to the fight in support of the ANA. Prior to September 2007, no such training or coordination support had been offered to the ANP, and as a result, the ANP in the rural districts of Kandahar were poorly trained and integrated with the CF.[41]

Initially, the P-OMLT and its associated mentored ANP were deployed in PSSs in the western parts of Zhari and Panjwayi, areas still replete with Taliban insurgents. The small CF teams and handful of ANP they mentored were entrusted with the task of protecting key roads through those districts. Taliban activity near these PSSs limited what the still-untrained and poorly equipped ANP could accomplish, and in some cases P-OMLT mentors and their affiliated ANP were attacked on an almost daily basis. Even with mentors present, the ANP were unprepared to assume a role better-suited to light infantry. By necessity, mentoring in these beleaguered PSSs was limited to improving the ANPs ability to fight and survive — there was little scope for teaching community-policing skills or investigative techniques.

Less than six months after the establishment of the P-OMLT, the most vulnerable PSSs in western Zhari and Panjwayi were handed over to the ANA or elements from the battle group. The P-OMLT teams and their affiliated ANP were relocated away from the most contested areas of those districts. The focus became a series of PSSs in central Zhari and Panjwayi, areas more secure and better suited to the ANP. The role remained largely the same, with P-OMLT teams and ANP detachments guarding and patrolling key routes on which much of JTF-A's logistical supplies moved. Development of the ANP by the Task Force (TF) 1-08 P-OMLT was still limited to improving survivability and patrolling skills, which were arguably very necessary given the continuing paramilitary role of the police

In September of 2008, the third rotation of P-OMLT mentors deployed to Afghanistan as part of Task Force 3-08 (TF-308).[42] Occupying the positions in central Zhari and Panjwayi that had been manned by the previous P-OMLT, the TF 3-08 police mentors initially assumed many of the same roles as their predecessors. However, the first FDD recruits began arriving in these two critical districts during the summer of 2008. These post-FDD ANP arrived from the RTCs with better survivability and fighting skills, as well as better equipment. Better weapons handling and patrolling skills were noted among the RTC trained police, and, generally, they demonstrated a fair level of competence in dismounted patrols.

As a result, the TF 3-08 P-OMLT assessed the training needs of post-FDD ANP and determined there was an opportunity to shift the mentoring focus away from simply improving the ANP survivability and fighting skills. A long-term mentoring plan was developed, whereby the TF 3-08 P-OMLT would mentor the ANP in an expanded array of topics. The foundation of the plan was four key skill areas, or "pillars," relating to the skills the P-OMLT leadership determined the ANP required. First, and of foremost importance, was the development of ANP leadership skills at the district, platoon, and squad levels. It was recognized that the vast majority of problems in the ANP could be traced back to corrupt, incompetent, or inexperienced leadership. What is more, it was noted that training and mentoring the rank-and-file policemen would only ever provide a short-term solution to the ANP's problems. Developing capable leaders was the only way of enabling the ANP to eventually reach higher levels of capability and ultimately function without mentorship.

Therefore, the TF 3-08 P-OMLT leadership decided to reorganize the sub-unit to allow for a greater focus on mentoring the ANP leadership in Zhari and Panjwayi. Previous P-OMLTs, for good reason, had focused most of their effort on developing the ANP squads with whom they were partnered, and relatively little effort was devoted to formally mentoring leaders above the squad level. The TF 3-08 P-OMLT created a platoon headquarters in each district that was responsible for mentoring the district chiefs-of-police and their staff.[43] The added benefit of these platoon headquarters was that individual P-OMLT teams of eight to twelve soldiers in the districts were now under the command of one headquarters, which enabled better coordination and control. Moreover, these headquarters provided a focus at the district level for co-operation with the myriad organizations implicated in police mentoring and development issues.

With the platoon headquarters established, the P-OMLT engaged in mentoring and advising the chiefs-of-police and their staff on a wide variety of issues, ranging from operational matters to personnel problems. The platoon headquarters developed their counterparts' ability to plan and conduct police operations, manage resources, handle personnel administration, and deliver training to their subordinates. The platoon commanders also had the sensitive task of confronting the chiefs-of-police with ethical or even criminal issues, such as corruption, extortion, theft, and the use of underage ANP officers. In all cases, the tact, patience, and wisdom of the young platoon commanders and their headquarters staff ensured the proper resolution of difficult situations.

At the ANP platoon and squad level, P-OMLT section commanders performed many of the same roles as their platoon commanders in developing leadership skills.[44] In addition to this mentoring relationship, Sergeant Roger Marcinowski, the P-OMLT operations warrant officer (WO), developed and delivered an ANP squad leader's course modeled on the CF junior leader course. Selected ANP squad leaders were put through two weeks of training, which included instruction on leadership and ethics, police law, battle procedure, patrolling, police operations, investigations, check points, and logistics. During this course, the candidates were required to plan and lead a patrol as a final test. The results were worth the effort. The P-OMLT operations WO insisted that the top candidates on the course could lead a CF patrol.

The second pillar of the TF 3-08 mentoring plan entailed the development of ANP policing skills. Used mainly as a paramilitary force or a more lightly armed version of the ANA, the ANP had received little in the way of police-specific training. Low literacy rates among even the chiefs-of-police meant that training the ANP in investigative techniques and forensics was difficult. Where such topics could be taught (during the squad leader's course, for example) they were, but otherwise the P-OMLT had to lower its expectations. Therefore, the emphasis at the squad level was placed on training the ANP in such topics as detainee handling, vehicle and building searches, and the conduct of checkpoints. These skills could be taught through demonstration and did not require literacy on the part of the ANP.

The P-OMLT leadership also recognized that to improve the ANP's ability to police the communities in which they operated, it was necessary to encourage them to interact with the population. While this may seem obvious, the ANP's use as a paramilitary force often meant its members adopted an aggressive posture when on patrol and seldom interacted with locals. Indeed, the ANP leadership in Zhari and Panjwayi were frequently more interested in hunting and engaging the Taliban than in interacting with the populace. While confronting and defeating the insurgents was a necessary function in those contested districts, so too was winning the support of the civilian population. Significant was the fact that the ANP did not have a good reputation among many of the civilians, owing to past incidents of extortion and heavy-handedness.

As a result, the P-OMLT strongly encouraged the ANP to develop relationships with village leaders and ordinary civilians. Patrols were tasked with simply talking to locals. Moreover, ANP policemen were exhorted to adopt a friendly demeanour when doing so. Additionally, a Canadian Tactical Psychological Operations (PSYOPS) Team was invited to instruct key ANP leaders and policemen in the conduct of *shuras*, or traditional Afghan meetings, and in the delivery of PSYOPS messages. This effort paid dividends as the ANP in Zhari and Panjwayi began leading shuras in some villages near their PSSs. Anecdotal evidence from the TF 3-08 P-OMLT platoon and section commanders also indicated that locals began to approach the ANP more frequently and displayed a more positive attitude toward patrols.

The efforts to develop the ANP's leadership and community-policing skills met with some success; however, greater difficulty was encountered in the third pillar — logistics. During TF 3-08's deployment, the ANP suffered from shortages of every imaginable form of supplies, ranging from trucks to ammunition to food. The P-OMLT leadership appreciated that this critical shortcoming would hinder the ANP's ability to perform even the most basic of tasks. Unfortunately, the P-OMLT was also relatively powerless to supply what the ANP needed. Therefore, the mentors at platoon and P-OMLT headquarters devoted a great deal of effort to getting the ANP supply system to work.

DynCorp and American military mentors at the ANP Provincial Headquarters were responsible for assisting the police in delivering logistical support. The P-OMLT headquarters, therefore, spent a considerable amount of time trying to convince and cajole those mentors to ensure the provision of much needed supplies. A parallel system was created, whereby the ANP district staff would submit a request for supplies to the Provincial Headquarters and the P-OMLT chain-of-command would forward a copy to the American mentors working there. Nonetheless, for unknown reasons, few of those requests were ever actioned and the ANP continued to lack critical supplies for much of the almost eight months of TF 3-08's deployment.

To compensate for the failings of the ANP logistics system, P-OMLT mentors resorted to using Canadian money to buy what was lacking. Both the Canadian CIVPOL and Department of Foreign Affairs and International Trade (DFAIT) teams in Kandahar had access to money that could be used to buy supplies such as boots, office supplies, and furniture. In co-operation with CIVPOL and DFAIT, the P-OMLT drew up and submitted for approval a list of critical supplies. Despite minor bureaucratic delays, some of these supplies were delivered and did help to alleviate the ANP's supply problems. Nonetheless, this was far from a perfect situation as the preference within the P-OMLT was to empower and enable the ANP to use their own system instead of creating a dependency on Canadian support.

The final pillar of the TF 3-08 P-OMLT mentoring plan entailed continued improvement to the ANP's survivability skills with two separate efforts: providing some modicum of training for policemen who had not yet received FDD training and building on the skills of those ANP who had been through an RTC. In the case of the former, much of the training centred on weapons handling and patrolling skills and was taught by the P-OMLT sections at the PSSs. Additionally, P-OMLT section commander Captain Hank Crawley developed and delivered a three-day basic training course for non-FDD trained ANP. For those ANP who had passed through the FDD process, the mentoring effort was largely focused on developing counter-improvised explosive device (counter-IED) skills. As the ANP were employed principally in the protection of key routes through Zhari and Panjwayi, this was an important skill set to have. Indeed, one P-OMLT section and ANP squad in Panjwayi were responsible for daily IED-clearance patrols along a stretch of road over twenty kilometres long. With training and mentoring, the ANP squad was able to independently conduct those IED sweeps by the end of TF 3-08's deployment.

Despite the progress that the TF 3-08 P-OMLT's efforts were beginning to show, by the end of the deployment in April 2009, the JTF-A leadership decided to eliminate the P-OMLT as a sub-unit. The P-OMLT sections of TF 1-09 were transferred to the PRT and were distributed among two new stabilization companies. The P-OMLT headquarters formed the command element of Stabilization Company "B" and therefore could no longer focus solely on police development. Three P-OMLT sections remained under command of this company, and three others redeployed to Kandahar City under command of Stabilization Company "A." Also included in these new companies were infantry platoons for force protections, civil-military co-operation teams, engineer project management teams, and district coordination centres.[45]

The obvious effect of this reorganization was that there was no longer one sub-unit responsible for coordinating CF police development efforts. In effect it was a reversion to the approach used before TF 3-08, where individual P-OMLT teams acted with greater autonomy. Lost in this new approach was much of the focus on developing the leadership of the ANP in Zhari and Panjwayi, although the benefit was increased mentoring of ANP in the vital districts of Kandahar City.

One constant throughout the short lifespan of the P-OMLT as a formed sub-unit was change. However, this change was not always positive, and there was a constant pressure to do away with the P-OMLT and "get out of the police mentoring business." Many CF officers failed to appreciate the importance of developing police forces in a counter-insurgency campaign. Likewise, few understood the need for police forces to act as actual police instead of a less well-armed version of the ANA. There were notable exceptions to these attitudes, but as explained below, the development of the P-OMLT is indicative of the overall mindset within the CF regarding police development. There are two principal reasons for this attitude within the CF. One is a lack of understanding with regard to what the P-OMLT is and what it does. The second is the limited understanding of the importance of police forces in a counterinsurgency campaign.

Firstly, and perhaps the most obvious, is the fact that very few officers or soldiers understand what the P-OMLT is and how it operates. This is completely understandable, as very few precedents and no doctrine exist for the P-OMLT. The P-OMLT is not primarily a kinetic force, and the results of P-OMLT activities generally cannot be seen immediately. Mentoring, coaching, liaising, and coordinating are all tasks that are difficult to quantify and do not lend themselves to simple explanation. Most in the army generally understand what a battle group does and how it does it. Therefore, it is relatively easy for the army as an institution to wrap its head around generating, training, and employing a battle group. With the P-OMLT, there is no such institutional understanding, as doctrine or TTPs (tactics, techniques, and procedures) do not exist. Material that does exist provides scant guidance, and, besides, was only published a year *after* the P-OMLT was actually created. This fact makes it difficult to quantify the value of the P-OMLT or justify its existence.

Adding to this general lack of awareness was the fact that developing police forces is not something that is intuitively within the realm of the military's responsibility. "Not surprisingly, then," a former senior U.S. Army police mentor explained, "the development of the Afghan army is well ahead of the development of the Afghan police, as we are much more comfortable building an army than a police force."[46] These words apply equally to the Canadian experience in mentoring the ANA and ANP as they do to the American experience. Even CF military police have had little experience, and no doctrine, that prepared them for the development of an indigenous police force in a counter-insurgency campaign.

A side effect of the general lack of knowledge regarding policing was that coalition commanders tended to employ the ANP like a paramilitary force. In this author's experience, there were numerous occasions where the ANP were expected to accompany CF elements on sweeps through insurgent-held territory. Occasionally, the ANP were expected to take part in the operations over several days, despite the fact they lacked everything from sleeping bags to portable rations. Protests from the P-OMLT leadership that the ANP were not equipped or trained for such operations and could be better used policing cleared areas were ignored.

This was no minor issue, as misemploying the ANP as light infantry affected their ability to provide security for the population. "Employ[ing] the police on counter-insurgency tasks to the exclusion of local law-and-order and rule of law activities," respected counter-insurgency expert David Kilcullen explains, "creat[ed] a governance vacuum at the district level, which the Taliban have filled."[47]

A second reason for the reticence in some minds regarding the utility of the P-OMLT stems from the fact that, up until very recently, there has been little literature or analysis concerning the importance of indigenous police forces in a counter-insurgency campaign. That which does exist pales in comparison to the writings on the tactical employment of coalition forces in a counter-insurgency context and is even drowned out by the research and literature concerning the development of indigenous armies and militias. In other words, there is a lot to read about how external and coalition forces — that is, non-indigenous forces — should operate in a counter-insurgency fight, but surprisingly little dealing with how and why indigenous police forces should operate. The earlier examples of police forces in Malaya, Cyprus, and Vietnam are relatively unknown and are certainly not taught in the CF military education system. It is understandable, therefore, that few except the most prescient or insightful officers could recognize the need for an organization like the P-OMLT.

This general lack of understanding regarding the need for developing police forces often meant the P-OMLT was low in priority of JTF-A units for personnel and equipment. The experience of the TF 3-08 P-OMLT provides a telling demonstration of this fact. Formed with a full sub-unit headquarters and nine mentoring sections in Canada, the TF 3-08 P-OMLT was cut to six teams before even deploying to Afghanistan. Those three teams would have been sufficient to mentor a third police district above and beyond Zhari and Panjwayi. Furthermore, once the

TF 3-08 P-OMLT deployed to Kandahar, all of the sub-unit headquarters' drivers, gunners, signallers and staff officers were stripped away to reinforce other organizations within the OMLT.[48] The three armoured vehicles of the P-OMLT headquarters were similarly re-assigned. These cuts were not due to an overall shortage of manpower within JTF-A, as the headquarters, battle group, and PRT all grew during this period, sometimes significantly. The fact that these cuts were made shows there was little interest in maintaining the current police mentoring efforts, let alone expanding the program. Again, while this is perhaps understandable given the general lack of awareness regarding indigenous police development, it represents a lost opportunity for the CF.

Personnel and vehicle shortages also meant the P-OMLT had to assume greater risks than other organizations within JTF-A. Whereas most other CF elements in Kandahar would not travel outside a forward operating base with fewer than three vehicles, the small P-OMLT teams often had to move in single vehicles. Dismounted patrols were no different: as few as three P-OMLT mentors conducted patrols with five to six ANP, while other units rarely patrolled with less than a platoon of about 30 soldiers. Considering the TF 3-08 P-OMLT completed over three hundred dismounted patrols, this was a significant risk. This blatant lack of resources is yet another telling indication of the value accorded to police mentoring by the CF.

Challenges to the CF police-mentoring effort did not only come from within. The fractured nature of the coalition police-mentoring effort in Afghanistan produced a number of problems. Not least among these was the number of organizations involved in developing the ANP. As mentioned earlier, Germany, the EU, the U.S. Department of State, and the U.S. Department of Defence have been or continue to be major players in police development. In addition to this, many nations within the International Security Assistance Force (ISAF) have independent police development programs within their PRTs.[49] Canada is no different with the CIVPOL contingent training ANP at the Kandahar PRT.

The result of this wide array of organizations is an equally wide array of approaches, philosophies, and priorities. Coordination between the various national and multinational programs was lacking as well. Andrew

Wilder of the Afghanistan Research and Evaluation Unit relates how, in Kunduz Province, "Dyn-Corp personnel at the Regional Training Centre were largely unaware of what the German police advisors were doing in the adjacent German PRT, and vice versa."[50] This anecdote could as easily apply to Kandahar Province, where there was little to no interaction between the RTC staff just outside Kandahar City, and any other police-mentoring organization.

The dearth of coordination had notable effects on the operations of the TF 3-08 P-OMLT. In both Zhari and Panjwayi, there were P-OMLT platoons, American PMTs, and Canadian CIVPOL. Each organization had differing objectives, chains-of-command, and mentoring approaches. Co-operation at the district level was often good, but true synchronization could not occur with three different organizations reporting to different headquarters. CIVPOL and the P-OMLT platoons generally worked well together, but force protection considerations meant the former were often limited in the mentoring they could do outside of forward operating bases. With the American PMTs, co-operation was usually good as well, although the problems of synchronization were often apparent. For example, on a few occasions P-OMLT sections travelled out to isolated ANP stations to conduct training and joint patrolling only to find that the ANP there had left on a patrol with the U.S. PMT. A lack of true synchronization at the district level meant the coalition's police-development efforts were often inefficient.

Different organizations also meant different approaches to mentoring the ANP. As mentioned above, Canadian CIVPOL tended to remain in forward operating bases, or back at the PRT, where they conducted formal training in policing skills. American PMTs also lived in forward operating bases, but they were separated from the ANP. In this author's experience, they rarely mentored or trained the ANP in any substantial way. What training they did was focused on paramilitary not policing skills, which is not surprising since PMTs most often had no military police or even reservists with police experience in their teams.

The P-OMLT took a different approach and lived with the ANP on a full-time basis. This had a number of benefits for both the ANP and the P-OMLT. Firstly, a full-time presence allowed the mentors to develop a strong relationship with their ANP counterparts; mentors must be seen as credible and have the trust of those they are mentoring. The ANP were far more reluctant to listen to, or trust, mentors they rarely saw. Secondly, this approach allowed mentors to lead by example and continuously monitor the ANP's progress. Having a section of professional Canadian soldiers living in a PSS provided a constant positive example. The *insitu* Canadian mentors were also able to get a feel for the true capacity of the ANP, something that cannot be done with a two-hour visit once a week. Finally, embedding P-OMLT sections in PSSs created a symbiotic relationship that benefited the ANP and JTF-A. The ANP gained a modicum of force protection and support from the Canadians, while JTF-A could be assured that the mentored ANP sections were actually doing what they were tasked to do. This last point is significant because un-mentored ANP often failed to perform tasks such as route sweeps or patrols.

The varied mentoring approaches resulted in a less than optimal methodology to developing the ANP in Kandahar. Without a clear, overarching mentoring plan that addressed the activities of all agencies and forces engaged in developing the ANP, there were inefficiencies and gaps in the coalition approach. The disjointed effort also set a bad example for the ANP and did little to improve their faith in the coalition efforts. If coalition forces could not even coordinate police development amongst themselves, how could they ask the ANP to do any better in organizing its affairs?

In addition to the limited effort the CF devoted to police mentoring and the problems of coordinating the multitude of police-development efforts in Kandahar, the ANP themselves presented the greatest single challenge to the P-OMLT. The problems with the ANP were numerous, although many could be traced to the leadership at all levels within the districts. While there were some exceptional, dedicated, and capable squad leaders and district staff, there were others who were corrupt, abusive thugs. Undoubtedly, this was the result of the fact that many of the ANP had come from tribal and warlord militias. Leaders who had stolen or extorted money from the population while in the militias simply carried on with that practice once in uniform — many were of the opinion that it was their right as police officers. It was the same mentality that motivated police leadership, up to and including provincial headquarters staff, to skim their subordinates' salaries or steal ammunition and supplies for sale on the black market.

This culture of corruption and criminality was a constant source of aggravation for the P-OMLT leadership. Considerable effort was devoted to changing this behaviour, and where that was not possible, to removing corrupt leaders. The TF 3-08 P-OMLT did manage to have one district chief-of-police, who was blatantly stealing and running illegal extortion schemes, removed. Frustratingly, this police leader was not arrested or even retired, but rather was simply transferred to another district, where he no doubt continued his unethical behaviour.

Unethical and criminal behaviour did not stop with corruption, graft, and extortion. On several occasions, P-OMLT section commanders had to deal with ANP drug and alcohol use. The section commanders, who lived in isolated PSSs that were often under attack, realized they could not afford to have security compromised by drunk or stoned policemen. The negative effects of drugs and alcohol on ANP discipline and readiness were unacceptable in such dangerous circumstances. On another level, the P-OMLT leadership fought hard against drug and alcohol use in order to improve the image of the ANP among the population. As the leadership repeatedly told the ANP chiefs-of-police and squad leaders, the police exist to enforce the laws, not break them. This approach had some effect, although the drug and alcohol problem was too pervasive for the P-OMLT to handle alone. Section commanders and platoon commanders did what they could, but in a force where as many as 60 percent of policemen are suspected of using drugs, progress was difficult.[51]

Drug use by the ANP also led to, and was indicative of, ties to Afghanistan's vast illegal narcotics industry. Police throughout the country accepted bribes and allowed drug production and smuggling to happen within their districts. Some police were directly involved in the drug trade, further diminishing their credibility in the eyes of much of the population.[52] The Ministry of the Interior reportedly "sold" ANP command positions that were known to produce lucrative bribes from the criminal gangs that produced and smuggled drugs. The TF 3-08 P-OMLT encountered one such ANP commander in an operation in eastern Zhari District.

As the P-OMLT and ANP were about to search a large, opulent compound for IEDs, an ANP squad commander from an un-mentored PSS, who supposedly made around $100 U.S. a month, arrived and announced the house was his. When asked how an ANP policeman could afford such a palatial home, other ANP officers quietly indicated he was linked to the drug trade. Although never proven, this provides but one example of the influence of the drug trade on the ANP. Locals could have little faith that the police were acting in the interests of the community when they were so clearly bought off by criminal elements.

Another ethical issue the TF 3-08 P-OMLT was forced to confront was the occasional use of under-age boys as police officers. On three separate occasions, P-OMLT section commanders had to confront ANP squad leaders about the presence of under-age policemen. Often it was simply a case of a father bringing his son to the PSS, where he could be fed and sheltered. More ominously, though, in some cases it was suspected by the P-OMLT leadership that the boys were there for use as sex slaves by the older policemen. While quick steps were taken to ensure these boys were removed from P-OMLT-mentored PSSs, it was difficult to convince the ANP leadership that such a practice was illegal. As with drug and alcohol use, bribery, and extortion, the use of boys as policemen detracted from the ANP's credibility in the eyes of the locals. Fortunately, incidents involving under-age policemen were relatively rare in Zhari and Panjwayi.

Combating corruption and unethical behaviour was critical not just for improving the quality of the ANP, but also for winning and maintaining the support of the population. In his book *Koran, Kalashnikov, and Laptop*, academic Antonio Giustozzi describes the effects of criminality among the police. "In Panjwayi," he wrote, "UN sources explicitly reported that abusive behaviour of national and border police seemed to have been a key contribution to turning part of the local population towards the Taliban."[53] The ANP were seen by many as thugs in uniform, which did little to engender support for the government of Afghanistan. As the ANP were often the only evidence of a central government most Afghans in rural areas ever saw, the behaviour of police was critical. Indeed, one poll showed that over 45 percent of Afghans see police once a week or more and 41 percent had seen the police doing something improper.[54] These discouraging numbers point to the need to devote serious effort to reforming the ANP leadership and enforcing strict rules regarding drug and alcohol use. As police constitute such a critical part of the counter-insurgency campaign, undisciplined and corrupt policemen have a tremendous impact on the effort to win the support of the population.

Less critical than criminality and indiscipline was the ANP's state of training and equipment. The FDD program helped to improve the general level of training but nonetheless represented only the most basic level required. "It's practically impossible to produce competent police officers in a program of only weeks," an anonymous former DynCorp executive stated.[55] Further training for leaders is necessary, as few have any experience in planning or leading a police force. Many of the logistical and organizational challenges that the ANP face are due to disinterested, corrupt, or incompetent leaders. Few know what they are doing, and none that worked with the TF 3-08 P-OMLT seemed to know or care what police were meant to do. Consequently, many fall back on their pre-ANP experiences with militias and use their police forces as a fighting force. Also, inculcating a culture of policing rather than fighting in the rank-and-file is necessary if the ANP are to be more than a poorly-armed adjunct to the ANA.

The use of the ANP as a paramilitary force had dire effects on the casualty rate of policemen. In Zhari District, where the ANP were authorized a force of ninety-two policemen, the annual casualty and loss rate was almost 100 percent. This meant that Zhari District lost almost ninety-two policemen each year from combat casualties, disease, desertions, and policemen refusing to sign on for additional service. This loss rate was both a reflection of low morale and a cause of it, especially with regard to combat casualties. It quickly becomes apparent that this rate was not conducive to the training of a competent police force, as few policemen were around long enough to learn their trade. The use of the ANP as "cannon fodder for the insurgency" has resulted in the police suffering casualty rates three times as high as the ANA.[56] If the ANP are to develop into a capable police force, they must be used as police and not as light infantry.

Many policing skills also require literacy, and less than one-third of ANP policemen can read or write. The TF 3-08 P-OMLT faced considerable difficulty in teaching the ANP investigative techniques, police law, or logistical procedures as a result of the general illiteracy of the force. If the ANP is to develop into a true police force, then a considerable literacy program will be required. As experience in Malaya indicated, the police must be capable of enforcing laws and able to investigate and arrest subversive, terrorist, or criminal elements. This cannot be done if the majority of policemen are ignorant of the law or incapable of conducting a basic investigation. Furthermore, Malaya demonstrated that police, due to their proximity to the people, can serve as a vital source of intelligence regarding the insurgency. Collection and transmission of intelligence becomes considerably more difficult when police leaders cannot read or write reports. Likewise, winning the support of the local population is considerably more difficult when the police are known to be incompetent and incapable of providing security.

The TF 3-08 P-OMLT tried to correct many of these deficiencies but could only do so much in seven months and with limited resources. Much more could have been done with a relatively small investment in personnel and resources. In spite of the historical examples and recent experiences that point to the criticality of developing indigenous police forces in counter-insurgency campaigns, the CF's efforts at developing the ANP represent a lost opportunity. Low priority given to the effort, coupled with a general lack of coordination with other Canadian agencies and international partners, has resulted in less than optimal results.

Encouragingly, more effort seems to be devoted to developing the ANP now than during TF 3-08's deployment. Increased mentoring up to the regional headquarters is a step toward addressing the critical failings of the ANP leadership. Similarly, the assignment of CF trainers to the Kandahar RTC is a reflection of the understanding that training must improve if the ANP are ever to be capable of policing Afghanistan. Developing the ANP is not an impossible task, but it does require considerably more effort than has been expended in the past. If the successful development of the ANA is any indication, progress in improving the

ANP is only a matter of time, money, and mentors — two of which the police development effort has lacked until very recently. As developing police forces in counter-insurgency is so critical, this is an opportunity the CF and the coalition cannot afford to lose.

10

Counter-Insurgency Versus "COIN" in Bazaar-e-Panjwayi and Panjwayi District, 2008–2010

An Illustrative Study of a Canadian Problem

DR. SEAN M. MALONEY

Canada's efforts to confront insurgent forces in the town of Bazaar-e-Panjwayi and the larger Panjwayi District in Afghanistan from 2009 to 2010 is a useful case study in exposing the ambiguity and limitations of counter-insurgency operations. Coalition forces slowly lost control of this particular area of operations, in part because of a lack of coordination in the development and governance spheres, and in part because of an inability to identify and then address how enemy operations affected governance. Confusion over what constituted counter-insurgency and its application, coupled with continuity issues, were, however, the primary culprits.[1]

Counter-insurgency sits between stabilization operations and conventional warfare on the spectrum of conflict. However, in the Afghanistan environment, serious blur exists within that counter-insurgency band: there is counter-insurgency and there is "COIN."[2] In terms of general definitions, counter-insurgency operations are the efforts taken to stop an insurgent movement from challenging the government. An insurgent movement may use a variety of methods to accomplish its aims. Counter-insurgency in this sense involves any and all measures taken by the government forces to compel the insurgents to cease and desist, no matter what types of activities the insurgent force employs. COIN, on the other hand, tends to be associated with historic low-intensity conflict techniques involving population engagement and protection, strengthening governance, security, and the horizontal integration of these activities. In some ways, COIN can be a subset of counter-insurgency. In many ways, however, the Canadians in Afghanistan during this period moved back and forth between COIN and counter-insurgency, mostly out of sync with what the enemy was doing.

What happens, then, when the insurgents vary how they do business and fluctuate their operations between population intimidation and near-conventional military operations? And then how do the counter-insurgents adapt their forces to deal with it all? COIN doesn't work at the near-conventional end of this spectrum, just as one cannot use conventional forces to prevent local intimidation. Indeed, the term "COIN effect" is often employed by Canadian practitioners in Afghanistan. Its precise meaning varies but tends to suggest the protection of the population from coercion and the fostering governance and development activities with the effect of moving the population toward supporting the government. Consequently, an informal doctrine exists whereby the Canadian Army practises "COIN" in the winter, when enemy activity has a particular pattern, and counter-insurgency in the summer, during the so-called "fighting season," when the enemy exhibits a different pattern of behaviour.

The constant refocusing of Canadian efforts in Kandahar Province since 2005 makes it difficult to examine any district from a counter-insurgency versus COIN perspective, as there tends to be little continuity of effort. For the most part, Canadian operations in Zharey District and Arghandab District have tended toward counter-insurgency, not COIN, because of the nature of enemy activity there. In Panjwayi District, however, it is easier to examine both. As such, the question must be asked, "How successful have Canadian counter-insurgency and COIN efforts been so far in Bazaar-e-Panjwayi and Panjwayi District?" And, "What can we learn from these experiences?"

A BRIEF INTRODUCTION TO PANJWAYI DISTRICT

Panjwayi District is located west of Kandahar City. It is a primarily rural district surrounded by large hills or "ghars," with the flatter areas dominated by grape production fields and compound living facilities. When combined, the fields and compounds constitute complex terrain that rivals that of an urban area. The larger population centres include Bazaar-e-Panjwayi, the capital; Nahkonay; Mushan and Mushan Bazaar; and Salavat. There is one paved main service route from Kandahar City to Bazaar-e-Panjwayi.

Bazaar-e-Panjwayi serves as the economic hub and transshipment point for agricultural produce, as much as it is the governance centre represented by the Panjwayi District Centre, located on the outskirts of the town. Socially, the bulk of the population is from the Noorzai tribal grouping, but there are important minority tribes, including the Alikazais and the Alokozais. There is normally a district leader who is appointed by the provincial governor and a district shura that serves as a governance forum. The district shura members are the elders representing the various communities. At the community level, that is, sub-district, the headman or malik is the primary elder, but there are also community mullahs, the religious leadership. The state of the relationship between malik and mullah varies considerably depending on the community.

As for policing, there were district-level police of varying levels of training led by a district police chief appointed by the provincial chief of police. The "police" in Panjwayi District transitioned from an untrained militia with no provincial-level control in 2004–2006 to a partially-trained militia with some degree of provincial control, and then to a trained militia with increased provincial and federal control by 2009.

In 2003–2004, the Afghan government initiated the National Solidarity Program (NSP). The NSP was supposed to establish Community Development Councils (CDC), whereby local people working with local leadership were to identify development projects. These were supposed to be submitted to a District Development Assembly, a sub-set of the district shura where the district leader and other leaders would prioritize CDC projects in the district. The monies for these projects were supposed to be handled through the Provincial Development Council, which reported to the provincial governor. In practise, the Canadian-led Provincial Reconstruction Team (PRT) acted as an ad hoc Provincial Development Council and at the same time was involved in the development relationship between the district and the province through Civil Military Cooperation (CMC) teams, the Canadian International Development Agency (CIDA), and the Department of Foreign Affairs and International Trade (DFAIT).

HISTORICAL PATTERNS OF INSURGENT ACTIVITY IN PANJWAYI DISTRICT BEFORE 2009

During the anti-Soviet jihad in the 1980s, mujahideen forces used Zharey District to the north of Panjwayi as a mounting base for ambush operations against Soviet convoys on Highway 1. The dense terrain discouraged pursuit, and Panjwayi District served as a rest and refit area for insurgents who would transit to the mounting base in Zharey, conduct operations, and then retire back to Panjwayi. The Soviets established a base in Bazaar-e-Panjwayi and used minefields to interdict insurgent movement at key junctures. This however, did not stop the mujahideen from mounting a spectacular raid against the Soviet administration facility in Bazaar-e-Panjwayi in the mid-1980s. This event entered into local legend, and the fighters involved remain to this day feted as heroes.

More recently, from 2001 to 2005, Zharey and Panjwayi districts are seldom mentioned during coalition operations. For the most part, the action was in northern districts like Shah Wali Kot, particularly in 2004–2005, as the primary enemy strongholds of the day were in adjacent Oruzgan, northern Helmand, and Zabol provinces. With the advent of the suicide improvised explosive device (IED) campaign in Kandahar City during late 2005, numerous indicators pointed to Zharey and Panjwayi districts as the base areas for IED cells and logistics nodes. These organizations were the waypoint for bombers and equipment that transited from Pakistan to Helmand to western Kandahar province and finally through a "ratline" into Kandahar City. Further analysis concluded that the ratline went from Bazaar-e-Panjwayi through Nahkonay and Salavat and into a number of compromised Afghan National Police (ANA) stations in the southwest part of the city. In late 2005, the Taliban increased their ambush activity along Highway 1, using Zharey as a base. These actions were comparatively limited.

In 2006, coalition operations in the province focused on the northern districts and then on Zharey, as indicators suggested that it would be used as a mounting base to conduct Tet-style attacks into Kandahar City (Sarposa Prison was one of the planned targets). Coalition spoiling operations were successful, but then the enemy reinforced Zharey and attempted positional near-conventional defence. At the same time, they attempted to use western Panjwayi District as a reinforcement route to back up operations in Zharey. They also tried to reinforce insurgent cells operating around Sperwan in order to draw off coalition forces from the fall 2006 Operation Medusa offensive over in Zharey.[3] These operations were limited in scope and time and were not designed to maintain a permanent presence in the district like they were in Zharey.

From late fall 2006 to summer 2007, there was minimal insurgent activity directed at Panjwayi District.[4] The focus of coalition operations was in a series of disruption operations in Zharey and on increased patrolling in Panjwayi. Afghan security forces expanded their operations in Panjwayi, particularly along the Mushan–Bazaar-e-Panjwayi road. There were numerous motives behind this security force approach, but it attracted limited enemy activity in 2007. Rather, insurgent activity was directed against the police checkpoints along the road and amounted to harassment more than anything. The sea-change in Panjwayi was signalled in June 2007, when nine Canadians were killed in two separate large-scale IED attacks — one near Sperwan Ghar and another along the Bazaar-e-Panjwayi–Nakhonay road. These events were disproportionate and didn't fit any existing pattern of enemy behavior in the district.

In late 2007, the decision was made to "harden" Afghan security force checkpoints along the Mushan–Bazaar-e-Panjwayi road and then, in time, pave that route down to Mushan. These decisions related to a plan to encircle insurgent forces in Zharey district while at the same time providing employment for people in Panjwayi District. The intent, quite simply, was to buy off fighting-age males.

However, once the checkpoint system was hardened, it attracted significant enemy activity. The use of large groupings of armoured vehicles on the western part of the route to resupply the police sub-stations attracted even more enemy attention in the form of large IEDs, and by the spring of 2008, a duel developed between insurgents in western Zharey and Panjwayi and Canadian forces, as they sought to resupply and relieve forces along the road. This confrontation drew in more and more coalition resources and produced record levels of violence in western Panjwayi District.

At the same time in early 2008, discreet insurgent operations conducted from Nahkonay against the relatively stable Dand District became a new cause for concern, but there weren't enough coalition resources to handle Zharey, Arghandab, eastern Panjwayi, and western Panjwayi at the same time.

By the summer of 2008, the insurgents significantly ramped up IED activity along the eastern end of the Mushan road and expanded suicide IED operations inside Bazaar-e-Panjwayi itself. The withdrawal of coalition forces from a number of combat outposts and attempts to use aerial resupply instead of armoured resupply columns resulted in an adaptation in enemy tactics, particularly the use of indirect fire against tactical infrastructure, the domination of terrain in the western part of the district, and the promulgation of an intimidation campaign against workers involved in road construction. In effect, the situation in Panjwayi District deteriorated from merely hosting a Taliban logistical "ratline" into the city in 2005 to acting as a whole new district "front," on par with Zharey and Arghandab districts in importance to the enemy effort in 2008.

THE WAR IN BAZAAR-E-PANJWAYI, 2008–2009

By early 2009, the 3rd Battalion, The Royal Canadian Regiment (3 RCR) Battle Group maintained a tank squadron and a mechanized infantry platoon in Forward Operating Base (FOB) Ma'Sūm Ghar, adjacent to

Bazaar-e-Panjwayi, an infantry company, and an M-777 artillery detachment in Patrol Base Sperwan Ghar. A Canadian Operational Mentor and Liaison Team (OMLT) was also based in Ma'Sūm Ghar and aligned with 2nd (Strike) *Kandak*, an Afghan National Army light infantry battalion — which had its weapons company in Ma'Sūm Ghar— and another infantry company situated near Sperwan Ghar. A Canadian Police Operational Mentor Team (P-OMLT), a mixture of military police and combat arms troops, worked with the Afghan Uniformed Police, an organization consisting of partially trained militia.

On the development front, the Construction Management Organization, a Canadian engineer sub-unit, deployed Construction Management Team-1 (CMT-1) to Panjwayi District to supervise a road paving project from Bazaar-e-Panjwayi to Sperwan Ghar. The Joint District Coordination Centre (JDCC), another Canadian-led and mentored organization, was established at Ma'Sūm Ghar to act as a security coordination centre and nexus between the three Afghan security forces (army, police, and National Directorate of Security) and the Canadian forces in the area. The JDCC was also responsible for running the 911-like phone system for the district.

Task Force Kandahar, the brigade-level headquarters, established Stability Box Juno in 2008. Stability Box Juno ran down eastern Zharey District to Bazaar-e-Panjwayi. The idea was to establish security in the box with coalition and Afghan forces, then focus Canadian and Afghan security and development resources on two critical areas: the Highway 1 to Bazaar-e-Panjwayi road and Bazaar-e-Panjwayi itself. The idea was to cajole the CIDA and DFAIT representatives from the PRT in Kandahar City to come out to Zharey and Panjwayi districts, so they could make closer contacts with their Afghan counterparts and carry out governance and development activities.

Some thought was given at this time to making the JDCC a kind of "PRT forward" at the district level and even bringing out the civilian police (CIVPOL) component of the PRT to work with the Afghan police and the P-OMLT. All of these activities were supposed to be conducted inside Stability Box Juno. However, there was little thought given to expanding activities outside of it for the time being — the "ink spot" theory was not in play.

The 3 RCR Battle Group's concept of operations usually involved bringing together the tank squadron and one or two infantry companies, as well as close air support, for a deliberate operation in either Panjwayi or Zharey district. It was usually Zharey because of its proximity to the vital Highway 1 main service route. The battle group's operations were not formally tied to the stability box, nor were those of the OMLT and 2nd *Kandak*. The reality was that 3 RCR Battle Group was pre-occupied with "killing the red icons" that popped up on the map (the enemy) and it possessed significant weight to do so — if the enemy was engaged in near-conventional operations, as he tended to in Zharey, or when he attempted to interfere with ground resupply operations directed toward the beleaguered Strong Point Mushan in western Panjwayi District.

It would be easy to draw boundaries on a map and declare that the coalition forces and their Afghan counterparts controlled those spaces and sortied out from time to time into enemy-controlled spaces to destroy them and return to the safety of their bases. Indeed, a future historian may make that mistake, looking at period maps that clearly delineate sub-unit boundaries and depict with apparent certainty insurgent logistical and command nodes, and assume a sort of linear reality.

There was another, more complex reality, however. The insurgent forces' structure in Panjwayi District was itself multi-faceted. There were what we might call "main force" Taliban, who were trained and organized guerrilla infantry with access to heavy weapons and communications. Some were local fighters, while others were out-of-area fighters from Pakistan. For the most part, these fighters were located west of Sperwan Ghar.

Then there were IED emplacers. There were, at this time, two or more specialized cells. One operated on the Bazaar-e-Panjwayi–Kandahar City highway to the east, while another operated in and around Bazaar-e-Panjwayi itself. One was from the district and another consisted of out-of area personnel.

The third type of insurgent was the intimidation teams. These consisted of small groups of young men on motorcycles and equipped with concealed pistols (so that they could not be targeted as insurgents). Operating at night, they would move north from the Sperwan Ghar area into Bazaar-e-Panjwayi for nocturnal activity. There was a relationship between the intimidation teams and the IED cell in the town.

The pattern of enemy activity involved all three types of insurgents. The "main force" guerrillas kept the battle group occupied by day west of Sperwan Ghar and at times moved in to shoot up coalition and Afghan tactical infrastructure in order to harass and provoke a response. Airpower and artillery might be used in response, or some form of combat-team-sized sweep might be mounted, from which the main-force insurgents would fire at and then quickly disengage, leaving the battle group punching into space. At night the IED cells interdicted the eastern main service route with anti-vehicle IEDs and lay anti-personnel IEDs to inflict damage on dismounted Afghan army and police patrols, while the intimidation teams coerced local leaders and pro-government people in Bazaar-e-Panjwayi. Control was not measured by what ground was staked out on a map by blue icons, rather, control varied depending on the time of day or night. Control of the population through intimidation was more important to the enemy than physical control of the structures that constituted the town of Bazaar-e-Panjwayi.

And that was not all. The internal politics of the district were such that there was friction between the district leader on one hand and the chief of police and another local power broker on the other. For the most part, this was related to the district leader's concerns that police from outside the district would examine his extracurricular economic activities. There was widespread belief that the district leader initiated a local protest against the police chief and staged the event in such a way as to demonstrate that the police were powerless. A second event involved a young man wearing a police uniform — but who was not police — shooting an individual in town. The coalition believed this to be another attempt to discredit the police chief. Taken together and then combined with enemy actions, it all contributed to seriously undermining the population's confidence in the police.

In reality, there was little or no security in the Bazaar-e-Panjwayi area at night. Despite the urgings of the P-OMLT, the police would not patrol. The OMLT was working on a nighttime army patrol schedule, but capabilities were limited by the lack of night vision and the lack of a responsive Afghan counter-IED and medical evacuation (MEDEVAC) capacity. The weapons company was not high enough up on the priority list for equipment. The insurgents eventually mounted their own local "spectacular" action, an event that resulted in the slaughter of an entire police check-point in Bazaar-e-Panjwayi, which was only five hundred metres from FOB Ma'Sūm Ghar. The insurgents even established a temporary checkpoint in the town itself, in the course of one night. Intimidation teams operated freely in the villages south of Bazaar-e-Panjwayi proper, and there was no nighttime security force response.

There were other indicators of a lack of control. Critically, the cellphone system in the area was shut down at night at the behest of the insurgents, who in past years conducted a scorched earth campaign against the cell towers in Panjwayi and Zharey districts. The cellphone companies acquiesced to the intimidation. Consequently, local people could not call the JDCC and report criminal and insurgent activity to the authorities.

Juxtaposed with all of this was the vibrant economy in Bazaar-e-Panjwayi, where all everyday and luxury items — by Afghan definition — were available. The insurgency appeared to have little or no effect on the economy per se. One school in Bazaar-e-Panjwayi was full of children and active, while another that lay just outside the Afghan security patrol area remained closed due to insurgent intimidation

The most positive aspect of the coalition forces presence in Bazaar-e-Panjwayi was Construction Management Team (CMT) 1. CMT-1, consisting of navy plumbers, air force construction engineers (and even a submariner), mounted in TLAV armoured vehicles, worked alongside four hundred locally-hired people and the Blue Hackle private security company. CMT-1 managed a paving project that slowly inched its way southwest from Bazaar-e-Panjwayi. This project attracted significant enemy activity starting in November 2008, including a mortar attack, small-arms fire, a suicide bomb attack directed at the administration site, and intimidation of workers through kidnapping, beatings, and subsequent release to psychologically impact the other workers. It is possible the intimidation was not, in fact, insurgent-based, and may be the result of the refusal by some workers to kick-back to the district leader or others.

Despite all of this, over 80 percent of the workers arrived for work regularly. As a group, they significantly improved their living standard. They wore close-toed shoes, had higher-quality clothing, and rode motorcycles to work instead of walking or riding bicycles. A micro-economy emerged in the adjacent communities to supply food and small goods to the workers. It is safe to say that the workers spent the bulk of their earnings in Bazaar-e Panjwayi in support of their families, which in turn boosted the vibrancy of the local economy as a whole. High pay appeared to override the insurgency's intimidation efforts. It was probable, however, that the insurgents received a kickback either from the workers or from district power brokers after they took their cut. Alternatively, the attacks against the project may not have been insurgent-based at all, and may have been designed to convince the workers to pay off local power brokers. The use of a suicide bomber, however, was a strong indicator that Taliban insurgents were involved in at least some of the attacks.

Unlike other coalition organizations in the area, CMT-1 developed relationships with the local mullahs along the project route. These were ad hoc, personality-based initiatives, in one case led by an infantry corporal who noticed that the local mosque speakers were rusted out and offered to help fix them. Local credibility was gained between the communities, the project workers, and CMT-1 as these relationships developed, and as a result, more information on what was going on around the project and in Bazaar-e-Panjwayi was acquired. Calls to the JDCC increased as relatives of the workers had more confidence to call in information on suspicious activity in the district and as far away as Kandahar City.

DIRECTIONS NOT TAKEN

Many of the pieces necessary for successful COIN operations in Bazaar-e-Panjwayi were in place. There was a high enough troop density. The town was geographically and economically important. So, why were the coalition and Afghan forces unable to generate the COIN effect inside the Bazaar-e-Panjwayi portion of Stability Box Juno in 2008–2009?

Local governance in the form of the district leader was a serious impediment. This took two forms. The first was his antagonistic relationship with the police: the police are critical to any COIN effort, in that they are the security forces with immediate day-to-day contact with the population — they are the immediate "face" of the government. One should not use the army to police the population.

The second form of impediment was the possibility that there was overlap between the district leader's interests and those of the insurgents when it came to the paving project. Had there been a strong coalition civilian governance presence in the district, his malfeasance might have come under scrutiny earlier. Having a governance specialist from the PRT visit on a near random basis was not enough.

The lack of effective security force coordination was another serious problem. In theory, the JDCC should have been the mechanism to get the police, the army, their mentors, and the district leader together to formulate a district security plan. In addition to the antagonism between the district leader and the police, there was also animosity between the police and the army, with the army viewing itself as a morally superior institution to the corrupt, untrained police. Canadian staff at the JDCC were new to Afghanistan and did not consist of specially-trained personnel, though there was a civilian police (CIVPOL) representative. The efforts of the OMLT and P-OMLT mentors became key connective tissue, particularly the P-OMLT.

The Canadian OMLT mentors could coordinate with the P-OMLT mentors laterally, and then each could work on the police and the army to get them to co-operate. The P-OMLT used its initiative and, despite being denied access to higher-level intelligence from the Canadian All Source Intelligence Cell at Kandahar Air Field, was able to collect intelligence with its allies and facilitate police raids that shut down one of the IED cells. The police also participated in IED clearance sweeps east of Bazaar-e-Panjwayi, thus deterring IED emplacement. These activities in turn boosted police morale but were unable to offset the other problems in the police-government relationship.

The CMT-1 experience should have been analyzed and systematized in conjunction with improvements to security force coordination. CMT-1 was generating effects that could have contributed to "COIN," but the experience was isolated. Indeed, the lack of any development facilitated by the Kandahar PRT team's CIDA and DFAIT representatives should be noted. Here was an ad hoc Canadian Forces sub-unit doing what the professional developers were not and having positive effects that had the potential to be widespread. CMT-1 operations, however, were at a lesser military cultural prestige level than, say, battle group combat team sweeps and advance to contact against insurgent "main force" guerrilla fighters.

All coalition and Afghan activities should have focused on "taking back the night" from the insurgents. This would have restored security in the eyes of the population to a significant degree, and from there this could have served as the basis for improved policing at all levels, which in turn would have resulted in better targeting data on insurgents of all types. The first step should have been to restore cellphone service, despite what the companies were doing elsewhere. The telephone is the connective tissue between the population and the police, via the JDCC. The police needed the capacity to respond to incidents. If the police needed reinforcement, there should have been army quick reaction forces to back them up.

None of these measures were put into play. Coalition efforts were stove-piped and uncoordinated, and there was a lack of will within the Afghan government camp. Consequently, the population in Bazaar-e-Panjwayi remained uncommitted to the Government of the Islamic Republic of Afghanistan and increasingly became a haven for insurgent forces to operate in — all of this while combat team operations conducted by the battle group ranged far and wide into western Panjwayi District and north into Zharey District. As a result, Bazaar-e-Panjwayi had two governments: Afghan government by day, insurgent rule by night.

THE SITUATION IN 2010

A year and half later, the situation had not significantly improved in Bazaar-e-Panjwayi, and in fact, it had deteriorated throughout Panjwayi District. The school closed and the town became loaded with fighting-age males with sullen looks; children made threatening gestures toward coalition forces.[5] Afghan patrols seldom left the main road through the town area. Economic activity, however, remained robust. The town thrived in terms of goods, variety of produce, and bustling activity. Solar-powered lampposts were in evidence. There was substantial shopping activity in the town during the day and at night. However, the coalition forces still had no idea what went on inside of the mosques in Bazaar-e-Panjwayi.

From 2009 onward, the insurgents expanded their activities and established four "defended areas" in eastern Panjwayi District. They also deepened their hold on western Panjwayi. They seriously contested the coalition forces for control over the population of these defended areas, using parallel governance techniques coupled with the establishment of defensive belts on the approaches of these comparatively isolated communities.

To counter enemy action in these communities, the battle group shifted from a counter-insurgency to a COIN approach. Infantry companies were dispersed to those communities and they conducted partnered operations with Afghan army and police. At the same time, civil military co-operation (CIMIC) teams tried to work with local leaders on reconstruction and aid projects. The difference between battle group operations in 2010 compared to 2009 is that the Canadian battle group area of operations was reduced to a single district from three, and there was a greater recognition in subsequent battle groups in 2009–2010 that "COIN" operations needed to predominate over counter-insurgency. This facilitated the grouping of the infantry companies in Panjwayi District, their dispersion to the threatened communities, and efforts to integrate development and security in their operating areas.

As the Canadian forces adapted, so too did the insurgents. The insurgent teams became smaller — four to six people, in order to present a small, fleeting target, and they increasingly concealed their weapons to complicate coalition force targeting. Insurgent tactics evolved to include the use of children as signallers in their early warning system, to assist with IED emplacement, and as shields to prevent aerial engagement of manoeuvring heavy weapons teams. The insurgents also engaged local combat coalition outposts and strong points with direct fire and used anti-personnel IEDs to contain any forces that attempted to project power from their bases.

These techniques were similar to those employed against the tactical infrastructure established along the Bazaar-e-Panjwayi–Mushan road in 2007–2008. The added difference is that, in 2010, their techniques were specifically designed to limit coalition forces interaction with the population. In effect, this kept coalition forces off balance and ensured that the populations in those areas remained uncommitted to the government.

The enemy's efforts at parallel governance grew dramatically since 2009 and moved from negative governance to positive governance.[6] By 2010 the enemy had

a. a court and dispute resolution system established in Zangabad, which administers the whole district. People may be transported there for "trial" or travel there of their own initiative for land dispute resolution. There is no equivalent functional government structure in Bazaar-e-Panjwayi;

b. co-opted "neutral" aid projects and used them to "PSYOP" the population;

c. established numerous illegal vehicle check points to exert population control measures;

d. conducted a systematic intimidation campaign against local elders both in insurgent-controlled areas and in other areas throughout the district; and

e. provided limited medical care in some areas using "neutral" or even government resources.

The inability of the coalition to establish a special program to identify, target, and disrupt parallel governance meant that the insurgents developed a deeper hold in the communities than they had two years earlier.

The Afghan National Army company responsible for Bazaar-e-Panjwayi was, by 2010, un-mentored by the OMLT. The OMLT policy, imposed by ISAF and endorsed by Canada, removed company-level mentoring by the summer of 2010. Even though this company belonged to 2nd

Kandak, an experienced unit, 4th Company was new and inexperienced. It did not conduct partnered operations with the coalition forces, nor did it conduct joint operations with the police. The ANA/OMLT and ANP/P-OMLT patrolling of Bazaar-e-Panjwayi and points south ceased to function. This was in contrast to what the OMLT and P-OMLT were doing in 2009.

The decision by Task Force Kandahar to stop mentoring at the company-level in early 2010 — combined with the turbulence that was created when the P-OMLT was reassigned by the brigade headquarters from the OMLT organization and given to the Task Force Kandahar Military Police Company — had detrimental effects on the security presence in Bazaar-e-Panjwayi. Any synergy that existed between the OMLT and P-OMLT disappeared.

Policing effectiveness was dramatically reduced. A Focused District Development (FDD) wasn't implemented at all. This would have been a national plan designed to remove insitu police, replace them temporarily with a federal gendarmerie, retrain the police, and then re-insert them back into the district. In 2010 the police were no better off in terms of equipment, motivation, and training than in 2009. In addition, the poor relationship between the Afghan police leadership and the district leader did not improve at all. Indeed, an effective chief of police that had an antagonistic relationship with the district leader was killed by an IED in June 2009, though it was not necessarily associated with insurgent activity.[7] The situation deteriorated further when his replacement lost his cool and assaulted the district leader during a meeting in July 2010.

This same ineffective and divisive district leader remained in place, generating the same problems as before, including the deliberate antagonism of the police leadership, which in turn generated constant turbulence in policing with the obvious and calculated knock-on effects. District development assembly meetings became moribund (and under threat because of the high-profile assassination of one of its more effective members, an individual who insisted that there be fair bidding on a road construction project). Furthermore, the district shura became unrepresentative of the population and psychologically cowed, and the community development councils became inoperative.

In fact, all decision making went through the illiterate, uneducated district leader and became projected through the nepotistic patronage lens held up by the district leader and his backers. Attempts to get governance support in the form of educated advisors came to naught. Line ministries did not, in general, come out to Panjwayi District. Government-controlled dispute resolution was practically non-existent at the district level, and insurgent mechanisms were increasing in influence at the same time.

Astoundingly, one and half years later, the cellphone system in the district remained off at night and on during the day. This in effect severed communications between the population and the police or government for almost 30 percent of the time, particularly during the critical hours of darkness. This in turn invalidated any local policing or counter-insurgent response plan at the community level and facilitated enemy intimidation operations.

The establishment of Operations Coordination Centre-District (Panjwayi), or the OCC-D(P), in 2010 was a significant improvement over the Joint District Coordination Centre both in terms of location, facilities, and effectiveness. Moving the coordination facility next to the district centre and away from the FOB at Ma'Sūm Ghar was a positive move. The Ma'Sūm Ghar facilities were primitive and did not physically facilitate good coordination (several maze-like buildings, on a hill, and inside ISAF tactical infrastructure). The new district centre was symbolic in a positive sense, in that it physically overlooked the southern part of the district as well as Bazaar-e-Panjwayi.

In addition, the establishment of a permanent District Stabilization Team (DST) to work from the OCC-D(P) was a dramatic improvement over the nearly random visits from the PRT, CIDA, and DFAIT representatives in the past. The idea of the JDCC or the OCC-D(P) acting as a "Provincial Reconstruction Team-Forward," marginalized nearly two years ago, almost became a reality in 2010. However, the turbulence generated by the dismantlement of the original PRT team structure in the summer of 2010 undermined the support base for a "PRT forward," which in turn forced the DST to act nearly independently. The American DST representatives used whatever influence or resources they had with a variety of American structures to get the job done, while the Canadian DST representative had little or no influence on anything.[8] "Handshake" relationships existed between the DST and the battle group, which allowed some coordination with the Engineer Construction Squadron (the Construction Management Organization's replacement in yet another re-organization), and the battle group CIMIC teams.

In many ways, the development situation regressed to 2005, in that the OCC-D(P) was in the same position that the Canadian PRT was when it started that year, and the various mechanisms designed to get projects out to the communities were no longer functional. In the summer of 2010, the Kandahar PRT was viewed by some as dysfunctional, unresponsive to Panjwayi District requirements, and too Kandahar City-centric. Indeed, during the tour from September 2009 to February 2010, the on-site Canadian commanders in Ma'Sūm Ghar noted that a DFAIT representative from the PRT stayed for five days in Panjwayi — two more than he wanted to because of an airlift issue. There was no CIDA representation in the district, nor were there any visits from CIDA personnel during that six-month period.

On the positive side, the P-OMLT teams were moved to the coordination centre, as were Canadian civilian police. This generated some positive effects on Afghan policing, but it is as if policing support programs started all over from scratch. This also applied to the reconstruction and development programs.

Disappointingly, the road-paving project on the Bazaar-e-Panjwayi–Mushan road completely collapsed in 2009. The construction management teams were moved to Dand District to support initiatives there by the summer, and paving was turned over to a Western contractor. This contractor was unable to work effectively with the district leader (that is, was probably unable or unwilling to come to a suitable financial "arrangement" with him) and violence increased against the workers. In one case, IEDs were laid under shaded trees where workers took their lunch. This afforded the contractor the excuse not to complete the project because of the security situation.[9]

Contractor-based solutions elsewhere in the district became for the most part inoperative for the same reasons. This may have been the result of commercial violence between competitors instead masquerading as insurgent violence. The spin-off benefits for the population in 2009 generated by the road paving project appeared to have all dried up.

LEGITIMACY IS KEY.... BUT THE LOCK IS BROKEN

First and foremost, neither counter-insurgency nor COIN addressed the problems of government legitimacy. As it stood in the summer of 2010, the coalition forces entered a stalemate in the province and Panjwayi District in particular. The insurgency increased its governance capacity in the rural areas it dominated. They continued to challenge the government for control of districts adjacent to Kandahar City and then mounted an urban terrorist campaign inside the city itself. The substantially increased coalition force troop density, as well as increased security measures in and around the city, held the situation in check. The bulk of the population, however, remained uncommitted in the struggle and tended to support whoever demonstrated strength in the districts.

Overlaying this state of affairs was the pervasive loss of legitimacy on the part of the federal, provincial, and local governments in Kandahar Province. The uncommitted portions of the population cannot shift allegiance to the government of Afghanistan if that governance is suspect and illegitimate. Consequently, the insurgency continued to hold out in these areas and increased its influence with their forms of governance. That was the state of affairs around Bazaar-e-Panjwayi and in Panjwayi District.

The perception by the population that the government lacks legitimacy in Kandahar Province and in Panjwayi District was, in 2010, pervasive at a number of levels:

a. **Federal Government**
The 2009 elections were seen to be fraudulent. The inability of the international community to intervene and correct the situation severely damaged the confidence of the population in both the international community and in the Karzai government. This event and its fallout may prove to have

been the tipping point in the increased level of violence seen since mid-2009. The inability of the federal government to reign in NGOs who provide tacit support for the insurgency by remaining "neutral" damaged the federal government's image at the local level.

b. **Provincial Level**

The appointment of demonstrably problematic governors by the president and the subsequent appointment of even more problematic district leaders by the governor was seen by the population as a suspect chain that linked the federal and provincial levels. The Provincial Council, though an elected body, was seen as remote and having little day-to-day impact on the lives of district residents, particularly those in Panjwayi district. The inability to facilitate the reconstruction of a functional justice system so that dispute resolution could take place had in effect ceded that terrain to the insurgency in the rural areas and reduced confidence amongst the population in the urban areas. Interference with the formation of a functional police service by the district leader ensured that dispute resolution could not take place in the rural areas and, indeed, the poor behaviour of the partially trained police contributed to the problem at the local level.

c. **Local Level**

Poorly-trained and undisciplined police were viewed as the protectors of the corrupt system. Coalition forces were seen as ignorant outsiders who don't really understand what is going on and leave every six months anyway. Every act of poor behaviour, perceived or otherwise, contributed to the picture of a bunch of infidel mercenaries defending an illegitimate system. Coupled with gender equality programs pushed by the development community and counter-narcotics operations pushed by the

Western law enforcement community, these perceptions were exploited by the insurgency via their religious representatives. NGOs that do not link their program with the government are not seen to be neutral — they were seen to be insurgent development projects since they were conducted at the suffrage of the insurgents;

d. **Religious Level**

The insurgency retained religious legitimacy at the local level in Panjwayi district because the coalition forces ceded that ground to them through absolute inaction since 2006. There was no realistic coalition strategy or Canadian policy for religious engagement.

e. **Tribal Level**

There are long-standing grievances at the tribal level pertaining to aid and development dispersions, water rights, land appropriation, and contracting inequalities. Some of these grievances pre-date the existing conflict. These issues complicate all of the above problems.

In effect, the coalition forces in Panjwayi District were dealing with a "system of illegitimacy" that undermined the ability to gain the support of the population. Each community consists, in varying proportions, of four types of people: pro-government (or anti-insurgency), uncommitted, apathetic, and pro-insurgency (or anti-government).

The objective of the coalition forces should be to decrease the number of apathetic people, convince the uncommitted to support the government, and have those three groups convince the anti-government people to cease and desist, or provide targeting data so they can be removed. However, the "system of illegitimacy" ensures that the number of apathetic people remains high and even pushes uncommitted people into siding with anti-government forces. Indeed, a state of despair may exist in some communities and one way out may be presented to young people with no jobs, namely jihad sanctioned by local religious leaders and influenced by anti-government clerics. Counter-insurgency and COIN as practised by the Canadian forces in Panjwayi District have been unable to address these issues and possibly cannot.

CONCLUSIONS

What are the lessons of the Canadian experience with Bazaar-e-Panjwayi and Panjwayi District? First, and most importantly, neither counter-insurgency nor COIN can address legitimacy, and the population will remain uncommitted until those problems are addressed. Counter-insurgency and COIN can effectively shield the development and governance efforts; the Canadian Army can figure out what the best balance is between counter-insurgency and COIN; but neither counter-insurgency nor COIN can replace development and governance.

Second, counter-insurgency and COIN, no matter how effective these efforts are, cannot address larger governance issues related to the system of dispute resolution and how that connects with national or provincial-level legal systems. Dispute resolution is a key element in legitimacy. Can or should military security forces be involved in dispute resolution — or should police? Of note, Canada's predilection toward using the army for "peacekeeping" may have raised internal army expectations too high in what the institution and its members could or could not accomplish in these areas. It is also probable that the lack of other government department support in this area led to a vacuum that was filled with an army "can-do" attitude.

The questions that must be asked are these: Where were the Canadian entities whose responsibility it was to handle governance and development issues at all levels? Were they present in the district and just ineffective? Were they effective or ineffective at the provincial and national levels? Or, did they focus elsewhere and not prioritize this key town and district, and if so, why? Why were their efforts not properly coordinated with those of the Canadian Army in order to produce the synergy needed to achieve success in a place like Bazaar-e-Panjwayi?

Third, the counter-insurgent forces can do all sorts of good things in terms of development using CIMIC and other resources, but they must be linked to development and governance, or there is no benefit to the activities, and the insurgents will merely exploit these efforts for their own objectives. For example, the CMT-1 paving project had positive economic benefits for the population, but it didn't seriously contribute toward shifting the population to supporting the government, because nobody established linkages.

Fourth, there was far too much turbulence in Canadian structures and approaches, and this produced serious inefficiencies. The constant regrouping of forces under each commander and nearly monthly refocusing of operations throughout the area of operations (inside and outside of Panjwayi District) produced a lack of continuity over an eighteen-month period. Poor conditions became normalized ("Oh, that's just the way it was when we got here, there's nothing that can be done about it") and then they were not addressed. The problem with the phone system and the district leader are two examples.

The insurgents are far more agile, keep their people on the ground until they are killed or promoted, and have a better feel for the operational environment than the Canadian Forces. They do not have multiple competing layers of bureaucracy and are not hampered by international legal constructs or international media and NGO scrutiny.

The Canadian experience in Bazaar-e-Panjwayi and Panjwayi District should serve as a cautionary case study. It is possible that, in the future, there must be established, recognized limits on what the Canadian Army *can* or *should* do in similar circumstances — regardless of what its members and representatives are *capable* of doing under similar conditions. Moreover, the higher-level headquarters must do what it can and say, "Enough!" to force the issue — before it spins out of control.

NOTES

Chapter One — Adjust Your Sights:
Leading Issues Likely to Arise in Any Counter-Insurgency Campaign

1. On general theories see Ted Gurr, *Why Men Rebel* (Princeton: Princeton University Press, 1970); Charles Wolf Jr. and Nathan Leites, *Rebellion and Authority: An Analytic Essay on Insurgent Conflicts* (R-462-ARPA, RAND, 1970); Eric R. Wolf, *Peasant Wars of the Twentieth Century* (New York: Harper and Row, 1969); and Peter Zagorin, "Theories of Revolution in Contemporary Historiography," *Political Science Quarterly* 88, no. 1 (March 1973): 23–52. Studies more proximate to contemporary events include Benedict Anderson, *Imagined Communities: Reflections on the Origin and Spread of Nationalism* (Brooklyn: Verso Press, rev. ed. 1990); Anonymous, *Through Our Enemies' Eye: Osama Bin Laden, Radical Islam, and the Future of America* (London: Brassey's Defence Publishers, 2002); Fawaz Gerges, *The Far Enemy: Why Jihad went Global* (Cambridge: Cambridge University Press, 2005); Mark Huband, *Warriors of the Prophet: The Struggle for Islam* (Boulder: Westview Press, 1999); Geraint Hughes, "The Insurgencies in Iraq, 2003–1009: Origins, Developments and Prospects," *Defense Studies* 10, no. 1 (October 2009): 152–176. For a deeper understanding of the problems associated with disentangling motives, see Eli Berman, Joseph Felter, and Jacob N. Shapiro, "Do Working Men Rebel? Insurgency and Unemployment in Iraq and the Philippines," NBER Working Paper No. 15547 (November 2009); Paul Collier, Anke Heoffler, "On Economic Causes of Civil War," *Oxford Economic Papers* 50, no. 4

(1998): 563–73; Paul Collier, Anke Heoffler, "Greed and Grievance in Civil War," Center for the Study of African Economies, CSAE WPS/2002-01 (13 March 2002); and James D. Fearon, "Rationalist Explanations for War," *International Organization* 49, no. 3 (1995): 379–414. Complex world views are also explored in Robert A. Pape, *Dying to Win: The Strategic Logic of Suicide Terrorism* (New York: Random House, 2006).

2. Jon Lee Anderson, in *Guerrillas: Journeys in the Insurgent World* (New York: Penguin, 2004), provides a rare comparative analysis of how five then-active insurgencies are organized to mobilize and maintain support and wage protracted struggles against difficult odds. David Charters and Maurice Tugwell, in *Armies in Low-Intensity Conflict* (London: Brassey's Defence Publishers, 1989), reveal in a rare comparative analysis how various armies have sought to combat such forces.

3. Ben Connable and Martin C. Libicki, in *How Insurgencies End; Key Indicators, Tipping Points, and Strategy* (National Defense Research Institute, RAND Corp., 2010), do a solid job dissecting some of the elements.

4. T.E. Lawrence, "The Evolution of a Revolt," *Army Quarterly and Defence Journal* (October 1920): 1–22; on the handling of the forces, he advised see Lawrence, "Twenty Seven Articles," *The Arab Bulletin* (20 August 1917). John A. English does a good and critical job of summarizing his thought in "Kindergarten Soldier: The Military Thought of Lawrence of Arabia," *Military Affairs* 1, no. 1 (January 1987): 7–11.

5. For details of this period of the Anglo-Irish War, see T. Bowden, "The Irish Underground and the War of Independence, 1919–1921," *Journal of Contemporary History* 8, no. 2 (April 1973): 3–23; Andrew Selth, "Ireland and Insurgency: The Lessons of History," *Small Wars and Insurgency* 2, no. 2 (1991): 299–322; and Charles Townsend, "The Irish Republican Army and the Development of Guerrilla Warfare, 1916–1921," *English Historical Review* 94, no. 371 (April 1979): 318–345. Such geopolitical constraints are often overlooked by analysts. For example, see Stephen Biddle, *Military Power: Explaining Victory and Defeat in Modern Battle* (Princeton: Princeton University Press, 2004). On the power potential of states, see *Measuring National Power* (U.S. National Defense Research Institute, RAND Corp., 2000).

6. Samuel B. Griffith II (Trans.), *On Guerrilla Warfare* (Champaign: University of Illinois Press, 1961); Francis F. Fuller, "Mao Tse-Tung: Military Thinker," *Military Affairs* 22, no. 3 (Autumn 1958): 139–145.

7. George Washington faced a rather similar problem of turning a revolutionary band into a force able to take on the strength of the British Army. See David McCullough, *1776* (New York: Simon and Schuster, 2005).

8. One might see the parallel to the intentions of modern PRTs.

9. William Hinton provides a first hand account of the Chinese revolution and action at the village level in *Fanshen: A Documentary of Revolution in a Chinese Village* (Berkerly: University of California Press, 1966). See Vietnamese effort to use similar methods in Truong Chinh, *Primer for Revolt: The Communist Takeover in Vietnam* (Santa Barbara: Praeger, 1963) and Vo Nguyen Giap, *Guerre du Peuple, Armee de Peuple* (Maspero, 1960).

10. Mao Tse-Tung, "Problems of Strategy in Guerrilla Warfare Against Japan," in *Selected Writings of Mao Tse-Tung* (Beijing: Foreign Language Press, 1966), 153–186.

11. Such an observation was not lost on the classic military theorist Baron Antoine Jomini, who remarked on it in his classic *Precis on the Art of War.*

12. See Anderson, cited above, and the cases of the Tamil Tigers in Sri Lanka, ZAPU and ZANU campaigns in Rhodesia, the ANC in South Africa, and the Shining Path in Peru for a short list of examples.

13. On the limited modern style, see Zhivan Alach, "The New Aztecs: Ritual and Restraint in Contemporary Western Military Operations," *Defense Studies* 10, no. 1 (October 2009): 248–27. Cf. David H. Petraeus, "Multi-National Force-Iraq Commander's Counterinsurgency Guidance," *Military Review* (September/October 2008): 210–212.

14. See Lionel Beehner, "What Sri Lanka Can Teach Us About COIN," *Small Wars Journal* 6, no. 8 (August 2010): 4–10.

15. See Connable and Libicki, *How Insurgencies End.*

16. See Peter Paret, *French Revolutionary Warfare from Indochina to Algeria* (New York: Princeton/Praeger Press, 1964); and Martin Alexander, "The French Experience 1919–1962: French Military Doctrine and British Observations, from World War One to the Algerian War," in John Gooch, ed., *The Origins of Contemporary Doctrine* (Strategic & Combat Studies Institute, The Occasional, Number 30, September 1997), 32–51.

17. Geraint Hughes, "The Insurgencies in Iraq, 2003–1009: Origins, Developments and Prospects," *Defense Studies* 10, no. 1 (October 2009): 152–176.

18. Contrast Susan L. Carruthers, *Winning Hearts and Minds: British Governments, the Media and Colonial Counter-Insurgency, 1944–1960* (Leicester: Leicester University Press, 1995); Robert M Cassidy, "Winning the War of the Flea. Lessons from Guerrilla Warfare," *Military Review* (September/October 2004): 2–12 with Mark Silinsky, "An Irony of War: Human Development as Warfare in Afghanistan," *Colloquium* 3, no. 3 (October 2010): 1–16; Joseph Soeters and Tibor Szvircsev Tresch, "Towards Cultural Integration in Multinational Peace Operations," *Defense Studies* 10, no. 1 (October 2009): 272–287; and Christian Tripodi, "Enlightened Pacification: Imperial Precedents for Current Stabilization Operations,"

Defense Studies 10, no. 1 (October 2009): 40–74. On the benefits and necessity of having a good local government administration, see Charles A. Joiner, "The Ubiquity of the Administrative Role in Counterinsurgency," *Asian Survey* (8 August 1967): 540–54; and Dennis J. Duncanson, "Symbiotic Insurgency in Vietnam Ten Years After," *International Affairs* (October 1978): 594–98. The problems of having to rely on a terribly ineffectual host government are anticipated in Charles Maechling Jr., "Our Internal Defense Policy — A Reappraisal," *The Foreign Service Journal* (January 1969): 19–21, 27.

19. Not all allies are created equal notwithstanding the NATO or other umbrella; some might well follow their own agendas and operate in a manner foreign to other partners. Such geopolitical realities require discernment and should not be a surprise, because all coalition warfare is marked with such division.

20. See, for instance, Jason T. Adair, "Learning on the Run: Company Level Counter-Insurgency in Afghanistan," *Canadian Army Journal* 10, no. 4 (Winter 2008): 26–35.

21. See Sir Robert Thompson, *Defeating Communist Insurgency* (New York: Praeger, 1966); Andrew Mumford, "Sir Robert Thompson's Lessons for Iraq: Bringing the 'Basic Principles of Counter-Insurgency' into the 21st Century," *Defense Studies* 10, no. 1 (October 2009): 177–194; and John A. Nagl, *Learning to Eat Soup with a Knife: Counterinsurgency Lesson from Malaya and Vietnam* (Chicago: Chicago University Press, 2005).

22. See the suggestive David Grange, Tim Heinemann, et al., *Irregular Warfare Leadership in the 21st Century: Attaining and Retaining Positional Advantage* (Chicago: McCormick Tribune Foundation, 2007).

23. Cf. Frank Kitson, *Intensity Operations — Subversion, Insurgency, Peacekeeping* (North Haven: Shoestring Press, 1971); John Kiszerly, "Learning About Counter-Insurgency," *RUSI Journal* (December 2006): 16–21; and Chistian Tripodi, "Enlightened Pacification: Imperial Precedents for Current Stabilization Operations," *Defense Studies* 10, no. 1 (October 2009): 40–74.

24. Michael A. Hennessy. *Strategy in Vietnam: The Marines and Revolutionary Warfare in I Corps, 1965–1972* (New York: Praeger, 1997); Richard A. Hunt, *Pacification: The American Struggle for Vietnam's Hearts and Minds* (Boulder: Westview Press, 1995); and Martin Ingram, *Stakeknife: Britain's Secret Agents in Ireland* (Dublin: The O'Brien Press, 2004).

Chapter Two — The Quagmire of Great Powers:
Dealing With the Afghan Way of War

1. Harvey Henry Smith, *Area Handbook for Afghanistan* (Washington: the

Supt. of Docs., U.S. Govt. Print Office, 1973), 5.

2. Ali Ahmad Jalali and Lester W. Grau, *The Other Side of the Mountain: Mujahideen Tactics in the Soviet-Afghan War* (Quantico, Virginia: U.S. Marine Corps, Studies and Analysis Division, 1999), xiii.

3. *Ibid.*

4. Arnold J. Toynbee and D.C. Somervell, *A Study of History, Volume 2: Abridgement of Volumes VII-X* (Oxford, England: Oxford University Press, 1987), 125. Modern Afghanistan lies between the Soviet Union, China, Pakistan, and Iran.

5. Adam Ritscher, "Brief History of Afghanistan" (speech, Students against War teach-in, Duluth, Minnesota), *www.afghangovernment.com/briefhistory.htm* (accessed 13 July 2010).

6. Michael Barthorp, *The North-West Frontier: British India and Afghanistan: a Pictorial History, 1839–1947* (Poole, Dorset: Blandford Press, 1982), 147–49.

7. Brigadier-General David Fraser, former Commander ISAF Multi-National Brigade Sector South, Kandahar, Afghanistan, presentation to Canadian Infantry Association Annual General Meeting, Edmonton, 25 May 2007.

8. Smith, *Area Handbook for Afghanistan*, 93: "Large landowners, such as are often found in other Middle Eastern countries, are relatively uncommon. A few large landholdings exist, but the marked difference between wealthy absentee landlords and landless peasantry is not a feature of Afghan social structure. Small holdings of individuals arid property held jointly by the tribe are the more usual types of land tenure. Wealth in land or animals is nonetheless a criterion of high social status in the villages; positions of status often devolve from lineage, as for example, one lineage may provide all the *mullahs* (Moslem religious leader). Literacy is another criterion of status in the village. The ability to do some reading and writing is both an economic and a social asset."

9. Seth G. Jones and Arturo Muñoz, *Afghanistan's Local War: Building Local Defense Forces* (Santa Monica, California: RAND Corp, 2010), 21. According to the report: "For those who are still tribally organized, the outward form of the tribe remains the same as that found among nomads." It goes on to state that the tribal structure extends over several villages, and the connecting links are provided by the kinship system.

10. *Ibid.*, 92. Depending on the specific location and situation, the *malik* could also be responsible for carrying out certain central or provincial government functions, such as presiding over weddings, collecting statistics, and keeping other types of village records.

11. *Ibid.*, 91.

12. *Ibid.*, 92. "This pattern reflects the Afghan view of authority and is often referred to as 'tribal democracy.' It is viewed by some Afghan intellectuals as being the seed for future democratic development. Those who attend the *jirgah* are themselves the heads of lineages or sub lineages to whose members they carry back the decions of *jirgah*. Criteria other than relative age and seniority also play a part in this essentially kin-based status system. Apart from holding a political office the two most important elements are wealth and armed strength. Wealth is either in animals, land or both, depending on the economic pursuits of the tribesmen."

13. Depending on the circumstances, religious leaders and influential chiefs may also have such authority.

14. Jalali and Grau, *The Other Side of the Mountain*, xiii.

15. Seth G. Jones and Arturo Muñoz, *Afghanistan's Local War*, 21–24.

16. Barthorp, *The North-West Frontier*, 147–48.

17. Donald P Wright, *A Different Kind of War: The United States Army in Operation Enduring Freedom (OEF), October 2001–September 2005* (Fort Leavenworth, Kansas: Combat Studies Institute Press, U.S. Army Combined Arms Center, 2010), 6. "Irrigation has allowed for the expansion of farming into other sections, especially in the southwest.... Despite its significant size, only 55,000 square km of the land is arable. Fertile areas are located primarily in the river valleys."

18. *Ibid.*, 7.

19. "Guerrilla Warfare," taken from the *US Military History Companion, www. answers.com/topic/guerrilla-1* (accessed 1 June 2010). "The word guerrilla comes from the Spanish meaning 'little war.'"

20. Stephen Tanner, *Afghanistan: A Military History from Alexander the Great to the Fall of the Taliban* (New York: Da Capo Press, 2002), 136.

21. Jalali and Grau, *The Other Side of the Mountain*, 384. Jalali and Grau do point out, however, that during the Soviet occupation some adaption was necessary: "Two modem systems, the helicopter and the antipersonnel mine, created severe tactical problems which were outside the [Afghans'] historical experience." They stress that, for the Afghans, "tactical innovation occurs only where tactical innovation is required and the [Afghans] eventually found ways to work around the problem technology." They note, however, that "where innovation was not required, the [Afghans] stayed with the tried and true. Thus the basic [Afghan] ambush and pursuit were little changed from last century."

22. Tanner, *Afghanistan*, 136.

23. Smith, *Area Handbook for Afghanistan*, 182. "Each member of the tribe has connections with his extended family, lineage, tribe, and ethnic

community. His strongest feelings of identity and loyalty relate to his extended family, then in diminishing degrees of intensity, to the larger social units. As a focal point of loyalty the national society comes last. Feelings of allegiance to the nation are filtered through the family and its extended relationships, tending to become meaningful only if they happen to coincide with the interests of the smaller groups."

24. *Ibid.*, 184. "Readiness to do battle is suggested not only by the traditional custom, now disappearing, of carrying daggers and firearms at all times, but also by patterns of village construction. The fortified village, with high towers, is seen in many regions throughout the country."

25. *Ibid.*, 185.

26. *Ibid.*, 185.

27. *Ibid.*, 184.

28. Graeme Smith, "Tribal animosity drawing Taliban recruits," *Globe and Mail*, March 25, 2008. According to Smith, some think that "NATO forces have been drawn into a tribal feud that underlines the conflict in southern Afghanistan." According to a *Globe and Mail* poll conducted in 2008, "a sample of ordinary insurgents, 42 fighters in Kandahar province were asked by to identify their own tribe, and the results point to a divide within the Taliban ranks: only five named themselves as members of the three major tribes most closely associated with the government, suggesting that tribal animosity has become a factor that drives the recruitment of insurgents."

29. Donald P. Wright, *A Different Kind of War*, 43. Also see Svetlana Savranskaya, "The Soviet Experience in Afghanistan: Russian Documents and Memoirs," *Volume II, Afghanistan: Lessons from the Last War*, 9 October 2001; Document 21, CC CPSU Letter on Afghanistan, 10 May 1988 (Alexander Lyakhovsky, *Tragedy and Valor of Afghan*, Iskon, Moscow, 1995, Appendix 8), *www.gwu. edu/~nsarchiv/NSAEBB/NSAEBB57/soviet.html*, accessed 20 January 2007.

30. Waldemar Heckel and John Yardley, *Alexander the Great: Historical Sources in Translation* (Oxford: Blackwell, 2004), 95. Although Darius, the Persian king, had been decisively defeated, he had not been captured, so Alexander decided to continue his advance against him. According to reports, he had taken refuge in Bactria. Shortly after this occupation of Persepolis, Alexander received news that Artaxerxes V (Bessus), satrap of Bactria, had killed Darius and declared himself king of the Persian Empire. However, Alexander decided he would have to pursue and defeat Bessus in order to legitimize his claim to the empire.

31. Meredith L. Runion, *The History of Afghanistan* (Westport, Connecticut: Greenwood Press, 2007), 34. "The Helmand River stretches for 1,150 km (715 miles). It rises in the Hindu Kush mountains, about 80 km (50 miles)

west of Kabul passing north of the Unai Pass. It crosses south-west through the desert of Dashti Margo, to the Seistan marshes and the Hamun-i-Helmand lake region around Zabol at the Afghan-Iranian border."

32. Tanner, *Afghanistan*, 39–40. For a map of the area in question, see "Ancient History," *www.livius.org/a/1/maps/sogdia_map.gif* (accessed 15 June 2010).

33. *Ibid.* Bactria, or Bactriana sometime later, had various names, including Tukharistan, Tokharistan, and Tocharistan, and was located between the range of the Hindu Kush and the Oxus River. It should be pointed out that there is some dispute among scholars as to whether Alexander actually took this route or not.

34. Robert B. Asprey, *War in the Shadows: The Guerrilla in History* (Garden City, New York: Doubleday, 1975), 6. Also see J. F.C. Fuller, *The Generalship of Alexander the Great* (London: Eyre & Spottiswoode, 1958), 8. Lacking sufficient timber to bridge the fast-flowing river, he "collected the hides the troops used for tent covers and ordered them to be filled with the driest possible chaff, and then to be tied down and stitched neatly together so as to be watertight. When they were filled and stitched together they were efficient enough to take the army across in five days." Also, satrap was the Persian name given to the governors of the provinces of the ancient Median and Achaemenid (Persian) Empires. *www.thefreedictionary.com/satrapies* (accessed 25 September 2010).

35. Tanner, *Afghanistan*, 43. Also see Frank Lee Holt, *Into the Land of Bones: Alexander the Great in Afghanistan* (Berkeley, California: University of California Press, 2005), 53.

36. A Scythian is a "member of a nomadic people originally of Iranian stock who migrated from Central Asia to southern Russia in the 8th and 7th centuries BC. The Scythians founded a rich, powerful empire centred on what is now the Crimea. The empire survived for several centuries before succumbing to the Sarmatians during the 4th century BC to the 2nd century A.D. Much of what is known of the history of the Scythians comes from the account of them by the ancient Greek historian Herodotus, who visited their territory. In modern times this record has been expanded chiefly by the work of Russian anthropologists. The Scythians were feared and admired for their prowess in war and, in particular, for their horsemanship. They were among the earliest people to master the art of riding, and their mobility astonished their neighbours." *www.britannica.com/EBchecked/topic/530361/Scythian* (accessed 12 November 2010).

37. James R. Ashley, *The Macedonian Empire: The Era of Warfare Under Philip II and Alexander the Great, 359–323 B.C.* (Jefferson, North Carolina: McFarland, 1998), 296. Also see Andrew Curry, "Frozen Siberian

Mummies Reveal a Lost Civilization," *Discover, http://discovermagazine. com/2008/jul/25-frozen-siberian-mummies-reveal-a-lost-civilization* (accessed 22 November 2010). The Scythians, "never constituting an empire, ... were a network of culturally similar tribes that ranged from Siberia to Egypt almost 3,000 years ago and faded away around A.D. 100."

38. J. R. Hamilton, *Alexander the Great* (Pittsburgh: University of Pittsburgh Press, 1973), 7–98. Also see Fuller, *The Generalship of Alexander the Great*, 234.
39. *Ibid.*, 98. The sixth and seventh are not mentioned.
40. Asprey, *War in the Shadows*, 6. See also Fuller, *The Generalship of Alexander the Great*, 8.
41. Francis Henry Skrine and Sir Edward Denison Ross, *The Heart of Asia: A History of Russian Turkestan and the Central Asian Khanates from the Earliest Times* (London: Methuen & Co, 1899), 7.
42. Hamilton, *Alexander the Great*, 98.
43. Fuller, *The Generalship of Alexander the Great*, 12–14.
44. Ashley, *The Macedonian Empire*, 305.
45. *Ibid.*
46. This action was the only serious defeat ever suffered by one of Alexander's columns during his time in Afghanistan.
47. Asprey, *War in the Shadows*, 8.
48. Flavius Arrianus, Aubrey de Sélincourt, and J.R. Hamilton, *The Campaigns of Alexander* (Harmondsworth, England: Penguin Books, 1976), 204.
49. Tanner, *Afghanistan*, 47. Also see Hamilton, *Alexander the Great*, 10.
50. Ilya Gershevitch, *The Cambridge History of Iran (Volume 2)* (Cambridge: Cambridge University Press, 1985), 48. They were an Iranian nomadic confederation in antiquity and had similar customs of dress and mode of living to the Scythians.
51. Ulrich Wilcken and Eugene N. Borza, *Alexander the Great* (New York: Norton, 1967), 160. Also see Tanner, *Afghanistan*, xx: "The Macedonian columns once again spread across the field, and this time Spitamenes, with a force of three thousand men, was caught by the column led by Coenus, and his force suffered eight hundred dead. Afterward, the Massagetae abandoned the cause. They seized Spitamenes and cut off his head, delivering it to Alexander as a peace offering."
52. Arrianus, Sélincourt, and Hamilton, *The Campaigns of Alexander*, 28. Oxyartes is first mentioned as one of the chiefs who accompanied Bessus on his retreat across the Oxus River into Sogdiana (329 B.C.E.).
53. "Alexander Captures the Sogdian Rock," *www.livius.org/aj-al/alexander/ alexander_t54.html* (accessed 15 July 2010).

54. Meredith L. Runion, *The History of Afghanistan* (Westport, Connecticut: Greenwood Press, 2007), 34.
55. *Ibid.*
56. Arrianus, Sélincourt, Hamilton, *The Campaigns of Alexander*, 322.
57. Asprey, *War in the Shadows*, 4. Also, Fuller, in *The Generalship of Alexander the Great*, states, "Unfortunately Arrian and other historians tell us little about what tactical changes Alexander introduced but whatever the changes, one thing is certain, they were based on mobility and flexibility, coupled with the use of a large number of military posts and military colonies that restricted his enemy's mobility while they added to his own."
58. *Ibid.*
59. It must also be remembered that part of Alexander's success was based on the fact that he was not afraid to launch punitive campaigns to systematically destroy enemy encampments or to summarily execute tribesmen believed to be supporting the resistance. That being said, whenever possible, he attempted to bring his enemies onto his side, providing defeated enemies with key appointments, and, when appropriate, encouraging his officers to marry local nobility.
60. Tanner, *Afghanistan*, 81.
61. *Ibid.*, 97. "The *qanat* irrigation system, with its thousands of holes and tunnels adjacent to communities, provided excellent hiding places for defenders (in addition to the caves naturally carved in the mountains)."
62. *Ibid.*, 97.
63. "Ahmad Shah Durrani," www.answers.com/topic/ahmad-shah-durrani (accessed 15 August 2010).
64. *Ibid.*
65. Karl Ernest Meyer and Shareen Blair Brysac, *Tournament of Shadows: The Great Game and Race for Empire in Central Asia* (Washington, D.C.: Counterpoint, 1999), 63.
66. Tanner, *Afghanistan*, 133.
67. W.J. Vogelsang, *The Afghans: The peoples of Asia* (Oxford, United Kingdom: Blackwell Publishers, 2002), 249. It did not help matters that British troops were increasingly being used for such things as tax collection.
68. Tanner, *Afghanistan*, 140.
69. *Ibid.*, 140.
70. *Ibid.*, 170.
71. Richard H. Shultz and Andrea J. Dew, *Insurgents, Terrorists and Militias* (New York: Columbia University Press, 2006), 163.
72. Frank Clements, *Conflict in Afghanistan: A Historical Encyclopaedia* (Santa Barbara, California: ABC-CLIO, 2003), 94.

73. Shultz and Dew, *Conflicts in Afghanistan*, 160.
74. *Ibid.*, 160.
75. "The Battle of Kabul and the Retreat to Gandamak," *www.britishbattles. com/first-afghan-war/kabul-gandamak.htm* (accessed 1 May 2010). See also Archibald Forbes, *The Afghan Wars, 1839–42 and 1878–80* (New York: C. Scribner's Sons, 1892); and Sir George Fletcher MacMunn, *Afghanistan: From Darius to Amanullah* (Lahore, Pakistan: Sang-e-Meel Publications, 2002)
76. This was done with an ultimatum on 30 October 1878.
77. The Second Anglo-Afghan War is often viewed as two campaigns, the first from November 1878 to May 1879 and the second from September 1879 to September 1880.
78. Martin Ewans, *Afghanistan: A Short History of Its People and Politics* (New York: Perennial, 2002), 70.
79. Jeffery J. Roberts, *The Origins of Conflict in Afghanistan* (Westport, Connecticut: Praeger, 2003), 18.
80. Mir Tamim Ansary, *Destiny Disrupted: A History of the World Through Islamic Eyes* (New York: Public Affairs, 2009), 240. As a result, British representatives were installed in Kabul and the British were given control of the Khyber and Michni passes.
81. Jeffery J. Roberts, *The Origins of Conflict in Afghanistan*, 19.
82. Martin Ewans, 77. Also see Archibald Forbes, *The Afghan Wars, 1839–42 and 1878–80,* (New York: C. Scribner's Sons, 1892).
83. Stanley Sandler, *Ground Warfare: An International Encyclopaedia* (Santa Barbara, California: ABC-CLIO, 2002), 452.
84. Seth G. Jones, *In the Graveyard of Empires: America's War in Afghanistan* (New York: W.W. Norton & Co, 2009), xi. Also see *www.britishempire. co.uk/forces/armycampaigns/indiancampaigns/campafghan1878maiwand. htm* (accessed 12 July 2010).
85. Amin Saikal, Ravan Farhadi, and Kirill Nourzhanov, *Modern Afghanistan: A History of Struggle and Survival* (London: I.B. Tauris, 2004), 34. Under the peace arrangement, Britain controlled Afghanistan's foreign policy.
86. Julian Paget, *Counter-insurgency Campaigning,* (London: Faber and Faber Limited, 1967), 23.
87. Michael Barthorp, *The North-West Frontier: British India and Afghanistan: a Pictorial History, 1839–1947* (Poole, Dorset: Blandford Press, 1982), 151. The Afghan regular army was not a very formidable force and was only able to muster about fifty thousand men. The Afghan command was counting on support from the tribes, which could gather up to twenty thousand or thirty thousand fighters.

88. Robert Wilkinson-Latham and Angus McBride, *North-West Frontier, 1837-1947* (London: Osprey Pub, 1977), 25. Also see *www.khyber.org/pashtohistory/aviationhistory/aviationhistory.shtml* (accessed 23 August 2010).

89. Tanner, *Afghanistan*, 143.

90. Cary Gladstone, *Afghanistan Revisited* (New York: Nova Science Publishers, Inc., 2001), 40-41.

91. Lester W. Grau, "The Soviet-Afghan War: A Superpower Mired in the Mountains," Foreign Military Studies Office, *http://fmso.leavenworth.army.mil/documents/miredinmount.htm* (accessed 1 December 2007).

92. *Ibid.*

93. *Ibid.*

94. Stephen J. Blank, *Afghanistan and Beyond: Reflections on the Future of Warfare,* (Pennsylvania: U.S. Army Strategic Studies Institute, 1993), 9–10.

95. J. Bruce, Amstutz, *Afghanistan: The First Five Years of Soviet Occupation* (Washington, D.C.: NDU Press, 1986), 132.

96. Ralph H. Magnus and Eden Naby, *Afghanistan: Mullah, Marx, and Mujahid* (Boulder: Westview Press, 2002), 135. The word *mujahid* is an Arabic participle drawn from the same root as the Arabic word *jihad*, "to strive or struggle." *Mujahideen* is simply the plural form of the same word. The term derives from the word *mujahid*, or "one who strives or struggles on behalf of Islam."

97. Grau, "The Soviet-Afghan War."

98. *Ibid.*, xiv. As the war progressed, heavy machine guns, recoilless rifles, and mortars were also used.

99. Ali Ahmad Jalali and Lester W. Grau, *The Other Side of the Mountain: Mujahideen Tactics in the Soviet-Afghan War* (Quantico, Virginia: U.S. Marine Corps, Studies and Analysis Division, 1999), 15. "The column consisted of 150 to 200 trucks full of many things such as food and furniture. Whatever we could take away, we did. Hundreds of Mujahideen came and looted the column. We captured 15 trucks for my group which we eventually moved to our base in Durow canyon. We torched the vehicles we could not take and left the area around 1300 hours. After we had finished, helicopters and aircraft came and bombed some areas around the ambush site. Despite our lack of warning when the lead vehicle came toward our ambush site, the ambush turned out well."

100. *Ibid.*, xiv. This was about 15 percent of their force, or fifteen thousand to twenty thousand troops. If they used more, they would have to take them from security duties in quiet areas.

101. R.H. Shultz Jr., R.L. Pfaltzgraff Jr., U. Ra'anan, W.J. Olson, and I. Lukes, *Guerrilla Warfare and Counterinsurgency: U.S.– Soviet Policy in the Third World* (Toronto: Lexington, 1989), 345.

102. Mohammed Yahya Nawroz and Lester W. Grau, *The Soviet War in Afghanistan: History and Harbinger of Future War* (Fort Leavenworth, Kan: Foreign Military Studies Office, 1995), 9.

103. *Ibid.*, 285. As a result, these people found themselves tightly targeted by the more direct and violent Soviet practices, which were based on the premise: "kill one, frighten a thousand."

104. Julian Paget, *Counter-Insurgency Campaigning* (London: Faber and Faber Limited, 1967), 169. This tactic is commonly referred to as the stick technique. There are several ways of employing the stick technique, which can include minor punishments such as curfews, fines, detention and various other restrictions. Paget emphasizes that "this is not likely to be an acceptable policy to any western power today, for it is morally unacceptable that any government should try to out do the average insurgent force in terrorism."

105. R. Klass, *Afghanistan: The Great Game Revisited*, (London: Freedom House, 1987), 174.

106. T.T. Hammond, *Red Flag Over Afghanistan: The Communist Coup, the Soviet Invasion, and the Consequences* (Boulder: Westview Press, 1984), 161.

107. Klass, *Afghanistan*, 341.

108. Amstutz, *Afghanistan*, 145.

109. Quoted in J. Laber and B.R. Rubin, *A Nation is Dying* (Evanston: Northwestern University Press, 1988), 62. The significance of these attacks was not lost on villagers: "The irrigation system was built through generations to make this landscape fitted for men to live in."

110. Amstutz, *Afghanistan*, 145.

111. Klass, *Afghanistan*, 91.

112. *Ibid.*, 173.

113. E.R. Girardet, *Afghanistan: Eight Years of Soviet Occupation* (Department of State Bulletin, Vol. 88, No. 2132, March 1988), 37. Also see *Lessons from the War in Afghanistan*, 6.

114. *Ibid.*, 37. The attempt was complicated by the extremely long and rugged nature of the border between these two countries — over 1,400 miles with approximately 320 mountain passes

115. Klass, *Afghanistan*, 180. When these actions failed, the Soviets started to carry out direct actions on both sides of the border. Although initially hesitant to violate Pakistani air space, by 1986 the Soviets had become so desperate they were striking all known rebel bases with air and artillery attacks. In fact, it is estimated that 700 air and 150 artillery attacks were carried out inside Pakistan throughout the latter part of the war.

116. O. Roy, *The Adelphi Papers: Lessons of the Soviet/Afghan War*, (London: Brassey's, 1991), 22. See also Col. F. Freistetter, "The Battle in Afghanistan:

A View from Europe," *Strategic Review* 9, no. 1 (winter 1981): 41.

117. Alex, Alexiev, *Inside the Soviet Army in Afghanistan* (Santa Monica, California: RAND, 1988), 4.

118. E.R. Girardet, *Afghanistan: The Soviet War* (New York: St. Martin's Press, 1985), 36.

119. *Ibid.*, 129.

120. Arnold, 97.

121. Shultz et al., *Guerrilla Warfare and Counterinsurgency*, 164.

122. Nawroz and Grau, *The Soviet War in Afghanistan*, 8.

123. James F. Hoge, and Rose Gideon, *How Did This Happen?: Terrorism and the New War* (New York: PublicAffairs, 2001), 88.

124. United States Army, *Lessons from the War in Afghanistan Part 1*, Introduction (National Security Archive: Declassified October 9, 2001), 22, *www.gwu.edu/~nsarchiv/NSAEBB/NSAEBB57/us.html* (accessed 1 November 2006). The initial Soviet objectives were to control the cities and town, secure the major lines of communications, and train and equip government forces.

125. Stephen J. Blank, *Afghanistan and Beyond: Reflections on the Future of Warfare* (Pennsylvania: U.S. Army Strategic Studies Institute, 1993), 21.

126. Grau, "The Soviet-Afghan War." The Soviets deployed and maintained a force of about 100,000 troops in Afghanistan, which was generally believed to have been totally inadequate for the task they were to undertake. According to CIA estimates, "An increase of perhaps 100,000 to 150,000 men might [have allowed] the Soviets to clear and hold major cities and large parts of the countryside or block infiltration from Pakistan and Iran, although it probably could not do both.... An even larger reinforcement of 200,000 to 400,000 men probably would [have allowed] Moscow to make serious inroads against the insurgency if the efforts could be sustained."

127. Nawroz and Grau, *The Soviet War in Afghanistan*, 7–9.

128. Raimo Vayrynen, "Focus on Afghanistan," *Journal of Peace Research* 17, no. 2 (Special Issue on Imperialism and Militarization, 1980): 93–102, *www.jstor.org/pss/423418* (accessed 28 October 2006).

129. Taru Bahl and M.H. Syed, *Encyclopaedia of Muslim world* (New Delhi: Anmol Publications, 2003), 131.

130. *Ibid.*, 132.

131. Robert D. Crews and Amin Tarzi, *The Taliban and the Crisis of Afghanistan* (Cambridge, Massachusetts: Harvard University Press, 2008), 4.

132. Rashid, Ahmed, *Taliban: Militant Islam, Oil, and Fundamentalism in Central Asia* (New Haven: Yale University Press, 2000), 27–29.

133. *Ibid.*

134. Meredith L Runion, *The History of Afghanistan* (Westport, Connecticut: Greenwood Press, 2007), 123.

135. "History of Afghanistan," *www.afghangovernment.com/briefhistory.htm* (accessed 15 September 2010). As the Northern Alliance was routing the Taliban, the Americans inserted additional ground forces to hunt for Bin Laden.

136. Vincent Morelli, and Paul Belkin, *NATO in Afghanistan: A Test of the Transatlantic Alliance* (Washington: Congressional Research Service, 3 December 2009), 1.

137. Brian Hutchinson, "Taliban again rule territory stained with Canadian blood: Insurgents use medieval justice, child soldiers to slowly regain control of region," *Edmonton Journal*, 4 September 2010. *www2.canada.com/edmontonjournal/news/story.html?id=1e98f5ca-f0be-43c1-b997-f302dbaf902b/*.

138. Morelli and Belkin, *NATO in Afghanistan*, 1.

139. *Ibid.*, 3.

140. *www.longwarjournal.org/archives/2008/08/taliban_kill_ten_fre.php* (accessed 15 November 2010).

141. Swapna Kona, "Afghanistan: The Spring Offensive," *Institute of Peace and Conflict Studies*, no. 44 (April 2007): 3–4.

142. *Ibid.*, 4.

143. Morelli and Belkin, *NATO in Afghanistan*, 1.

144. International Security Assistance Force, "Key Facts and Figures," *www.isaf. nato.int/troop-numbers-and-contributions/index.php* (accessed 4 September 2010).

145. The Atlantic Council of the United States, *Saving Afghanistan: An Appeal and Plan for Urgent Action* (Strategic Advisors Group, Issue Brief, March 2008), 1.

146. *Ibid.*

Chapter Three — Public Opinion Matters: The Struggle for Hearts and Minds

1. Colonel John R. Boyd as cited in Major Jason Hayes, "Preparing Our Soldiers for Operations within Complex Human Terrain Environments," *Australian Army Journal* (winter 2009), 104.

2. COIN, according to the *U.S. Army Counterinsurgency Handbook*, "is military, paramilitary, or other political, economic, psychological, and civic action taken by a government to defeat insurgency." Department of Defence, *U.S. Army Counterinsurgency Handbook* (New York: Skyhorse Publishing Inc., 2007), 1.

3.   Headquarters, U.S. Forces-Afghanistan, International Security Assistance Force, Kabul, Afghanistan, APO AE 09356m, 10 November 2009.

4.   There are a variety of techniques used to study public opinion, including "election returns, consumer behaviour, stock market fluctuations," and "public meetings and demonstrations." These techniques often rely on four methods of public opinion assessment, "survey research or polling, focus groups, experimental research, and the analysis of mass media content." Notably, these tools do not mean that public opinion is in any way easy to measure. Carol J. Glynn, Susan Herbst, Garrett J. O'Keefe, Robert Y. Shapiro and Marc Lindeman, *Public Opinion*, 2nd edition (Boulder: Westview Press, 2004), 73.

5.   Glynn et al., *Public Opinion*, 6.

6.   *Ibid.*, 11. Notably, Glynn et al. are only referring to the Vietnam War.

7.   According to Robert Osgood, "Limited Wars are military interventions that are bound by time, resource, political aims, kinetic effect, and geography. Moreover ... Limited Wars should only be resourced to a level directly proportional to the desired objective." As cited in Paul Carcone, "Examination of Limited War's Relevance in the Post Cold War Era," *www. suite101.com/content/examination-of--limited-wars-relevance-in-the-post-cold-war-era-a256318* (accessed 1 September 2010).

8.   According to the dictionary of military terms, asymmetric warfare includes "threats outside the range of conventional warfare and difficult to respond to in kind (e.g., a suicide bomber)," *www.au.af.mil/au/aul/bibs/asw.htm* (accessed 2 August 2010).

9.   Interview with Colonel Fred Lewis by Adam Day, *Legion Magazine*, November 2006.

10. Cori E. Dauber, *YouTube War: Fighting in a World of Cameras in Every Cell Phone and Photoshop on Every Computer* (CreateSpace, November 2009), 3.

11. Bruce Jackson, "Where's your Schwerpunkt?" *Vanguard* (May–June 2010): 27.

12. Russell Hampsey and Sean P. McKenna, "Afghan's Unique Surge: The Fight Can Only Be Won by Listening to Afghan Voices," *www.afji.com/2010/06/4646076* (accessed 4 June 2010).

13. Gerald Woodil, Ewen Stockbridge, and Mike Cumberland. *Counter Insurgency Campaign Assessment and Direction in Regional Command South*, DRDC CORA TM 2010-08 (January 2010): 1–2.

14. As the U.S. Counterinsurgency Field Manual points out, "Not everyone is good at COIN. Many leaders don't understand it, and some who do can't execute it." As cited in Hampsey and McKenna, "Afghan's Unique Surge."

15. Michael G. Mullen, "From the Chairman: Strategic Communication: Getting Back to Basics," *Joint Force Quarterly* (4th Quarter, 2009), *www.jcs.mil/newsarticle.aspx?ID=142.*

16. As an American Special Forces member explains, "The local and personal approach requires … 'drinking lots of tea.'" As cited in "The McChrystal Rules," *www.strategypage.com/htmw/htsf/articles/20100528.aspx* (accessed 5 June 2010).

17. For more on the benefits of CQ in the COE see Emily Spencer, *Solving the People Puzzle: Cultural Intelligence and Special Operations Forces* (Toronto: Dundurn Press, 2010).

18. Major Jason Hayes, "Preparing Our Soldiers for Operations Within Complex Human Terrain Environments," *Australian Army Journal* (winter 2009): 107. Spencer, in *Solving the People Puzzle*, 115: "Echoing age-old truisms about insurgency and counter-insurgency warfare, in 2004, retired American Major-General Robert H. Scales commented, 'This new era of war requires soldiers equipped with exceptional cultural awareness and an intuitive sense for the nature and character of war.'" Additionally, as American veteran Special Operations Forces officer Russell D. Howard remarked, "Special Forces captains will have to be much more than culturally *aware*, which is the current requirement. They will have to achieve cultural *competency*, which is when the Special Forces officer demonstrates not only awareness but also cultural knowledge and sensitivity combined with an ability to gain trust and modify the behavior of allies, neutrals, or potentially divisive persons or groups to achieve a desired outcome or accomplish a mission." Russell D. Howard, "Educating Special Forces Junior Leaders for a Complex Security Environment," Joint Special Operations University Report 09-6 (July 2009): 14–15.

19. As reporter Grace V. Jean explains, "The human terrain maps lay out where tribes, ethnic groups and religious sects are located. They also capture attitudes, for instance it maps out a population's beliefs and values. In addition they report where certain behaviours tend to occur or not occur." As she surmises, "In essence, human terrain analysts zero in on the things that matter to the populations that they study. This in turn assists the military personnel in winning, or at least not alienating, a given population group." Grace V. Jean, "Human Terrain," *National Defense* (February 2010): 22.

20. In a speech at the Australian Strategic Policy Institute, Australian chief of the army Lieutenant-General Ken Gillespie echoed these benefits of human terrain analysts. He observed that "contemporary operations are characterized by the need for our deployed land forces to work *among the*

people, and establish a broad relationship with the supported population." He continues, "Such warfare requires small teams of highly skilled and flexibly employed soldiers, who can rapidly transition between different types of operations ... and it leads us to an environment that demands we prepare our people for levels of contextual awareness, flexibility, expertise sensitivity and precision which have rarely been required of the soldier in past conflicts." As cited in Major Jason Hayes, "Preparing Our Soldiers for Operations within Complex Human Terrain Environments," *Australian Army Journal*, (winter 2009): 104.

21. Dauber, *YouTube War*, 13.

22. Hayes, "Preparing Our Soldiers for Operations within Complex Human Terrain Environments," 106.

23. Dauber, *YouTube War*, ix.

24. *Ibid.*, 2.

25. Lee Winsor, David Charters, and Brent Wilson, *Kandahar Tour: The Turning Point in Canada's Afghan Mission* (Mississauga: John Wiley & Sons Canada, Ltd., 2008), 210.

26. General (Ret.) Paul Manson, "Afghanistan is at the crossroads while Canadians Sleepwalk," *Veritas* (Spring 2010): 48.

27. As cited in Dr. Robert Bergen, "Censorship; the Canadian News Media and Afghanistan: A Historical Comparison with Case Studies," *Calgary Papers in Military and Strategic Studies*, Occasional Paper Number 3 (2009): 48.

28. *Ibid.*, 56.

29. *Ibid.*, 57.

30. Bergen, "Censorship; the Canadian News Media and Afghanistan," 34.

31. As cited in Matthew Rosenberg, "US Special Operations Ordered Deadly Afghan Strike," *Dow Jones Reprints* (22 February 2010), *http://online.wsj.com/article/SB10001424052748704057604575080640203691352.html* (accessed 22 February 2010). See also Rod Norland, "Military Officials Say Afghan Fight Is Coming," *www.nytimes.com/2010/02/04/world/asia/04taliban.html* (accessed 6 February 2010).

32. Government of Canada, "Canada's Engagement in Afghanistan," *Quarterly Report to Parliament for the Period of July 1 to September 30 2009*, 4.

33. As cited in Eric Talmadge, "Canadian General Talks Tough," *Star*, 31 January 2010, *www.thestar.com/news/canada/afghanmission/article/758291--canadian-ge* (accessed 6 February 2010).

34. As cited in Thomas H. Henriksen, *Afghanistan, Counterinsurgency, and the Indirect Approach*, Joint Special Operations University Report 10-3, April 2010, 4.

35.   The Army Capstone Concept, "Operational Adaptability: Operating under Conditions of Uncertainty and Complexity in an Era of Persistent Conflict 2016-2028," TRADOC Pam 525-3-0, 21 December 2009, 20.

36.   As cited in Thomas H. Henriksen, "Afghanistan, Counterinsurgency, and the Indirect Approach," Joint Special Operations University Report 10-3, April 2010, 4.

37.   Author Matthew Rosenberg, in "US Special Operations Ordered Deadly Afghan Strike," phrases the issue quite succinctly: "Coalition airstrikes or raids that kill Afghan civilians repeatedly hand Taliban propaganda victories." Additionally, as a recent Kandahar District Narrative explained, "The Kandahar PRT [Provincial Reconstruction Team] commander in late 2009 ordered his troops to remove the 'STAY BACK!' signs from their armored vehicles, open the hatches and wave to locals, and to reduce the size of their patrols. He also demanded they obey local traffic laws, such as stopping at stop signs, slowing down, and honking their horns less frequently." As a result, the report continues, "it was quickly apparent that local residents were responding favorably to the new approach." The evidence: "Upon returning from his first patrol under this new approach, a Canadian soldier reported that 'a woman in a burkha waved back for the first time.'" The Stability Operations Information Center (SOIC-South) Kandahar Airfield, "Kandahar City Municipality & Dand District: District Narrative Analysis," 30 March 2010, 14.

38.   McRaven as cited in Laura King, "U.S. Army Chief Pleas Afghans to Forgive," *Los Angeles Times*, 9 April 2010.

39.   The Stability Operations Information Center (SOIC-South) Kandahar Airfield, "Kandahar City Municipality & Dand District: District Narrative Analysis," 30 March 2010, 54–55.

40.   Dauber, "YouTube War," 3.

41.   International Crisis Group, "Taliban Propaganda: Winning the War of Words?" *Asia Report*, no. 158 (24 July 2008), 1.

42.   As cited in International Crisis Group, "Taliban Propaganda," 1.

43.   Hampsey and McKenna, "Afghan's Unique Surge."

44.   Winsor, Charters, and Wilson, *Kandahar*, 180.

45.   General (Ret.) Paul Manson, "Afghanistan is at the crossroads while Canadians Sleepwalk," *Veritas* (Spring 2010): 48.

46.   International Crisis Group, "Taliban Propaganda," *ii*.

47.   Carl Forsberg, "The Taliban's Campaign for Kandahar," *Executive Summary, Afghanistan Report 3* (December 2009), 35.

48.   International Crisis Group, "Taliban Propaganda," *i*.

49.   Forsberg further describes that, at this time, "Kandaharis staged a public

protest blaming Canadian troops when handicapped children were killed in an explosion in February 2009. A subsequent ISAF investigation concluded that the deaths were caused by an enemy IED; however, this did not alter public perception. In subsequent months, a number of additional protests were staged in Kandahar over claims of civilian deaths, which NATO steadfastly denied." Forsberg, "The Taliban's Campaign for Kandahar," 47.

50. *Ibid.*, 7, 44. As Forsberg explains, "Prior to 2004, small groups of Taliban fighters conducted minor attacks in Kandahar City, including the assassinations of pro-government mullahs, ineffective rocket and mortar attacks, and the distribution of night letters, called *shabnameh* in Dari and Pashtu, warning citizens against cooperation with the government. These attacks succeeded in driving most international non-governmental organizations (NGOs) out of the province by the end of 2003." *Ibid.*, 22–23.

51. Ruhullah Khapalwak and David Rohde, "A Look at America's New Hope: The Afghan Tribes," *www.nytimes.com/2010/01/31/weekinreview/13rohde. html* (accessed 6 February 2010).

52. Forsberg, "The Taliban's Campaign for Afghanistan," 47.

53. Jonathan Steele, "Afghanistan: is it time to talk to the Taliban?" *Guardian Online*, 4 May 2010, *www.guardian.co.uk/world/2010/may/04/afghanistan-taliban* (accessed 9 May 2010).

54. As *New York Times* reporter Eric Schmitt notes, "Mullah Baradar [the captured Taliban deputy commander] is describing in detail how members of the Afghan Taliban's leadership council, or shura, based in Pakistan, interact, and how senior members fit into the organization's broader leadership, officials said. He is also offering a more detailed understanding of what prompted Mullah Omar to issue a new code of conduct for militants last year that directed fighters to avoid civilian casualties. American officials say the code was meant to project a softer image to the Afghan people." Schmitt, "Captured Leader Offers Insight into the Taliban," *New York Times Online*, http://www. nytimes.com/2010/05/06/world/asia/06baradar.html?hp (accessed 9 May 2010). Notably, however, Mullah Omar has recently been cited as being harsher than the Taliban code of conduct would recommend. This reversal of strategies prompted German Brigadier-General Josef Blotz to remark, "This [order] proves the Taliban are willing to ignore their own Code of Conduct when they sense they are losing influence and control, as today's attack [18 July 2010] against several Afghan civilians [who] were killed and injured by a suicide attack in a residential area in Kabul today demonstrates." Josef Blotz as cited in Thomas Joscelyn and Bill Roggio, "Mullah Omar orders Taliban to attack civilians, Afghan women," *www.longwarjournal.org/archives/2010/02/ the_talibans_top_lea.php* (accessed 8 August 2010).

55. Forsberg, "The Taliban's Campaign for Kandahar," 34.
56. John F. Burns, "Into Kandahar, Yesterday and Tomorrow," *New York Times Online, www.nytimes.com/2010/05/23/weekinreview/23burns.html? pagewanted=1&hp* (accessed 30 May 2010).
57. Forsberg, "The Taliban's Campaign for Kandahar," 15.
58. International Crisis Group, "Taliban Propaganda: Winning the War of Words?" *Asia Report*, no. 158 (24 July 2008): 34.

Chapter Four — Coalition Counter-Insurgency Warfare in Afghanistan

1. U.S. Joint Chiefs of Staff Joint Doctrine Division, *Department of Defence Dictionary of Military and Associated Terms* (Washington, D.C.: Joint Publication (JP) 1-02, 12 April 2001, amended version 30 May, 2008), 92.
2. *Ibid.*, 31.
3. By *strategy* I mean a cognitive exercise that appreciates foreign policy and acknowledges the national interests at stake, deriving from these clear objectives for operations, force requirements for the achievement of these objectives, and a plan for executing operations using these forces over time to secure the peace desired.
4. The America, Britain, Canada, Australia Standardization protocols reflect the reality of an enduring alliance between these four linguistically and culturally aligned countries.
5. Contemporary coalitions utilizing confidential bilateral arrangements between the lead nation and individual members to determine commitments, areas of responsibility, support requirements, information sharing, and command arrangements have inherent tensions and jealousies. In American-led coalitions, the relationship between the United States and each partner is widely varied, determined through bilateral discussions between American authorities and political and military leaders of that nation. The apportionment of American logistic, materiel, or financial support to one partner, the result of a bilateral arrangement between the United States and that country, can cause jealousy amongst other partners. Alliances, in contrast, have more open and equitable practices deliberately designed to prevent such inter-alliance tensions or rivalry.
6. Russel W. Glenn, *Band of Brothers or Dysfunctional Family?: A Military Perspective on Coalition Challenges During Stability Operations* (Santa Monica, California.: RAND Corporation, 2009), 11–20.
7. OEF efforts in Afghanistan commenced with several variations of ARCENT Land Component Command in Afghanistan and transitioned to Combined Forces Coalition — Afghanistan in 2003. There were two commanders

CFC-A before disbandment of headquarters CFC-A in 2007, after which command of OEF forces migrated to commander Combined Security Training Command — Afghanistan. The first nine commanders of ISAF were European and Canadian Corps Commanders. General Richards (U.K.) commanded ISAF during the assumption of US OEF forces. After May 2007, the U.S. has provided the ISAF commander four different general officers being assigned to that command between 2007 and 2010. See Ian Hope, *Unity of Command in Afghanistan: A Forsaken Principle of War* (Carlisle, Pennsylvania: Strategic Studies Institute, U.S. Army War College, November 2008).

8.　The author has participated in three of the planning efforts and has reviewed the products created by the other attempts. Contributing to the inability of the coalitions to produce unifying campaign plans is the fact that the various departments of the United States government, and various communities in the United States military, have competing capstone doctrine. The Department of State recognizes the primacy of Stability Operations doctrine, while the Department of Defence holds its counter-insurgency doctrine as most relevant. United States Special Forces Command, however, prefers to perceive most operations as part of larger efforts codified in its irregular warfare doctrine. Each document represents a competing community of interest with congressional and budgetary representation. These divisions present obstacles to coherent American strategy formulation.

9.　Canada's effort in Kandahar is illustrative. While Canadian efforts have been described by journalists and politicians as "strategic," they have never risen above the purely tactical (local) level and have suffered from a complete want of long-term coherency. Canada has changed focus and method with the arrival of each new general officer and senior diplomat into Kandahar. Mobile counter-insurgency in 2006 gave way to investment in static "tactical infrastructure" in 2007, which was superseded by an emphasis on civilian-led "whole of government" in 2008, a tactical COIN-focused "model-village" approach in 2009 (a poor man's local version of a "strategic hamlet"), followed by the "ring of security" around Kandahar City in 2010. With each new commander comes a new concept, each formulated in isolation or in the absence of higher coalition plans.

10.　Credit for this assessment must be given to several anonymous officers of the Afghan NDS (Department of National Security), who in June 2006, in Kandahar, provided the author with a paper analyzing Taliban strategic plans. The paper reviewed Taliban activity in their defensive stage 2002–2006 and predicted the surge of Taliban activity in 2006 in efforts to establish bases of operation inside Afghanistan to begin widespread guerrilla activity. Whilst not mentioning Mao, anyone schooled in the theory of communist revolutionary warfare could easily recognize the influence of Mao strategic thought throughout this prescient document.

11. This chapter utilizes Mao's prescriptions as set down in Combat Studies Institute, eds., *Selected Military Writings of Mao Tse-Tung* (Leavenworth, Kansas: U.S. Army Command and General Staff College, 1991), 167–263.

12. Initial media claims of "thousands" of Taliban casualties during Operation Medusa in 2006 have been discredited. While official figures of reported and estimated Taliban casualties vary, all consistently indicate that the Taliban suffered less then five hundred casualties, which seems consistent with the claims of local Afghans. Still, the fighting of 2006 remains the most intensive in Kandahar since 2001 and did succeed in regaining the tactical initiative from the enemy.

13. David Galula, *Counter-Insurgency Warfare Theory and Practice* (New York: Praeger, 1968).

14. *Ibid.*, 17–42.

Chapter Five — Campaigning in Afghanistan: A Uniquely Canadian Approach

1. This work is primarily based on a presentation given by Lieutenant-General (Ret.) Michel Gauthier, former Commander Canadian Expeditionary Forces Command (CEFCOM) (2005–2009), to National Security Programme 2 at the Canadian Forces College in Toronto, Ontario, on 20 May 2010, as well as email correspondence between the co-authors from June to October 2010.

2. In accordance with current Canadian doctrine, "a campaign is a set of military operations planned and conducted to achieve a strategic objective within a given time and geographical area, which normally involve maritime, land and aerospace forces." Canada, Department of National Defence, *Canadian Forces Joint Publication (CFJP) 01 Canadian Military Doctrine* (Ottawa: Canadian Forces Experimentation Centre, 2009), 6-3, para 0610.

3. Carl von Clausewitz, *On War*, Michael Howard and Peter Paret, eds. and trans. (Princeton: Princeton University Press, 1976), 87.

4. John English, "The Operational Art," in *The Operational Art: Developments in the Theories of War*, B.J.C. McKercher and Michael A. Hennessy, eds (Westport, Connecticut: Praeger Publishers, 1996), 7–8.

5. The term doctrine at its most fundamental level is used to represent the common understanding that is generated by standardized methods of practice. Doctrine is a distillation of history, theory, and accepted techniques. It

is not prescriptive but can be likened to a sheet of music that all players may read and interpret, using their own instrumental method.

6.　See Howard G. Coombs, "In The Wake of a Paradigm Shift: The Canadian Forces College and the Operational Level of War (1987–1995)," *Canadian Military Journal* 10, no. 1 (Spring 2010): 19–27.

7.　Comprehensive discussion concerning the levels of war is contained in the various chapters of Allan English, Daniel Gosselin, Howard Coombs, and Lawrence Hickey, eds., *The Operational Art — Canadian Perspectives: Context and Concepts* (Kingston: Canadian Defence Academy Press, 2005).

8.　In 1981, the "A" in NORAD changed from "Air" to "Aerospace" in recognition of the growing importance of space to continental defence.

9.　Defence analyst and Queen's University professor Dr. Doug Bland argued that at the beginning of the twenty-first century one could still discern these trends in the employment of the Canadian Forces. Douglas Bland, "War in the Balkans Canadian Style," *Policy Options* (October 1999): 18–21.

10.　See Howard G. Coombs with Richard Goette, "Supporting the *Pax Americana*: Canada's Military and the Cold War," in *The Canadian Way of War: Serving the National Interest*, Colonel Bernd Horn, ed. (Toronto: Dundurn Press, 2006), 265–96.

11.　The current Canadian Forces College, which educates senior officers in the competencies required of the profession of arms, was originally the Royal Canadian Air Force Staff College (1943–1965), then, as a result of the unification of the Canadian military, it became the joint Canadian Forces Staff College (1966–1975), following that was renamed the Canadian Forces Command and Staff College (1975–1988), and in 1988 was finally designated the Canadian Forces College. See Howard G. Coombs, "In Search of Minerva's Owl: Canada's Army and Staff Education (1946–1995)," Unpublished Ph.d. diss., Queen's University, January 2010.

12.　Canada, Department of National Defence, Canadian Forces College Archives, *Canadian Forces Command and Staff College Calendar* (1980–1981), 9.

13.　Canada, Department of National Defence, Canadian Forces College Archives. *Canadian Forces Command and Staff College Calendar* (1985-1986), 21.

14.　William McAndrew, "Operational Art and the Canadian Army's Way of War," in *The Operational Art: Developments in the Theories of War*, B.J.C. McKercher and Michael A. Hennessy, eds (Westport, Connecticut: Praeger Publishers, 1996), 97.

15.　After the closure of the National Defence College in 1994, two shorter courses were instituted at the Canadian Forces College to replace the longer single course. The Advanced Military Studies Course (AMSC) commenced in 1998, and the National Security Studies Course (NSSC) was started in 1999. In 2006 these latter courses were renamed the Advanced Military Studies Program (AMSP) and the National Strategic Studies Program (NSSP). These programs have since been superseded by the National Security Program (NSP). This most recent course commenced in September 2008 and amalgamated the AMSP and NSSP into one course of study. Much of the debate concerning the operational level of war initially took place within the AMSC and manifested itself in the form of argumentative papers by students and instructors — some of which were included as chapters within English et al., eds., *The Operational Art — Canadian Perspectives*.

16.   See Canada, Department of National Defence, "Report of the Somalia Commission of Inquiry," *www.dnd.ca/somalia/somaliae.htm* (accessed 18 August 2010).

17.   See Colonel J.H. Vance, "Tactics without Strategy or Why the Canadian Forces Do Not Campaign," in *The Operational Art — Canadian Perspectives*, Allan English et al., eds. (Kingston, Ontario: Canadian Defence Academy Press, 2005), 271–92.

18.   See Howard G. Coombs, "Perspectives on Operational Thought," in *The Operational Art — Canadian Perspectives*, Allan English et al., eds. (Kingston, Ontario: Canadian Defence Academy Press, 2005), 75–96.

19.   Examples of Canadian officers commanding at the operational level of war in the late 1990s and early 2000s were the command within a coalition exercised by a commodore who was responsible for Task Force 151 in the Persian Gulf, or the command of alliance forces in Bosnia and Afghanistan exerted by a general officer.

20.   These activities are derived from the exercise of other elements or instruments of national power, and these are diplomatic, informational, and economic in nature. In the United States, the acronym commonly used with reference to these components is DIME, for Diplomatic, Informational, Military, and Economic, but at the same time there are a number of other paradigms also used to represent this idea.

21.   Canada, Department of National Defence, "B-GL-300-001/FP-00 Conduct of Land Operations" (1 July 1998), 37–47.

22.   The expression "whole-of-government" in the Canadian context has evolved over time and during various periods has been referred to as interagency, "Diplomacy, Defence and Development" or "3D," and "comprehensive approach" — all trying to express the same idea of pan-government cooperation to achieve common national goals. "Whole-of-government" is the most recent and commonly utilized articulation of this idea.

23. See United Nations, "S/RES/1510 (2003) Resolution 1510 (2003) — Adopted by the Security Council at its 4840th meeting, on 13 October 2003," *http:// daccess-dds-ny.un.org/doc/UNDOC/GEN/N03/555/55/PDF/N0355555. pdf?OpenElement* (5 August 2010).

24. This is taken from a presentation given by Brigadier-General Dean Milner, Commander Joint Task Force Afghanistan 5-10, to the Conference of Defence Associations in Ottawa, Ontario, on 18 June 2010.

25. The report of the "Independent Panel on Canada's Future Role in Afghanistan" was known as the "Manley Report," after its chair, The Honourable John Manley. See Canada, "Independent Panel on Canada's Future Role in Afghanistan" (Ottawa: Minister of Public Works and Government Services, 2008); and also, Canada, House of Commons of Canada, *39th Parliament, 2nd Session Journals*, no. 53 (25 February 2008.), *www2.parl.gc.ca/HousePublications/Publication.aspx?pub=Journals&doc= 53&Language=E&Mode=1&Parl=39&Ses=2* (accessed 5 August 2010).

26. "The ATA replaced the Afghan Interim Authority (AIA). In accordance with the Bonn Agreement, the ATA organised a Constitutional *Loya Jirga* in late 2003 to pave the way for the election of an Afghan government by early 2004." Due to a number of factors, the election was delayed until October 2004 and resulted in the inauguration of President Karzai that December as the chief executive of today's Government of the Islamic Republic of Afghanistan (GIRoA). "Government of Afghanistan," in *Peacebuilding in a Regional Perspective, www.cmi.no/afghanistan/background/ata.cfm* (accessed 14 February 2005).

27. These ISAF and Canadian officers were the precursor of the Strategic Advisory Team, established in 2005 until 2008 to assist the Afghan government with similar problems pertaining to the rebuilding Afghanistan. See Lieutenant-Colonel Michel-Henri St-Louis, "The Strategic Advisory Team in Afghanistan — Part of the Canadian Comprehensive Approach to Stability Operations," *Canadian Military Journal* 9, no. 3 (autumn 2009): 58–67.

28. For a detailed discussion of this process, see Howard G. Coombs and General Rick Hillier, "Planning for Success: The Challenge of Applying Operational Art in Post Conflict Afghanistan," *Canadian Military Journal* 6, no. 3 (autumn 2005): 5–14; and also Afghanistan, Islamic Republic of Afghanistan, *Afghanistan National Development Strategy: An Interim Strategy for Security, Governance, Economic Growth & Poverty Reduction*, n.d., *www.nps.edu/ programs/ccs/Docs/Pubs/unands_Jan.pdf* (18 August 2010); for information on the formulation of the ANDS, see Sayed Mohammed Shah, "Discussion Paper — Afghanistan National Development Strategy (ANDS) Formulation

Process: Influencing Factors and Challenges" (Kabul: Afghanistan Research and Evaluation Unit, February 2009).

29. Canadian Expeditionary Forces Command (CEFCOM) was established in 2006 as part of Canadian Forces "Transformation," or major restructuring, initiated by Hillier as one of his first acts as Chief of the Defence Staff. CEFCOM's mission is to "... conduct assigned global operations across the spectrum from humanitarian assistance to combat in concert with national and international partners in support of Canada's national interests." See "National Defence and the Canadian Forces — What We Do," *www.cefcom.forces.gc.ca/pa-ap/about-notre/index-eng.asp* (accessed 18 August 2010); interestingly, CEFCOM was established at the same time as the first major Canadian deployments to southern Afghanistan.

30. Presentation by Lieutenant-General (Ret.) Michel Gauthier, National Security Programme 2, at the Canadian Forces College in Toronto, Ontario, on 20 May 2010.

31. For details regarding Canada's current participation in Afghanistan, see "Canada's Engagement in Afghanistan," *www. afghanistan.gc.ca* (accessed 5 August 2010). Quote from *www.afghanistan.gc.ca/canada-afghanistan/ documents/r01_10/appendix-annexe.aspx*.

32. North Atlantic Treaty Organization, International Security Assistance Force (ISAF), COMISAF's Counterinsurgency Guidance (Kabul, Afghanistan: Headquarters ISAF/United States Forces — Afghanistan, 1 August 2010), 1, *usacac.army.mil/blog/blogs/coin/archive/2010/08/02/general-petraeus-issues-new-comisaf-coin-guidance.aspx* (accessed 10 August 2010).

33. See Dr. Doug Bland in "Canada's Contributions to Peace Operations, Past, Present and Future," Canadian Peacebuilding Coordination Committee, n.p., *http://forum.peacebuild.ca/content/view/13/27/* (accessed 29 August 2007).

Chapter Six — Sustaining Those Who Dare: Logistic Observations from Contemporary Afghanistan

1. The Disaster Assistance Response Team (DART) is of course the one prominent Canadian exception. The DART is designed for short-term deployments and is configured exclusively for movement by air.

2. For example, during the U.S. Civil War (1861–1865) General Ulysses S. Grant's Union forces were able to move quickly and decisively against the Army of Tennessee, taking advantage of the overall north–south orientation of the major waterways. Furthermore, the absence of good north–south rivers in the eastern theatre was advantageous to the defence of the Confederacy. Richard M. McMurray, *Two Great Rebel Armies: An Essay in Confederate*

Military History (Chapel Hill: University of North Carolina Press, 1989), 10. An engaging discussion is put forward by the author throughout on the benefit and challenges of rivers in the U.S. Civil War.

3.   Louis Dupree, *Afghanistan* (Princeton: Princeton University Press, 1980), 33.

4.   RC South, one of the four Regional Commands organized by NATO ISAF in Afghanistan. RC South was the area of responsibility of the Canadian-led Multinational Brigade in 2006 and, along with RC East, was one of the most volatile of the four Regional Commands under NATO ISAF.

5.   The Canadian-led effort to unclog the silt-infested Dahla Dam has made only incremental progress to date. The project on the Dahla Dam faces significant engineering and security challenges at the time of writing, and even the most optimistic among us can sense the vultures circling.

6.   The popular explanation at the time was that the altitudes in Afghanistan would render the payload capacities of a Canadian Gryphon Helicopter nearly useless. This proved to be inaccurate, as Gryphon squadrons would be deployed to RC South from Canada subsequent to our tour.

7.   I recall, at a post-reconnaissance discussion chaired by the Chief of the Land Staff, Lieutenant-General Marc Caron, that President Bush had to sign a waiver in order for these first four guns off the line to be pressed into Canadian service.

8.   The M777 gun carriage tire drew the attention of our most senior visiting general officers from Canada. As it turned out, sixty-five spare tires was the comfortable stocking number to sustain the four M777s.

9.   Highway 611 is a north-running route in Helmand Province used by the Charlie Company for deployment to the Sangin District.

10.   This group of Canadian Forces personnel in Kabul and Bagram were dubbed "The Kabul 100" by Colonel Steve Noonan's (then Commander Task Force Kabul) staff during the early planning of the move from Camp Julien down to Kandahar. I am told that the popular moniker stuck well beyond our 2006 tour.

11.   I do not mean to imply that the HLVW was a bad piece of major logistics equipment, but rather that it was dated by the time we picked up our sword in Kandahar. The HLVW was of Austrian design and was manufactured for the Canadian Forces by UTDC of Kingston, Ontario, in the late 1980s. Frequent trips by the author to the Kingston-based factory during the production of the truck inspired confidence and satisfaction in the production values and care that the firm put into this vehicle. The HLVW, which entered Canadian service in August 1990, is a thin-skinned workhorse, tailored to the lift requirements of the Cold War and the linear battlefield. In 2006 the after-market armour plating welded to the truck for

service in Kandahar was sub-optimum and afforded very little blast and ballistic protection for logistics soldiers.

12.   Notes from the June 2006 Multinational Brigade Logistics Brief, Kandahar Airfield, from the author's personal collection.

13.   The Arnes trailer is a civilian pattern, long flatbed trailer upon which the HLVW wrecker dragged/scraped the damaged LAV IIIs. A very cumbersome and time-consuming operation that proves lethal on the lava-lamp battlefield in Kandahar.

14.   This tool was the M548 tow bar. In reality it was employed with limited success to recover the LAV III and the Coyote. Lugging the 310-pound tow bar around the battlefield and properly hooking up the vehicle casualty, often under enemy contact, became understandable and limiting factors.

Chapter Seven — More Than Meets the Eye:
The Invisible Hand of SOF in Afghanistan

1.   This is somewhat understandable, as operational security is a fundamental prerequisite for special operations forces. It underscores everything SOF as individuals, units, or formations do. Its importance is rooted in two essential pillars. The first is based on a moral obligation to do everything possible to ensure the protection and safety of their personnel, particularly in the context of the type of operations that they conduct, the environments they conduct them in, and the nature of the enemy they face. The second pillar is the need to guarantee mission success. As the force of last resort, entrusted with "no fail" tasks, there is no margin for error. Important to note is that the significance of operational security extends to the protection of allies as well, for the same two reasons as already given. Moreover, failure to do so also jeopardizes the relationship with others, complete with dramatic consequences like the withdrawal of support such as intelligence, research and development (R&D), the provision of enablers (e.g. aviation, air, ISTAR) for operations, and support in general. Clearly, degradation in this realm could often have significant impact on the ability to achieve mission success.

2.   For a brief overview of the history between the Americans, Osama bin Laden, and al Qaeda (AQ), see Chapter 8, endnote 7.

3.   According to one official source, only "110 CIA officers and 316 Special Operations Forces personnel were initially deployed." Thomas H. Henriksen, "Afghanistan, Counterinsurgency, and the Indirect Approach," Joint Special Operations University Report 10-3, April 2010, 39.

4.   The air campaign had a great impact. For example, air strikes brought down by one of the first SF teams in country, aided by a lone air force combat controller, are credited with killing as many as 3,500 fighters and destroying up to 450 vehicles. Glenn Goodman, "Tip of the Spear," *Armed Forces Journal International* (June 2002): 35; Michael Ware, "On the Mop-Up Patrol," *Time* (25 March 2002): 36–37; Thomas E. Ricks, "Troops in Afghanistan to Take Political Role Officials Say Remaining Fights to be Taken by Special Forces, CIA," *Duluth News Tribune*, 7 July 2002, 1; and Massimo Calabresi and Romesh Ratnesar, "Can we Stop the Next Attack?" *Time*, 11 March 2002, 18.

5.   Maulvi Mohammad Haqqani, a Taliban fighter at the time, conceded, "I never thought the Taliban would collapse so quickly and cruelly under U.S. bombs." He lamented, "The bombs cut down our men like a reaper harvesting wheat." As cited in Sami Yousafzai and Ron Moreau, "The Taliban in Their Own Words," *Newsweek.com*, 5 October 2009, 36.

6.   Ahmed Rashid, *Taliban: Militant Islam, Oil and Fundamentalism in Central Asia* (New Haven: Yale University Press, 2010), 220.

7.   "Chapter 11 — Special Operations," NATO Publication AJP-1 (A), Third Draft, March 1998, 11-1.

8.   This is the official Canadian Special Operations Forces Command doctrinal definition. Special operations differ from conventional operations in the degree of physical and political risk, operational techniques, modes of employment, independence from friendly support, and dependence on detailed operational intelligence. Canada, *CANSOFCOM Capstone Concept for Special Operations 2009* (Ottawa: DND, 2009), 4.

9.   *Ibid.*, 4.

10. "Non-Kinetic" options refer to a wide range of skills and task sets that include provision of strategic advisory teams, security force assistance, information operations, psychological operations, and support to other military, paramilitary, or law enforcement agencies.

11. The negative publicity is largely based on civilian deaths and collateral damage that results from alleged air strikes during SOF missions and night raids, which are viewed negatively by Afghans. Other perceptions are reflected in the view of one Afghan official at the presidential palace, who insisted, "Nobody has an idea what were they [SOF] are doing there because they don't share anything with the Afghans." He added that SOF "arrest people and they raid houses without keeping the Afghans in the loop." Matthew Rosenberg, "US Special Operations Ordered Deadly Afghan Strike," *Dow Jones Reprints*, 22 February 2010, *http://online.wsj.com/SB10001424052748704057604575080060203691352.html?mod=WAJ_World_LEFTSecondNews* (accessed 22 February 2010). The sharing of

information is a sensitive issue because information shared with Afghans often, if not invariably, leaks out.

12. Department of Defence, *Special Operations Forces Reference Manual, 2nd ed.* (Tampa, Florida: JSOU, 2008), 1–5. The U.S. Army John F. Kennedy Special Warfare Center hosted a conference at which a new definition was developed. The new recommended doctrinal definition for UW is "activities conducted to enable a resistance movement or insurgency to coerce, disrupt or overthrow a government or occupying power by operating through or with an underground, auxiliary and guerrilla force in a denied area." Quoted in Robert Haddick, "Do We Still Need Special Ops?" *http:// smallwarsjournal.com* (accessed 23 April 2010).

13. Department of Defense, *Security Force Assistance FM3-07.1* (Washington D.C.: Department of the Army, May 2009), v.

14. The U.S. doctrinal definition for FID is "participation by civilian and military agencies of a government in any of the action programs taken by another government to free and protect its society from subversion, lawlessness, and insurgency. SOF's primary contribution in this interagency activity is to organize, train, advise, and assist host nation (HN) military and paramilitary forces. The generic capabilities required for FID include instructional skills; foreign language proficiency; area and cultural orientation; tactical skills; advanced medical skills; rudimentary construction and engineering skills; familiarity with a wide variety of demolitions, weapons, weapon systems, and communications equipment; and basic PSYOP and CA skills." Department of Defence, *Special Operations Forces Reference Manual, 2nd ed.* (Tampa, Florida: JSOU, 2008), 1–5. The similar Canadian concept is known as Defence, Diplomacy, and Military Assistance (DDMA), which refers to operations that contribute to nation building through assistance to select states in the form of the provision of specialized military advice, training, and assistance. *CANSOFCOM Capstone Concept for Special Operations 2009*, 10.

15. Sean D. Naylor, "Visa Roadblock," *Army Times*, 22 March 2010, 18.

16. Sean D. Naylor, "Afghans at the forefront," *Army Times*, 26 July 2010, 22. Colonel Don Bolduc acknowledged that the SOF focus evolved from earlier years when the emphasis was on kinetic operations. He explained his theory has transitioned from "pressure, pursue, punish" to "presence, patience, and persistence."

17. Sean D. Naylor, "Special Partnership," *Army Times*, 14 June 2010, 16.

18. Sean D. Naylor, "The Jewel in the Afghan Army," *Army Times*, 31 May 2010, 28.

19. Naylor, "The Jewel in the Afghan Army," 28.

20. James Gordon Meek, "Afghan Tribesman Going Commando," *New York Daily News*, 8 August 2010, 10.

21. Naylor, "The Jewel in the Afghan Army," 28. An Afghan team sergeant explained the professionalism and SOF approach to Commandos. He stated, "The Commandos have three words: bravery, speed, and power." However, he explained, "in Special Forces, before you show your power, your bravery or anything else, you've got to think about it. You've got to use your mind. You've got to think through the ramifications." He continued, "Most missions in the Commandos were aggressive: go after a bad guy and detain him if possible; if not, just shoot him. This was a killing game. When I came to Special Forces, I learned there were other ways to solve problems. In Special Forces I can learn so many other ways besides fighting the bad guys." Sean D. Naylor, "Afghan Special Forces," *Army Times*, 24 May 2010, 20.

22. Naylor, "The Jewel in the Afghan Army," 28.

23. *Ibid.*, 28.

24. James Gordon Meek, "Afghan Tribesman Going Commando," *New York Daily News*, 8 August 2010, 10.

25. Sean D. Naylor, "Making Bad Guys Good Guys," *Army Times*, 9 November 2009, 20.

26. Michael G. Mullen, "From the Chairman: Strategic Communication: Getting Back to Basics," *Joint Force Quarterly*, 4th Quarter, 2009, www.jcs.mil/newsarticle.aspx?ID=142. He also observed, "That's the essence of good communication: having the right intent up front and letting our actions speak for themselves. We shouldn't care if people don't like us; that isn't the goal. The goal is credibility. And we earn that over time." General David Petraeus stated, "This effort is a contest of wills.... We must never forget that the center of gravity in this struggle is the Afghan people; it is they who will ultimately determine the future of Afghanistan." ISAF News Release, "General Petraeus Issues Updated Tactical Directive," 2010-08-CA-004, issued 1 August 2010.

27. See Mark Schafer and Chris Fussell, "The Role of SOF Direct Action in Counterinsurgency," *2010 JSOU and NDIA SO/LIC Division Essays* (Hurburlt Field: JSOU Report 10-4, 2010), 85.

28. See Bernd Horn, *No Lack of Courage: Operation Medusa, Afghanistan 2006* (Toronto: Dundurn, 2010) for a detailed account of Operation Medusa.

29. TF-31 was a sub-unit from the 1st Battalion, 3rd Special Forces Group (3 SFG) or "Desert Eagles." The unit, under the command of Lieutenant-Colonel Donald Bolduc, was starting its fifth rotation in Afghanistan. Major Jamie Hall, the OC of the American SF "C" Coy, which consisted of

six Operational Detachment — Alpha (ODA) teams, was responsible for the Kandahar area, therefore, he was assigned to Operation Medusa. Each of his six ODAs also had a thirty-man ANA company attached to it.

30. Lieutenant-Colonel Shane Schreiber, interview with author, 18 October 2006.

31. *Ibid.*

32. Captain C. Purdy, interview with author, 17 October 2006.

33. Captain Michael Irwin, "Integrating Intelligence With Operations," *Special Warfare* 21, no. 1 (January–February 2008): 16.

34. Thom Shanker, Helene Cooper, and Richard A. Oppel Jr., "Elite U.S. Units Step up Effort in Afghan City Before Attack," *New York Times, www.nytimes. com/2010/04/26/world/asia/26kandahar.html?emc=eta1* (accessed 1 May 2010).

35. Peter Goodspeed, "Battle for Kandahar: Success or Failure of Obama's Troops to Surge Lies in Kandahar City," *National Post,* 27 May 2010, *www. nationalpost.com/news/world/story.html?id=3084975* (accessed 4 June 2010); and Shanker et al., "Elite U.S. Units Step Up Effort in Afghan City Before Attack."

36. See Lee Winsor, David Charters, and Brent Wilson, *Kandahar Tour: The Turning Point in Canada's Afghan Mission* (Mississauga: John Wiley & Sons Canada, Ltd., 2008), 198, for just one example. As they describe, "Boomer's tank-infantry force fought into the midst of the Taliban position, fixing the enemy to a wild gunfight to their front. That was when U.S. Army Blackhawk helicopters swept in to land the Special Forces teams behind the enemy to prevent their escape."

37. Sean D. Naylor, "A-Team in Afghanistan," *Army Times,* 21 June 2010, 16.

38. Mark Schafer and Chris Fussell, "The Role of SOF Direct Action in Counterinsurgency," *2010 JSOU and NDIA SO/LIC Division Essays* (Hurburlt Field: JSOU Report 10-4, 2010), 85.

39. Sean D. Naylor, "U.S. Stops Spec Ops Raids into Pakistan Tribal Areas," *Army Times,* 6 October 2008, 10. JSOC has been pushing hard for years to increase raids into the tribal safe areas along the Afghanistan-Pakistan border. As one JSOC officer stated, "We got to hit where their sanctuaries are." The 3 September 2010 raid was a direct result of the 13 July 2008 Taliban attack on a U.S. outpost in the Konengal Valley. In addition to the raids, Predator drones have been used on numerous occasions to target Taliban commanders in the FATA.

40. The Army Capstone Concept, *Operational Adaptability: Operating under Conditions of Uncertainty and Complexity in an Era of Persistent Conflict 2016-2028.* TRADOC Pam 525-3-0, 21 December 2009, 13. The deployed

forces did not bring artillery, based on the assumption that surveillance and precision fires from the air could destroy any targets. However, they experienced severe limitations due to difficulties with determining target locations.

41. Justin Kelly and Mike Brennan, *Distributed Manoeuvre 21st Century Offensive Tactics*, Land Warfare Studies Centre Working Papers Series, The Australian Army, June 2009, 25.

42. Quoted in Adam Day, *Witness to War* (Ottawa: Magic Light / CDA Press, 2010), 130.

43. Sean D. Naylor, "Beyond Bin Laden Petraeus: Success in Afghanistan," *Army Times*, 27 October 2008, 28.

44. *CANSOFCOM Capstone Concept for Special Operations 2009*, 10.

45. Sean D. Naylor, "U.S. Spec Ops Unit Hits Haqqanis," *Army Times*, 13 September 2010, 22. It is important to note that on two thirds of our targets there are no shots fired. The ratio for Canadian SOF is even higher in this regard; Sean D. Naylor, "The Deadliest Insurgents," *Army Times*, 20 September 2010, 18.

46. Kimberley Dozier, "Analysis: Gen. Petraeus Promotes Special-Ops Success to Show Part of Afghan War US is Winning," *www.foxnews.com/ world/2010/09/03analysis-gen-petraeus-promotes-special-ops-success-af-ghan-war-winning* (accessed 7 September 2010).

47. Naylor, "U.S. Spec Ops Unit Hits Haqqanis," 22; Naylor, "The Deadliest Insurgents," 18.

48. Jon Gambrell, Rahim Faiez, "Afghan President Moves to Stop NATO Night Raids Amid Anger over Civilian Casualties," Associated Press, 28 May 2011.

49. Sean D. Naylor, "Inside a U.S. Hostage Rescue Spec Ops Soldiers Conduct Night Raid in Afghanistan Mountains," *Army Times*, 17 November 2008, 8. According to one SOF operator, the rescue "sends a very clear message to any extremist group that [kidnapping Americans] will be handled with vigilance and unrelenting persecution."

50. Rick Hillier as cited in Julian Borger, "Linda Norgrove: US Navy SEAL Faces Disciplinary Action over Grenade Death," *Guardian.co.uk* (accessed 13 October 2010).

51. Paul Robinson, "We can't just take them out; it's tempting to simply fire a missile or sniper bullet and be done with suspected terrorist leaders — but it's a lot more complicated than that", *The Ottawa Citizen*, 27 May 2008.

52. Naylor, "The Deadliest Insurgents," 18.

53. *Ibid.*, 18.

54. Naylor, "The Deadliest Insurgents," 18.

55. *Ibid.*, 18.
56. Lieutenant-Colonel Rob Walker, interview with author, 5 October 2008.
57. Lee Winsor, David Charters and Brent Wilson, *Kandahar Tour: The Turning Point in Canada's Afghan Mission* (Mississauga: John Wiley & Sons Canada, Ltd., 2008), 167.
58. Kimberley Dozier, "Analysis: Gen. Petraeus Promotes Special-Ops Success to Show Part of Afghan War US is Winning," *www.foxnews.com/world/2010/09/03analysis-gen-petraeus-promotes-special-ops-success-afghan-war-winning* (accessed 7 September 2010).
59. *Ibid.*
60. Sean D. Naylor, "Officials: Al-Qaida Forces in Pakistan Battered but Resilient," *Army Times*, 3 August 2009, 21.
61. *Ibid.*, 21.
62. Major General Jim Molan, "How Much is Enough in Afghanistan," *Australian Army Journal*, (winter 2009): 21.
63. Sean D. Naylor, "Making Bad Guys Good Guys," *Army Times*, 9 November 2009, 20.
64. SOF was also responsible for a seminal DA raid in Pakistan that killed Osama Bin Laden on 1 May 2011. Based on evidence removed from his home, the CIA assessed Bin Laden was still "acting as a CEO of terror." In fact, he was working on plans to poison drinking water and destroy rail lines. CTV News, 7 May 2011.
65. An IED is a device placed or fabricated in an improvised manner incorporating destructive, lethal, noxious, pyrotechnic, or incendiary chemicals, designed to destroy or incapacitate, harass or distract. It may incorporate military stores but is normally devised from non-military components. NATO unclassified Releasable to PfP [Partnership for Peace] and ISAF, Joint Operational Guideline for Counter Improvised Explosive Devices Activities, Version 3.0, August 2008, 5.
66. Spencer Ackerman, "Drones Surge, Special Ops Strike in Petraeus Campaign Plan," *www.wired.com/dangerroom/2010/08/petraeus-campaign-plan/#more-29588* (accessed 18 August 2010). The Key to Adversary's success is vested in highly organized IED cells operating in isolation and in small numbers. Typically, each cell has a variety of members who specialize in different tasks. At the tactical level, the organization is based on local leaders, bomb makers, bomb couriers, bomb layers, triggermen (ambush teams), and exploitation teams (video recording of incident and first responders for future analysis). At the strategic level, the focus is funding, planning, training, logistics and resource allocation. Defeating the IED system requires the targeting of the opposition's political, social, and cultural systems. It involves

activity undertaken simultaneously at the political, strategic, operational, and tactical level intended to disrupt the network. The aim of defeating the system is to undermine the ability and will to construct and employ IEDs. Such operations will certainly take longer to initiate and apply but, overall, will have a more penetrating effect on the IED system. Activities may include deterrence, information operations campaigns, law enforcement, interdicting the IED re-supply apparatus, apprehending belligerents, and encouraging external pressure to stop the use of IEDs. NATO unclassified Releasable to PfP and ISAF, Joint Operational Guideline for Counter Improvised Explosive Devices Activities, Version 3.0, August 2008, 7-10.

67. Dozier.
68. Sean D. Naylor, "Gates Plans for 2,800 More Spec-Ops Personnel," *Army Times*, 20 April 2009, 16.
69. Michelle L. Malvesti, *To Serve the Nation: U.S. Special Operations Forces in an Era of Persistent Conflict* (Center for a New American Security, 2010), 4.

Chapter Eight — Lesson Learned:
Operation Medusa and the Taliban Epiphany

1. See Bernd Horn, *No Lack of Courage: Operation Medusa, Afghanistan* (Toronto: Dundurn, 2010) for a detailed account of the operation.
2. Quoted in Paul Wells, "The Final Battle Begins," *Maclean's*, 26 April 2010, 22. Major Wade Rutland told Leslie "the bad guys have complete freedom of manoeuvre in and around three villages, Zangabad, Mushan and Talukan," what Rutland called the area's "insurgent axis of evil." *Ibid.*, 22.
3. Sean D. Naylor, "A bigger, badder enemy," *Army Times*, 16 November 2009, 16. Journalist Adam Day wrote, "Even though the battlegroup is now tightly focused on eastern Panjwai and they / the U.S. has its COIN philosophy somewhat firmly in place, the place is more unruly than ever. Shots were fired every single time I went on patrol, even getting in a firefight while clearing an "insurgent stronghold" in the King's Garden just off the main road in Bazaar-e-Panjwai itself (within sight of the wire at MSG [Ma'Sūm Ghar]. I truly would have expected the population-centric approach would have paid some dividends after 14 months, but Slavat, for example, which was a very quiet place last year, is now an utter battlefield. It's not even like a stalemate. It's worse." Adam Day, email to author, 16 September 2010.
4. John F. Burns, "Into Kandahar, Yesterday and Tomorrow," *New York Times Online, www.nytimes.com/2010/05/23/weekinreview/23burns.html? pagewanted=1&hp* (accessed 30 May 2010). See also Alissa J. Rubin, "U.S. Report on Afghan War Finds Few Gains in 6 Months," *New York Times*

Online, www.nytimes.com/2010/04/30/world/asia/30afghan.html (accessed 1 May 2010). The report also noted that "the insurgents have succeeded in establishing at least a facsimile of government. They have named shadow governors, raised taxes and set up courts. Relying on their own lessons learned, they have relented on some of their harsher measures; now they allow children to fly kites and villagers to play soccer, and they have banned, in a decree issued by Mullah Muhammad Omar who was one of the founders of the Taliban in a village outside Kandahar in 1994, public beheadings for alleged miscreants. (His preference: firing squads)."

5.   Quoted in United Kingdom, Parliament, House of Commons Library, International Affairs & Defence Section, Research Paper 01/72, 11 September 2001: the response, 31 October 2002, 17, *www.parliament.uk/commons/lib/re-search/rp2001/rp01-112.pdf* (accessed 7 March 2007). The history between the Americans, Osama bin Laden, and al Qaeda (AQ) was long standing. They had tracked Bin Laden from Sudan to Afghanistan. On 28 August 1998, the Americans were able to convince the Security Council to pass UN Security Council Resolution (UNSCR) 1193 that demanded that "Afghan factions ... refrain from harboring and training terrorists and their organizations." More specifically, UNSCR 214, passed on 8 December 1998, affirmed that the Security Council was "deeply disturbed by the continuing use of Afghan territory, especially areas controlled by the Taliban, for the sheltering and training of terrorists and the planning of terrorist acts" and reiterated that "the suppression of international terrorism is essential for the maintenance of international peace and security." The Americans continued their U.N. offensive. On 15 October 1999, the US secured the adoption of UNSCR 1267, which expressed concerns about the "continuing violations of international humanitarian law and of human rights [in Afghanistan], particularly discrimination against women and girls," as well as "the significant rise in the illicit production of opium." Importantly, the resolution specifically criticized the Taliban for offering "safe haven to Osama bin Laden and to allow him and others associated with him to operate a network of terrorist training camps ... and to use Afghanistan as a base from which to sponsor international terrorist operations." As such the Security Council demanded "that the Taliban turn over Osama bin Laden without further delay" so that he could be "effectively brought to justice." The council also instituted the same economic and financial sanctions on the Taliban regime that had been recently imposed by the United States. The Taliban failed to comply, and on 12 October 2000, the AQ attacked the USS *Cole* in the harbour at Aden, killing seventeen U.S. sailors and wounding thirty-nine. To exacerbate the looming showdown, bin Laden took full credit for

the operation, prompting the Security Council to pass UNSCR 1333 on 19 December 2000. This resolution reaffirmed the charges made just a year earlier and added the stipulation that the Taliban were to ensure the closing "of all camps where terrorists are trained." In addition, economic sanctions were strengthened, Taliban offices were to be closed in the territory of member states, landing rights for Afghan national airways was revoked and all assets linked to Osama bin Laden and al-Qaeda were frozen. Once again the Taliban regime did nothing As a result, yet another UNSCR was passed on 30 July 2001, which described "the situation in Afghanistan .... as a threat to international peace and security in the region." As such, in the weeks leading up to 9/11, Afghanistan had already been identified as a major threat centre for American national interest. See United Nations Security Council Resolution 1193, 28 August 1998; Resolution 1214, 8 December 1998; Resolution 1267, 15 October 1999; Resolution 1333, 19 December 2000; Resolution 1363, 30 July 2001; and Ahmed Rashid, *Taliban: Militant Islam, Oil and Fundamentalism in Central Asia* (New Haven: Yale University Press, 2001), 80; Daniel Benjamin and Steven Simon, *The Age of Sacred Terror* (New York: Random House, 2002), xiii and 289. See also Steve Coll, *Ghost Wars* (New York: Penguin Books, 2004) for a comprehensive account of the US / Bin Laden / AQ interrelationship.

6.   North Atlantic Council Statement, 12 September 2001, Press Release (2001)124, *www.nat.int/docu/pr/2001/p01-124e.htm* (accessed 7 March 2007); and NATO, *NATO Handbook* (Brussels: NATO Office of Information and Press, 1995), 232.

7.   Statement by NATO Secretary General Lord Robertson, 4 October 2001, *www.nato.int/docu/speech/2001/s011004a.htm* (accessed 7 March 2007). See also Tom Lansford, *All for One: Terrorism, NATO, and the United States* (Aldershot: Ashgate Publishing, 2002), 126.

8.   See United Nations Security Council Resolutions 1368, 12 September 2001 and UNSCR 1373, 28 September 2001. Interestingly, the U.N. had already, in essence, given its approval to NATO on 28 September when they invoked Chapter VII of the United Nations Charter, which authorized the use of military force.

9.   Maulvi Abdul Rehman Akhundzada cited in Sami Yousafzai and Ron Moreau, "The Taliban in their Own Words," *Newsweek.com*, 5 October 2009, 36.

10.   Ahmed Rashid, *Taliban. Militant Islam, Oil and Fundamentalism in central Asia* (New Haven: Yale University Press, 2010), 220.

11.   See Rashid, *Taliban* and Coll, *Ghost Wars* for a detailed account of the rise of the Taliban. In short, Carl Forsberg summarized, "This senior Islamic

court [clerics in Kandahar] was 'independent of any of the Resistance political parties and had the final authority on all political-military-juridical matters.' These clerics benefited from their close ties to the population and had a 'more widespread basis of legitimacy' than Kandahar's militia commanders. The clerics who formed the Taliban likewise had a concrete connection to the larger sections of the population in Kandahar alienated from their leadership, and the Taliban rose to power as a popularly supported clerical response to these tribal strongmen." He went on to explain, "The Taliban professed limited aims at their inception, promising to wipe out corruption, provide security, and establish a fair judiciary based on sharia (Islamic law). The Taliban's dramatic demonstrations and noble promises convinced many that Omar and his followers were committed to good governance and could provide relief from the oppression and extortion of local strongmen." "The Taliban's Campaign for Kandahar," *Executive Summary, Afghanistan Report 3* (December 2009), 15.

12. One analyst explained, "Taliban field commanders are brought into the operational planning process through a rotation system, which allows them to spend a portion of their year in Quetta. During their time in Quetta, commanders are updated on the Taliban's strategy and tactics and discuss developments in lessons-learned sessions. A lull in combat operations from October to April, which was an annual occurrence until 2008, gave the Taliban an opportunity to formulate a campaign plan for the coming year, which could then be adjusted during the summer months." Forsberg, "The Taliban's Campaign for Kandahar," 22.

13. One Taliban fighter acknowledged, "The American invasion of Iraq was very positive for us. It distracted the United States from Afghanistan." Maulvi Mohammad Haqqani as cited in Sami Yousafzai and Ron Moreau, "The Taliban in Their Own Words," *Newsweek.com*, 5 October 2009, 39–40.

14. Forsberg, "The Taliban's Campaign for Kandahar," 22–23.

15. Maulvi Mohammad Haqqani as cited in Sami Yousafzai and Ron Moreau, "The Taliban in their Own Words," *Newsweek.com*, 5 October 2009, 39–40.

16. Strategic analyst Carl Forsberg explained the initial discomfort with the new tactics. He noted as the Taliban "consolidated their lines of communication across southern Afghanistan, the Taliban embarked on a new and more sophisticated bombing campaign in Kandahar City in the fall of 2005. The campaign was led by Mullah Dadullah Akhund, who served as the Taliban's overall field commander and had connections to suicide bombing units in the Kabul area. Dadullah's suicide bombing campaign in 2005 polarized the Taliban's senior leadership, which was concerned by Dadullah's reputation for inflicting violence. As a Taliban commander in

the 1990s, he was removed from command on multiple occasions for terrorizing local populations and perpetrating mass killings of non-Pashtuns. Mullah Omar and Mullah Osmani, had reservations about Dadullah's use of suicide bombers. In the end, Mullah Omar compromised; Pakistani suicide bombers could be employed for suicide bombings, but locals would not be." Forsberg, "The Taliban's Campaign for Kandahar," 55.

17. *Ibid.*, 23.

18 *Ibid.*, 23.

19 Bari Khan as cited in Sami Yousafzai and Ron Moreau, "The Taliban in Their Own Words," *Newsweek.com*, 5 October 2009, 40.

20. Lieutenant-Colonel Pat Stogran was the commanding officer. During their six months in Afghanistan, 3. PPCLI Battle Group performed tasks ranging from airfield security to combat operations.

21. The International Security Assistance Force (ISAF) is a United Nations-mandated operation, but NATO-led. It was authorized by United Nations Security Council Resolutions (UNSCRs) 1386, 1413, 1444, and 1510. UNSCR 1386 (20 December 2001), as well as UNSCR 1413, authorize ISAF to operate under Chapter VII of the U.N. Charter (peace-enforcing). Furthermore, under UNSCR 1444 (27 November 2002) the role of ISAF remained to assist in the maintenance of security and to help the Afghan Transitional Authority (Afghan TA) and the initial activities of the United Nations in Kabul and its environs — nowhere else. However, UNSCR 1510 (13 October 2003) authorized the expansion of the ISAF mandate beyond the original provision of security in the Kabul area into the rest of Afghanistan. The first ISAF troops deployed as a multi-national force (without Canadian participation) initially under British command on 4 January 2002.

22. The latest deployment consisted of close to two thousand Canadian troops who were deployed to Kabul as part of Operation Athena. Their task was to provide security in the Kabul area and reinforce the Afghan Transitional Authority. The deployment carried over five successive six-month rotations; Canadian troops conducted foot patrols and surveillance tasks that established a presence and capability within the ISAF area of responsibility. These tasks also generated intelligence and situational awareness. In addition, Canadian soldiers assisted and facilitated the rebuilding of the democratic process in Afghanistan.

23. The last Canadian material assets were moved and shipped to Kandahar on 29 November 2005 and Camp Julien, the Canadian base in Kabul, was officially handed over to the Afghan Ministry of Defence.

24. On 17 May 2006, Parliament voted to extend the Canadian military mission in Kandahar Province as well as the work of the PRT up to February

2009. The Americans created the PRT construct in November 2002, as part of OEF. It became a critical component of the U.S. efforts to stabilize Afghanistan. PRTs were conceived as a way to integrate diplomats, development officials, military assets, and police officers to address the causes of instability — namely poor governance, weak institutions, insurgency, regional warlords, and poverty. Canada, "Managing Turmoil: The Need to Upgrade Canadian Foreign Aid and Military Strength to Deal with Massive Change," An Interim Report of the Standing Senate Committee on National Security and Defence, October 2006, 150. See also Michelle Parker, "Programming Development Funds to Support a Counterinsurgency: A Case Study of Nangarhar, Afghanistan in 2006," Case Studies in National Security Transformation, Number 10, 2.

25. Canada, "Managing Turmoil." The PRT in Kandahar focused on three major areas: good governance, security sector reform (including providing training and equipment to Afghan police), and reconstruction and development. The specific PRT tasks were to promote the extension of the Afghan central and provincial government, implement development and reconstruction programs, assist in stabilizing the local security environment, and support security sector reform. The aims of the CF in Kandahar Province were first and foremost "to provide the people of Afghanistan with the hope for a brighter future by establishing the security necessary to promote development and an environment that is conducive to the improvement of Afghan life." In addition, the CF was to conduct operations in support of the ANSF, strengthen and enhance Afghan governance capacity, and help extend the authority of the Government of Afghanistan throughout the southern regions of the country. Finally, the CF effort was to support the larger Canadian integrated whole of government team to facilitate the delivery of programs and projects that support the economic recovery and rehabilitation of Afghanistan, as well to assist in addressing humanitarian needs of Afghans by supporting Canadian governmental organizations and NGOs whose efforts meet Canada's objectives.

Canada, "Canadian Forces Operations in Afghanistan," DND Backgrounder, 15 May 2007: the Canadian efforts were in support of the internationally supported Afghanistan Compact, which was developed in London 31 January to 1 February 2006. The Afghan Compact commits international community (more than sixty countries and international organizations) along with the GIRoA and the U.N. to achieve progress in three critical and interrelated areas of activity for the period 2006–11: security; governance, including rule of law, human rights and tackling corruption; and economic and social development. The Afghan Compact aimed to triple the

Afghan army to 70,000 troops; disband all illegal militias by 2007; reduce by 70 percent the amount of land made unusable by land mines by 2010; reduce the number of people living on less than $1 a day by 3 percent per year, and the proportion of those who are hungry by 5 percent per year, create functioning justice institutions in every province by end of 2010, including prisons with separate facilities for women and juveniles; upgrade the country's main ring road, central to government plans to revive Afghanistan's historic role as a land bridge between Central and South Asia; bring electricity to 65 percent of urban homes and 25 percent of rural homes by end of 2010; enroll 60 percent of girls and 75 percent of boys in primary school by 2010.

26. NATO took control of ISAF in 2003. Since then it expanded to the north in 2004 (Stage I), to the west in 2005 (Stage II) and its plan to move to the south (Stage III) transpired in 2005–2006. This new evolution of the Canadian mission was called Operation Archer.

27. The 1 PPCLI Battle Group (BG) consisted of 1 PPCLI, a tactical unmanned aerial vehicle (TUAV) troop, an HSS, a company, a forward support group (FSG), and the Kandahar Provincial Reconstruction team (PRT). Their mission: "Task Force Orion will assist Afghans in the establishment of good governance, security and stability, and reconstruction in the province of Kandahar during Op Archer Rotation (Roto) 1 in order to help extend the legitimacy and credibility of the Government of Afghanistan throughout the Islamic Republic of Afghanistan and at the same time help to establish conditions necessary for NATO Stage 3 expansion." Hope stated that he chose the name Orion to give everyone a common identifier: "I chose Orion from the constellation — representing the mythical Greek hunter of mountain beasts — that I knew blessed the Afghan skies, so that our soldiers might look up and seeing it, feel part of a larger entity, enduring and meaningful." Ian Hope, "Reflections on Afghanistan: Commanding Task Force Orion," in Bernd Horn, ed., *In Harm's Way. The Buck Stops Here: Senior Officers on Operations* (Kingston: CDA Press, 2007), 212. See also Lieutenant-Colonel Ian Hope, *Dancing with the Dushman: Command Imperatives for the Counter-Insurgency Fight in Afghanistan* (Kingston: CDA Press, 2008); and "1st Battalion Princess Patricia's Canadian Light Infantry Battle Group (Task Force Orion) — Operational Summary," 12 August 2006.

28. The Senlis Council, "Canada in Kandahar: No Peace to Keep: A Case Study of the Military Coalitions in Southern Afghanistan," London, June 2006, v.

29. *Ibid.*, xi.

30. *Ibid.*, 31.

31. Rashid, *Taliban*, 229.

32. Christie Blatchford, *Fifteen Days* (Toronto: Doubleday Canada, 2007), 13.

33. Lieutenant-Colonel Shane Schreiber, Operations Officer MNB HQ, 1 CMBG briefing, 22 January 2007.
34. Schreiber, 1 CMBG briefing, 22 January 2007.
35. *Ibid.*
36. For a detailed account of the battle(s), see Blatchford, *Fifteen Days* and Hope, *Dancing with the Dushman.*
37. Blatchford, *Fifteen Days*, 250.
38. Brigadier-General David Fraser, interview with author, 21 October 2006.
39. This refers to the Maoist model of insurgency: Phase 1 — Strategic Defence: focus on survival and building support. Bases are established, local leaders are recruited, cellular networks and parallel governments created; Phase 2 — Strategic Stalemate: guerilla warfare ensues. Insurgents focus on separating population from government; Phase 3 — Strategic Offensive: Insurgents feel they have superior strength and move to conventional operations to destroy government capability.
40. Brigadier-General David Fraser, interview with author 21 October 2006.
41. *Ibid.*
42. *Ibid.*
43. Blatchford, *Fifteen Days*, 251.
44. One reporter noted, "NATO is hoping to bring a new strategy to dealing with the Taliban rebellion: establishing bases rather than chasing militants, and is also hoping to win the support of local people by creating secure zones where development can take place. But questions remain whether they can quell the violence enough to allow aid workers to get to work in a lawless and impoverished region where [Kandahar province] about a quarter of Afghanistan's huge opium crop is grown, and the narcotics trade fuels the insurgency." Fisnik Abrashi, "NATO takes command in Afghanistan," *The Kingston Whig-Standard*, 31 July 2006, 10.
45. Lieutenant-Colonel Shane Schreiber, interview with author, 18 October 2006.
46. Brigadier-General David Fraser, interview with author, 21 October 2006.
47. Lieutenant-Colonel Shane Schreiber, interview with author, 18 October 2006. Schreiber noted, "And a very sophisticated C2 node. Somebody actually reinforcing, directing reinforcements to exact positions. Somebody actually controlling the battle."
48. Lieutenant-Colonel Shane Schreiber, ACOS, Multi-National Brigade HQ, 1 CMBG briefing, 22 January 2007.
49. An Army report also noted that their gunnery, "particularly with the SPG [73mm / 82mm recoilless rifle] was very good resulting in the defeat of a LAV 3 and support vehicles during one assault." Memo, Director Army Training to Commander Land Force Development Training System, "Tactical

Reconnaissance Report — Training Assessment OP Archer Rotation 3," 21 September 2006, 3. SPG refers to the Soviet designation Stankovyy Protivotankovyy Granatamet, or literally translated, mounted anti-tank grenade launcher. In NATO terminology, it refers to an anti-tank recoilless rifle.

50. General Hillier explained in an interview, "The challenge is that marijuana plants absorb energy, heat very readily. It's very difficult to penetrate them with thermal devices ... And as a result you really have to be careful that the Taliban don't dodge in and out of those marijuana forests. We tried burning them with white phosphorous — it didn't work. We tried burning them with diesel — it didn't work. The plants are so full of water right now ... that we simply couldn't burn them. A couple of brown plants on the edges of some of those [forests] did catch on fire. But a section of soldiers that was downwind from that had some ill effects and decided that was probably not the right course of action." "Canada Troops Battle 10-foot Afghan Marijuana Plants," *CNN.Com*, *www.cnn.com/2006/WORLD/Americas/10/12/Canada.troops.marijuana.reut/index.html* (accessed 13 October 2006).

51. Memo, Director Army Training to Commander Land Force Development Training System, "Tactical Reconnaissance Report — Training Assessment OP Archer Rotation 3," 21 September 2006, 3.

52. Brigadier-General David Fraser, interview with author, 21 October 2006.

53. Janice Gross Stein, *The Unexpected War: Canada in Kandahar* (Toronto: Viking, 2007), 219.

54. Brigadier-General David Fraser, interview with author, 21 October 2006.

55. Donald McArthur, "Canadian Troops Pressed Ahead on Operation Medusa," *Canadia.com*, 6 September 2006, *www.canada.com/components/print.aspx?id=5e81f24-dd05-4eb6-88c1-bbd5e09251f8&k=50060* (accessed 10 September 2006). Despite the encouraging rhetoric the reality on the ground was completely different. It became a largely Canadian fight. "Promises of *in extremis* assistance were a placebo to take the sting away from the constant 'no' that always came following requests to send troops to the south, and meant nothing," stated General Rick Hillier the CDS at the time. "We were," he angrily recalled, "essentially in it by ourselves." The Americans and British were already engaged in combat elsewhere in Afghanistan and were hard-pressed to assist, although they did what they could. Overall, the Europeans failed their allies and refused to participate. The Dutch declined to assist in the actual combat but did take over FOB Martello, which freed up additional Canadian resources that were fed into the battle. FOB Martello was built on the Tarin Khowt Road, on the way to the Dutch AO in the province of Uruzgan, by the

1 PPCLI battle group in order to secure the northern part of Kandahar Province to support NATO's expansion into that province. In the aftermath of Operation Medusa, Hillier told his peers, "Canada feels like we've been abandoned by our allies in the Kandahar province fight." See General Rick Hillier, *A Soldier First: Bullets, Bureaucrats and the Politics of War* (Toronto: HarperCollins Publishers Ltd., 2009), 475–76.

56. The 1 RCR / 1 PPCLI RIP occurred from 24 July to 24 August 2006.

57. Commander's Entry, TF 3-06 War Diary, 19–31 August 2006.

58. Colonel Omer Lavoie, "Leadership in Combat and RMC's Role," article for RCR ROIC candidates, 9–10 April 2010, Petawawa. And true to combat throughout the ages, Lavoie noted that "everything that could have possibly gone wrong, seemed to; the enemy was attacking from all directions, serious confusion occurred with regard to identifying friendly Afghan Security Forces in the same battle, ammunition was beginning to run low, there was only one way on to and off of the position, numerous vehicles broke down or got stuck and one LAV III even rolled over."

59. Warrant Officer Mike Jackson, interview with author, 13 October 2006.

60. Lieutenant-Colonel Omer Lavoie, interview with author, 8 October 2006.

61. The concept was that once the enemy had been heavily attrited through the sustained employment of joint fires, they would be forced to withdraw using their exfiltration routes to the south near Siah Choy, where they would be interdicted by SOF elements and completely destroyed. Manoeuvre was actually initiated earlier than initially planned because of the window of availability for key enablers such as the Predator Unmanned Aerial Vehicle (UAV), which were required for Operation Mountain Fury in Regional Command East (RC (E)), which was running concurrently with Operation Medusa. Memo, Director Army Training to Commander Land Force Development Training System, "Tactical Reconnaissance Report — Training Assessment OP Archer Rotation 3," 21 September 2006, 4.

62. "H-Hour" is the designated time given for coordination of movement and fires for all engaged forces for any given operation.

63. The prospect of the large concentration of Taliban fighters escaping unscathed concerned senior NATO commanders. Lieutenant-Colonel Schreiber revealed, "When Major-General Benjamin Freakley [ISAF Deputy-Commander for Security] heard that the enemy may be escaping he said 'they're leaving, you're letting them out of the bag.' That was his big fear is that the Taliban would get out of the bag and we'd have to fight them again later. So, he said 'the Taliban are leaving so you have to get in there and get after them.' Lieutenant-General Richards [the ISAF commander]

agreed with him, so we started to get a significant amount of pressure to get in there and to actually find out what was going on in Objective Rugby." Lieutenant-Colonel Shane Schreiber, ACOS, Multi-National Brigade HQ, 1 CMBG briefing, 22 January 2007. Brigadier-General Fraser himself conceded, "I would say there was a tremendous amount of pressure from ISAF to 'get it done!'" Interview with author, 21 October 2006.

64. Fraser acknowledged, "This was the ground the enemy had chosen to defend. [Objective] Rugby [the approximate area around the school complex] was where we assessed that the Taliban wanted us to fight them. That was their main battleground." The Brigade Commander elaborated, "Their whole defence was structured to have us coming across the Arghandab River in the south and fight into Rugby." He added, "And the schoolhouse was the area in the centre, where there were big killing fields to the east and the north." The school was built in 2004 with funds from the US Commander's Emergency Reconstruction Program (CERP). As quoted in Day, "Operation Medusa: The Battle for Panjwai, Part 1."

65. Major Matthew Sprague, interview with author, 19 November 2007.

66. Brigadier-General David Fraser, presentation — Canadian Infantry Association Annual General Meeting, 25 May 2007.

67. The ISAF commander was not enamoured with the revised slow Canadian approach. However, Fraser simply stated that they could not risk taking many more casualties because of the national political ramifications. Richards refused to accept this rationale and called Fraser's national command. However, in the end, the ISAF commander was forced to relent.

68. As quoted in Day, "Operation Medusa: The Battle for Panjwai, Part 3." Major Ivey noted, "Scattered on the ground were the leaflets dropped there by NATO, warning the locals that an operation was coming through. The locals had also been warned over the radio and all the local Afghan troops knew the plan as well. This operation was no surprise attack." Major Greg Ivey, interview with author, 17 October 2006.

69. Lieutenant-Colonel Omer Lavoie, interview with author, 8 October 2006.

70. Brigadier-General David Fraser, interview with author, 21 October 2006.

71. Major Greg Ivey, interview with author, 17 October 2006.

72. Captain C. Purdy, interview with author, 17 October 2006.

73. Once they had captured the ground it became fully apparent the scale of the enemy preparation. "They had extensive fortifications," remembered Captain Pappin, "bunkers, loopholes in thick walls and buildings, and some bunkers were built in the courtyards of mosques." Lieutenant Hiltz explained, "I was able to get a good look at the actual position itself. He described one of the positions "as a bunker system with approximately four feet of earth

over top of it, a steel I-beam reinforced roof and the actual interior of it was almost done similar to the crack filling on a wall in a house." He added, "It was done smooth and it could have held anywhere from 15 to 25 personnel. They were able to move into that bunker with pretty much impunity through a ditch system, essentially an irrigation system that was actually ringed with trees, which would have concealed them." He elaborated, "And again, they were low enough that it would have given them cover, so they would have been able to pull back into the bunker unmolested." Hiltz concluded, "In essence, there was quite a significant amount of trench system and bunker systems that they had built." Captain Piers Pappin, interview with author 14 July 2008; and Lieutenant J. Hiltz, interview with author, 16 October 2006.

74. Brigadier-General David Fraser, interview with author, 21 October 2006. One strategist noted:

> The Taliban's losses during Operation Medusa in 2006, which were estimated to be as high as 1,100, were staggering, given that the Taliban's southern force was estimated to consist of approximately 6,700 fighters during the summer of 2006. The Taliban also suffered the loss of several important commanders in early 2006. A combination of heavy casualties and leadership changes may explain the lack of large scale Taliban offensives in the south in 2007. But while there was no Taliban offensive of the scale seen in 2006 or 2008, the Taliban continued to pursue a subtle but aggressive campaign throughout 2007 with the ultimate goal of retaking Kandahar City. Because of the Taliban's success in tying down the Canadians in Zhari in Panjwai, they were able to pursue two key goals in Kandahar. The Taliban were able to develop institutions of governance in Taliban-held areas of Kandahar, especially in Zhari and Panjwai, as a means of winning legitimacy for the Taliban movement. The Taliban were also to wage a successful offensive to move into Kandahar City from the north through Arghandab district circumventing the ISAF deployment in Zhari and Panjwai.

Carl Forsberg, "The Taliban's Campaign for Afghanistan," Institute for the Study of War, *Afghanistan Report*, December 2009, 31–32.

75. *Ibid.*

76. "Audio Report by Mark Laity, NATO's civilian spokesman in Afghanistan," NATO Speeches, 22 Nov 06, NATO Library online, *www.nato.int/docu/ speech/2006/s060922b.htm* (accessed 26 November 2006).

77. NATO Allied Command Operations, "ISAF concludes Operation Medusa in Southern Afghanistan," SHAPE News, 17 September 2006, *www.nato. int/shape/news/206/09/060917a.htm* (accessed 24 November 2006).

78. "Operation Medusa Foiled Taliban Plans, NATO Commander Says," 20 September 2006, *london.usembassy.gov/afghn187.html* (accessed 24 November 2006).

79. "Aid arriving in Panjwayi following Taliban Defeat," *ISAF News*, no. 116, 1.

80. House of Commons Defence Committee, *UK Operations in Afghanistan. Thirteenth Report of Session 2006-07* (London: The Stationary Office Ltd, 18 July 2007), 16.

81. David McKeeby, "NATO's Operation Medusa Pushing Taliban from Southern Kandahar," 18 September 2006, usinfo.state.gov/xarchives/display.html?p=washfile-english&y=2006&m=September&cx=20060918160 51idybeckcm0.9616358 (accessed 24 November 2006).

82. CTV news staff, "Operation Medusa a 'significant' success: NATO," 17 September 2006, *www.ctv.ca/serviet/ArticleNews/story/CTVNews/20060917/ suicid bomb 060917?sname=&noads=24Nov06* (accessed 24 November 2006).

83. Graeme Smith, "Taliban 'Eliminated' from Pivotal District," *Globe and Mail*, 18 September 2006, A14.

84. Richard Foot, "Afghanistan sliding into Chaos," *Montreal Gazette*, 6 Jan 2007, A3.

85. Paul Koring, "The Afghan Mission — A thin Canadian line holds in Kandahar," *Globe and Mail*, 6 December 2006, A26.

86. Quoted in Janice Gross Stein, *The Unexpected War: Canada in Kandahar* (Toronto: Viking, 2007), 219.

87. Discussion at NDHQ, 8 May 2007.

88. CTV news staff, "Operation Medusa a 'significant' success: NATO," 17 September 2006, *www.ctv.ca/serviet/ArticleNews/story/CTVNews/20060917/ suicid bomb 060917?sname=&noads=24Nov06* (accessed 24 November 2006).

89. Lieutenant-Colonel Shane Schreiber, ACOS, Multi-National Brigade HQ, 1 CMBG briefing, 22 January 2007. General James Jones stated number of killed about one thousand, "but if you said 1,500 it wouldn't surprise me." "Operation Medusa Foiled Taliban Plans, NATO Commander Says," 20 September 2006, *usinfo.state.gov/xarchives/display.html?p=washfile-english&y=2006&m=September&cx=20060920172756adtbbed0.444072* (accessed 24 November 2006).

90. Brigadier-General Dave Fraser, interview with author, 21 October 2006.

91. Major Mark Gasparotto, "Route Summit Phase 1 — Squadron Combat Team," in Mark Gasparotto, ed., "Clearing the Way: The Story of 23 Field Squadron in Operation Medusa and Building Route Summit," unpublished manuscript, December 2008.

92. Declan Walsh, Richard Norton-Taylor, and Julian Borger, "From soft hats to hard facts in battle to beat Taliban," *The Guardian*, 18 November 2006, 4.

93. CTV news staff, "Operation Medusa a 'significant' success: NATO," 17 September 2006, *www.ctv.ca/serviet/ArticleNews/story/CTVNews/20060917/ suicid bomb 060917?sname=&noads=24Nov06* (accessed 24 November 2006).

94. Graeme Smith, "The Afghan Mission: Knowing the Enemy: The Taliban," *Globe and Mail*, 27 November 2006, A1.

95. Graeme Smith, "Noise of War Gives Way to the Sound of Rebuilding," *Globe and Mail*, 13 January 2007. In short, the locals saw ISAF as largely responsible for the damage that was done due to Operation Medusa. More importantly, reparations seemed very slow in coming.

96. Brigadier-General Dave Fraser, interview with author, 21 October 2006.

97. Memo, Director Army Training to Commander Land Force Development Training System, "Tactical Reconnaissance Report — Training Assessment OP Archer Rotation 3," 21 September 2006, 5.

98. "Bloody Monday bomber blows up a crowd of children," *ISAF newspaper*, no. 116, 4.

99. Graeme Smith, "Taliban Vow to Retake Panjwai Redoubt," *Globe and Mail*, 18 September 2006, A1. Another Taliban insurgent named Ashoor laughed, saying, "You cannot stop us. We've been using these tactics for hundreds of years and they have always worked." He stated, "After an attack fighters can easily stash their weapons among villagers sympathetic to their cause [and] they can then melt in with the local population and move on to another village, where there are more caches of weapons available to them for mounting another attack." Adnan R. Khan, "Prepare to Bury Your Dead," *Macleans*, 20 March 2006, *www.macleans.ca/topstories/world/article.jsp?co ntent=20060320_123593_123593* (accessed 24 November 2006).

100. One soldier revealed, "The Taliban are going to snipe at us, literally and figuratively. They are going to try to increase the cost of doing business. They can do that at their will, because they can hit us anywhere they want, when they choose. We might be able to hit back hard, but they still control the pace of what goes on, not us. So they really hold the upper hand." Peter Goodspeed, "Battle for Kandahar: Success or Failure of Obama's Troops to Surge Lies in Kandahar City," *National Post*, 27

May 2010, *www.nationalpost.com/news/world/story.html?id=3084975* (accessed 4 June 2010).

101. Interview with Lieutenant-Colonel Peter Williams, Joint Effects Coordination Officer, 22 October 2006.

102. Lieutenant-Colonel Shane Schreiber interview with author, 18 October 2006.

103. The Stability Operations Information Center (SOIC-South) Kandahar Airfield, *Kandahar City Municipality & Dand District: District Narrative Analysis*, 30 March 2010, 62.

104. Maulvi Mohammad Haqqani cited in Sami Yousafzai and Ron Moreau, "The Taliban in their Own Words," *Newsweek.com*, 5 October 2009, 39–40.

105. CNN Tonight, 29 march 2010. An IED is defined as a device placed or fabricated in an improvised manner incorporating destructive, lethal, noxious, pyrotechnic, or incendiary chemicals and designed to destroy or incapacitate, harass or distract. It may incorporate military stores but is normally devised from non-military components. NATO, *Joint Operational Guideline for Counter Improvised Explosive Devices Activities*, Version 3.0, August 2008, 5.

106. Stewart Bell, "Targeting Taliban Bombs," *National Post*, 6 June 2009, A4. The military is spending tens of millions on technological fixes such as robots that flail the ground for buried bombs, vehicles that detect explosives up to one hundred metres away and destroy them with a laser, and airlifting troops around the battle space to defeat Taliban IEDs. Colonel Omer Lavoie, the commander of the Counter-IED Task Force, insisted the most effective strategy to defeat the IED was to go directly after the Taliban IED network from the individual who buries the device to the parts suppliers, financiers, and bomb makers. One reporter noted, "Meanwhile the military is spending $80 million on programs such as Project 1112, which uses surveillance towers and aerial balloons to keep a constant eye on roads and Project 1199 a trio of vehicles that can detect and clear roadside bombs." Since 2007 alone, the Americans have "pumped more than £10 billion into research and technology designed to detect and neutralise the IEDs that cost the Taliban just £20 to make." Miles Amoore in Kabul, "Inside the Mind of a Taliban Bomb Master," *Times Online*, 30 May 2010, *timesonline.co.uk/tol/news/world/afghanistan/article7140135.ece* (accessed 5 June 2010).

107. Adam Day, *Witness to War: Reporting on Afghanistan 2004–2009* (Ottawa: Magic Light Publishing, 2009), 222.

108. Miles Amoore in Kabul, "Inside the Mind of a Taliban Bomb Master."

109. Steve Bowman and Catherine Dale, *War in Afghanistan: Strategy, Military Operations, and Issues for Congress* (Washington D.C.: Congressional

Research Service, 8 June 2010), 25. Kinetic events are defined as all attacks whether by IED, indirect fire, or direct.

110. Forsberg, "The Taliban's Campaign for Afghanistan," 29. Forsberg assessed the Taliban's IED campaign was aimed at limiting Canadian freedom of movement and forcing the Canadians to devote their attention to force protection. He believed the key objectives of the Taliban's campaign were the lines of communication that connected Canadian positions in Zhari and Panjwayi to KAF. Forsberg assessed, "The IED campaign in Zhari and Panjwai had the net effect of taking the initiative away from the Canadians, whose military resources were increasingly focused on force protection and targeting of IED cells, rather than on separating the Taliban from the local population through counterinsurgency operations."

111. *Ibid.*, 46. A DoD report to Congress in June 2009 noted that insurgent attacks increased 60 percent over the same reporting period in 2008 and that military casualties (both international and Afghan) increased by 48 precent. Steve Bowman and Catherine Dale, War in Afghanistan: Strategy, Military Operations, and Issues for Congress (Washington D.C.: Congressional Research Service, 8 June 2010), 25.

112. Day, *Witness to War,* 246.

113. David McCandless, "Information Is Not Beautiful: Afghanistan," *Guardian,* 13 November 2009, *www.guardian.co.uk/news/datablog/2009/nov/13/ information-beautiful-afghanistan* (accessed 28 February 2010).

114. CBC News, "Afghanistan Violence up significantly," *cbc.ca,* 19 June 2010, *news.ca.msn.com/top-stories/cbc-article.aspx?cp-documentid=24627323,* accessed 19 June 2010; and United Nations General Assembly Security Council, "The situation in Afghanistan and its implications for international security. Report of the Secretary-General," 10 March 2010, 7. Similarly, CBC news reported, "Suicide attacks occurred at a rate of about three a week, half in the restive south. Such bombings have tripled this year compared with 2009." CBC news, "Afghanistan Violence up Significantly," *www.cbc.ca/world/ story/2010/06/19/afghanistan-violence-un.html* (accessed 19 June 2010).

115. Phil Stewart, "Threat Rising from Homemade Afghan Bombs: U.S. Army Chief," Reuters, 6 May 2010, *www.reuters.com/article/idUSTRE6456FI20100506* (accessed 9 May 2010). In January 2010 alone, there were already one thousand attacks by homemade bombs. Miles Amoore in Kabul, "Inside the Mind of a Taliban Bomb Master," *Times online,* 30 may 2010, *timesonline.co.uk/tol/ news/world/afghanistan/article7140135.ece* (accessed 5 June 2010).

116 Anthony H. Cordesman, "The Afghan War: A Campaign Overview," Center For Strategic and International Studies, 7 June 2010, 8.

117. Stewart Bell, "Targeting Taliban Bombs," *National Post,* 6 June 2009, A4.

The 2009 figure was taken from Miles Amoore in Kabul, "Inside the Mind of a Taliban Bomb Master."

118. Phil Stewart, "Threat Rising from Homemade Afghan bombs: U.S. Army Chief."

119. Captain Tim Button, interview with author 9 January 2009.

120. Vincent Morelli and Paul Belkin, "NATO in Afghanistan: A Test of the Transatlantic Alliance," CRS Report for Congress, 23 January 2009, 2. The prestigious *Economist* magazine reported that "since January [2007] almost 6,000 people have been killed, a 50% increase on last year. They included 200 NATO soldiers and more than 3,000 alleged Talibs. Insurgent violence is up by 20% on 2006." "Afghanistan's Taliban — War without End," *The Economist*, 25 October 2007, www.economist.com/world/asia/displaystory.cfm?story_id=10026465, (accessed 14 November 2007). By November 2009, the coalition as a whole had lost 1,142 troops since October 2001. Dr. Liam Fox (British MP), "Beyond the Smoke: Making Progress in Afghanistan," speech to the International Institute for Strategic Studies, *www.iiss.org/recent-key-addresses/liam-fox-address* (accessed 9 October 2009).

121. Bowman and Dale, *War in Afghanistan*, 26.

122. Forsberg, "The Taliban's Campaign for Afghanistan," 47.

123. *Ibid.*, 47.

124. "French army chief rules out military victory in Afghanistan," *http://afp.google.com/article/ALeqM5jd3DKrlYPLUzIwIfryRK7U8tAPYQ* (accessed 18 October 2008).

125. *Ibid.*

126. Bill Graveland, "Report: Taliban Growing Stronger," *The Chronicle Herald*, 9 December 2008, *http://thechronicleherald.ca/World/1094914.html* (accessed 9 December 2008). A senior officer of the Afghan Directorate of National Security clearly professed, "This war has no tactical solution if we do not fight the Taliban at the theatre level as well and that is to attack their leadership and their headquarters where they are." A. Saleh, "Strategy of Insurgents and Terrorists in Afghanistan," Report by the Afghan National Directorate of Security, 5 May 2006.

127. Bowman and Dale, *War in Afghanistan*, 26.

128. CTV News Net, 10 March 2009.

129. General Stanley McChrystal, "ISAF Commander's Counterinsurgency Guidance," Headquarters ISAF, Kabul, Afghanistan, September 2009.

130. General Stanley McChrystal, speech, International Institute for Strategic Studies, London, U.K., 1 October 2009.

131. CNN Live, 3 November 2009.

132. Bill Roggio, "Taliban Contest or Control Large Areas of Afghanistan," *www.*

longwarjournal.org/archives/2009/12/taliban_contest_or_c.php (accessed 6 December 2009). In the areas under control, the Taliban operated a parallel political administration and often declared Sharia law, ran courts, recruiting centres, and tax offices, as well as maintained security forces.

133. Sean D. Naylor, "A bigger, badder enemy," *Army Times*, 16 November 2009, 16.

134. Government of Canada, "Canada's Engagement in Afghanistan," Quarterly Report to Parliament for the Period of July 1 to September 30, 2009, 2. The report also noted, "At the same time the widely acknowledged fraud in the landmark [2009] presidential election poses an equally serious crisis of credibility within Afghanistan and in nations whose soldiers are fighting and dying on Afghan soil."

135. United Nations General Assembly Security Council, "The situation in Afghanistan and its implications for international security. Report of the Secretary-General," 10 March 2010, 7.

136. Matthew Fisher, "No Life Like It: Taliban Just One of the Perils Faced by Infantry," *National Post*, 2 August 2010, *www.nationalpost.com/news/canada/Somnia/3350984/story.html* (accessed 8 August 2010). For example, in mid-May 2010, a nine-year old boy and his four-year old spotter died when an IED they were laying blew up. On 6 June 2010, two Afghan kids, aged eleven and eight, were caught in the act of planting an IED. Paul Watson, "On the Battlefield, Canadian Soldiers Get Permission to Shoot," *Star*, *www.thestar.com/news/canada/afghanmission/article/836407--on-the-batt* (accessed 27 July 2010).

138. See, for instance, Ahmed Rashid, "How to End the War in Afghanistan," *BBC News*, *http://news.bbc.co.uk/2/hi/8490710.stm* (accessed 17 April 2010). Rashid noted, "There is broad agreement that talking to the Taliban is the only way to bring the insurgency to an end. No longer are the US, Nato or Afghanistan's neighbours talking about militarily defeating the Taliban, rebuilding the country from top to bottom or promoting democracy. Instead there is a single purpose in mind — how to provide sufficient security for development while at the same time allowing foreign forces to leave."

Chapter Nine — Opportunity Lost:
The Canadian Involvement in the Development of the Afghan National Police

1. Much of this chapter is based on the author's experiences on two separate deployments, totaling almost 20 months in Afghanistan. The first, from September 2005 to August 2006, was with the Canadian Strategic Advisory Team — Afghanistan, which provided a glimpse into the strategic-level issues surrounding the development of the ANP. The second

was from September 2008 to April 2009, as officer commanding the Task Force (TF) 3-08 Police Operational Mentor and Liaison Team (P-OMLT) in Kandahar Province. This latter tour provided a tactical perspective regarding the issues relating to developing a police force in a counterinsurgency campaign. In addition to these experiences, this essay is based on studies, reports, articles, and books about Afghanistan and the ANP prepared by government agencies, academics, military officers, and counter-insurgency experts. The essay is limited in its scope to the examination of the CF effort to develop the ANP and then only up to the summer of 2009. The broader Canadian diplomatic, civilian police, and developmental programs, outside the purview of the CF, are beyond the scope of this study. They are mentioned only insofar as they influence the CF's efforts at developing the ANP.

2. Nick Grono, "Policing in Conflict States — Lessons from Afghanistan" speech, The Hague, 16 June 2009, *www.crisisgroup.org/home/index.cfm?id=6167&1=1* (accessed 24 August 2009).

3. Highlighting these difficulties is not done to disparage the efforts of the men and women of the CF at all levels who have worked tirelessly to train and mentor the ANP. Rather, it is intended to foster further discussion and awareness of the importance of police development in a counterinsurgency campaign.

4. James S. Corum, *Training Indigenous Forces in Counterinsurgency: A Tale of Two Insurgencies* (Carlisle, PA: Strategic Studies Institute, 2006), 8.

5. *Ibid.,* 10.

6. *Ibid.,* 15–21.

7. Frank Kitson, *Low Intensity Operations: Subversion, Insurgency, Peacekeeping* (London: Faber and Faber Limited, 1971), 95.

8. Sir Robert Thompson, *Defeating Communist Insurgency: The Lessons of Malaya and Vietnam* (New York: Frederick A. Praeger, Publishers, 1966), 105.

9. Corum, *Training Indigenous Forces,* 23.

10. *Ibid.,* 27

11. Ian F.W. Beckett, *Modern Insurgencies and Counter-Insurgencies* (London: Routledge, 2001), 155.

12. *Ibid.*

13. Corum, *Training Indigenous Forces,* 29–34.

14. Robert Taber, *War of the Flea: The Classic Study of Guerrilla Warfare* (Washington, D.C.: Potomac Books Inc., 2002), 93.

15. William A. Nighswonger, *Rural Pacification in Viet Nam: 1962–1965,* dissertation, ARPA, 1966, *www.dtic.mil/cgi-bin/GetTRDoc?AD=AD483323&Location=U2&doc=GetTRDoc.pdf* (accessed on 23 September 2009).

16. Sir Robert Thompson et al, *Report on the National Police Force: Republic of Vietnam* (1971), 5, *www.counterinsurgency.org/1971%20Thompson%20 Police/Thompson%20Police.htm* (accessed on 24 September 2009).

17. Seth G. Jones, "Counterinsurgency in Afghanistan," *RAND Counterinsurgency Study* 4 (2008), 72.

18. International Crisis Group, *Reforming Afghanistan's Police*, 15.

19. Department of National Defence, B-GL-323-004/FP-003 *Counter-Insurgency Operations* (Ottawa: Public Works and Government Services Canada, 2008), 5–36. Original emphasis.

20. *Ibid.*

21. Department of the Army, *FM 3-24 Counterinsurgency* (Washington, D.C.: Government Printing Office, 2006), 6–19.

22. Department of the Army, *FM 3-07.1 Security Force Assistance* (Washington, D.C.: Government Printing Office, 2009), v.

23. Joint Center for International Security Force Assistance Website, "Who is JCISFA?" *https://jcisfa.jcs.mil/Public/WhoIsJCISFA.aspx?Page=Who%20 Is%20JCISFA* (accessed 24 September 2009).

24. Ministry of Defence, *JDP 3-40 Security and Stabilization: The Military Contribution* (London: MoD, 2009), 5–10.

25. International Crisis Group, *Reforming Afghanistan's Police — Asia Report no. 138* (Brussels: International Crisis Group, 2007), 7.

26. David Kilcullen, *The Accidental Guerrilla: Fighting Small Wars in the Midst of a Big One* (New York: Oxford University Press, 2009), 61.

27. For a summary of the issues and problems with the Ministry of the Interior, see Anthony H. Cordesman, Adam Mausner, and David Kasten, *Winning in Afghanistan: Creating Effective Afghan Security Forces* (Washington, D.C.: Center for Strategic and International Studies, 2009), 103–04.

28. The term "policemen" is used to describe the lower-ranking members of the ANP, known as *Satunkai* in Dari. Higher ranking *Satanman* (non-commissioned officers) and *Saran* (officers) are collectively referred to as police officers.

29. Robert M. Perito, "Afghanistan's Police: The Weak Link in Security Sector Reform," *United States Institute of Peace Special Report* (Washington, D.C.: United States Institute of Peace, 2009), 4.

30. *Ibid.*

31. Department of State and Department of Defense. *Interagency Assessment of Afghanistan Police Training and Readiness* (Washington, DC: Government Printing Office, 2006), 49, 55.

32. *Ibid.*, 11, 15.

33. The ANP consisted of a number of branches. The bulk of district police were

referred to as the Afghan Uniformed Police (AUP) after the implementation of FDD. The ANCOP were a better trained and equipped force, of sixteen battalions in 2009, which was intended for use in countering riots and in fighting the insurgency. There are similarities between the ANCOP of the Malayan Police jungle companies described earlier. Other branches of the ANP included the Afghan Border Police (ABP), Counter Narcotics Police of Afghanistan (CNPA), and the Criminal Investigative Division (CID).

34. Perito, "Afghanistan's Police," 6.
35. Government Accountability Office, "Afghanistan Security: U.S. Efforts to Develop Capable Afghan Police Forces Face Challenges and Need a Coordinated, Detailed Plan to Help Ensure Accountability," Testimony of Charles Michael Johnson Jr. before US House Subcommittee on National Security and Foreign Affairs (Washington, D.C.: Government Printing Office, 2008), 6.
36. Perito, "Afghanistan's Police," 10.
37. JTF-A consisted of a number of units. The Battle Group was the largest and, as its name implies, was the principal Canadian fighting force in Kandahar. Based on an infantry battalion, it included a tank, artillery, reconnaissance, and engineer sub-units. Other JTF-A units included the already mentioned PRT, the Operational Mentor and Liaison Team (OMLT) that oversaw CF efforts to develop the ANA and ANP in Kandahar, as well as the National Support Element that was responsible for logistical and administrative support to all of JTF-A.
38. Canadian Expeditionary Forces Command Fact Sheet, "Operational Mentor and Liaison Teams," *www.comfec-cefcom.forces.gc.ca/pa-ap/ops/fs-fr/omlt-eng.asp* (accessed 24 Aug 2009).
39. *Ibid.*
40. The 1st Brigade of the ANA 205th 'Hero' Corps was deployed in Kandahar Province. By mid 2008, this brigade had expanded to include three infantry *kandaks*, one combat support *kandak*, and one combat service support *kandak*.
41. See "Afghanistan's Police Force a Weak Link: General," *CTV.ca*, *www.ctv.ca/servlet/ArticleNews/story/CTVNews/20080514/Afghanistan_army_080514/20080514?hub=TopStories* (accessed 25 Aug 2009).
42. The first was created in theatre from elements of the TF 3-07 OMLT and MP Company, as mentioned above. TF 1-08 deployed with a formed P-OMLT and assumed responsibility for mentoring the ANP in February 2008 and was itself replaced by TF 3-08 in September 2008.
43. The platoon headquarters consisted of an infantry captain and a military police master corporal.

44. A P-OMLT section consisted of 8-12 soldiers, about half of whom were infantry and the remainder military police. Sections were led by infantry or military police sergeants, warrant officers or captains.

45. Captain Gary Silliker, "Construction Management Organization Comes to Deh-e-Bagh," *Oromocto Post Gazette*, 8 August 2009, *http://static.canadaeast.com/archives/postgazette/20090808/XFP0808B0264.pdf* (accessed 26 Aug 2009).

46. Lewis G. Irwin, "Reforming the Afghan National Police," *Joint Forces Quarterly* 52 (1st Quarter 2009), 75.

47. Kilcullen, *The Accidental Guerrilla*, 62.

48. Ten personnel in total were transferred from the P-OMLT headquarters to other organizations at the beginning of TF 3-08's rotation.

49. Perito, "Afghanistan's Police," 10.

50. Andrew Wilder, "Cops or Robbers: The Struggle to Reform the Afghan National Police," *Afghanistan Research and Evaluation Unit Issues Paper Series* (Kabul: Afghanistan Research and Evaluation Unit, 2007), 28.

51. Andrew Legon, "Ineffective, Unprofessional, and Corrupt: The Afghan National Police Challenge," Foreign Policy Research Institute E-Note (June 2009), *http://fpri.org/enotes/200906.legon.afghannationalpolice.html* (accessed 24 August 2009).

52. Perito, "Afghanistan's Police," 7.

53. Antonio Giustozzi, *Koran, Kalashnikov, and Laptop: The Neo-Taliban Insurgency in Afghanistan* (New York: Columbia University Press, 2008), 177.

54. ABC News/BBC/ARD Poll, "Afghanistan: Where Things Stand," 30 December 2008 to 12 January 2009, *http://abcnews.go.com/images/Polling Unit/1083a1Afghanistan2009.pdf* (accessed 24 August 2009).

55. T. Christian Miller, Mark Hosenball, and Ron Moreau, "The Gang That Couldn't Shoot Straight," *Newsweek*, 29 March 2010.

56 Legon, "Ineffective."

Chapter Ten — Counter-Insurgency Versus "COIN" in Bazaar-e-Panjwayi and Panjwayi District, 2008–2010: An Illustrative Study of a Canadian Problem

1. This study is based on the author's in the field observations of coalition and Afghan operations in Bazaar-e-Panjwayi and Panjwayi district over a five-year period. The author visited the operating area, accompanied patrols, and interviewed participants in winter 2005, summer 2006, summer 2007, spring 2008, summer 2008, spring 2009, and summer 2010.

2. COIN is the official doctrinal abbreviation for counterinsurgency.

3. See Colonel Bernd Horn, *No Lack of Courage: Operation Medusa, Afghanistan 2006* (Toronto: Dundurn, 2010) for a detailed account of Operation Medusa.

4. Insurgent forces from outside Panjwayi district did transit the district. During Operation Medusa, a substantial enemy force operating in a near-conventional fashion was destroyed by a U.S. Special Operation Task Force around Sperwan Ghar.

5. They draw their thumb across their necks, or make an "explosion" by splaying their fingers out in an upwards gesture while smiling or spitting.

6. Sean M. Maloney, "Taliban Governance: Can Canada Compete?" *Policy Options*, June 2009, 63–68.

7. This device also killed Corporal Martin Dube, who was trying to disarm it.

8. Most likely due to this individual's young age, lack of experience, and gender.

9. This contractor, Bennett-Fouch and Associates, was apparently bilking the Afghan Government to the tune of $33 million. How exactly this organization got the contract really needs to be explored in another venue. See *www.economywatch.com/in-the-news/US-companies-not-paying-afghan-partners-14-07.html* (accessed 14 July 2010); Megan Kelly, "US Contractors Breaking Trust," *www.globalenvision.org*; Carlotta Gall, "US Companies Cheat Locals Out of Millions," *New York Times*, *www.nytimes.com/2010/07/08/world/asia/08contract.html?pagewanted=all* (accessed 7 July 2010).

GLOSSARY OF ABBREVIATIONS

3D	Development, Diplomacy, and Defence
ABCA	America, Britain, Canada, Australia
ADZ	Afghan Development Zone
ANA	Afghan National Army
ANCOP	Afghan National Civil Order Police
ANDS	Afghanistan National Developmental Strategy
ANP	Afghan National Police
ANSF	Afghan National Security Forces
AO	Area of Operations
AQ	al Qaeda
ATO	Afghan Theatre of Operations
BG	Battle Group
C2	Command and Control
C4ISR	command, control, communications, computers, intelligence, surveillance, and reconnaissance
CAS	Close Air Support
CDC	Community Development Councils
CDS	Chief of the Defence Staff
CEFCOM	Canadian Expeditionary Command
CENTCOM	Central Command
CF	Canadian Forces

CFB	Canadian Forces Base
CIA	Central Intelligence Agency
CIDA	Canadian International Development Agency
CIMIC	Civil Military Cooperation
CIVPOL	Civilian Police
CJSOTF-A	Combined Joint Special Operations Task Force – Afghanistan
CJTF 76	Coalition Joint Task Force 76
CMT	Construction Management Team
CO	Commanding Officer
COE	Contemporary Operating Environment
COIN	Counter-insurgency
CPP	Chinese People's Party
CQ	Cultural Intelligence
Coy	Company
Coy Gp	Company Group
C/S	Call Sign
CSC	Corrections Services Canada
CSTC-A	Combined Security Transition Command – Afghanistan
DA	Direct Action
DDMA	Defence, Diplomacy, Military Assistance
DFAIT	Foreign Affairs and International Trade Canada
DND	Department of National Defence
DST	District Stabilization Team
EMT	Embedded Military Training [Team]
EU	European Union
EUPOL	European Police Mission
EW	Electronic Warfare
FAC	Forward Air Controller
FATA	Federally Administered Tribal Area
FDD	Focused District Development
FID	Foreign Internal Defence
FOB	Forward Operating Base
FOO	Forward Observation Officer
GIRoA	Government of the Islamic Republic of Afghanistan
GWOT	Global War on Terrorism

HLVW	Heavy Lift Vehicle Wheel
HN	Host Nation
HQ	Headquarters
HTT	Human Terrain Teams
HUMINT	Human Intelligence
IED	Improvised Explosive Device
INL	International Narcotics and Law Enforcement Affairs
IO	Information Operations
ISAF	International Security Assistance Force
ISB	Interim Staging Bases
ISR	Intelligence, Surveillance, Reconnaissance
JDCC	Joint District Coordination Centre
JSOC	Joint Special Operations Command (JSOC)
JTF-A	Joint Task Force Afghanistan
KAF	Kandahar Airfield
KIA	Killed in Action
KM	kilometre
KMT	Kuomintang Party
KPRT	Kandahar Provincial Reconstruction Team
LAV	Light Armoured Vehicle
LDI	Local Defence Initiative
LoC	Lines of Communication
MEDEVAC	Medical Evacuation
MNB	Multi-National Brigade
MND	Minister of National Defence
MP	Military Police or Minister of Parliament (depending on context)
NA	Northern Alliance
NATO	North Atlantic Treaty Organization
NCO	Non-Commissioned Officer
NDS	National Directorate of Security
NGO	Non-Governmental Organization
NORAD	North American Aerospace Defence
NSE	National Support Element
NSP	National Solidarity Program

OC	Officer Commanding
OCC-D(P)	Operations Coordination Centre-District (Panjwayi)
OEF	Operation Enduring Freedom
OMLT	Operational Mentoring and Liaison Team
OP	Observation Post or Operation (depending on context)
PMT	Police Mentor Teams
P-OMLT	Police Operational Mentor and Liaison Team (P-OMLT)
PPCLI	Princess Patricia's Canadian Light Infantry
PR	Public Relations
PRT	Provincial Reconstruction Team
PSS	Police Sub Stations
PSYOPS	Psychological Operations
QIP	Quick Impact Project
QRF	Quick Reaction Force
RAO	Remote Area Operations
RC (S)	Regional Command (South)
RCMP	Royal Canadian Mounted Police (RCMP)
RCR	Royal Canadian Regiment
RIP	Relief in Place
RoCK	Representative of Canada in Kandahar
ROEs	Rules of Engagement
RPG	Rocket Propelled Grenade
RSM	Regimental Sergeant Major
RTC	Regional Training Centre
SF	Special Forces
SFA	Security Force Assistance (SFA)
SFOR	(NATO) Stability Force
SOF	Special Operations Forces
SPG	Stankovyy Protivotankovyy Granatamet (translation - anti-tank grenade launcher).
TB	Taliban
TF	Task Force
TIC	Troops in Contact
TOCA	Transfer of Command Authority
TTP	Tactics, Techniques, and Procedures

Glossary of Abbreviations

UAV	Unmanned Aerial Vehicle
UN	United Nations
UNAMA	United Nations Assistance Mission to Afghanistan
US JPS	United States Joint Planning System
USMC	United States Marine Corps
UW	Unconventional Warfare
WIA	Wounded in Action
WoG	Whole of Government
WTC	World Trade Centre

CONTRIBUTORS

Major Tony Balasevicius is an infantry officer and member of The Royal Canadian Regiment (RCR). He has served as a platoon and company commander and in various positions with the Canadian Airborne Regiment. In 1995 he took over responsibility for the Army's interim parachute capability and in 1998 was posted to Ottawa. In 2002 he became the deputy commanding officer of 1 RCR and was subsequently posted to the Directorate of Land Requirements in Ottawa. Major Balasevicius is currently a staff officer with Canadian Defence Intelligence at the National Headquarters in Ottawa.

Lieutenant-Colonel John Conrad is a combat logistics officer with twenty-seven years of experience with the Canadian Forces. He holds a master's degree from the Royal Military College of Canada (RMC) and has commanded at every level of army logistics. He has served in Cambodia, Bosnia, and most recently Kandahar, where he commanded the Canadian logistics battalion in 2006. He was decorated with the Meritorious Service Medal for his leadership on the Kandahar tour. His most recent book, *What the Thunder Said*, a logistics retrospective on the Canadian experience in Kandahar, was published in 2009. Conrad currently works as a senior manager with the Government of Ontario and as a reserve battalion commander in Toronto.

Dr. Howard G. Coombs is an assistant professor of the RMC and a serving army reserve officer, affiliated with the Princess of Wales' Own Regiment. In 2004 he served in Afghanistan as a strategic planner, and in 2010–2011 he returned to theatre attached to Joint Task Force Afghanistan 5-10 as a civilian advisor.

Lieutenant-General (retired) Michel Gauthier served thirty-six years in the Canadian Forces, retiring in 2009 after almost four years as the first commander of the Canadian Forces Expeditionary Command. Over that period, he served in tactical to strategic level command and staff appointments in both Canada and abroad. Lieutenant-General Gauthier has attended professional courses in Canada, the United States, and overseas, including the Canadian Forces Command and Staff College, the U.S. Army War College, and the U.S. Pinnacle Course, which is focused on joint and combined warfighting for senior commanders. He currently lives in Ottawa, Ontario.

Major Alex Haynes is an infantry officer with The Royal Canadian Regiment. He has served in the CF since 1994. Since then he has also completed his B.A. in history and political science from Simon Fraser University in British Columbia and has worked toward the completion of an M.A. in war studies from the RMC. Major Haynes has deployed overseas as a platoon commander in Kosovo, as an advisor with the Strategic Advisory Team — Afghanistan, and as officer commanding the Task Force 3-08 Police Operational Mentor and Liaison Team. He is currently a student on the Joint Command and Staff Programme at the Canadian Forces College in Toronto.

Contributors

Dr. Michael A. Hennessy is an associate professor of history and war studies at RMC who specializes in naval and intelligence history. He is currently the dean of Continuing Studies at RMC.

Lieutenant-Colonel Ian Hope served as a strategic planner in counter-terrorism operations with United States European Command in Stuttgart, Germany, a strategic planner with Headquarters International Security Assistance Force in Kabul, the Canadian liaison officer to Headquarters United States Central Command, and as commander the 1st Battalion Princess Patricia's Canadian Light Infantry Battle Group (Task Force Orion) in Kandahar from January to August 2006. He is a graduate of the United States Army School of Advanced Military Studies and the United States Army War College and is currently finishing his Ph.D. in history with Queen's University. He has taught courses in coalition warfare and in counter-insurgency operations at the United States Army War College and the RMC.

Colonel Bernd Horn is an experienced infantry officer who has commanded at the unit and sub-unit level. He has filled key command appointments such as the deputy commander Canadian Special Operations Forces Command, commanding officer of the 1st Battalion, The Royal Canadian Regiment, and officer commanding 3 Commando, the Canadian Airborne Regiment. Dr. Horn has a Ph.D. from the RMC, where he is also an adjunct professor of History. He has authored, co-authored, edited, and co-edited in excess of thirty books and over one hundred chapters and articles on military history and military affairs.

Dr. Sean M. Maloney is a history professor at the RMC and taught in the war studies program for ten tears. He is currently the historical advisor to the chief of the Land Staff for the war in Afghanistan. He previously served as the historian for 4 Canadian Mechanized Brigade, the

Canadian Army's primary Cold War NATO commitment, right after the re-unification of Germany and at the start of Canada's long involvement in the Balkans. Dr. Maloney has extensive field experience in that region, particularly in Croatia, Bosnia, Kosovo, and Macedonia from 1995 to 2001. His work on the Balkans was interrupted by the 9/11 attacks, and from 2001 Dr. Maloney has focused nearly exclusively on the war against the al Qaeda movement and particularly on the Afghanistan component of that war. He has travelled regularly to Afghanistan since 2003 to observe coalition operations in that country, and he is the author of a number of books dealing with the conflict there.

Dr. Emily Spencer is the director of research and education at the CANSOFCOM Professional Development Centre and a research associate with the Canadian Forces Leadership Institute. She is the author of *Solving the People Puzzle* and the editor of *The Difficult War*. She lives in Kingston, Ontario.

Major-General Jonathan H. Vance is an experienced infantry officer who has commanded 2 RCR, 1 Canadian Mechanized Brigade Group and Joint Task Force — Afghanistan. He is currently a senior army staff officer at National Defence Headquarters in Ottawa.

INDEX

1 Canadian Mechanized Brigade Group, 108

3D. *See* Development, Diplomacy, and Defence

11 September 2001 (9/11), 8, 14, 60, 139–40, 146, 164–65, 169

Afghan Development Zone (ADZ), 173–74, 187

Afghan National Army (ANA), 62, 116, 120, 136, 147, 151–52, 182, 186, 189, 212, 216–17, 219, 222–23, 230–31, 237, 239, 247–48

Afghan National Civil Order Police (ANCOP), 148, 213

Afghan National Police (ANP)
    Canadian development efforts, 116, 120–21, 186, 199–232
    Corruption, 116, 236–37
    German development program. 210–12, 225–26,
    U.S. Department of State/Defense development program, 212, 225–26

Afghan National Security Forces (ANSF), 62, 110, 149, 181

Afghanistan
    Task Force, *see* Joint Task Force Afghanistan
    Transitional Authority, 110
    Study Group, 61, 195

Afghanistan National Developmental Strategy (ANDS), 111, 118

Akbari, Ghulam Yahya, 159

Algeria, 23–24

Alikazais and Alokozais, 235

Alliance, 27, 38, 40, 59–60, 84–85, 88–90, 102, 140, 146–47, 165–66

Al Qaeda (AQ), 13–14, 60, 88, 107, 139–41, 159, 161, 165–67, 169

America, Britain, Canada, Australia Standardization (ABCA), 86

Amu Darya River, 42, 126

Anglo-Irish War, 19–20

Arab Revolt, 18–19

Arghandab River, 126, 176–77

Asymmetric warfare, 69, 81, 133, 164, 190–92, 195, 197

Article 5, 165

Bagram, 127, 131
Bayenzi, 182, 186, 192
Bazaar-e-Panjwayi, 179–81, 233–55
Bin Laden, Osama, 60, 140–41, 165–66
Bland, Dr. Doug, 118
Blatchford, Christie, 172
Boer War, 19
Bolduc, Colonel Don, 148
Bosnia, 104–05
Britain, 20, 46, 86, 196
Button, Captain Tim, 194–95

C4ISR, 146
Camp Julien, 108
Camp Souter, 131
Campaign
    Assessment, 71, 114–15,
    Design, 19, 22, 26, 105, 114,
    Plan, 25–27, 85–86, 90, 105,
        113–15, 128
Canadian Expeditionary Command
    (CEFCOM), 111–16, 189
Canadian Forces (CF), 7, 13, 74, 101,
    103–04, 108–09, 111–15, 119–20,
    124, 130, 171, 199, 238–39,
    245–46, 254–55
Canadian Forces Base (CFB) Borden,
    130
Canadian Forces College, 103–04,
    279–81
Canadian International Development
    Agency (CIDA), 109, 170, 236,
    239, 245, 249–50
Carleton-Smith, Brigadier Mark, 196
Central Command (CENTCOM), 86,
    89, 112
Central Intelligence Agency (CIA), 62,
    140–41, 157, 166, 270, 285, 291

Centre of Gravity, 69–70, 72, 97, 105,
    173–74
Chief of the Defence Staff (CDS),
    111–12, 156, 189, 283, 300
China, 20, 125
Chinese Communist Party, 20
Chinese People's Party (CPP), 20–21
Civil Military Cooperation (CIMIC),
    9, 246, 250, 255
Civilian Police (CIVPOL), 208,
    214–16, 221, 225–26, 239, 244,
    250, 310
Clausewitz, Carl von, 101, 109
Coalition, 10, 14–16, 24–26, 29,
    61–62, 70–71, 76, 83–99, 102,
    108, 127, 134, 140, 145, 147, 149,
    151–52, 159–60, 165–66, 168,
    170, 173, 174, 177–78, 180, 188,
    190–97, 209, 210, 213–17, 223–
    25, 227, 231–33, 236–48, 251–53,
    260, 275, 278, 281, 308, 313
Coalition Joint Task Force 76 (CJTF
    76), 127
Cold War, 102–04, 130, 184, 284
Combined Joint Special Operations
    Task Force — Afghanistan
    (CJSOT-A), 148
Combined Security Transition
    Command — Afghanistan
    (CSTC-A), 212–16
Community Development Councils
    (CDC), 235, 248
Commando program, 148–49, 288
Comprehensive approach, 208, 281–82
Construction Management Team
    (CMT), 239, 242, 250
Contemporary Operating
    Environment (COE), 68, 77, 154
Corrections Services Canada (CSC),
    109

Index

Counter-insurgency (COIN), 9–10,
17–27, 41, 57–58, 64, 67, 69–72, 77,
81, 83–99, 106–08, 129, 147–50,
157, 160–61, 164, 195, 198–200,
203–11, 215, 223–24, 230–55,
271–73, 278, 292, 310, 313
Culture, 16, 22, 68, 72, 97, 99, 131,
145, 154, 167, 228, 230
tribal, 31–32, 34
Cultural Intelligence (CQ), 72, 273
Cyprus, 204–07, 224

Dand District, 238, 250
Department of Foreign Affairs and
International Trade (DFAIT), 109,
170, 221, 236, 239, 245, 249–50
Department of National Defence
(DND), 109, 115–16, 170
Development, Diplomacy, and
Defence, 111, 281
District Stabilization Team (DST), 9,
249–50
Doctrine, 9, 24, 34, 75, 98–99, 102–06,
114, 118–19, 147, 207–09, 223, 234
DynCorp, 211–14, 221, 230

European Police Mission (EUPOL),
214–16
European Union (EU), 214–15, 225

Federally Administered Tribal Areas
(FATA), 147, 153, 289
Flynn, Major-General Mike, 196–97
Focused District Development (FDD),
213–14, 216, 218, 221–22, 230,
248, 312,
Foreign Internal Defence (FID), 147,
287
Forward Operating Base (FOB), 9,
225, 238, 242, 249, 300

Fraser, Brigadier-General David, 31,
108, 151, 154, 171, 173–74, 176,
178–79, 182–83, 185–87, 190, 302
Freakley, Major-General Benjamin, 301

Galula, David, 83, 95–98
Gauthier, Lieutenant-General Mike,
189
Georgelin, General Jean-Louis, 196
Germany, 86, 168, 210–12, 214, 225–26
Governance, 10, 26, 29, 60, 79–80,
111, 116–20, 128, 147–50, 160,
170, 173, 175, 195, 197, 224,
233–35, 239, 244, 246–47, 249,
251, 254–55, 295, 297–98, 303
Government of Afghanistan (GoA),
14, 79–80, 92, 174, 187, 229, 251,
282, 297–98
Government of the Islamic Republic
of Afghanistan (GIRoA), 111,
116, 147, 152, 170–71, 173, 176,
191, 197, 245, 282, 297
Gunbad Safe House, 129

Haqqani network, 157
Hari Rud River, 126
Harper, Stephen, 196
"Hearts and minds," 67–82, 150, 160,
187
Hekmatyar, Gulbuddin, 155–56
Helmand, 108, 123, 126, 130, 134, 158,
168, 171–72, 188, 236, 284
Helmand-Arghandab River system,
126
Herat, 43, 47, 148, 159, 191
Hezb-i-Islami militant group, 156
Highway 1, 175–76, 187, 189, 193,
236–37, 239–40
Hillier, General Rick, 110–14, 119,
156, 189, 283, 300–01

Himalayas, 128
Hindu Kush mountains, 35, 42–43, 128,
  263–64
Hope, Lieutenant-Colonel Ian, 130,
  170–73, 175, 179, 181, 216, 298,
Host nation (HN), 16, 70, 72, 81,
  146–47, 153, 160, 208, 287
Human intelligence (HUMINT), 154
Human terrain analysts, 72, 273
Human Terrain Teams (HTT), 26

Imperial Japanese Army, 20–22
Improvised explosive device (IED),
  61, 73, 129–30, 132, 150, 160, 168,
  192–93, 222, 236–38, 240–42, 244,
  246, 248, 276, 291–92, 306–07, 309
Information operations (IO), 77–79,
  286, 292
Insurgency, 8–10, 14, 17–20, 22–23,
  36, 58, 63, 83, 89, 91–99, 106,
  119–20, 124, 137, 147, 160, 164,
  188, 195–97, 201, 203–07, 230–
  31, 242, 251–53, 299, 309–10, 312
intelligence, 26, 39, 41, 55, 59, 65, 86,
  89, 146–47, 151–55, 158, 164,
  171–72, 175, 177, 183, 194, 196,
  201–206, 231, 244, 285–86, 289,
  296
Intelligence, surveillance, and reconnaissance (ISR), 146, 153, 175,
  177, 181
Interagency, 118, 160, 281, 287
International Crisis Group, 78, 81, 207
International Narcotics and Law
  Enforcement Affairs (INL),
  211–12
International Security Assistance
  Force (ISAF), 8, 14, 31, 60, 63,
  71, 74–75, 78–79, 83–84, 86,
  88–90, 92, 93, 96, 98–99, 107–08,

110–118, 149–50, 156–58, 160,
  163, 167–71, 174, 178–79, 181,
  186–89, 191, 193, 196, 225, 247,
  249, 261, 276, 278, 282–84, 288,
  291–92, 296, 298, 301–03, 305
Iran, 35, 43, 63, 97, 125, 148, 261, 270
Iraq, 24, 68, 87–88, 94, 107, 127,
  166–68, 207, 295
Ireland, 19–20, 23
Ivey, Major Greg, 185

Jackson, Warrant Officer Michael,
  70–71, 180
Jingle trucks, 134–35
Joint District Coordination Centre
  (JDCC), 239, 242–45, 249
Joint Special Operations Command
  (JSOC), 76, 148, 153–55, 289
Joint Task Force Afghanistan (JTF-
  A), 7, 104, 110, 113, 115–16, 118,
  215–17, 222, 224–25, 227, 312

Kabul, 9, 14, 35, 43, 45–48, 52, 55,
  59–60, 61, 63, 74, 79, 89, 92, 107–
  08, 110, 126, 131, 134, 140, 157,
  166–69, 172, 189, 191, 210–11,
  213, 215, 264, 267, 272, 276, 284,
  295–96, 308
Kandahar
  Airfield (KAF), 110, 123, 125–26,
    130, 137, 179, 187, 193, 307
  City, 59, 61, 79, 92–93, 150, 158,
    163–64, 168–75, 181, 187,
    189, 195, 215–16, 222, 226,
    235–40, 243, 250–51, 276,
    278, 295, 303
  Province, 11, 14, 106, 108, 117,
    120, 134, 136–37, 150, 157,
    163, 170, 172–73, 199, 216,
    226, 234, 236, 251, 263,

Index

296–97, 299, 300–01, 310, 312

Provincial Reconstruction Team (KPRT), 110, 119, 298

Kandak, 148–49, 216, 239–40, 248, 312

Karzai, Hamid, 79, 95–96, 110, 116, 128, 148, 163, 251, 282

Khalid, Assadulla, 188

Kilcullen, David, 224

Kitson, General Frank, 202, 207

Kunar Province, 156

Kunduz Province, 226

Kuomintang Party (KMT), 20–22

Lash Kar Gah, 126

Lavoie, Lieutenant-Colonel Omer, 132, 179–84, 301, 306

Lawrence, T.E., 18–20

Leslie, Lieutenant-General Andrew, 74, 163, 292

limited war, 27, 69, 81, 272

local defence initiative (LDI), 148

Lussier, Major Andrew, 184

M109, 135–36

M777, 128, 284

Malaya, 200, 202–06, 224, 231

Mao, 20–22, 54, 83, 91–93, 99, 278–79, 299

Marcinowski, Sergeant Roger, 219

Mass media, 67–68

Ma'Sūm Ghar, 179–80, 182–83, 239, 242, 249–50, 292

Mazaar-e-Sharif, 60, 141, 166

McAndrew, Dr. Bill, 103–04

McChrystal Lieutenant-General Stanley, 75–76, 124, 196

Military police company, 248

Ministry of the Interior (Afghanistan), 211–13, 228, 311

Montreal, 125

Mujahidin, 52–59, 64, 168, 172, 195, 236, 268,

Mullen, General Mike, 150

Multi-national brigade (MNB), 31, 108, 150, 173–74, 187

Mushan, 235, 237–38, 240, 247, 250, 292

National Directorate of Security (NDS), 147, 239

National Solidarity Program (NSP), 235, 281

National Support Element (NSE), 312

NATO, 14, 29, 31, 60–63, 79, 84, 89, 93, 102, 106–08, 118, 120, 127–28, 136, 155, 157, 163, 165, 170, 173–74, 176, 178–79, 182, 187–90, 196–97, 260, 263, 296, 298–302, 308–09

Stability Force (SFOR), 127

Non-governmental organizations (NGOs), 111, 145, 156, 168, 252–53, 255, 276, 297

Noorzai, 235

Norgrove, Linda, 156

North Atlantic Treaty Organization (see NATO)

Northern Alliance (NA), 60, 88, 140, 146, 165–66, 271

Objective Rugby, 186, 192, 301–02

OEF (see Operation Enduring Freedom)

Omar, Mullah, 80, 140–41, 166, 172, 276, 293, 295–96,

Operation
Apollo, 169
Archer, 298

Athena, 169, 296
Desert Storm, 87–88
Enduring Freedom (OEF), 8, 14,
  83, 107, 125, 140, 165–66
Medusa, 15, 150, 163–198, 237,
  279, 288–89, 301, 303
Operational Mentor and Liaison
  Team (OMLT), 239, 310, 312
Operations Coordination Centre-
  District (Panjwayi) (OCC-D(P)),
  249

Pakistan, 43, 55, 58–60, 62–63, 88–89,
  93, 97, 117, 125, 128, 141, 147, 150,
  153, 156–59, 166–68, 172, 176, 197,
  236, 240, 269–270, 276, 291, 296
Panjwayi, 11, 74, 110, 169, 171–73, 175,
  179–82, 186, 193, 197, 216–18,
  220, 222, 224, 226, 229, 233–55
Pappin, Captain Piers, 302–03
Paramilitary, 140, 146–47, 153, 206,
  210–11, 217, 219–20, 223, 226, 230
Pashmul, 15, 150, 171, 173–83,
  186–87, 191
Pentagon, 140, 159, 164, 193–94
Petraeus, General David, 118, 149,
  154, 160, 288
Police Mentor Teams (PMTs), 214
Police Operational Mentor and
  Liaison Team (P-OMLT), 310
Police Sub Stations (PSS), 216, 238
Princess Patricia's Canadian Light
  Infantry (PPCLI)
  1st Battalion (1 PPCLI), 125, 129,
    132, 298, 300–01
  3rd Battalion (3 PPCLI), 14, 169
Propaganda, 76, 78, 93, 96, 201, 275
Provincial Reconstruction Team
  (PRT), 14, 26, 110, 112, 119,
  169–70, 215–16, 222, 225–26,

236, 239, 244–45, 249–50, 275,
  296–298
Psychological Operations (PSYOPS),
  220, 286
Public opinion, 67–82, 272
Public relations (PR), 74
Purdy, Captain Chris, 151

Qala Bist, 126
Quetta *Shura*, 167
Quick Impact Projects (QIPs), 174–75

Regestan Desert, 150
Regional Command (South) (RC(S)),
  108, 173, 186, 191
Regional Training Centres (RTCs),
  211
Remote Area Operations (RAO), 153
Representative of Canada in
  Kandahar (RoCK), 110
Richards, Lieutenant-General David
Royal Canadian Mounted Police
  (RCMP), 109, 170
Royal Canadian Regiment (RCR)
  1st Battalion (1 RCR), 132, 179,
    184, 186–87,
  3rd Battalion (3 RCR), 14, 238,
    240

Rules of Engagement (ROEs), 143

Sangin District, 130, 136
Sarposa Prison, 237
Scheffer, General Jaap de Hoop, 178
Schreiber, Lieutenant-Colonel
  Shane, 151, 173, 175–77, 189,
  192, 301
Security Force Assistance (SFA), 147,
  149, 168, 208–09, 286
Senlis Council, 171, 196

Shura, 71, 148, 167, 220, 235, 248, 276
Soviet 40th Army, 127
Special Operations Forces (SOF), 14, 60, 112, 139, 139–61, 166, 273, 285–86
Sperwan Ghar, 151–52, 237, 239–41
Sprague, Major Matthew, 182–83
Stability Box Juno, 239, 243–44
Stabilization companies, 222
Suicide bomber, 14–15, 77, 168, 191–92, 243

Tactics, Techniques, and Procedures (TTPs), 15, 67, 223
Tajik Taliban, 159
Tajikistan, 125
Tamil Tigers, 23
Task Force (TF)
  3-06, 179, 186
  3-08, 218–22, 224–31, 310
  Kandahar (TFK) (*see also* TF 3-06 and 1 RCR BG), 110
  Orion, 170, 179, 182, 298
Terrorism, 13, 33, 52, 69–70, 73, 77–79, 81, 86, 88, 91, 93, 140, 159, 164–67, 170, 191, 195, 197, 200–04, 231, 251, 293
Thompson, General Sir Robert, 25, 99, 203, 207
Tora Bora mountains, 141, 166
Total war, 67–68
Turkey, 125
Turkmenistan, 125

Unconventional warfare (UW), 146
United Nations (U.N.), 55, 60, 102, 104, 107, 118, 140, 165, 169, 186, 193, 196–97, 296,
  Security Council, 60, 107, 140, 165, 293–94, 296

Resolution (UNSCR), 293–94, 296
United States Joint Planning System (US JPS), 103
United States Marine Corps (USMC), 129, 208
Unity of command, 99
Unmanned Aerial Vehicle (UAV), 154, 298, 301
Uruzgan, 168, 171–72, 188, 300–01
Uzbekistan, 125

Vance, Brigadier-General Jon, 104
Vietnam, 68, 92, 94, 103, 185, 203, 206–07, 224
  South, 94, 206–07

War of Irish Independence, 19–20
Wardak Province, 149, 155
Whole of government (WoG), 25, 95, 99, 106, 108–09, 114, 116, 118–19, 278, 281, 297
Williams, Lieutenant-Colonel Peter, 192
World Trade Centre, 140, 164
Wright, Major Mike, 33, 180

Young, Commissioner Sir Arthur, 201

Zabul, 152, 168, 172
Zhari, 169, 171–72, 181, 187–88, 193, 216–18, 220, 222, 224, 226, 228–30, 303, 307

OF RELATED INTEREST

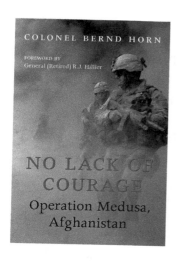

No Lack of Courage
Operation Medusa, Afghanistan
by Colonel Bernd Horn
978-1554887668
$30.00

No Lack of Courage is the story of the North Atlantic Treaty Organization's Operation Medusa, the largely Canadian action in Afghanistan from 1 to 17 September 2006, to dislodge a heavily entrenched Taliban force in the Pashmul district of Afghanistan's Kandahar Province. At stake, according to senior Afghan politicians and NATO military commanders, was nothing less than the very existence of the reconstituted state of Afghanistan, as well as the NATO alliance itself. In a bitterly fought conflict that lasted more than two weeks, Canadian, Afghan, and Coalition troops defeated the dug-in enemy forces and chased them from the Pashmul area.

In the end, the brunt of the fighting fell on the Canadians, and the operation that saved Afghanistan exacted a great cost. However, the battle also demonstrated that Canada had shed its peacekeeping mythology and was once more ready to commit troops deliberately to combat. Moreover, it revealed yet again that Canadian soldiers have no lack of courage.

Solving the People Puzzle
Cultural Intelligence and
Special Operations Forces
by Dr. Emily Spencer
978-1554887507
$24.99

The twenty-first century has brought the perfect storm of conditions to create substantive global instability. This contemporary operating environment (COE) is characterized by complexity, ambiguity, volatility, and constant danger. It is a human invention that requires a human solution.

Special operations forces (SOF), a group comprised of highly trained personnel with the ability to deploy rapidly and apply special skills in a variety of environments and circumstances, is the logical force of choice to achieve success in the COE. Increasing their effectiveness is cultural intelligence (CQ) — the ability to recognize the shared beliefs, values, attitudes, and behaviours of a group of people and then apply that knowledge toward a specific goal. Empowered by CQ, SOF are positioned to dominate in the COE.

Solving the People Puzzle makes a convincing argument for the powerful union of the "force of choice" with the "tool of choice." This book will inspire and inform.

Available at your favourite bookseller.

DUNDURN
www.dundurn.com

What did you think of this book?
Visit www.dundurn.com for reviews, videos, updates, and more!